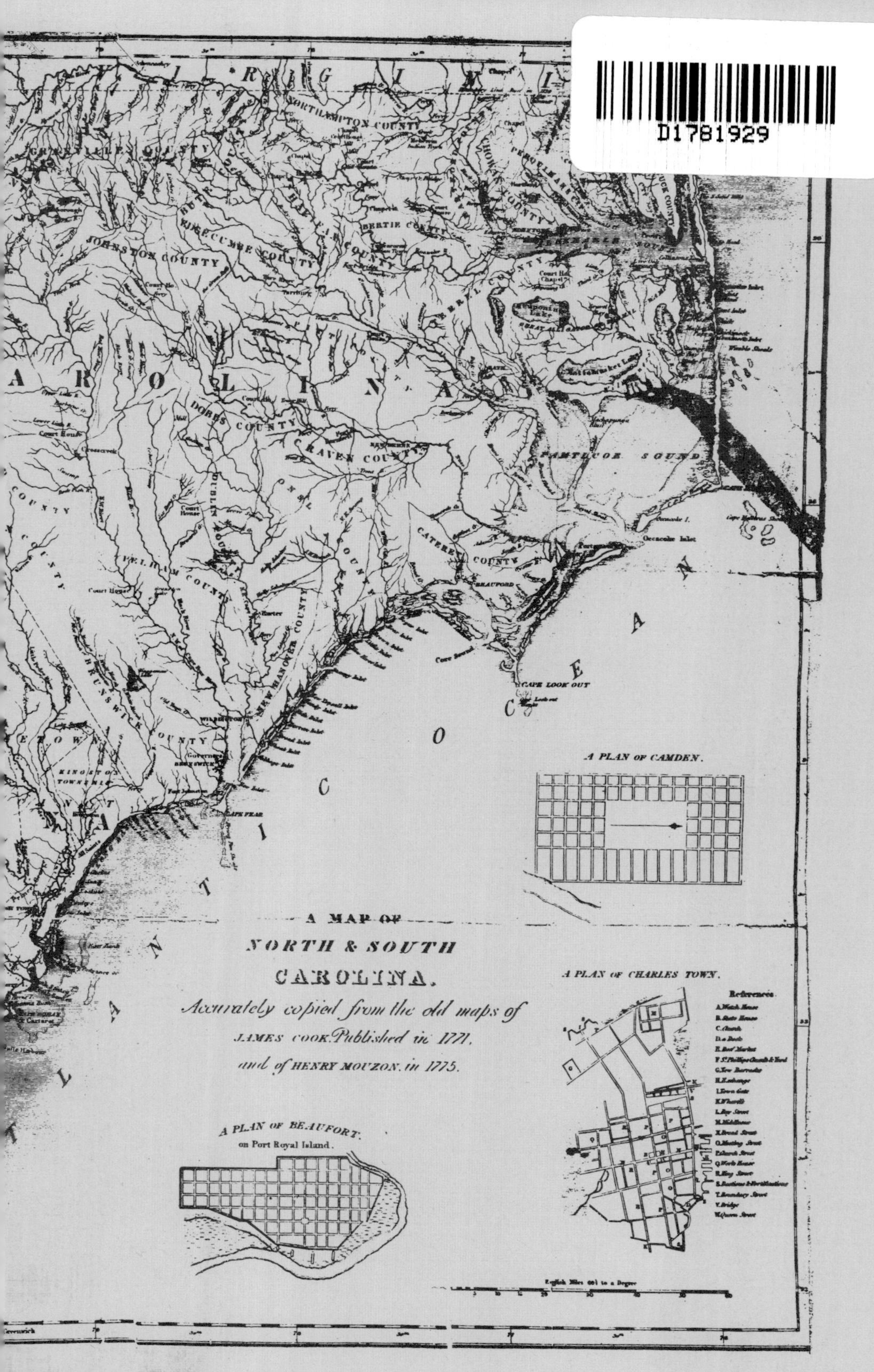
A MAP OF
NORTH & SOUTH
CAROLINA.
Accurately copied from the old maps of
JAMES COOK. Published in 1771,
and of HENRY MOUZON. in 1775.
A PLAN OF CAMDEN.
A PLAN OF CHARLES TOWN.
A PLAN OF BEAUFORT.
on Port Royal Island.
VIRGINIA
CAROLINA
ATLANTIC OCEAN
NORTHAMPTON COUNTY
JOHNSTON COUNTY
DOBBS COUNTY
CRAVEN COUNTY
BERTIE COUNTY
CARTERET COUNTY
NEW HANOVER COUNTY
BRUNSWICK COUNTY
PELHAM COUNTY
DUBLIN COUNTY
PAMTICOE SOUND
CAPE LOOK OUT
CAPE FEAR
Occacoke Inlet
English Miles 69½ to a Degree

THE DISORDERS OF WAR

The HARBOUR of CHARLES TOWN in South Carolina
from the Surveys of Sr. Jas. Wallace Captn. in his Majestys Navy & Others
with
A VIEW of the TOWN from the SOUTH SHORE of Ashley River.
Statute Miles
Nautical Miles
SPENCES INLET
LONG ISLAND
Mount Pleasant
HOG ISLAND
WANDO RIVER
COOPER RIVER
CHARLES TOWN
ASHLEY RIVER
Wappoo Creek
Shutes Folly
REBELLION ROAD
SULLIVANS ISLAND
Rattle Snake
NORTH CHANNEL
The Ten feet Bank
Fort Johnson
PART of JAMES ISLAND
Cummins Point
Two feet CHANNEL
Stone Breakers
North Breaker
SHIP CHANNEL
South Breaker
The Light House W by S.
The Light House W by N
SOUTH CHANNEL

THE DISORDERS OF WAR

THE REVOLUTION IN SOUTH CAROLINA

By

JEROME J. NADELHAFT

University of Maine at Orono Press
Orono, Maine 1981

The maps on pages 15, 101, and 130 have been adapted with permission of Princeton University Press. The originals appear in *Atlas of Early American History: The Revolutionary Era, 1760–1790.* Copyright ©by Princeton University Press, and published for the Newberry Library and the Institute of Early American Culture.

First edition

Manufactured in the United States of America

ISBN 0-89101-049-1

9 8 7 6 5 4 3 2 1

To Ruth

Table of Contents

Preface

For most of the almost 200 years since publication of David Ramsay's *History of the Revolution of South Carolina* in 1785, historians paid but scant attention to South Carolina's revolutionary history. Directing their attention northward to Virginia and Massachusetts, New York and Pennsylvania, and to leaders the likes of John and Sam Adams, George Washington, Patrick Henry, and Benjamin Franklin, they abandoned the state to military historians and laymen who, each praising his or her own hero, crossed and recrossed the state with eighteenth-century armies and besieged readers with books about battles, campaigns, and high-ranking officers.

While the partisan generals Francis Marion, Andrew Pickens, and Thomas Sumter have been the subjects of biographies, the civilian leaders, and the political and constitutional events they participated in, remain obscure and unknown. John Rutledge's life awaits scholarly treatment; the only biography of Henry Laurens appeared in 1915. There are no extended studies of Rawlins Lowndes, Arthur Middleton, Aedanus Burke, or even Christopher Gadsden. There is as yet no detailed treatment of the state's economy in the 1780s or of its turbulent politics. No one has accurately summarized the Carolina constitutions of 1776, 1778, and 1790.

The need for serious work on South Carolina's revolutionary history is demonstrated by two recent, useful books. *Perspectives in South Carolina History: The First 300 Years,* edited by Ernest M. Lander, Jr. and Robert K. Ackerman (Columbia, S.C., 1973), contains only one article to deal with any aspect of the Revolution: Robert H. Woody's deservedly well-known "Christopher Gadsden and the Stamp Act." One skips then from 1765 to the 1790s, with not a glance at the consequences of the Revolution. In contrast, there are eight articles on the Civil War and Reconstruction. Louis B. Wright's survey, *South Carolina: A Bicentennial History* (New York, 1976), describes the bloody warfare of the Revolution. But again, there are no descriptions of constitutional, political, or economic developments. Peace is declared on one page and the cotton gin is introduced on the next to begin the story of the 1790s.

Perhaps historians neglected South Carolina because the more populous Massachusetts and Virginia seemed more active in precipitating the Revolution and because they produced men who became Presidents and Vice Presidents. Perhaps, also, they were wooed by the published collections of Revolutionary era documents and the massive unpublished private papers. By comparison, few of South Carolina's records have been published and few private papers have survived. There is little personal material for Christopher Gadsden, less still for John Rutledge, and less still for Alexander Gillon.

But there are good sources. The South Carolina Department of Archives and History has gathered court records and has carefully organized legislative papers, petitions, tax records, and other official documents. Recently, first under the direction of J. Harold Easterby and now under Charles Lee, it has begun to publish collections of records — legislative journals, treasury books, and papers relating to Indians. And, scattered in libraries and historical societies up and down the East Coast, there are some important letters written by South Carolina's leaders. Equally valuable are the excellent and numerous newspapers.

Using these sources with great imagination, Jack P. Greene, George C. Rogers, Robert M. Weir, Peter H. Wood, and several others have within the last two decades written perceptively about the Revolutionary Era. *The Disorders of War* is my attempt to help redress the old imbalance, to describe the consequences of American Independence and the Revolutionary War in South Carolina.

For the last several years, each time I was finishing the *final* draft of this book, I would on request patiently explain to my children that we would not be rich and famous but that we might recover the typing expenses. Fortunately, other costs were partly met by research grants. The American Philosophical Society extended aid early, and the State University of New York and the University of Maine, Orono, provided me with summer research grants. The first draft was written while I was living on my wife's salary and the generosity of the National Endowment for the Humanities.

I have been helped by librarians too numerous to name. In every library I visited as an impoverished graduate student they graciously allowed me, often under trying conditions, to do my own microfilming so that I could be sped on to the luxuries of the next city's YMCA. Charles Lee and the staff of the South Carolina Department of Archives and History — especially Francis M. Hutson, Wylma Wates, and Alexia J. Helsley — outperformed all others.

At the University of Wisconsin Merrill Jensen and David Lovejoy introduced me to early American history and to research. Merrill Jensen accepted one draft of this study as a dissertation, and he and Jackson Turner Main read the first postdoctoral version. I thank them for the mistakes they caught — and hold them partly responsible for those they missed. Dave Smith, of the University of Maine History Department, and my colleagues in AFUM, the faculty union, unknowingly pushed this book forward by keeping me sane in the chaotic, often idiotic world of the twentieth-century university.

The most support came from people close to me. According to the Talmud, as reported by Chaim Potok in *The Chosen,* a person should do two things for himself: acquire a teacher and choose a friend. I have chosen well, being triply blessed. Tina and Bill Baker, colleagues and dear friends, have been an integral part of my life daily for a decade. I am a wiser and better person for it. Ruth is colleague, teacher, wife, and friend. More than any person I know, she integrates wifehood, motherhood, and vocation. The words she has used to describe the theme and concern of a favorite author, Elizabeth Gaskell, are words I would use to describe hers: "the private relationships as the supreme expression both of the individual and of the world at large." Overworked herself, she was scarcely ever directly involved with this book except to improve its style immeasurably. Indeed, without her interruptions — and those of our daughter, Erica, and son, Matthew, who thankfully never paid attention to the old "Daddy is in his study" routine — I might have finished this South Carolina work years earlier. But it would not have been the same book, and not a good one at all. The books Ruth made me read, the ideas she introduced, changed me, perhaps too slowly and not enough, and this book. She has been my teacher. Since I cannot improve on the words Richard Steele used for Lady Elizabeth Hastings, I will borrow them for Ruth: "To love her is a liberal education."

Bangor, Maine
August 1981

ONE
Unity and Division Before Independence

No love of innovation, no desire of altering the constitution, no lust for independence has the least influence upon our counsels.
Provincial Congress, 21 June 1775.

The Men of property begin at length to see that the many headed power the People . . . have discovered their own strength and importance. . . .
Lieutenant Governor William Bull, 28 March 1775.

Part I: Unity

AFTER the close of the French and Indian war, England renewed its intent to reform relations with the American colonies, adding a new concept of taxing Americans to help with the financial drain caused by the war. The plan to reassert political power and raise a revenue in America ran afoul of independent thinking Americans in all colonies. South Carolinians joined in opposition rather than slip passively "from one degree of slavery to another." In January 1776 Josiah Smith accurately summed up the feelings of many of his countrymen: they were not anxious for "bloody work," but, their "cause being just," they were prepared to die rather than submit themselves, their offspring, and all dear to them, "to the will & controul of a haughty and abandoned sett of rulers."[1] Not all leaders agreed, but enough did to carry the point.

During the 1760s and 70s, South Carolina's protest was led by men elected to the Commons, the dynamic lower house of the legislature. Their arguments were constitutional — and often prophetic. The danger of Parliamentary taxation worried the colony's leaders, as the native Lieutenant Governor William Bull noted when reporting their fear that the British would soon impose on Americans all the schemes used to raise money in Great Britain.[2] Thomas Heyward, Jr., studying law at the Middle Temple in 1767, sent home news of a plan to raise £400,000 in the colonies. Parliament defeated the scheme, but the debate revealed people who wanted to make Americans "the most abject slaves." Perhaps the Carolinians' fears were exaggerated and unreal, but because of England's rapidly changing ministries, the colonists did not believe English assurances that Parliamentary taxes would never reduce them to poverty.[3]

But for those politically-minded Carolinians who, in Bull's words, entered "deep into Principles," the danger of unlimited taxation was only part of the issue raised by England. From 1765 on, when the period of serious opposition began, South Carolina placed Parliamentary actions in a larger and less materialistic context. Members of the Carolina Commons objected to the Stamp Tax not only because they had not levied it themselves, but also because they could not allow their "Provincial legislature to be subordinate to any legislative power on earth."[4]

In 1769 thirty-seven members of the Commons unanimously adopted the strong Virginia resolutions which condemned as "arbitrary and cruel," "oppressive and illegal," England's plan to revive a sixteenth-century statute for the transportation of colonists to England for trial. When in 1774 England tried to punish and subdue Boston and Massachusetts for the tea party in particular and revolutionary activity in general, South Carolina was the first among the colonies outside New England to raise money and provisions for Boston. Unawed by what Henry Laurens called Britain's plan to "terrify the other colonies," Carolinians saw that what happened to Massachusetts was to be resisted because it might otherwise someday happen to them. "The cause of Boston," wrote Josiah Smith, "has really become the cause of all America. . . ."[5]

During this decade and more of agitation and ill-will, when South Carolina joined forces with other colonies over common grievances, two local constitutional fights gave evidence of intense legislative devotion to principle. The dispute over Christopher Gadsden's election predated the Stamp Act and prepared the ground for that Act's rejection by the colony. The Wilkes fund controversy, which involved the lower house's control over the appropriation of money, occurred after 1769, when other colonies were relatively quiet, and kept South Carolina in active opposition to England.

The Gadsden election controversy began in April 1762 and lasted until 1764 when Gadsden and the Commons won an almost total, though unacknowledged victory. Because of a minor violation of the election act, Governor Thomas Boone refused to administer the oath that would enable Gadsden to take his seat in the Commons. But Boone went on to challenge the very foundations of Carolina's government: the people possessed no inherent rights to a legislature, and such a body owed its existence solely to England's approval of an election law.[6]

In response, the Commons upheld a broad constitutional doctrine, basing its right to a legislature on the "ancient Constitution of our Mother Country." Boone's action reduced "the Power and Authority of the House to an Abject dependence on, and Subserviency of the Will, and

Opinion of a Governor." On 16 December 1762 the Commons decided to do no more business with Boone until he apologized for violating its privileges. Not until 1764, when the unapologetic Boone sailed to England, where he was reprimanded for having "more Zeal than prudence," did the Commons function again as a legislative body.[7]

A few years later the lower house again fought for claimed rights. English officials were visibly annoyed when in 1769 the South Carolina Commons, without the approval of governor or council, ordered the treasurer to advance £1,500 sterling to the Wilkes fund for "the support of the Bill of Rights" in England. England's John Wilkes, who had been convicted of seditious libel for his violent criticism of George III, was repeatedly denied his seat in Parliament. His supporters created a radical organization for political reform in England, to which Carolina now contributed. England, made aware by the deliberate insult of the lower house's complete control over finances in the colony, instructed the royal governor not to approve any more bills appropriating money for nonprovincial purposes without the king's special consent. The Commons replied by defending in familiar terms its exclusive right to determine the forms of money bills and by denouncing the governor's additional instruction as one "opposite to Reason, Law, and the Constitution of the Colonies." The conflict unresolved, the Commons in 1772 again resorted to its forceful policy of inaction. After 1769 no tax bill was passed, after 1772 no legislation of any kind.[8] Although the British backed down in 1775, their silent concession was too late to be of any significance, for other events and other issues, notably the Boston Tea Party and the Coercive Acts, had replaced local concerns with a concern for the future of all America.

Few dissenters from South Carolina's legislative protest came forward; those who did, like William Wragg, a wealthy planter, a member of the Commons and, after 1769, of the Council, retained their colleagues' respect, at least until war approached. In the decades preceding the conflict, the members of the lower house had come to speak with one voice. Because England had destroyed the independence of the South Carolina Council by appointing to it men financially dependent on the Crown, Carolinians achieved political status from membership in the Commons, a body which represented the lowcountry, South Carolina's coastal region. Their political society was small and voters were few. In 1770 the Commons contained forty-eight members. St. John Berkeley, which elected three representatives, had seventy-six white males between sixteen and sixty on a road census in 1762. Ninety-four voters participated in the election in St. Paul which began the Gadsden-Boone fight in 1762. In that year there were only an estimated 3,500 free white adults in parishes surrounding Charleston and another 1,300 adult white males in the port.[9]

The lowcountry was one of the wealthiest sections of the mainland colonies. Planters, lawyers, and merchants sometimes made annual profits of between £1,000 and £3,000 sterling. Probate records of the 1760s and 1780s, which underrepresent the poor, evaluate only 3% of estates at under £100 (personal property — not including land). Tax records place the proportion of poor at about 12%. More than 60% of the estates were valued over £1,000 sterling. In Charleston almost 30% of the men left estates worth more than £1,000, in contrast to Boston where only approximately 20% left estates of that size.[10]

Individually, members of the Commons acquired recognition while they served their colony and protected their interests. Like their constituents they were rich. In 1765 over two-thirds of the representatives had property worth at least £5,000 each, while each of the others owned property worth more than £2,000. Not all the representatives had inherited their wealth. The introduction of indigo had provided men with a chance to move up. Probably between 20 and 40 percent of the members of the 1765 Commons were self-made men. Two of the twelve most active representatives between 1762 and 1765 were immigrants, and four or five were the sons of immigrants. Others who sat between 1762 and 1768 were men of little education and, probably, had but recently climbed the economic ladder.[11] Membership in the Commons meant that they had arrived.

Convinced of their own virtue and talent, cherishing the individual independence which wealth gave them, the legislators, unlike those in other colonies, divided into no permanent factions or opposing groups.[12] Those chosen to rule were intimately acquainted, meeting formally in Charleston to conduct colony business and gathering informally and socially to escape the summer heat of their plantations and their winter boredom. Their children intermarried. Fathers and sons, brothers, brothers-in-law, uncles, nephews, and cousins sat together in the Commons. Between 1762 and 1768 only seventy-five different people were members. At least forty-seven were related by marriage or blood (first cousin or closer). Twenty-five of the sixty-four whose residences are known lived in Charleston, sixteen lived there part of the year, twenty lived in lowcountry parishes, and only three in the interior of the colony. Peter Manigault, Speaker of the Commons, spoke for all its members when he remarked in 1768 that he was "well acquainted with the Circumstances of most . . . Inhabitants."[13]

With their wealth, Carolinians acquired an air of superiority which was sometimes justified. They traveled abroad, sent their children to England for education, and created in Charleston a flourishing center of cultural activity and communal entertainment. Their dances, concerts, and stage productions, their horse races, and their clubs filled their leisure hours. Wealth, culture, and education gave ruling Carolinians a sense of accomplishment. Lawyers, who were trained in London's Inns of Court and who watched English courts function and Parliament debate, like other Carolinians, concluded that they were at least equal to the English in their ability to govern themselves. Further proof of superiority and ability was found in the possession of blacks, some men counting as their own more than 200 slaves whose lives they could control down to the most private and most gruesome detail.[14]

The closeness of the legislators and their constituents was more than political, more than social and familial. Rulers and ruled, they were also drawn together by a self-imposed danger. Whites were surrounded, dangerously so, by black slaves whose numbers had increased rapidly enough to provide their masters with ample leisure and physical comfort but too rapidly for them to feel secure. By 1760 the plantation areas of South Carolina and Charleston contained close to 20,000 whites and more than 50,000 slaves. In 1762 the 76 adult white males in St. John Berkeley lived amongst 1,064 male slaves between sixteen and sixty; about the time of the Revolution St. Stephen's parish could muster only 126 white men while on its lands lived about 5,000 blacks.[15] Because the blacks were unpredictable, because the whites believed the slaves "barbarous, wild [and] savage," they feared that their wealth, their status, their lives could end momentarily. During the Stono Rebellion of 1739, in which more than twenty whites were killed, all Carolinians were "shocked" at the "Danger daily hanging over their Heads."[16] Tension was increased by the master's ignorance of his slaves' attitudes. Some humane owners were convinced that their slaves were "strongly attached" to them, but others were not sure. At least one Georgian argued after the 1739 rebellion that kindness would not produce loyal servants, because every man was "naturally fond of liberty." Fear of an uprising or of individual acts of violence led whites to avoid lasting controversy among themselves lest they appear divided and weak. Henry Laurens understandably thought splits within the colony "more awful and more distressing than Fire Pestilence or Foreign Wars."[17]

The danger and the anxiety grew in times of change or crisis. When the British government expelled French citizens from Canada during the French and Indian war, more than 1,000 were shipped to South Carolina. Carolinians worried that the newcomers would "join with the Negroes." Charles Pinckney, long-time member of the lower house, anticipated that slaves would be encouraged "to rise upon their masters and cut their throats in hopes of obtaining freedom."[18]

The controversy with England reawakened the lowcountry's fears of its blacks. In December 1765, a rumor of rebellion led acting governor William Bull to enlist the aid of Catawba Indians and the usually despised seamen in port. By 1773 many people feared insurrection, and the ensuing years brought no relief. The Charleston General Committee of Safety warned one parish in May 1775 that slaves would be incited to rebel. Henry Laurens heard and spread the news: the British would encourage "insurrections of our negroes attended by the most horrible butcheries of innocent women & children."[19]

The colony's response was as quick as it was predictable. In St. Bartholomew one black was executed and in Charleston vigilance uncovered two slaves who accused a prosperous free black, Thomas Jeremiah, known as Jerry, of plotting to smuggle guns to slaves. Jerry was tried, convicted, and executed, while the royal governor, Lord William Campbell, expressed his helplessness. "My blood ran cold," he wrote, "when I read on what ground they had doomed a fellow creature to death," but his intervention, he was told by one prominent figure, would "raise a flame all the water in Cooper River would not extinguish."[20]

Fear that the British would incite a race war increased after Lord Dunmore, royal governor of Virginia, issued his proclamation in November 1775 declaring free all the rebels' slaves and servants who would join the British. Edward Rutledge thought Dunmore's proclamation tended "more effectually to work an eternal separation between Great Britain and the Colonies, — than any other expedient, which could possibly have been thought of." In April 1776 John Rutledge, South Carolina's newly elected governor, told the state's legislators that "humanity must revolt" at the plans "to make the ignorant domesticks subservient to the most wicked purposes." The Council of Safety had already ordered Indians out to catch runaways, and the legislature followed with a law imposing the death penalty on slaves joining British land or naval forces. Two blacks were soon sentenced to be hanged for attempting escape in a schooner.[21]

Black slaves were more than a threat, however. White Carolinians measured their own freedom against the realities of black enslavement. They would not be made "the most abject slaves" or be led "from one degree of slavery to another."[22] They prided themselves on free will, independence, the "*right to think and act*" for themselves. "Servile submission" would make Americans "groan and sweat under a slavish life." America would be forced "to bow the Neck to Slavery." Christopher Gadsden was only one important Carolinian to use the compelling analogy: oppressed by British rule, he wrote in 1769, "we are as real SLAVES as those we are permitted to command."[23] Even inland settlers, with few blacks in their midst, made the connection. Complaining about their own bad treatment by the colonial legislature, they labelled themselves "Fifty Thousand Prime Slaves . . . Lately imported from Great Britain, Ireland, and the Northern Colonies." Edmund Burke, taking his lessons from history as well as from the events around him, understood. Southerners, like slaveowners of the ancient world, Burke said in Parliament, were "attached to liberty." "The haughtiness of domination combines with the spirit of freedom, fortifies it, and renders it invincible."[24]

For politically powerful Carolinians, therefore, protest was a matter of principle; it was not, for them, a matter of economic necessity. They did not fear immediate economic crises as many Northerners did, and they did not experience the realities of prolonged depression. England's policy of raising revenue by means of a duty on foreign molasses affected only those colonies whose distilleries turned molasses into rum; South Carolina imported rum ready made. Economically, the only legislation Carolinians deemed harmful was the Currency Act of 1764, which prohibited the further issuance of legal tender paper money and hampered the payment of debts. In 1766, therefore, the Carolina Commons protested, arguing that without more circulating medium the colony might be forced to discontinue importing from Great Britain. Again, however, other colonies suffered greater hardships. Some Charlestonians were pinched, but merchants circumvented the law and the colony as a whole was not seriously hurt.[25]

The colony's economic fate depended on the success of its two great staples, rice and indigo, both of which were affected by Parliamentary legislation. Rice had been enumerated in 1704 (it could then be shipped only to Great Britain or British colonies), but its fate had been unlike that of tobacco, the enumerated staple of Virginia and Maryland. Carolinians found a good, large, and legal market for their rice in the British West Indies. Furthermore, in 1730 Parliament opened up the valuable markets of Spain and Portugal, and in 1764 it allowed direct shipment of Carolina rice to the French and Spanish West Indies. Of the 130,601 barrels of rice exported between 1 November 1770 and 10 October 1771, ports in Great Britain received only 73,235½ barrels.[26]

The second staple, indigo, introduced in the 1740s in an attempt to diversify the colony's agriculture, was first exported in 1747. With the bounty provided by Parliament in 1748, indigo rapidly became the second most important South Carolina export, its value even exceeding that of rice in 1757 and 1758.[27]

During the 1760s and 70s, while political and constitutional controversy raged throughout America, and while other colonies suffered economic depressions, Carolina prospered. Both the quantity and value of the colony's exports rose. In 1756 approximately 83,000 barrels of rice were exported, in 1760, 64,000. In 1768, 132,000 barrels were shipped out, in 1773, 133,000. In 1756 the wholesale price in Charleston for rice had been 4.9 shillings per hundred pounds; it was 8.2 shillings in 1766, and 9.3 in 1768. The high was 11.7 shillings in 1772. Production of indigo likewise increased. In 1756 almost 400,000 pounds were exported, 450,000 pounds in 1764, and 599,000 in 1766, and though that figure was not again reached until 1773, in each intervening year, with but one exception, more than 460,000 pounds of indigo were exported.[28]

"The Planters here all got rich," wrote Robert Wells, printer of the *South-Carolina and American General Gazette,* in August 1765. The colony's success was reflected in the planters' increased demands for imported luxuries and necessities: their money making had "not a little rais'd their ambition and inclined too many of them to be very extravagant in their purchases," Josiah Smith reported.[29] In the purchase of slaves, necessities for most and ostentatious luxuries for some, the planters' extravagance showed clearly. An estimated 4,612 slaves were imported in 1769, 3,000 in 1771, almost 5,000 in 1772, and 8,000 in 1773.[30]

As was the custom, the planters bought on credit and created a large debt. Immediately before the outbreak of fighting, Carolinians owed British creditors £412,000 sterling, a debt second only to the more than £2,000,000 owed by the Virginia planters.[31] But since the debt was roughly equal to the value of one year's exports, it was not of much concern.

South Carolina's basic economic interests were not threatened by Parliamentary legislation. No one would complain about the indigo bounty. Few people spoke up about the regulations which remained on the shipments of rice. Few, if any, urged revolution as a means of forestalling or cancelling the payment of debts.

Part II: Division

Despite the unanimity of Carolinians in their dealings with slaves and the near unanimity of colonial leaders on what Henry Laurens called "the grand essential points" — most vital being the need to remain free from British tyranny — there were many-faceted, serious divisions among Carolinians. They were deepened by the revolutionary crisis. Disputes over methods of opposition were neither extraordinary nor unexpected. Far more dangerous was the division which in simple but inadequate terms pitted west against east, backcountry against lowcountry. Often, however, lowcountry parishes near North Carolina and Georgia joined the interior in opposition to the parishes in the immediate vicinity of Charleston and to the few dominant families who resided there. In the port of Charleston, numerous artisans and mechanics challenged old rulers. The disagreement among the active rebels over means of protest arose only because there was a revolutionary crisis. The geographic division and the split within Charleston existed independently of the crisis, but because of it they became crucial. The splits seriously affected the speed and extent of change in South Carolina.

Although by June 1775 the direction of the colony's internal affairs had been taken over by an extralegal government, a provincial congress, most members of the Commons House simply moved into the new and larger revolutionary bodies where they fought among themselves and with others to determine policies appropriate for the battle with England.[32] Observers noted their disagreements over tactics: What forms should opposition take? How far should it go? Alexander Innes, secretary of the royal governor (and a secret political informer of Lord Dartmouth, Secretary of State for America), thought that moderates were separated from radicals by wealth. "The Opulent and Sensible," he reported, "wish to avoid . . . desperate measures," but the "Violent, who are in general the needy," opposed them, feeling that they "might in the struggle mend their situation.'' Printer Peter Timothy, of the violent faction, agreed in part. He found the ''Plebeians'' supporting war and ''the noblesse perfectly pacific.''[33]

But even if the needy plebeians were more extreme as a group than the opulent noblesse, there was little economic distinction between the leaders of the violent and moderate parties. In 1775 the radical party, which sought to prepare for war and distinguish friend from foe, was led by Arthur Middleton, a Middle Temple lawyer and son of Henry Middleton (president of the Continental Congress in May 1775 and owner of hundreds of slaves); William Henry Drayton, a wealthy planter, former councilor and supreme court judge, and Christopher Gadsden, a rich merchant. They were opposed by a more moderate group led by another wealthy planter, Rawlins Lowndes (nicknamed *Ralinus postponator* by Arthur Middleton), and two rich merchants, Miles Brewton, who eventually left for England, and Henry Laurens.[34] To Arthur Middleton these were ''timid, lukewarm'' people who were willing ''to make a *retrograde progress.*'' To Innes they were leaders afraid of ''the lengths already gone'' and ready ''to check the torrent.''[35]

Yet Innes knew that too much could be made of these open splits. He reported the five men chosen to represent the colony at the second Continental Congress ''ready to cut one another's throats,'' knowing, however, that they agreed on ''the grand point of distressing Britain.'' The fights, Lieutenant Governor Bull wrote, were ''not between the friends of government and of democracy, but between demagogues of different opinions.'' Some men, a writer to the *South Carolina Gazette* observed, hesitated when decisive action was required. But their conduct was only ''the Offspring of Timidity.''[36]

That ''men may agree in general'' as Laurens had written, ''but no two men believe in all points exactly alike,'' became more obvious with the debate over independence. By 1775 many Englishmen believed that the colonists were striving for ''Independancy.''[37] What the English did not understand was that ''Independancy,'' at least for leading Carolinians, meant only the old arrangement which allowed Americans to control their internal affairs. Formal independence was not desired; but for many it became the only means of gaining what England would not grant. As a tactic it aroused much opposition, for it was radical, perhaps irrevocable, and dangerous.

Many Carolinians hoped Great Britain would ''awaken out of her lethargy'' and return the colonists to the conditions under which they had lived before 1763. Their attitude was apparent when, early in 1776, in response to a recommendation of the Continental Congress, South Carolina's Congress began to consider a constitution. On 6 February William Henry Drayton, president of the South Carolina Provincial Congress, declared that members could choose between independence and slavery.

Christopher Gadsden, who had just returned from the Continental Congress armed with the colony's first copy of Thomas Paine's *Common Sense,* supported independence. But Henry Laurens thought the idea "indecent"; John Rutledge found it treasonable; and Rawlins Lowndes was shocked.[38] The arguments in Paine's work were "too strong to be gainsay'd," wrote Josiah Smith, yet the pamphlet was called "*Nonsense.*" A committee buried Gadsden's proposal. The colony's constitution, adopted in March 1776, was to last only until "the unhappy differences" between Britain and America were resolved.[39]

Laurens's hesitancy about independence was understood by men not as ready to place their thoughts on paper. "One more year," he wrote in February 1776, "will enable us to be independent. Ah! that word cuts me deep — has caused tears to trickle down my cheeks." When in less than a year independence came, he returned again to the painful thought. He felt like a "dutiful son, thrust by the hand of violence out of a father's house into the wide world."[40]

Men of Laurens's class had longstanding ties with England. They visited there (Laurens was there as late as 1774) and sent their children there for education (John Laurens was still in England when the fighting in America broke out). Many had business associates there. The ties were not easily broken.

Undoubtedly at least as important for the members of the provincial congress and their constituents who opposed independence was the fear of an unruly mob and new political forces. The fear, shared by leaders in other colonies, was born not of ignorance but of their knowledge of South Carolina's internal divisions and of experience perhaps stimulated by their own ideas and actions. "Your Lordship will easily see with what art the *Herd* has been led on from one step to another," Alexander Innes told Lord Dartmouth, who had already learned from William Bull that men of property were beginning to see danger in the "many headed power the People," for they were becoming independent.[41] Some men of property had seen the danger earlier. In October 1765 Charleston crowds had burned effigies, buried the coffin of "American Liberty," forced their way into Henry Laurens's house, searched for the hated stamps, and generally carried on in a boisterous enough way to prompt the *South Carolina Gazette* to report that "the richer folks were terrified at a spirit which [they] themselves had conjured up. . . ." Merchant Benjamin Smith hailed repeal of the Stamp Act not only because it restored liberty to America but also because "the lower class who have been made men of consequence in the late comotions" saw that their consequence "is now sunk into nothing."[42]

Some of the new political figures whose activities frightened the colony's leaders were artisans and mechanics in Charleston. Although the presence of slaves kept down the number of white craftsmen — and poor whites — the shipwrights, coopers, cobblers, and other mechanics were numerous. Many were successful enough to realize social and economic ambitions. Cabinet maker Thomas Elfe purchased town lands and tenements. John Paul Grimké and Jonathan Sarrazin, silversmiths, owned plantations, as did Daniel Cannon, a carpenter. Sarrazin was one of many mechanics to engage in shipping enterprises. And, because of the scarcity of white laborers, craftsmen became slaveowners. Of the 194 identifiable mechanics listed as heads of families in the 1790 census, 159 owned slaves.[43] Slavery was a mixed blessing, however, since the craftsmen were training workers who often became competitors.

But their success notwithstanding, the craftsmen did not exercise political power or substantial influence, even though they could easily meet the property requirement for voting — payment of a twenty shilling currency tax. Following the traditional pattern, they elected to represent them resident plantation owners, merchants, or lawyers. They were equally powerless in the running of Charleston, which was governed by the planter-dominated legislature. Despite the repeated protests of grand juries, mechanic groups, and individuals, the legislature stubbornly refused to incorporate the port.

The conflict with England gave artisans and mechanics their chance. They opposed the Stamp Act with public protests and demonstrations. While Benjamin Smith might be pleased that repeal of the act denied "the lower class" a stage, the setback was brief. The years of controversy after 1765 were years of growing political consciousness and action for Carolinians of different orders and locales. Between 1765 and 1768 mechanics founded the John Wilkes Club, which nominated candidates, still of the upper class, however, for office. Whereas in the past the Commons' concern for harmony had required recognition of only three major interests — four planters, four merchants, and four lawyers were the most important legislators between 1762 and 1765 — by 1774 everyone, "the Gentleman & Mechanic, those of high and low life, the learned & illiterate," was discussing politics and "American affairs" and influencing policy.[44] Charleston's artisans and mechanics pushed a nonimportation plan through popular meetings in 1769 with planter support and in the face of merchant opposition. Then they highlighted their success and the very legitimacy of their participation by joining with others to create a thirty-nine-member committee of enforcement that included equal numbers of planters, merchants, and mechanics.[45]

Artisans and mechanics were motivated not only by opportunity, but also by economic need. They were the only Carolinians consistently affected adversely by English policy. The shortage of currency, the decline of trade with New England, and the Townshend duties on glass, lead, painters' colors, and some paper, restricted their economic chances. And they were always competing for customers with merchants who sold British

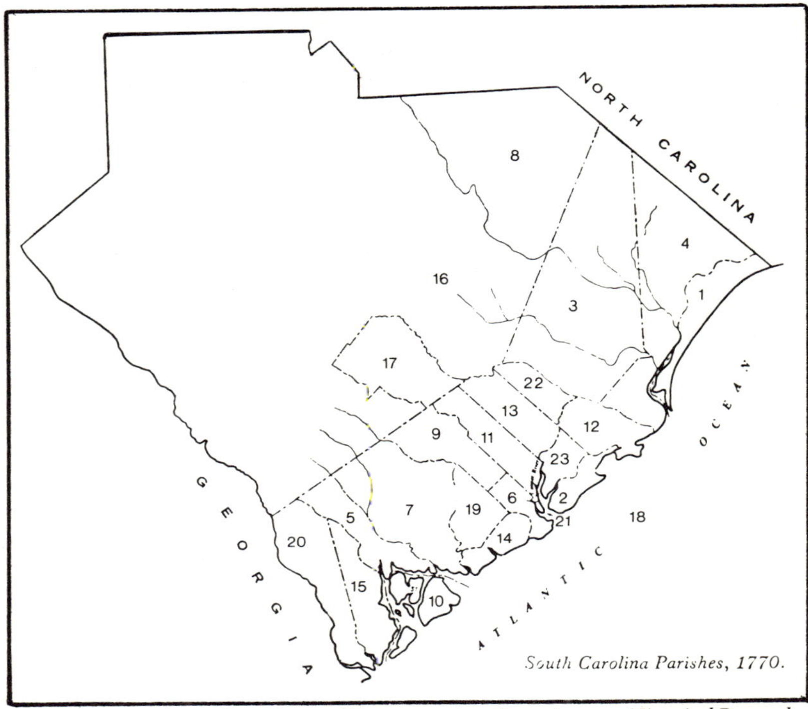

South Carolina Parishes, 1770.

Courtesy, South Carolina House of Representatives Committee on Historical Research

goods. The craftsmen most ardently pushed nonimportation in 1769; the scheme finally approved closed the port to British imports and struck at their competitors by prohibiting the importation of Negroes and by banning purchases of British goods from transient traders. But repeal of the Townshend Revenue Act in 1770 ended the craftsmen's hope that Carolina manufactures would be stimulated. Artisans and mechanics could not enlist planter support to continue nonimportation until the tea tax was repealed.[46]

The other political newcomers whose appearance was feared by the colony's leaders were the westerners. On the eve of war the most pressing split within the colony was between west and east. Backcountry and lowcountry differed geographically and culturally. The lowcountry consisted of the sea islands, the most important ones lying along the southern coast of the colony, the coast adjoining the islands, and the lower pine belt, together making a strip of land roughly sixty miles wide. When the legislature divided the colony into circuit court districts in 1769, the lowcountry districts became known as Georgetown, Charleston, and Beaufort. Georgetown, in the north, extended from the North Carolina border to

Apportionment among the Colonial Parishes 1716–1775

	Parish	1716	1719	1721	1734	1745	1747	1751	1754	1757	1765	1767	1768	1775
1	All Saints											2		
	Christ Church	2	2	2	2	2	2	2	2	2	2	2	2	2
	Prince Frederick				2	2	2	2	2	2	2	2	2	2
	Prince George Winyah			2	2	2	2	2	2	2	2	2	2	2
5	Prince William					2	2	2	2	2	2	2	2	2
	St. Andrew	4	3	3	3	3	3	3	3	3	3	3	3	3
	St. Bartholomew	3	4	4	4	4	4	4	4	4	4	4	4	4
	St. David													
	St. George Dorchester			2	2	2	2	2	2	2	2	2	2	2
10	St. Helena	3	4	4	4	3	3	3	3	3	3	3	3	3
	St. James Goose Creek	3	4	4	4	4	4	4	4	4	4	4	3	3
	St. James Santee	1	2	2	2	2	2	2	2	2	2	2	2	2
	St. John Berkeley	3	3	3	3	3	3	3	3	3	3	3	3	3
	St. John Colleton				3	3	3	3	3	3	3	3	3	3
15	St. Luke											2		
	St. Mark									2	2	2	1	1
	St. Matthew										2	2	1	1
	St. Michael							3	3	3	3	3	3	3
	St. Paul	4	4	4	3	3	3	3	3	3	3	3	3	3
20	St. Peter						1	1	1	1	1	1	1	1
	St. Philip	4	5	5	5	5	5	3	3	3	3	3	3	3
	St. Stephen								1	1	1	1	1	1
	St. Thomas & St. Dennis	3	3	3	3	3	3	3	3	3	3	3	3	3

the Santee River, Charleston from the Santee to the Combahee River, and Beaufort from the Combahee to the Savannah River, which separated the colony from Georgia. The backcountry was the area of upper pine belt, red and sand hills to the north and west of the coastal districts.[47]

Differences between backcountry and lowcountry settlers and settlements were as clear as, and more important than, geographical differences. Most of the maritime parishes, particularly those between the Santee and Combahee rivers, had been settled long before by a mixed group of colonists attracted by the proprietors' promotional campaign and by promise of religious toleration. Before 1700 English Presbyterians and Baptists, Presbyterian Scots, and French Huguenots had settled the area close to Charleston. Although most of the dissenting groups had fought political battles with English Anglicans who migrated from Barbados, the battles along religious lines had long since ended. The Church of England became the established church, financially supported by Anglican and non-Anglican alike; many Huguenots converted, and families intermarried.[48] Settled early, these parishes, all close to Charleston, dominated the colonial government. By 1717 ten parishes had been established around the port. In 1757 the entire colony had nineteen parishes, including two for Charleston. Only St. Mark was more than sixty miles from the coast. It was the lowcountry whose economy was dominated by the staple crops, rice and indigo, and whose labor force was black.

Beginning in 1730, under Governor Robert Johnson, settlement of the interior was encouraged to provide the lowcountry with greater military protection from slaves, Indians, and the agents of competing European governments. Townships stretching across the frontier were established and peopled by Germans, Swiss, Dutch, Irish, Scots, Scots-Irish, Welsh, and English. Some came directly from Europe, others from colonies to the north. They were Presbyterians, Seceders (Reform Presbyterians), Lutherans, Baptists, Anglicans, French Huguenots, and Quakers. And, partly because of the isolation of the backcountry, many were "destitute of a regular parochial attendance on divine worship."[49]

Backcountry settlers, like those of the coastal parishes, lived with the threat of violence from hostile, alien people. But their fears were often realized. The violence of their lives was frightening and brutalizing. Early in 1760, Cherokee Indians, angered by clashes in Virginia, attacked whites all over the backcountry. Large parties of settlers fleeing to safety were ambushed. Nine children whose scalps had been slashed were brought into Augusta, Georgia, on one day. Danger and suffering were constant: twenty-seven people killed at Rayburns Creek; a short time later, twenty-five killed at Congaree Creek; six Negroes carried off from one plantation; several whites killed when they left the protection of a fort to tend their lands. When the whites mobilized and resisted, their anger intensified the savagery. After one battle, whites joyfully fed Indian scalps to dogs.[50]

Settlers who escaped their farms and outran the Indians huddled, inadequately fed and clothed, in overcrowded backcountry forts. One small fort on the Enoree housed 400. All told, almost 1,500 people spent the winter in thirty forts. Smallpox spread through the interior, and fourteen people died of it at Ninety Six.

The war dragged on into 1761, but the Indians were weakened by an unusually hard winter. They made peace in December after a summer campaign by British regulars and provincials destroyed their Middle Towns.

The effects of the war were serious and lasting. Settlers fortunate enough to survive were economically ruined or set back. Many were victimized after the war by criminals whose habits were formed during the war. As David Ramsay wrote after the Revolution, "the wrong-doers lived easily at the expense of the absentees. . . ." They became "pests of society," having discovered that "to steal was easier than to work."

The Cherokee War, demonstrating that the colony's small size left it vulnerable, provided new impetus for the settlement of the interior. French Protestants, Germans, and Scots-Irish from Europe and northern colonies arrived in the new wave and increased the population of the interior from about 20,000 in 1759 to over 50,000 in 1775. Almost all settled

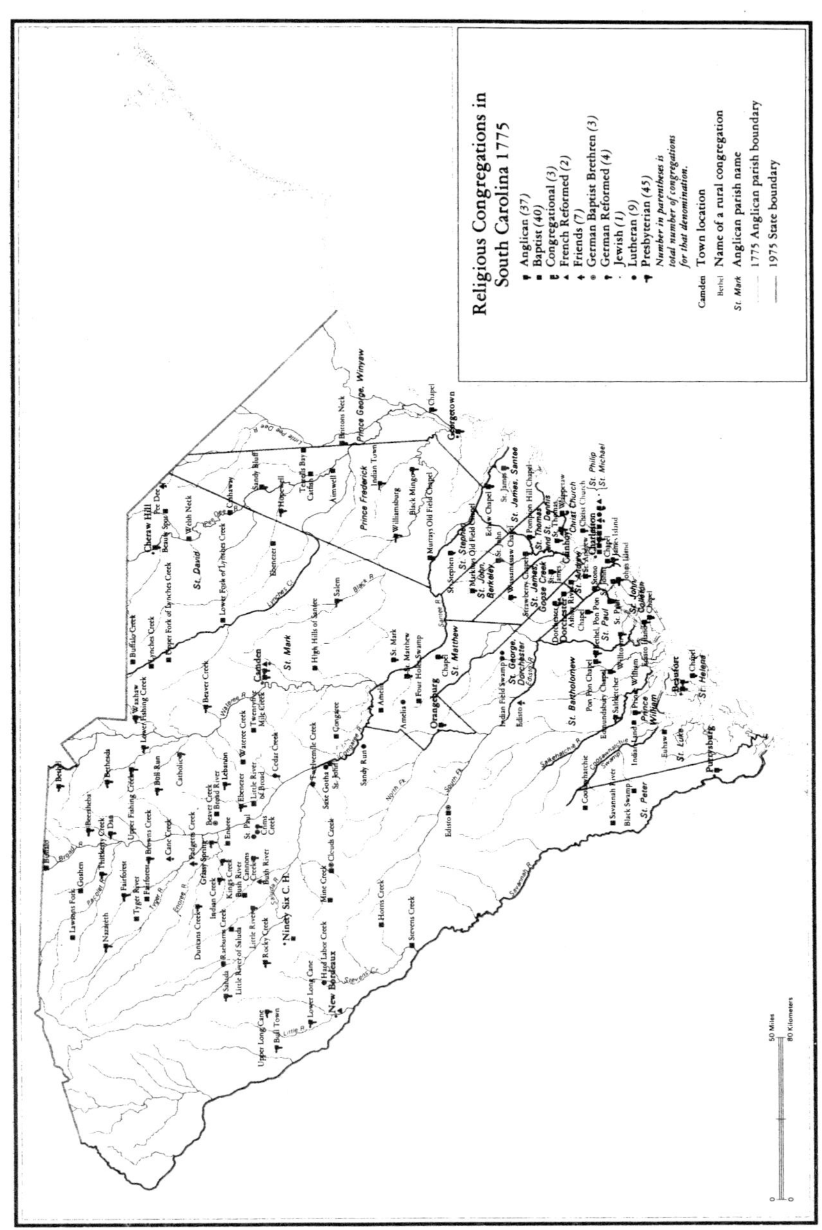

Adapted by permission, Princeton University Press

on small farms where, without the aid of substantial numbers of blacks, they produced provision crops of corn and wheat, and, in some areas, tobacco and indigo.[51]

As the colony edged closer to war, lowcountry political leaders had cause to worry about opposition to their policies that would trap them between the British and hostile inland settlers. Their fears stemmed from bitter confrontations with backcountry settlers.

In the late 1760s settlers in the backcountry and the northeastern part of the lowcountry, pointedly denouncing their lowcountry rulers, had joined forces to better their lives by whatever means necessary. They sought no scapegoats for personal failings; their problems were real, serious, and not particularly of their own making. Rapid growth following the Cherokee War, together with the disorganization caused by ruinous Indian raids, disease, and an almost unbelievable influx of criminals operating in an intercolonial ring, created overwhelming problems. The Reverend Charles Woodmason, a spokesman for the enraged settlers, poignantly described a part of the distress when he wrote of the theft and destruction of cows, horses, and property, of the ravishing of married women, the deflowering of virgins, "and other unheard of cruelties committed by these barbarous Ruffians."[52]

Perhaps encouraged by the Commons' fight against English actions, the backcountry settlers began to petition and protest. Borrowing the rhetoric of the lowcountry, they objected that legislators made "such Noise about Liberty" while oppressing "*Free-Men* — British subjects — Not Born *Slaves.*" And, because "Oppression will make Wise Men, Mad," they took the law into their own hands to punish criminals terrorizing them.[53]

The defiant settlers, calling themselves "Regulators" because of their immediate desire to establish order, had old complaints, some apparently trivial to the unaffected but taken together, as they were experienced, testifying to the daily burdens that wore down backcountry people. In 1765 the interior had only about forty justices of the peace, the local officials appointed by the legislature who not only decided civil cases involving less than £20 currency, but who also controlled free blacks and slaves, licensed taverns, and sent men to jail to await trial or released them on bail. And many of the incumbent justices were incompetent. Too few road commissioners were appointed to supervise the work needed for the improvement of travel and trade. Although the parishes which served lowcountry residents extended inland, their vague boundaries left people confused and the territories encompassed so large as to make impossible collection of any poor tax or care for the poor. There were too few ministers (which was not the responsibility of the government), and the lack of schools meant that children grew up ignorant "of ev'ry Thing, Save Vice — in which they are Adepts."[54] Westerners did not even have ready access to the colony's laws, for there was no digest or code, and new legislation was apparently not publicized inland. The Reverend Woodmason summed up most of the annoyances: "is it not Slavery to be without wise Magistrates — Without Religion — Without Laws — Without Police — Without Churches — Without Clergy. . . ? And is it not Slavery," he asked, "for to have no Roads, Ferries, or Bridges. . . ?"[55]

In taking immediate steps to alleviate their problems, the Regulators acted in the violent manner which had become ordinary in the backcountry. They rounded up and viciously flogged criminals, one receiving 500 stripes from a band of about 50 Regulators; they burned the houses of people suspected of aiding the criminals. And, apparently suffering from a labor shortage, they turned their attention to the idle and lazy. South Carolina was the only southern colony without a vagrancy law. Regulators adopted their own, whipping vagrants and setting to work idle persons they thought reclaimable. So violent and arbitrary did their methods become, however, that they were finally opposed by people known as Moderators.[56]

To suppress the criminals and to ease their lives by reducing or eliminating what could be a 200 mile trek to Charleston (and back) for justice, the Regulators demanded a system of county and circuit courts. It was not a new plea, for Governor Glen had requested an expansion of the judicial system in 1754. But as it was, captured criminals and witnesses to their actions had to be transported to Charleston, there to wait until lowcountry judges and juries with no knowledge of backcountry life announced their decisions. Civil cases not handled by local justices involved the same inconvenience. The unjust system of justice was "*Slavery,*" too, said Woodmason.[57]

The Regulators' grievances were many, so numerous that an "Advertisement" in a Charleston newspaper argued the cause of the unfortunate settlers by satirically announcing the sale of "Fifty Thousand Prime Slaves . . . Lately imported from Great Britain, Ireland, and the Northern Colonies." Perhaps the fundamental complaint, however, was their lack of adequate representation in the Assembly.[58] It is, wrote Woodmason, "to this Great Disproportion of Representatives on our Part, that our Interests have been so long neglected, and the Back Country disregarded."[59] Before 1765 the legislature had laid out only one backcountry parish, St. Mark, and that probably as much to protect the rights of the traditional lowcountry rulers as to give the residents what they deserved. Thomas Lynch, a planter, and Paul Trapier, a merchant, both wealthy, had begun in the late 1740s to dominate the political affairs of Prince Frederick, a lowcountry parish extending north and west and containing a rapidly growing population. But by 1754 the people of the more remote regions outvoted the Lynch and Trapier supporters and replaced them with new representatives. The legislature met the situation by creating St. Mark in 1757, which allowed Lynch and his friends to reassert their leadership in Prince Frederick.[60]

For most of the period, the legislature's response was meager. Laws were not collected and published, and education was not provided, low-country leaders apparently assuming that those who deserved schooling would somehow provide for it themselves. Justices of the peace, as well as road commissioners, were finally increased in number, but they were not given the additional powers requested and perhaps not chosen with the best interests of the backcountry in mind. In December 1774 the grand jury of Ninety Six District complained of the appointment of magistrates acceptable to Charleston merchants and therefore presumably unsympathetic to backcountry purchasers. Governor Glen's suggestion in 1754 for inland courts died after its first reading in the Commons.[61] But the low-country did understand the problem, however unsympathetic its actions. When the Commons protested the proposed stamp tax, it argued that in addition to all its other sins the tax increased legal costs, "which, to our back settlers, that live some at two hundred or three hundred miles distance from Charles Town, must be very distressing indeed."[62] When the lower house finally attempted to provide some judicial relief, England and the Council stood in the way. The Commons, however, could simply have created additional courts under the precinct act of 1721, which had provided for the establishment of courts outside Charleston, and which had never been repealed.[63]

Lowcountry legislators seldom explicitly denounced the residents of the interior, but their behavior betrayed their belief that the area was a desperate place filled with hardened criminals and sinners, and that help need not be extended to the virtuous. Quite possibly John Rutledge did call the Regulators "a Pack of Beggars," as Woodmason charged, but whether he wished in the Commons "that the Back Country was at Bottom of the Sea," or not, it is easy to see why the Regulators did not trust the legislature and why they rejected what had "for many Years been the Prescription of . . . [their] Political Quacks": the advice to "Have Patience — Have Patience!"[64]

When pressure mounted, in the form of the Regulators' vigilante movement, resistance to the decrees of Charleston courts and officials, and the mobilization of backcountry settlers to vote in the coastal polling places, the legislature responded with one major reform, an expanded court system. In 1768, the Commons, Council, and governor finally approved the creation of six circuit courts, four of them for the backcountry. During the drafting of the bill, however, a much wanted provision for county courts was deleted, to the surprise and despair of the Regulators. The legislature further complicated the judicial picture by providing that the new judges receive good behavior appointments, which was almost certain to arouse the opposition of England because it denied the royal government the right to remove the judges whenever it saw fit. When England for that reason disallowed the act, the legislature removed the clause and passed in 1769 a circuit court act which was not to be put into operation until jails and courthouses were built in each district. That took until 1772.[65]

For the continuation of some difficulties, the Commons might blame England. In 1765 the South Carolina legislature had joined two backcountry townships to form St. Matthew parish, which it allowed two representatives. But two years later the English disallowed the act and instructed governors not to approve laws changing the size of the legislature.[66] The veto left the backcountry in a position of political impotence. The legislature partially circumvented the royal disallowance by granting St. Matthew one representative while taking one away from St. James Goose Creek.[67] But since such reapportionment would ultimately deprive the lowcountry of its political power, it was not likely to continue.

If England was a source of grief, however, the Regulators did not acknowledge it. They denounced the lowcountry for all their troubles. "Our cries must have pierced their ears, though not entered into their hearts," wrote the Reverend Woodmason, while Peter Timothy, of the *South Carolina Gazette,* privately noted that the "Solicitations" of backcountry settlers were "too much disregarded."[68] The Regulators sensed that the legislators were not doing all they could. Since the Commons, during its fight with Governor Boone, had strongly defended the people's right to representation in a legislature, it should have greeted England's denial of representation for over half the population with equally forceful resolutions. None were passed. The Commons was too busy defending its right to appropriate money to the Wilkes fund, indicating to Regulators that its own refined legislative rights were more important to the lowcountry leaders than backcountry representation.

Admirable in theory, the lower house's defense of selected principles threatened backcountry lives. During the Boone-Gadsden dispute, when the lower house refused to deal with the governor, the frontier was beset by Indian trouble. Late in 1763 the Creeks attacked western settlers and once again drove them into frontier forts. Governor Boone, perhaps hoping that the incidents would force the Assembly to act, called the legislature into special session. Boone discovered, as the Regulators soon would, that people who lived securely "near the sea coast" turned deaf ears to the cries of the inland settlers.[69] Gadsden, emphasizing principle, put their inaction in better light, but "that he would rather submit to the destruction of one half of the Country than . . . give up the point in dispute with the Governor" was anything but comforting to the unrepresented backcountry settlers whose lives and property were being sacrificed.[70]

The underlying attitude of the legislators began to change early in the 1770s. The Regulator movement had drawn attention to the area, some lowcountry people who visited it, impressed by its beauty and potential, began, like Pierce Butler, to buy large quantities of land. Because of such ties, the backcountry gathered support; although the Commons did not succeed in getting through the Council a bill to increase representation for the interior in defiance of England's instruction not to alter the size of the legislature, Woodmason was still able to write in 1771 that "the Back Inhabitants are (at Last) carrying the Points they've so long labour'd for."[71] For the lowcountry, the difficulties with England and the threat of slave rebellions in subsequent years made union more desirable.

South Carolina's colonial rulers recognized their problem. Few in number, they were caught between numerous, often hostile, westerners who were demanding new power and English officials who were claiming an old authority. "We must have *peace* or rather *union* let it cost what it may," wrote Arthur Middleton in 1775, while Henry Laurens was sufficiently optimistic to think possible at least a "promise [of] absolute neutrality" from the backcountry.[72] Seeking peace, neutrality, or union, a five-man mission was sent inland by the colony's Provincial Congress to explain the American cause to the uncommitted and disaffected. The five men were well chosen for their task. William Henry Drayton was accompanied by two dissenting ministers, the Reverend William Tennent, pastor of the Presbyterian Church in Charleston, and the Reverend Oliver Hart, pastor of the Baptist Church of Charleston for more than twenty-five years, and two influential backcountry settlers, Joseph Kershaw, a merchant from the Camden area, and Colonel Richard Richardson, first elected to the Commons in 1754 by the remote residents of Prince Frederick, and a military hero during the Cherokee campaigns of 1759, 1760, and 1761.[73]

The mission ignored the area between the town of Camden and the Little Pee Dee River, the northeastern area where the Regulators had been particularly strong, and concentrated on the lands south of the Congaree River (Saxe-Gotha township) and between the Broad and Saluda rivers. The northeast, which probably had a larger percentage of settlers from other colonies and from the Carolina coast than other frontier areas, did not worry the lowcountry leaders as much as the western territory, with its Germans, Scots-Irish, and Irish. Apparently afraid that disloyalty would cause the king to annul their land grants, many of the Germans and their neighbors had taken an oath to support "his Majesty's Government."[74] Lowcountry leaders worried that the royal governor would try to suppress the rebellion with the loyal population. Drayton especially made moving speeches, but "notwithstanding the Watery Eyes of the Mynheers & their Frows," the mission made little progress.[75]

There was enough division so that conflict occurred. Drayton averted one battle between the 1,000 men aiding him and a 1,200 man Tory force by agreeing to a treaty. The Tories indicated that they wanted only to live in peace; they would not join the British. They promised to deliver to the proper authorities any person who opposed the actions of the provincial congress. The treaty, however, was denounced by other leading Tories, and fighting soon began. When lowcountry rebels sent powder and lead to the Cherokees, hoping to ensure their loyalty, nervous backcountry settlers led by Patrick Cunningham, whose Tory brother had been arrested in Charleston, intercepted the supplies in fear that the Indians would make war on them. By a margin of two votes, the Provincial Congress then decided to seize the leaders of the opposition. With between four thousand and five thousand men, three thousand of them from the backcountry, Colonel Richardson broke up backcountry resistance. A rebel force of 1,300 defeated the Tories. About 130 were taken prisoner, a massacre apparently prevented only by the leadership of Colonel William Thomson.[76]

The threat of armed opposition, however, was but one aspect of the backcountry challenge. Another was political: the backcountry would demand extensive internal political changes to increase its virtually nonexistent power and to gain more favorable recognition of its dissenting religions. The native colonial rulers reacted to the demand for such change as they reacted to lower-class participation in political life. But they could not prevent change. Partly because the lowcountry was itself divided, containing large sections whose people might join in protest with settlers further inland, the political leaders were forced to make substantial concessions whether they had any "love of innovation" or not.

The division within the lowcountry was visible as early as January 1775, when it first emerged as a tactical split over the Continental Association. The split, however, proved to be primarily economic and political rather than tactical, and not at all an isolated phenomenon. When in January the Provincial Congress met in Charleston, bitter debate was evoked by the Association, the three-month-old agreement of the Continental Congress to interdict trade with Great Britain, Ireland, and the West Indies. Because the legal trade some colonies had with Europe could continue, South Carolina's delegation sought to have exception made for Carolina's enumerated products, rice and indigo. Failing, they compromised on rice, so that after 10 September 1775, of all the myriad articles of trade previously exported to Great Britain, Ireland, or the West Indies, only rice ultimately destined for Europe could be shipped to England.[77]

Even though the delegation set forth a scheme by which indigo growers could be compensated for their lost trade, some Carolinians began to talk of censuring their "late Deputies for partiality in favouring the exportation of Rice."[78] Christopher Gadsden, the one delegate to the Continental Congress who had opposed favoring either rice or indigo, rose in the Provincial Congress and denounced the actions of his four colleagues, John and Edward Rutledge, Thomas Lynch, and Henry Middleton. Gadsden and a great many others, considering "their interests as sacrificed to the emolument of the Rice Planters," demanded total nonexportation. To the idea that compensation might be paid indigo planters, they responded that it should then also be paid "the Hemp Grower, the

Lumber Cutter, the Corn Planters. . . . That, as we were all one people, we should all suffer alike.'' But the ''Indigo party'' lost a close vote after an all-day argument when, instead of taking the vote as usual, by acclamation, it was put individually. ''Each man's name was called, and he declared himself *yea,* or *nay,*'' so that ''some were overawed, either by their diffidence, circumstances, or connexions. . . .'' A complicated and unworkable compensation scheme was approved and rice growers were free to plant and market their crops.[79]

Too often, the lowcountry has been described as a monolithic region of plantations producing both rice and indigo. Governor James Glen may have been responsible for the error. Indigo, he had noted in the 1750s, was a perfect second crop for diversification because it could be grown on the high lands surrounding the rice swamps. Furthermore, the indigo season ended in the summer, allowing planters to ''manufacture Rice in the ensuing Part of the Year.'' The impression Glen gave at a time when indigo was fast becoming an important crop led to the idea that indigo and rice were often grown together. But Edward Rutledge accurately described later agricultural developments when he wrote in 1787 that rice, indigo, and tobacco were grown ''in different divisions of the Country; & scarcely any two of them by one & the the same persons.''[80]

The most important indigo lands, the sea islands off the southern coast, the land around the Santee, Congaree, and Wateree rivers, and, in the northeast, the land around the Pee Dee and Black rivers, were separate and distinct from the rice lands. Edisto Island's indigo supposedly ''sold at a higher rate than any other manufactured in the State,'' and St. Helena island was so devoted to the crop that as late as 1791 it was still ''wholly attentive to the Cultivation of Indigo.'' St. Stephen parish, just south of the Santee River, was settled by French Huguenots and made rich by indigo.[81] Further west along the southern side of the river, indigo was grown in the section of Orangeburg District that had become St. Matthew parish. Along the Wateree River in Camden District, like Orangeburg outside the lowcountry, indigo brought considerable money to the planters.[82] And east of Camden, indigo, the best in the colony some thought, was grown along the Pee Dee and Black rivers in Cheraw and Georgetown districts. As early as 1755, some of Georgetown's prospering indigo planters founded the educational and charitable Winyaw Indigo Society.[83]

The planters who produced indigo were newly wealthy and politically deprived. Like the backcountry, Georgetown had been settled late, large numbers not coming until the 1740s and 50s. Many of the settlers were non-English, the Welsh and French being numerous. And again like the backcountry, both Georgetown District and Beaufort District, close to Georgia, were hopelessly underrepresented. In 1771, when the Commons was still functioning, the predominantly rice-growing Charleston District with its thirteen parishes elected thirty-six of the forty-eight members of the lower house. With roughly the same area and with at least half of the white population of Charleston District (the city included), Georgetown elected only four; the smaller Beaufort District, with perhaps half Georgetown's white population, elected five. The interior proper elected three. People along the Pee Dee River, and along smaller rivers and streams in Georgetown District, were as troubled and harassed by the lack of courts and sufficient local officials as backcountry residents. They too became Regulators.[84]

During the 1760s, only one of the twelve most important members of the Commons, Thomas Lynch, Sr., of Prince George Winyaw, was elected by a parish outside the Charleston District. Of the twenty-one members whose committee assignments indicated their prime importance in any session between 1761 and 1775, only four came from the lowcountry outside the Charleston District. Lynch was one; the three others, Thomas Evance, Thomas Middleton, and John Rattray were from Prince William, one of the parishes near Georgia, and both Evance and Middleton had at times represented Charleston District parishes. In the Council of Safety, one of the revolutionary bodies, eight of the thirteen members were from Charleston itself, and the remaining five from parishes close to the city.[85]

Although it was common throughout America for control to rest in the hands of those who lived near the legislatures' meeting places, simply because it was easier for such members to attend, others, and the people they represented, justifiably felt belittled. When those without consequence found their interests or desires being overlooked, as they seemed to be in South Carolina when the colony's delegates secured exemption for the exportation of rice, they could well become resentful. Eventually, residents and representatives of the backcountry and of some lowcountry parishes would demand substantial changes in their government.

The wealthy residents of Carolina's lowcountry assumed that they alone were to govern, that theirs should be the dominant voice because theirs was the most competent and experienced voice. They expected to pass on to their children their wealth, fame, and power. Elizabeth Rutledge, whose husband was the most important political leader in South Carolina during the Revolutionary era, obliquely expressed the goal. In 1789, even after some startling political changes brought about by the Revolution, she expressed surprise that her son John would think of returning from Europe when his father had offered him a longer stay. What could he gain from a premature return? "I suppose you know you cant serve in the Continental Legeslature till you are twenty five years of age, & you are now, not quite twenty three. . . ."[86] No one, she implied, could question his right to serve the instant he chose to. Little wonder that one English official and close friend of a South Carolina governor had described the members of the Carolina assembly as "sordid Legislators . . . that no King can govern nor no God . . . please."[87] Little wonder, too, that when changing circumstances deprived the Commons of opportunities to govern, its members moved smoothly into newly formed revolutionary congresses. Forty-three of the forty-eight members of the Commons were elected to sit in the first Revolutionary Congress. Three of the remaining five were chosen for the second. From the Commons came the leaders of the Provincial Congress: the first president, Colonel Charles Pinckney, a political power for twenty-two years; the second president, Henry Laurens, with service in the lower house from 1757 to 1772; Rawlins Lowndes, almost continuously a member of the Commons after 1749 and many times its speaker. John Rutledge sat, and so, of course, did Christopher Gadsden.[88] Individually and collectively the elite had grown too powerful to abdicate.

But they were no longer powerful enough to rule unchallenged. Opposition to England brought an end to the enforced silencing of dissident groups which had produced official unity. In 1774, a political system including westerners and city workers began to emerge. In July, not yet four months after England closed the port of Boston as partial punishment for the Boston Tea Party, 104 inhabitants, drawn to Charleston by letters sent to every parish and section of South Carolina, met until midnight on three consecutive days to consider American rights and the election of delegates to the First Continental Congress in Philadelphia. Then they set up a General committee to run the colony. The meetings, said Peter Timothy, editor of the *South Carolina Gazette,* were "such an example of pure democracy as has rarely been seen since the days of the Ancient city republics."[89]

In November 1774, after the delegates had returned from the Congress in Philadelphia, the General Committee called for the election of a Provincial Congress to better represent the entire colony. Fifty-eight of the 184 seats were set aside for backcountry spokesmen. And when elections were held, in addition to the new westerners, thirteen men closely identified with the fortunes of Charleston's artisans and mechanics were chosen.[90] The new groups were active, either brought to a state of political awareness by England and by the actions of Carolina's rulers or instinctively responding when presented with their first real opportunities.

Brought face to face with strangers, the political elite had real fears and difficult choices. The old rulers were surrounded by growing political power — exercised in America by hitherto subservient, apathetic, or simply ineffective people, in England by Parliament challenging their control of Carolina. No matter where they turned there was potential trouble. In 1769 William Henry Drayton refused to join the nonimportation scheme because the policy had been formed in consultation with people who knew only how to work with their hands. The English-educated Drayton despised the "*profanum vulgus,*" as did Francis Kinloch, also the

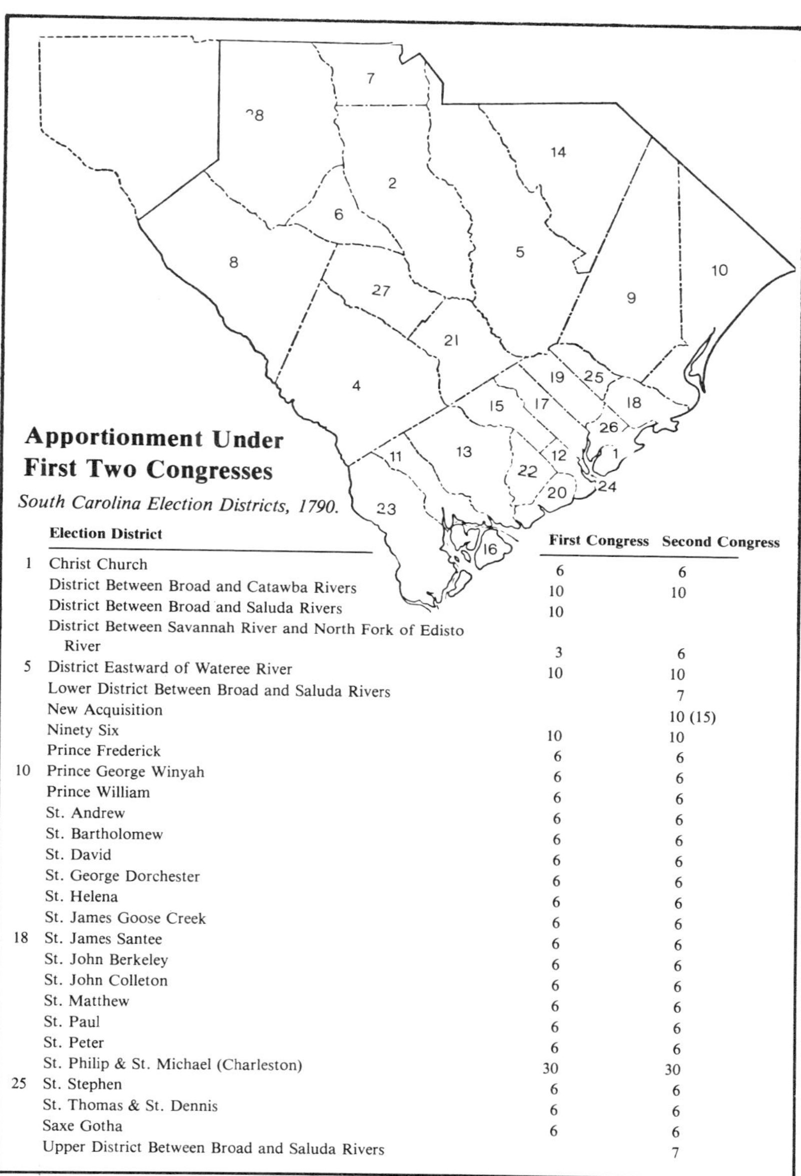

Apportionment Under First Two Congresses

South Carolina Election Districts, 1790.

	Election District	First Congress	Second Congress
1	Christ Church	6	6
	District Between Broad and Catawba Rivers	10	10
	District Between Broad and Saluda Rivers	10	
	District Between Savannah River and North Fork of Edisto River	3	6
5	District Eastward of Wateree River	10	10
	Lower District Between Broad and Saluda Rivers		7
	New Acquisition		10 (15)
	Ninety Six	10	10
	Prince Frederick	6	6
10	Prince George Winyah	6	6
	Prince William	6	6
	St. Andrew	6	6
	St. Bartholomew	6	6
	St. David	6	6
	St. George Dorchester	6	6
	St. Helena	6	6
	St. James Goose Creek	6	6
18	St. James Santee	6	6
	St. John Berkeley	6	6
	St. John Colleton	6	6
	St. Matthew	6	6
	St. Paul	6	6
	St. Peter	6	6
	St. Philip & St. Michael (Charleston)	30	30
25	St. Stephen	6	6
	St. Thomas & St. Dennis	6	6
	Saxe Gotha	6	6
	Upper District Between Broad and Saluda Rivers		7

Courtesy, South Carolina House of Representatives Committee on Historical Research

beneficiary of English schooling. "To be confounded in a heap of butchers, bakers, blacksmiths," wrote Kinloch, "is dreadful for a man of any education. . . ." In 1775 Henry Laurens witnessed "the Country people'' becoming active and denounced the idea that ''no Man is now supposed to be unequal to a share in Government.'' Such an idea, he thought, would lead to ''trouble & confusion.'' New representatives were not accustomed to debate or thought; they were of the opinion that ''every thing might have been completed with no more words than are necessary in the bargain and sale of a cow.''[91]

When the Commons had sat with forty or fifty men, its members, knowing each other, had known what to expect. By 1775 those contemplating the transition had to consider the artisans and mechanics, butchers and bakers, the country people, and the size of the political unit in which they would participate. One could work and anticipate success in a small Commons that contained a few unknowns. But how did one behave and predict the turn of a debate in a body of 184, even if no more than 100 attended? Often, a traveler reported after the war, proposals urged ''with all the charms of eloquence'' by the well-educated lowcountry representatives were defeated by the silent opposition of backcountry voters too afraid or too embarrassed to speak.[92] Votes in the Provincial Congress in the winter of 1775–1776 were close and unpredictable: 51 to 49 on November 8; 49 to 48 six days later; in February, 53 to 49, 54 to 46, 49 to 49. For some people, the change, the problems, the suspense were too great.

John Laurens, who would rush home to fight, saw the dilemma; he saw that some people, ''illy calculated to move in the most limited ministerial spheres [were] unfortunately suffered to have a voice in matters of the greatest Intricacy and Importance.'' But he accepted the risk, because to desist from opposition to Great Britain because new people were entering political life would bring even greater evil. One had to resist England and struggle to keep Carolina free of internal change. So, in 1775 the Provincial Congress noted that ''no love of innovation'' or ''lust for independence'' influenced its decisions.[93] Some Carolinians, fearing their inability to prevent change, drew back from radical measures of opposition.

Sincerely and often South Carolina legislators warned of the dangers of British encroachments. They viewed such innovations as unconstitutional and contrary to the rights of Englishmen. But unconstitutional or not, England's policies directly threatened the legislature and the people who sat in it. Had the members of the Commons been content to allow a dissipation of their power, their worth would have sunk low in the eyes of those electing them, and the colony would have lost its very real right to govern itself. If the ''Gentlemen of Carolina'' needed a cause, as one Carolinian would later write, because they had ''grown too opulent to be confined to the care of their estates & stood in need of some scope to that ambition, which of itself takes place in the breasts of those who are rich, idle, & well educated,'' England gave them one, a good one.[94] In seizing it, however, the wealthy ruling class was reluctantly and knowingly giving scope as well to the ambitions of diverse and hitherto powerless Carolinians.

TWO
The Revolutionary Constitutions

We now feel every joyful and comfortable hope . . . in the present Constitution, . . . a Constitution founded on the strictest principles of justice and humanity; where the rights and happiness of the whole, the poor and the rich, are equally secured. . . .

Grand Jury of Cheraw, 29 May 1776.

So many circumstances concur to give the capitol and adjacent Parishes the advantage in representation, that there is great danger that the government of this state in time will degenerate into an oligarchy.

The Reverend William Tennent, 17 September 1776.

IN March 1776 South Carolina's Provincial Congress adopted a temporary "mode" of government to last until the disagreements between England and America were settled. The constitution confirmed many familiar arrangements and introduced some change. Two years later, with independence declared, armies crossing the American countryside and occupying cities, and all likelihood of amicable settlement ended, the state replaced the temporary frame of government with a more permanent one, which, while reaffirming some old practices, was revolutionary. Given the starting point, total domination of colonial affairs by a few people and a small area around Charleston, the internal revolution wrought by the constitutions was dramatic.

By late 1775 the Anglo-American crisis was causing chaos in the colonies. Royal governors were fleeing or had fled, and legislatures had been dissolved. To some it was obvious that no matter what the end sought, the colonies would have to assume new governments. In November a committee of the Continental Congress, chaired by South Carolina's John Rutledge, replied to a request from New Hampshire for advice regarding government by recommending that the colony's convention "call a full and free representation of the people, and that the representatives, if they think it necessary, establish such a form of government, as, in their judgment, will best produce the happiness of the people." The day after the committee and Congress advised New Hampshire, John Rutledge received similar advice for South Carolina.[1]

Eight states wrote constitutions in 1776; two more followed in 1777. In almost all states there was intellectual excitement, lengthy debate, a clash of ideologies, hope and fear as people tried to make what they could out of the Revolution. For some, the mood was exultant, for the Revolution was opportunity to start over, "boldly to chalk out a new plan," to "exclude kings . . . [and] tyranny," to enter "a new era in politics."[2] But in South Carolina, in 1776, the dominant moods were reluctance and satisfaction. The reluctance was evident in the attempts to delay the formation of a regular government, the satisfaction in the terms of the government formed.

On 11 February 1776 the South Carolina Provincial Congress, disregarding the suggestion to call a "full and free representation of the people," but recognizing the importance of the matter, elected by ballot a committee of eleven — John Rutledge, Charles Pinckney, Henry Laurens, Rawlins Lowndes, Henry Middleton, Thomas Bee, Thomas Heyward, Jr., Christopher Gadsden, Arthur Middleton, Thomas Lynch, Jr., and chairman Charles Cotesworth Pinckney — to prepare a constitution. Although John Rutledge was only thirty-seven and three others, including the chairman, were under thirty-five, the committee was dominated by experienced rulers. Henry Middleton and Rawlins Lowndes had first been elected to the Commons in the 1740s, Charles Pinckney, Henry Laurens, and Christopher Gadsden in the 1750s, and John Rutledge, Thomas Bee, and Arthur Middleton before 1765. As usual in Carolina government, the men were closely related and drawn from a small area. Henry and Arthur Middleton were father and son, Charles and Charles Cotesworth Pinckney cousins, Henry Middleton and Charles Cotesworth Pinckney father- and son-in-law, Arthur Middleton and Charles Cotesworth Pinckney brothers-in-law. John Rutledge's sister Mary had married the brother of Thomas Bee's wife, and his brother Edward was married to Henry Middleton's daughter, Arthur's sister. Six of the committee members had been elected to the Provincial Congress by the city of Charleston, four by the surrounding parishes. Only Lynch, from Georgetown, represented the distant low-country parishes. None sat for the interior.[3]

The committee was controlled also by moderates who had opposed extreme retaliatory actions against England. Only Gadsden, Lynch, and Arthur Middleton may have differed from the others in outlook; they had favored strong, hence to many, radical, measures.[4] But since Gadsden's proposal for independence had been defeated a few days before by people who called Thomas Paine's ideas nonsense, the radicals probably had few remaining ideas about government different from the others on the committee. Certainly Arthur Middleton was no social or constitutional radical. His agreement with men like Rutledge was later evident when both opposed a more democratic form of government in 1778. His beliefs were probably close to those of another radical, William Henry Drayton. Drayton was so radical as to lay the idea of independence before the Provincial Congress, yet he had been appalled that men who knew only how "to cut up a *Beast in the Market,* . . . or to build a *necessary* House" had been involved in political decisions, for "*such Men*" were not meant to be "*profound Politicians* or *able Statesmen.*"[5] If Drayton had been on the committee (he was president of the Provincial Congress), his ideas would have differed little from those of Rutledge or Laurens. Only Christopher Gadsden, partly on the basis of his behavior after 1776, may be considered a "constitutional" radical. His earlier behavior certainly had isolated him from many of the committee members: he had been feuding with Henry Laurens for more than fifteen years; he had openly attacked Rutledge, Lynch, and Henry Middleton for their partiality to the rice planters and in turn had been pointedly denounced. Edward Rutledge had found him "if possible, worse than ever" at the Continental Congress, and the elder Lynch had both complained about his presence and rejoiced that at his departure business could move "Swimmingly." And Gadsden, since the days of the Stamp Act, had been the voice of Charleston's artisans and mechanics, urging merchants and planters on to more extreme measures.[6]

The committee on the constitution reported to the provincial Congress on 5 March; its plan was debated almost every day until it was adopted on the twenty-sixth by a Congress which had so steadily diminished in size that the remaining members had been forced to order 22 absent delegates living close at hand to attend. On 7 February 102 had voted on one question; five weeks later 70 voted on a clause of the proposed constitution. On 21 March only 52 voted. Some delegates, apparently thinking that acceptance of any constitution was too radical an act, sought to delay the adoption of even a temporary one by staying away. Others argued that the Congress lacked the power to write a constitution. But most objections to proceeding were silenced by news on 21 March of the parliamentary act which virtually declared war on America by pronouncing the colonies in "open rebellion and defiance," their vessels and goods forfeit when seized at sea.[7]

The constitution of 26 March 1776, only the second adopted by an American colony during the Revolutionary era, gave Carolina a government more democratic in form yet more suited to the native aristocracy than what it had enjoyed or endured through the British connection. Representation was broadened, regular elections guaranteed, and the higher offices of government opened to anyone who could qualify to sit in the lower house of the legislature.[8] But the equal distribution of power incorporated into the new frame of government satisfied the old rulers and made South Carolina different from the other Revolutionary states, most of which would soon adopt new constitutions.

The most noticeable and important difference between the government of 1776 and that of the colonial period lay in the realm of representation. The constitution legitimatized the system of representation developed

SOUTH-CAROLINA.

In a Congress,

Begun and holden at *Charles-Town*, on *Wednesday* the first day of *November* one thousand seven hundred and seventy-five, and continued, by divers adjournments, to *Tuesday* the twenty-sixth day of *March*, one thousand seven hundred and seventy-six.

A

CONSTITUTION,

OR

FORM OF GOVERNMENT,

Agreed to, and Resolved upon,

BY

The Representatives *of* South-Carolina.

WHEREAS the British Parliament, claiming of late years a right to bind the North-American Colonies by law, in all cases whatsoever, have enacted statutes for raising a revenue in those colonies, and disposing of such revenue as they thought proper, without the consent and against the will of the colonists. And whereas, it appearing to them, that (they not being represented in Parliament) such claim was altogether unconstitutional; and, if admitted, would at once reduce them from the rank of Freemen to a state of the most abject Slavery; the said colonies, therefore, severally remonstrated against the passing, and petitioned for the repeal of those acts—but in vain. And whereas the said claim being persisted in, other unconstitutional and oppressive statutes have been since enacted, by which the powers of the Admiralty Courts in the colonies are extended beyond their ancient limits, and jurisdiction is given to such Courts in cases similar to those which in Great-Britain are triable by jury—Persons are liable to be sent to, and tried in, Great-Britain, for an offence created and made capital by one of those statutes, though committed in the colonies—the harbour of Boston was blocked up—people indicted for murder in the Massachusetts-Bay, may, at the will of the Governor, be sent for trial to any other colony, or even to Great-Britain—the chartered constitution of government in that colony is materially altered—the English laws and a free

within the previous two years by revolutionary bodies forced to enlist the entire colony in the opposition movement. Charleston, which after 1771 had been allowed 7 representatives in the Commons, was given 30, each lowcountry parish 6, and backcountry parishes and districts 6, 10, or 12. The result was the creation of a large Assembly of 202 to replace the colonial Commons of 48 and the Provincial Congress of 184. Charleston District, retaining its 96 representatives from the Congress, remained dominant but could no longer govern without regard for other areas. The lowcountry parishes far from Charleston still had only 30 representatives, but the backcountry's representation was increased from 58 to 76, partly through the creation of new districts. While representation was still not adequately apportioned according to population, the colonial imbalance had been considerably corrected, more so than historians have realized. Most writers, treating the lowcountry as a unit despite the differences in settlement and agriculture, have assigned the area 138 representatives instead of 126, leaving the interior 64; a few have divided the legislature 144 to 58.[9] Although everyone was aware that the population was not stationary and the sections not growing at the same rate, the framers of the constitution did not provide for reapportionment.

Colonial suffrage qualifications were kept by a clause referring to the election act of 1721, which had granted the vote to adult white males owning fifty acres of land or paying a 20s. currency tax. Since England had granted fifty acres to anyone applying for it while the colonial government had taxed all free adult males 20s. currency, the suffrage was widespread.[10]

The structure of government, the relations among its various parts, and the methods by which some officials were chosen reflected the current desires of the political elite and the lessons it had learned. Because natives filled all the positions of government and because they were assumed to be good, there seemed no need to limit authority, jealously guard power, or distinguish between one branch of the legislature and another. The office of governor showed that individuals were to be trusted.

So fearful were people of other states of executive power, "ever restless, ambitious, and ever grasping" for more, that they stripped their new governors "of most of those badges of domination," and made them into mere administrators; Pennsylvania went one step further and abolished the office altogether. Six of the nine states besides South Carolina which wrote constitutions in 1776 and 1777 provided for the annual election of governors; seven limited the number of successive years they could serve, the Maryland constitution explaining that continued re-election of an executive was "dangerous to liberty." All denied them the power to veto legislation.[11]

Everywhere but in South Carolina the governor was a figurehead, a weak individual surrounded by suspicious people. In South Carolina, the governor, now called president, was a power. Elected by the General Assembly and Legislative Council from "among themselves, or from the people at large," the president served a two-year term. Since there was no enforced rotation in office, he, along with the vice-president and privy councilors provided for in the constitution, was always eligible for re-election. An attempt in the Provincial Congress to limit successive terms to two had failed. The fixing of the president's yearly salary at £9,000 currency gave him additional freedom of action and a benefit denied royal governors and other American Revolutionary executives. In no other Southern state was the executive granted a fixed salary. Elsewhere he depended on the legislature for both his election and his income. The powerless governors of other states were further handicapped by councils, whose advice and consent they were required to seek. South Carolina's president was given a Privy Council, but he was not "bound to consult" it.[12]

South Carolina's executive differed from others in another and most important way. Bills approved by the legislature were sent on to "be assented to or rejected by the President." Only Massachusetts in 1780 would allow the governor to veto legislation by himself, and there the legislature could override him with a two-thirds vote. Elsewhere it was assumed that one man could not be entrusted with the power to "abrogate at pleasure" acts passed by "Representatives of the people."[13]

Like the governors of other states, however, South Carolina's could not "commence War, or conclude Peace, or enter into any final Treaty" without the legislature's consent. Nor could he adjourn, prorogue, or dissolve the legislature.

The president shared legislative authority with a two-house legislature. The General Assembly was chosen by voters for a two-year term, although the committee drafting the constitution, accepting the prevalent Whig belief that annual elections were a defense against tyranny, had recommended the one-year term which every other state would adopt in 1776 and 1777.[14] Almost all states provided for upper houses that would utilize the wisdom of "men of worth" whose lack of "popular qualities" might prevent them from winning elections. Senates were either composed of men possessed of more property than those in the lower house or were elected by larger property owners. Chosen usually by the people, senators served longer terms than representatives. The differences provided the benefits of mixed government.[15] But South Carolina's Legislative Council was elected by the General Assembly "out of their own body . . . for the same time as the General Assembly." New elections filled the seats vacated in the Assembly by the election of thirteen councilors.

Before the Revolution, the wealthy members of the lower house, angry at outside interference and angry too that none of them grown old could bask in the glories of high office because of the English placemen, had successfully fought governors and councilors. Governors dependent for their salaries on the humor of the legislature could, when necessary, be kept wanting. Councilors could be ignored, as they were during the Wilkes fund dispute and again in 1773 when they had printer Thomas Powell arrested for a breach of their privileges. Edward Rutledge secured Powell's release through two assistant justices, Rawlins Lowndes and George Gabriel Powell, members of the Commons, by arguing that the

Council did not have the same rights as a House of Lords; it was not, in fact, an upper house at all, only a Privy Council to advise the governor.[16]

In 1776 with natives in office and with the election of councilors removed from the hands of the people, there seemed no need to set one branch against another by varying property requirements for office or by making one branch overwhelmingly superior to the other. The qualifications for the Assembly remained what they had been: white males, aged twenty-one, owning a "settled" plantation and ten slaves or property valued at £1,000 currency in the province, "construed to mean clear of debt," which was to guarantee that independence of thought and action legislators were supposed to possess. Neither the constitution nor the required oath of office ruled out non-Protestants.[17]

The Provincial Congress did not establish a lower house with significantly greater powers than the Council. As in the colonial period, money bills originated in the lower house and were not amendable by the Council, although in practice the Council amended them. Justices of the peace were nominated by the Assembly and commissioned by the president. But in all other matters of patronage and selection — in the choice of president, vice-president, privy councilors, judicial officers, sheriffs, field officers in the army and captains in the navy — the Council shared equal authority with the popularly elected Assembly. The Council, however, was not allowed to expel its own members.[18]

The president's fixed salary, his veto, and his unlimited right to succeed himself indicated a faith in the virtues of the likely rulers that ran counter to the suspicions of constitution writers throughout the rest of America. So did the failure to provide annual elections. Other provisions were no less trusting. Although 202 representatives sat in a full lower house, only 49 were needed for a quorum. The city of Charleston, where the legislature would sit for years, itself elected 30 representatives. Seven of the thirteen councilors were a quorum in the upper house.

Other states sought to keep the legislatures pure and "preserved from all suspicion of corruption" by banning "persons possessed of any post of profit under the Government," justices of the peace often excepted. South Carolina required such officeholders to resign from the legislature, but allowed them to serve if re-elected. Some states named judicial officers for specified terms; South Carolina chose the more indefinite "good behaviour" appointment, which allowed the removal of judges only on the demand of the legislature. Most states made provision for the impeachment of state officials, some even including legislators as vulnerable officeholders. South Carolina's constitution contained no impeachment clause.[19]

The constitution writers in South Carolina had seen no need for drastic experimentation. For the hitherto powerless settlers outside the Charleston area, the constitution did little but grant fixed representation. No provision was made for reapportionment; nothing promised to redress complaints about the inadequacies of the legal system. And, because the Anglican Church of the lowcountry leaders remained the established church, dissenters, the vast majority of the state's white population, were liable to be taxed for its support.

Satisfied with old ways, the lowcountry rulers had innovated little. They were unafraid of the misuse of power and unwilling to admit that they themselves might not represent everyone's best interests. Balance in government was what they sought and achieved.

The constitution was put into effect by the Provincial Congress, declared by the new frame of government to be the first General Assembly. Neither in South Carolina nor in other states in 1776 and 1777 were new constitutions submitted to the people for ratification. After the General Assembly chose the upper house, the two branches jointly elected John Rutledge president and Henry Laurens vice-president.

To John Adams, amassing information from all the colonies, the news about South Carolina's constitution brought ecstasy. Assumption by the colonies of the right and authority to govern themselves was to him independence in fact if not in name, a way around the timid Americans trying to avoid a final break with England. South Carolina "has aroused and animated all the continent," wrote Adams. Two visitors from South Carolina told Adams that Carolinians would "never give up" their new government.[20]

But Adams's informants were more enthusiastic than many other South Carolinians. John Rutledge closed the first session of the legislature by urging members to make known to their constituents "the indispensable necessity" there had been for forming a government. They were to address themselves to those rights which Britain had recently violated, including the right to trial by a jury of the vicinage and the right to be taxed by one's own representatives. Those "inestimable" rights were "the birthright of the poorest man and the best inheritance of the most wealthy." Echoing Rutledge, the grand jury of Cheraw expressed satisfaction: the constitution "equally secured" the "rights and happiness of the whole, the poor and the rich."[21]

The praise, however, was limited, and criticism soon surfaced, partly because of dramatic events since the spring of 1776. Some people thought it absurd to function under a plan which looked forward to accommodation with Great Britain when the thirteen colonies had united in a Declaration of Independence. Perhaps more importantly, South Carolina had become a battleground. Charlestonians, having worked months to prepare their defenses, had heroically turned back a massed British naval attack in June 1776. The backcountry too had seen action and far more bloodshed when in July, the Cherokees, encouraged by British agents, struck at men, women, and children. They were joined by Tories. Between July and October, a South Carolina force of more than 4,000 men, including some from North Carolina and Virginia, pacified the backcountry. About 2,000 Indians were killed, their Lower and Middle Towns destroyed. They were forced to cede a large territory to South Carolina. Backcountry Tories were defeated and silenced. Many, upset by the use of Indians, joined the rebels.[22]

Following independence and the outbreak of fighting, Judge Henry Pendleton charged the grand juries of Beaufort and Ninety Six with making recommendations for constitutional revision, and when the legislature met in special session in September, Christopher Gadsden moved for the appointment of a committee to propose changes in the constitution, which in fact had no provision for amendment. Far more was at stake in the criticism of the constitution than the simple alteration of phrases to change a colony into an independent state. Proposed amendments attacked the "capitol and adjacent Parishes," whose political advantage one legislator feared would cause the government to "degenerate into an oligarchy."[23]

The danger of the oligarchy came largely from the upper house, which was chosen in a way that gave almost inordinate power to a small area, as the first two elections demonstrated. Because several men resigned to fill other positions or declined to serve, seventeen men had to be chosen by and from the members of the lower house to complete the thirteen-man Legislative Council. Eleven were from parishes in or close to Charleston, four from the backcountry, and only two from the coastal parishes near Georgia; none at all were from the parishes north of the Santee River in Georgetown district. Of the fourteen elected to the second Council, six were from the parishes surrounding Charleston, and five, including President Rutledge's brother Hugh, who would be speaker, were from the city of Charleston. Only three were from the backcountry, and none from lowcountry parishes in Georgetown or Beaufort Districts, the indigo-producing districts whose fate, some thought, could not be left in the hands of self-serving rice planters.[24]

Because of its membership, Gadsden's committee did not suggest changes which reflected a consistent political philosophy, although it did propose making the government more representative of the state as a whole and more like the newly created governments of New Jersey, Delaware, and Pennsylvania. Five of the nine members of the committee — Gadsden, Rawlins Lowndes, Charles Pinckney, Thomas Bee, and Thomas Heyward, Jr. — had been on the committee which drafted the state constitution, but Alexander Moultrie, John Mathews, John Edwards, and Paul Trapier, Jr., were new, not only to the committee but to the legislature as well. Only Edwards, a leading Charleston merchant, had served in the colonial Assembly, and he had first been elected in 1772, the same year Heyward entered the government. Both Moultrie and Mathews were lawyers trained in England. Both had been re-elected to the Assembly after being chosen by the legislature in March to fill legal positions, Moultrie as attorney general and Mathews as an assistant judge. Trapier, who represented a parish in Georgetown District, was from an important family, although he had not served in the colonial legislature.[25]

The committee proposed to delete from the oath of office required of people in government the words indicating that the constitution would be operative until the differences between England and America were settled. It called for the establishment of an appeals court and of a chancellor's position, taking away from the vice-president and Privy Council the power to sit as a Court of Chancery. It suggested that proper people throughout the state be empowered to "prove wills, grant administrations, and do such other matters as are incident to a Court of Ordinary." In the future, the committee proposed, no ministers should be allowed to sit in the legislature, and, after the necessary information became available, the number of representatives in the lower house should be reduced and reapportioned on the basis of the white population and property.

The committee suggested two changes for the legislative council and one for the office of president. It recommended that the assembly elect councilors from its own membership or from the people at large, the constitution only allowing election of assemblymen. And, if the assembly chose to elect assemblymen councilors, then the seats vacated in the lower house would not be filled. Finally, the principle of rotation was to be applied to the president: no man should be eligible for re-election for six years after his first term.[26]

The Assembly considering the committee's report was small, only 61 of a possible 202 voting on one recommendation. The Reverend Tennent noted that backcountry representatives had stayed away, partly because of the Indian war and partly because of "that indolence by which it is easy to foresee the interest of those Districts will always suffer." However, committee assignments suggest that more backcountry and distant lowcountry representatives showed up in September and October than in March, which perhaps accounted for the attacks on the "oligarchy" of the "capitol and adjacent Parishes."[27]

When the two alterations of the council were debated, the lower house called for more drastic change. The Assembly decided that councilors should not be chosen by the legislature at all, but that each parish and district should elect one member of the Legislative Council. "One avenue for family intrigue seems to be obstructed," Tennent wrote. John Lewis Gervais, a Charleston merchant involved in backcountry trade and a representative for a backcountry district, thought the change would destroy the power by which "party & faction" elected councilors from "one or two parishes."[28]

The proposal to rotate the President out of office was approved unanimously. Tennent reported that "ambitious people" disliked the idea, but that "none dared oppose it openly."[29]

The House agreed to the need for a chancellor; by a unanimous vote it approved the request for an appeals court and for the appointment of officials throughout the state to perform the duties of a chancery court. And the House removed the clause banning ministers from the legislature.[30]

Nature and numbers conspired against democratic reformers when the Assembly, with the Speaker casting the deciding vote after a thirty to thirty division, agreed to reduce the number of representatives and apportion them on the basis of white population and taxable property. Tennent attributed that single successful attack on "the privileges of the people" to Charleston's "excessive" representation and the slowness of one of his supporters on a "call of nature."[31]

After altering the proposed amendments, the General Assembly ordered the committee which had prepared them to bring in an appropriate bill. That no such bill was passed by the legislature was not a major defeat for people seeking substantial change. Had one been passed, further amendment would have been more difficult. With the *status quo* continued, demands for change would produce more sweeping proposals.

After the close of the legislative session in October, Tennent mobilized some of the opposition to the constitution, writing and distributing to the interior petitions protesting the continued support of the Church of England. Printed copies of other proposed changes were sent throughout the state prior to the election of a new assembly on 28 and 29 October, so that according to David Ramsay, an elected member, the new representatives were specifically chosen to alter the constitution.[32]

The dissenters' petitions, signed by thousands of men and women, were taken up in January 1777. Tennent and Gadsden, one of the few non-Anglican revolutionary leaders, led the fight. Tennent, in the only surviving speech on the petition, noted that Carolinians could legally be married only by Anglican clergy (although in fact they were married by others); and, more importantly, that seventy-nine dissenting congregations were taxed to support twenty established churches, almost all of them in the lowcountry. Tennent appealed not only to the representatives' humanity and justice but also to their hopes for the future greatness of the state. "Religious establishments," he said, "discourage the opulence and cramp the growth of a free state. . . ." Richard Hutson, son of a former minister of a Charleston Congregational Church, joined Gadsden and Tennent in support of the measure.[33]

The strong support given to the state by dissenting ministers like the Presbyterian Tennent and the Baptist Oliver Hart did not silence the opponents of disestablishment, although it probably weakened them. Rawlins Lowndes and Charles Pinckney most strenuously defended the old order, apparently joined by some legislators who reasoned that an established church should continue so that the poor could be cared for and elections conducted by church wardens. By a close vote of seventy to sixty,

Tennent's petitioners won in the lower house, which then also went on to remodel the constitution completely.[34]

In February the Legislative Council ordered the Assembly's new proposals printed. Apparently the legislature took no action in its thirteen-day session in September. On 19 March 1778, however, the legislature and governor approved a new constitution which closely followed the lower house's recommendations of the previous year.[35]

Almost certainly the draft of 1777 and the constitution of 1778 were the work of dissenters, distant lowcountry planters, backcountry settlers, Charleston radicals, and opponents of the Rutledge family, in overlapping groups. The changes in the nature of government and the relations between church and state introduced by the new plan were numerous and important. The Anglican Church was disestablished, although the "Christian Protestant Religion" became the established religion, the peaceful and faithful adherents of any of its sects entitled to "equal religious and civil Privileges." (Consistently, the draft had referred to Christians; the constitution spoke of Protestants.) Any fifteen male Protestants over twenty-one could form a church and petition the legislature for incorporation, which would give the church the right to own and control religious property.

The Protestants clearly fared best, but in some ways other religious groups also benefited. No one had to contribute to a church he did not voluntarily join. All religions could worship freely, the constitution carefully providing that no one was to disturb "any religious Assembly," for that would disturb the peace and hinder conversions. Quakers, settled in a few backcountry areas, were additionally protected by a clause allowing one called on "to make an Appeal to God, as a witness to Truth," to do it according "to the Dictates of his own Conscience."

Perhaps recalling some incidents of previous years, the legislators wrote into the constitution a ban on people saying "any Thing, in their religious Assembly, irreverently, or seditiously, of the Government of this State." In 1774, the Reverend John Bullman, assistant minister of St. Michael's in Charleston, had denounced the "silly Clown[s] and illiterate Mechanic[s]" who criticized their ruler. Although Bullman was himself censuring disloyalty he was more importantly attacking the extralegal authority emerging in the colony. The church vestry quickly dismissed him, and then adopted an oath of loyalty to the state which ministers were required to take.[36]

While the new constitution gave all people the right to worship in their own ways, it took away some of the political rights they had enjoyed. Only Protestants could now be elected to serve in the state government, and ministers were declared ineligible for office.[37] Jews and other non-Protestants, however, could still vote: all free white men, resident one year in the state and meeting the old property requirements could vote if they acknowledged God and "a future State of Rewards and Punishments."

Christopher Gadsden undoubtedly inspired an attack on the Rutledges which influenced the form of the new government. John Rutledge, his political foe, was the most powerful individual in the state. After studying law at the Middle Temple and entering the Commons in 1761, Rutledge had climbed quickly to the top of Carolina's wealthy legal profession. He represented the colony at both the Stamp Act Congress and the Continental Congresses, and in 1776 he was elected the first president of the state. His brother Edward, ten years his junior, followed the same course: law in England and politics in Carolina. After the Rutledges and Gadsden clashed in 1775 over the Association, the brothers supporting the exportation of rice and Gadsden denouncing the favoritism shown rice planters, Edward labeled Gadsden "wrong-headed" and "violent."[38]

The opposition to the Rutledges was joined to a general effort to protect the people from political corruption. Rather than rely on the goodness of their officeholders, as they had in 1776, the legislators sought to protect themselves against the worst. They reduced executive authority, rotated some officials out of the government, and provided for impeachments. In their effort more jealously to guard their freedoms, they adopted a plan of government resembling the plans of other states.

The constitution of 1778 retained provisions for the election of the governor, formerly president, by the legislature. But the office was considerably weakened. No longer would the governor have a fixed salary (the draft gave him and other officials specific salaries), the new constitution simply stating that yearly salaries would be allowed public officials, which meant that the amounts might vary from year to year according to the discretion of the legislature. The governor's capacity to scheme in his own interest and therefore his ability to corrupt political processes was lessened by a limited term: no man could be re-elected governor for four years after the expiration of his two-year term. A more serious blow to executive authority was the loss of the veto power. Since South Carolina had written its first constitution, most states had adopted plans which, centering power in the legislature, denied the executive any share of the legislative power. Following these examples, Carolina stripped Rutledge and succeeding governors of the veto.

The principle of rotation in office was also applied to sheriffs, commissioners of the treasury, the attorney general, and numerous other officials, some of whom, however, were allowed to serve four years before being retired for four years. It was applied also to an enlarged Privy Council, half of which would be elected each year, whose makeup was further limited by excluding, "for the time being," the "Father, Son, or Brother to the Governor." Another Rutledge brother, Hugh, was president of the Legislative Council and a member of the Privy Council.[39] The Privy Council was required to keep a journal, entering votes and the arguments of any member who wished to be recorded; the journal would be turned over to the legislature when either house requested it.

Recognizing that government officials might be guilty of "mal and corrupt Conduct," Carolinians, like the people of six other states before them, gave their legislature the power of impeachment.[40] (The draft contained no provision for impeachment.) Impeachments, agreed to by two-thirds of the members present in the lower house, would be tried before the senators and state judges (excepting judges who were members of the lower house) under rules to be determined later by the legislature. The accused were entitled to lawyers. No judgment except acquittal could be determined unless agreed to by a two-thirds vote of those present.

Further to reduce corruption, and to remove temptation and even the suspicion of wrongdoing, the constitution limited plural officeholding. Neither the governor nor the lieutenant governor could hold any other civil or military commission, aside from any they might have in the militia. Members of the legislature could also hold commissions in the militia and as justices of the peace, and they could serve as delegates to the Continental Congress, but if they were chosen to any other office they had to resign their legislative seats. A legislator could be re-elected, but not if he had been appointed a commissioner of the treasury, sheriff, clerk of a court or of a branch of the legislature, or chosen to fill one of several other positions.

Honesty, voluntary or forced, was desirable, but not sufficient to ensure good government. The new constitution, therefore, made the government more representative of people throughout the state and set forth a few inviolable rights. The Legislative Council, which Gadsden's committee had tried to change, was abolished, and in its place was established a Senate, chosen not by the lower house but by the people voting by parish or district.[41] Although apportionment in the lower house remained the same, the new composition of the upper house seriously lessened the power of Charleston and the neighboring parishes, which could now elect thirteen senators, while Beaufort and Georgetown were to elect five, and the backcountry eleven.[42] The newly created, popularly elected Senate could still not introduce, alter, or amend money bills, but in all other matters it was equal to the lower house. Jointly with the lower house, it could now nominate justices of the peace, whom the governor commissioned, and with the lower house it still elected sheriffs and all other officials.

The inequities and difficulties caused by the virtual freezing of representation during the colonial period had been only partially solved by the provincial congresses and the first constitution. In 1778, however, the legislators pledged that seven years after the new constitution was written, and every fourteen years after that, representation in the lower house would be reapportioned "in the most equal and just Manner," on the basis of the number of white inhabitants and taxable property. Four other states provided for periodic reapportionment.[43]

Perhaps also to make more difficult any attempts to disregard the interests of parts of the state, the new constitution required the attendance of more legislators. The quorum in the 202-man lower house was raised from forty-nine to sixty-nine. Although the proportion of members required in the upper house declined, from seven of thirteen to thirteen of thirty-nine, the change in election procedures guaranteed more widespread representation.

Following the suggestion made in 1776 by Gadsden's committee, the legislators provided in the new plan for the appointment of ordinaries throughout the state; most importantly, the ordinaries proved wills and granted administrations. And, finally meeting one of the demands of the Regulators, legislators agreed that as soon as possible the state should be divided into districts and counties for the creation of county courts. The new constitution corrected one of the oversights of the first one by providing for future amendments by the approval of a majority of the members of the Senate and House of Representatives.

The constitution dealt with some subjects not mentioned in the 1777 draft. It guaranteed religious freedom to all people and declared that a freeman could not be "imprisoned or disseised of his Freehold, Liberties or Privileges, or outlawed, or exiled, or in any Manner destroyed, or deprived of his Life, Liberty or Property, but by the Judgment of his Peers, or by the Law of the Land." It made the military "subordinate to the Civil Power of the State" and emphasized the need to "inviolably" preserve "the Liberty of the Press." It called for reform of the penal laws, punishments to be made "in some Cases, less sanguinary, and, in general more proportionate to the Crime."

While the new constitution generally extended the rights and powers of the people and made the government more democratic, it introduced a few changes and continued some provisions which set some people and officials over others. The elected Senate gave South Carolina a bicameral legislature and a mixed government, for it was not a small version of the lower house. Senators had to have been residents of the state for five years, representatives for three. Senators had to own settled estates and freeholds worth £2,000 currency, free of debt, representatives a settled plantation and ten slaves or property valued at £1,000 currency, free of debt, which was the same qualification set down in the colonial period and in the constitution of 1776. Nonresidents of a parish or district could sit in the Senate or House for any area if they owned enough property in the area which elected them to meet higher requirements. No one could be a senator unless he was thirty years old (perhaps it was coincidence that Edward Rutledge was only twenty-nine); a representative had to be twenty-one. Curiously, no minimum age was established for the governor, but no one could fill that position unless he had been a resident of the state for ten years and owned a settled plantation or freehold worth £10,000 currency, clear of debt. And the offices of governor, lieutenant governor, privy councilor, senator, and representative were restricted to Protestants.

On 5 March, John Rutledge vetoed the new constitution, reasoning that he had taken an oath to govern the state according to the constitution of 1776 and he could not in good conscience agree to its alteration. Although everyone knew, according to John Lewis Gervais, that the Assembly had been elected to change the constitution, "& that printed reports of the intended alterations had been sent over the Country previous to the Election," it mattered not in the least to Rutledge. He was convinced that only the people, and not the legislature, could write a new constitution and then only "on a dissolution of government, or subversion of the constitution."[44]

But Rutledge objected to more than what he considered the unconstitutional nature of the new constitution. The new plan was too democratic. "The people," he said, "preferred a compounded or mixed government to a simple democracy, or one verging toward it," because the effects of democratic power are "arbitrary, severe, and destructive." He specifically repudiated the new method of choosing the upper house. Talking as though he knew what the people wanted, and apparently unimpressed by the new property requirements, he informed the legislators that Carolinians preferred the old way because it was "more likely" that representatives would choose from their own membership men of greater "integrity, learning and abilities" than the people would elect in their local districts. He did not add that the old way had kept the upper house in control of a few who, one observer thought, were "in the interest of the Rutledge family."[45]

Resorting once more to his assumed knowledge of what the people wanted, Rutledge objected to the loss of the veto. It had been decided by "the Congress of 1776," he wrote Henry Laurens, that the legislature should have three branches, "so that we have the sentiments of the people, by their representatives in that Congress," on the issue.[46] In short, Rutledge was trying to bind the state to a constitution written by a provincial congress not called to write one and hardly representative of the colony, rationalizing nevertheless that it expressed the will of the people.

In his message to the legislature, Rutledge gave one more reason for his veto. Despite the Declaration of Independence and continued fighting, he looked forward still to a desirable accommodation with Great Britain. The new constitution would prevent reunion, he thought.[47]

Rutledge's veto surprised the legislature, as did his immediate resignation, one month before his term expired. After Arthur Middleton, a brother-in-law of Edward Rutledge and one of the 'radicals' on the committee which had drafted the constitution of 1776, declined the governor's office because he too disapproved of the new constitution, Rawlins Lowndes was chosen over Gadsden. Lowndes accepted both the post and the constitution while Gadsden unhappily became lieutenant-governor, feeling others had so honored him merely to remove him from the legislature.[48] In or out of the legislature, Gadsden most certainly had a hand in the unsuccessful but "great opposition" to a resolution thanking Rutledge for his previous services.[49]

The new constitution contained features which may be considered undemocratic — high property qualifications for officeholders, reapportionment based on population and taxable property, the exclusion of ministers and non-Protestants from elected state positions. And it was not put to a popular vote. But it represented nonetheless in the method by which it was written and in its substance a democratic advance over the first constitution and the colonial government.

Most important, the government was a product of the Revolution. Attempts were made to protect the people from the potential corruption of some of their rulers by enforcing rotation, ending some plural officeholding, allowing impeachment, and denying one man a right to override the decisions of the state's elected legislators. And if the government was not representative of all the people, it was at least now drawn from the entire state. After 1771 the backcountry had elected only three men to the Commons, the lowcountry parishes near Georgia and those north of the Santee nine. The Charleston area had sent thirty-six. The Charleston area remained the most powerful, but it was no longer stronger than all other areas combined. Under the constitution of 1778 it had thirteen of twenty-nine seats in the Senate, and in the lower house, 96 of 202. That the government would now serve the entire state was implicit in the promise of county courts and ordinaries.

Colonial South Carolina had been divided between backcountry and lowcountry, dissenters and Anglicans, rice and indigo planters, merchants and mechanics, "Plebeians" and "noblesse." But the revolutionary crisis had provided political and religious dissenters with the opportunity to force changes on an entrenched power. The opportunity had not been wasted. There was, too, a likelihood that those dissenters, with their added power, would in the future continue to play an equally active role in Carolina affairs.

In 1776, a few months after independence had been declared, Henry Laurens anxiously wrote to his son about the future. "I am now by the will of God brought into a new world," he wrote, "and God only knows what sort of a world it will be. . . ."[50] By 1778 John Rutledge and others were finding out that it was a world remarkably different from the one they had known.

THREE
Cruelty and Retaliation: The Revolution in Mind, Heart, and Country

> I will not expatiate upon the excesses of the British Army; it would . . . make you and every worthy Englishman blush for the degeneracy of the Nation.
>
> Francis Kinloch, 1 October 1782.

> I wish I could give you a proper Idea of the distressed situation of this country, & temper of the people; & this I assure you has undergone a great & serious revolution. . . .
>
> Aedanus Burke, 25 January 1782.

IN 1775 Alexander Innes had predicted that South Carolina would soon be ruined by the "Division, Riot, Anarchy, and Confusion" of its leaders.[1] Freed from English restraints and scarcely threatened by the war which occupied the north, Carolina in 1778 almost fit Innes's description. The legislature had been thrown "into Great Confusion" by John Rutledge's resignation;[2] but that was neither the first nor the last major political change between Innes's appearance in 1775 and the establishment of real independence in 1783. Tumultuous political controversies continued. Though they were powerless, the new executives, Governor Lowndes and Lieutenant Governor Gadsden, were nonetheless so quickly attacked and so long slighted that Gadsden responded to the "monstrous . . . insult" by requesting leave of the legislature to resign. His request was denied.[3]

The controversy which upset Gadsden involved a declaration of loyalty to South Carolina. It was exacerbated by the Rutledges and their friends. On 28 March 1778 the legislature passed an act requiring every free male inhabitant to swear allegiance to the state. Lowndes, with Gadsden's advice and in the spirit of a recommendation from the Continental Congress, extended by proclamation of 5 June the time allowed for taking the oath, as a means, he wrote, of "conciliating Peace and Union." Reaction was instantaneous. Bells rang; people gathered and persuaded printers not to publish the proclamation and magistrates not to abide by it. A delegation to the governor intimated that there would be "fatal consequences" if he failed to "recall the Proclamation." Lowndes was already troubled, in anguish over the recent death of a son and the likelihood that another would soon die, but both he and Gadsden stubbornly resisted the protestors and made known their intention to administer oaths themselves if other magistrates remained cowed.[4]

Denouncing the "restless, flighty Men" for wanting to run "upon every Fancy to the meetings of [the] liberty Tree," Gadsden urged his critics to impeach the executive if they thought the objectionable proclamation unconstitutional. But mostly Gadsden ignored the pawns, the "managed misinformed part of the Town," and struck out at those schemers who for political reasons were attacking the new administration. He had learned that "E[dward] R[utledge]" had written one resolution adopted at the mass meeting and that had "Mr. R. been president Nothing of this Sort would have happen'd."[5]

Apparently making the most of an opportunity to embarrass its opponents, the Rutledge group, whether or not responsible for the initial tumult, dragged the controversy out in the legislature. In September Lowndes sent the lower house documents relating to "the affair of the Riot," then under investigation by a committee of eight. When the House postponed action until the next session, Gadsden immediately attacked the "negative censure" of the executive implied by the refusal to condemn the actions of the "artful and indefatigable Cabal."[6] The issues were momentous to him. He worried not so much about men running to the liberty tree but about those who were capitalizing on one executive act to undermine the present governors and to alter the new constitution. Gadsden did not name his enemies, but, because of their opposition to the constitution of 1778, he undoubtedly saw the Rutledges as the "ill-intending, restless, disappointed, self-important men behind the scenes" who wanted a government "modeled more to their gout."[7]

Other witnesses agreed. John Wells, Jr., a printer who had refused to publish the proclamation to avoid being a "*Scape Goat,*" noted that when Lowndes succeeded Rutledge as governor, he "gained . . . the ill will of that powerful family, which by their opponents is stiled '*The Family Compact.*'"[8] John Lewis Gervais, a member of the legislature, reported that Edward Rutledge and Attorney General Alexander Moultrie had attended the popular meeting. He saw politics behind the House's investigation, its "whole aim" being "to censure the president & to let the people get clear." Edward Rutledge was one of the five city members of the investigating committee unanimous in not supporting the executive. Three country members opposed them.[9]

Gervais's conclusion, "that we can't agree 6 months with a Governor of our Own chusing," was true, but too limited.[10] The fight indicated not only the existence of two antagonistic political groups but also a continuing disagreement over the desirability of change. Apparently the Rutledges and their friends still opposed the constitution of 1778 because it was too radical.

Innes had been respectably accurate. There had been no "Anarchy," but for many people there was more than enough "Division, Riot . . . and Confusion." And only three months after the denunciations of Lowndes's proclamation, Charleston was the scene of a far more serious outburst. Expanded trade brought to the port large numbers of foreign sailors, perhaps up to 1,000 at a time, who combined with the crews of privateers to keep some Charlestonians uneasy and the militia busy protecting persons and property.[11] The intrusion of outsiders increased when America, early in 1778, secured the support of the French in the war. On 6 September 1778 there was "a most violent riot" in Charleston. Fire was exchanged between Americans on shore and the French on their vessels. And, whether the trouble was stimulated by Tories, as Gadsden believed, or by a clash of European and American values, as Lowndes believed, or, as one French observer wrote, by prejudice and guilt — "the French are not liked at all and in spite of the need that is felt for them they are subject to all sorts of unpleasantness" — it was serious. Four men died, three of them French sailors.[12]

But despite the obvious stresses, always with the fear of slave rebellions present, the chaos was not the disaster some people expected. Carolinians could now afford the luxury of dissent among rebels because their war had disappeared. Since the defeat of the Tories and Cherokees, and the successful defense of Charleston in 1776, it had gone elsewhere, leaving behind stories, some of them no doubt imaginary, of wonder and bravery and frustrated ambitions. Richard Hutson wrote immediately and romantically of the "awfully pleasing sight" of the British army and navy being "most shamefully repulsed," and he spread the tale of one sergeant, "McDougal by name," who "rivals Epaminondas in fame; when breathing his last, 'My brave lads,' he cries, 'I am just expiring, but for heaven's sake let not sweet liberty expire with me.'"[13]

For some Carolinians, however, liberty did soon expire. Dissenting rebels were acceptable; loyalists were not. The legislature's attempt to enforce allegiance in 1778 was less harsh than the actions of militia units. After the loyalist defeat in 1775, patriot forces suppressed political dissent, prevented loyalists from resisting, organizing, or aiding the British. Thomas Brown, a loyalist who fled to St. Augustine, becoming a colonel of the Florida Rangers, wrote that rebels watched loyalists "with the most jealous eye . . . and upon the least suspicion . . . take them into custody and hurry them to some distant place of confinement."[14] Loyalists faced daily intimidation.

Such actions, crucial to maintaining the cause of independence, were not glorious enough for Charles Cotesworth Pinckney. In an effort to find battle in 1777, Pinckney, whose military ardor had led him in 1768 to the Royal Military Academy at Caen, France, went north to Washington's camp.[15] Most Carolinians obviously stayed home, many to take ad-

Miss Carolina Sulivan, a cartoon by Mary Darly.

vantage of new economic opportunities. Rice and indigo prices soared, and indigo, exported to new French markets, continued to bring extremely high returns after rice declined. Georgetown District prospered. Trade with Bermuda, especially for salt, increased. Because the war disrupted the North's normal trade patterns, South Carolina became more involved in American trade, sending imports north by coastal packet or overland wagon. Indeed, the British heard that South Carolina's trade had "in a great measure supported the rebellion." "At least 250 wagons were continually going backwards and forwards" to Philadelphia.[16]

Confident of the state's continued existence, some people began to plan more seriously than ever before "for the education and instruction of youth." In 1777 and 1778 the Mount Sion Society and the Catholic Society of Camden District, the Salem Society of Ninety Six District, and St. David's Society of Cheraw District were incorporated for the general purpose of supporting schools in areas where there had been few opportunities for formal study. In 1779 a society was established for similar purposes in St. John Colleton.[17]

There was money for investment and speculation. In 1777 and 1778 the newly formed Bank Company of South Carolina lent the state a total of £26,000; in those years also more individuals advanced the state money for the cause of independence, one British informant naively reporting that some individuals had loaned "as far as one hundred thousand pounds sterling." Furthermore, guardians and executors violated their trusts to support rebellion.[18] People monopolized goods for higher prices or bought and sold for quick profits. One Charlestonian, a brewer, turned over five townhouses in a week. People were "preying on each other like vultures," wrote the Reverend Oliver Hart in 1779.[19]

The prosperity, as Hart probably knew, was not universal. The new trade brought in the currencies of other states and prices soared with the depreciation. Goods from France were advanced 1,000 percent on their original cost, according to merchant Josiah Smith. The vestry of St. Philips's Church, complaining for years of their "very great want of Money for the relief of the Poor," needed £120,000 currency in 1779 for relief because of "the very extravagant prices of every necessary of life," including medicine, which cost so much that Dr. George Logan felt unable to attend the parish poor.[20] Food quickly became scarce and expensive. Wages lagged behind rising prices. Artisans felt cheated: they bought their materials for cash, they said, and sold on credit to purchasers who waited for inflation and a court suit before paying their debts.[21]

Life was hardest on the victims of South Carolina's brief war. The Provincial Congress had resolved in November 1775 to support people "maimed or disabled in the publick service," as well as the "families of such as might be killed," but men who volunteered thinking their families would be secure were tragically mistaken. In 1778 the legislature voted survivors a maximum of £200 current money a year, but the daily worsening inflation made the money inadequate. Slaveowners were better protected, for the legislature determined that masters who lost slaves in public service would be indemnified at a rate set by "two indifferent freeholders," which meant that they could take into account the latest depreciation.[22]

What prosperity there was ended and the distress became more acute when, beginning in 1778, the war with Great Britain moved south with increasing fury, ending the freedom which had allowed liberty and some license in South Carolina. With the war came disorder and change of a different kind. With it also came suffering and sacrifice far greater than most people could have envisioned when pledging their willingness "to hazard all" or to "die in the defence of . . . just rights." Had people known what to expect, had they somehow experienced already "the miseries of Civil War," as Pierce Butler said eleven years later when thinking about the French Revolution, they would have proceeded "with caution." To an area which had done little to precipitate war, and which therefore had little opportunity to make pledges, war brought revolution.[23] There it called forth not only the best that people were capable of but the worst. It encouraged vicious behavior not easily controlled in the years of fighting or abandoned afterwards.

Colonel Archibald Campbell's capture of Savannah, Georgia, in the closing days of 1778 was coincidental with South Carolina's first elections under its new constitution. Urged by Lowndes to be careful in choosing an executive, the legislature early in 1779 turned again to John Rutledge. With the state's position highly precarious, and with no political principles at stake, the legislature recognized in Rutledge a man of decision. But Rutledge could not keep the British out.

There were success and failure in Britain's expedition of 1778-1779. When General Benjamin Lincoln, sent by Congress to defend Carolina, invaded Georgia in April 1779, England's Augustine Prevost moved along the coast toward Charleston. General Prevost sought only to draw Lincoln back, but resistance was so light, panic so widespread, and Lincoln so slow to return that he threatened the city; and had his naval support not been deficient, Prevost thought, he would have taken it.[24] The British eventually withdrew, but they took with them ample profit. Beaufort and the neighboring area, rich in indigo, were indiscriminately robbed of "many millions." Former Lieutenant Governor Bull's plantation was looted, and other royal supporters were "shamefully plundered." Some plunder walked into the British camp. "Allured with hopes of freedom," slaves fled their owners. About three thousand were taken from the state by Prevost's men, many, probably, to be sold into slavery in the West Indies.[25]

The British profited also from increased knowledge of Carolina's internal problems. Prevost's men marched almost unhindered through the southern coastal region; the people "not only submitted and received protection," wrote James Simpson, a former attorney general of the colony, but many "gave more aid than, considering their situation, was consistent with prudence." Too, the presence of the British army near Charleston caused the state's Privy Council to propose making Charleston a neutral port and allowing South Carolina, at the end of the war, to share whatever fate the other twelve states met.[26]

For the British, however, and for Carolinians, there were signs of the disasters to follow. After capturing Savannah, Archibald Campbell called on loyalists to rise up, and he promised protection to people who affirmed allegiance to the crown and supported it with "their Arms." But the attempt to enlist loyalists failed. Patriot militia threatened anyone who did not return to the rebel side within three days. The rebels' strong response, their "depredations," the British said, made loyalists "apprehensive of joining us heartily." Many, in fact, became "zealous supporters of the rebel cause."[27] At Kettle Creek, Georgia, the militia defeated about 600 loyalists (not the expected thousands) who had moved through South Carolina.[28]

Even Prevost, despite his unexpected success, learned that the British might encounter serious problems. Rebels had passed laws "so severe and awful in execution, with such a spirit of faction and barbarity," that "the most zealous" loyalists would not join the British army. Without British troops nearby, Carolinians would not "shake off the yoke under which they are oppressed."[29]

Less than a year after Prevost's incursion, the British were back, with renewed vigor, a greater degree of certainty, and more permanence. By 1779, they had decided that their best chance to seize and maintain an offensive position in the war lay in concentrating efforts in the South, where, they still believed, their operations would enlist the support of slaves — "Intestine Enemies" — and large numbers of whites. The abortive Carlisle Commission, sent by the British in 1778 to negotiate a peace, had returned with information about great disaffection in America. And James Simpson had reported that the British could reduce South Carolina "without the risk or much opposition," because "very considerable numbers of the inhabitants" would assist them.[30]

Such loyal support became essential to British war plans when Parliament became more and more loath to send additional troops across the ocean. Even Lord George Germain, who was directing the war, wrote that Britain would fail, despite its great efforts, if it could not enlist the support of Americans.[31]

England's shift of the war to the South in search of allies worried Americans, who understood that "dominion over the black . . . [was] founded on opinion," which would "keep pace with our maintaining or giveing ground." The enemy's appearance in Carolina demanded the immediate dispatch of troops.[32] In 1778, however, with few troops available, Congress responded only by sending Lincoln to take command and by recommending that the state arm 3,000 slaves. Slaves were already employed as pioneers and laborers, tearing down houses, building defences, and working in boat yards and hospitals. They performed more skilled service for the navy, navigating pilot boats at Charleston, Stono Inlet, Georgetown, and Beaufort. As their importance was recognized, the state took out insurance for them. But the slaves, officially at least, did not fight.[33]

To arm 3,000 slaves as Congress suggested would have been a break with the past only in terms of numbers. In all of the state's numerous eighteenth-century wars slaves had fought or been ready to. Even after the Stono Rebellion of 1739 dampened the enthusiasm to arm slaves, necessity often dictated that slaves fight. A 1742 expedition to Georgia included armed blacks. During the French and Indian War slaves were used to garrison the post at Ninety Six. In all, of course, relatively few blacks were veterans of battles, even though in 1757 more than 3,000 were enrolled in the colonial militia. One colonial proposal to arm a large number, 500, was defeated during the French and Indian War by the deciding vote of the speaker of the lower house. To encourage those blacks who did fight, the government gave freedom in exchange for killing or capturing one of the enemy or for taking any of his colors.[34]

In 1779, however, Congress's proposal "much disgusted" Carolinians. They thought it "a very dangerous and impolitic Step." In February 1780 the lower house determined not to arm blacks but to allow them to work as pioneers, fatigue men, oarsmen, and mariners. At the same time it defeated a proposal to free slaves who behaved well while in the "said service."[35] No bill embodying any of these proposals was passed by the full legislature. South Carolina's slaves, accustomed to hard use, still found themselves in the strange and unenviable position of being "volunteered" for potentially dangerous service which brought money to their masters, while being denied what they had often enjoyed, the opportunity to fight for their freedom in a time of emergency, the emergency this time ironically being a war for freedom and self-government.[36]

The expedition from which the British expected so much began in December 1779. In February 1780, a British fleet and troops under Sir Henry Clinton and Admiral Marriot Arbuthnot neared Charleston. Moving cautiously, the troops took until late March to approach the city overland. General Lincoln was in a hopeless situation. Afraid to withdraw his troops lest Carolina make a separate peace (the evidence of the proposed neutrality in 1779 was still fresh), he did not feel free to evacuate the city. Yet he had little hope of resisting successfully. He delayed too long to fight his way out of the state, and, on 12 May he surrendered the city and more than 5,000 troops, Rutledge and others in the government having first escaped. The rest of the "opulent, populous, and very important colony," as the *New York Royal Gazette* described it, fell to Clinton almost without a struggle. Garrisons were established by the British at

Ninety Six, Camden, Cheraw, and Georgetown.[37] The state was in enemy hands, and, it seemed to the British from the response of Charlestonians, likely to stay that way.

Charleston in 1780

On 5 June 1780 more than 200 inhabitants of Charleston, many from the respectable and prosperous class, congratulated the British commanders "on the restoration of this capitol and province to their political connection with the Crown," and in July an address from some of Georgetown's leading citizens pledging "fidelity and loyalty" was forwarded to Charleston by a British officer. Shortly thereafter, some of the state's leaders switched sides. Rawlins Lowndes accepted British protection, as did Colonel Charles Pinckney, first president of the Provincial Congress, and Daniel Huger, members of the Privy Council. Pinckney and Huger had left Charleston before the surrender, but both returned willingly to accept British rule. Henry Middleton, an ex-president of the Continental Congress, joined Huger, Pinckney, and Lowndes. Altogether, according to a British list, 381 persons accepted protection.[38] Their motives varied.

Prewar revolutionary leaders had opposed what they considered arbitrary, oppressive Parliamentary legislation. Most, like Pinckney and Lowndes, who led the fight against disestablishment, sought little, if any, social or political change. But change came; first independence, a revolting doctrine which "originated in the more northern colonies," said the Addressors (congratulators) of Clinton and Arbuthnot, and then a dissolution of the old government. The Addressors denounced the creation of "a rank democracy," because it was a kind of "tyrannic domination, only to be found among the uncivilized part of mankind, or in the . . . dark and barbarous ages of antiquity." Perhaps that was what "people of the first fortunes" were thinking when they told James Simpson that disaster was "inevitable" unless their old government, which was "preferable to any they can ever hope to establish," was restored.[39]

To those who had hoped to restrain the hitherto politically weak and, in their eyes, uneducated lower orders while opposing Great Britain, the surrender of Charleston and the occupation of the state was neither a disaster nor a tragedy. Their war was over. After making their humble plea to be accepted once more as British subjects, the Addressors took care to point out that the oppressive English statutes had been repealed. They lamented that America had not seriously considered the overtures of reconciliation made through the Carlisle Commission in 1778.[40] Before sending the commission, Parliament had agreed not to tax America again. The commission itself had submitted proposals that would have given the colonies independence within the Empire. "There can be no doubt," Henry Laurens (still a rebel) had written, "that the people of America would joyfully have embraced" the proposals had they been made two years earlier.[41] With the city and state in British hands, and with Parliament made wise about the folly of taxing America and ready to make other concessions, many Carolinians could acknowledge their allegiance to the Crown and remain perfectly true to their prewar principles. They were traitors to what the Revolution had become, but not to its origins. The distinction was sometimes difficult to remember.

Rawlins Lowndes was denounced in 1785 as an enemy of his country for having said, as he surrendered to the British, that he was happy to return to his former allegiance. When Lowndes sued for damages, the parade of witnesses, of all factions, began. Laurens testified that no man could have been a greater friend to his country, Gadsden that only Lowndes's zeal had enabled South Carolina to send delegates to the Stamp Act Congress, Thomas Bee that Lowndes was the first person he knew who believed that England could not legally tax America, and even Dr. John Budd, one of the leaders of the 1778 demonstration against Lowndes, reiterated that no one could find fault with Lowndes's public conduct. Lowndes won the case — the jury apparently deciding he had not been a traitor — and was awarded damages.[42]

But not all the Addressors disliked the many changes that had come to the state or wished to return to the old form of government. Many of the less fortunate signers were forced to condemn the "rank democracy" by British agents whose threats took in "the unwary." Thomas Elfe was told in a "violent and threatening Manner" that he would be "removed from his Family, business, and Friends" if he refused to sign. Some Charlestonians, prisoners on parole by virtue of the surrender terms, felt compelled to pledge their allegiance so that, as British subjects, they could sue for debts before a Board of Police. Soon paroled citizens who did not return to British allegiance were also forbidden to follow their trades without permission.[43] To many artisans and mechanics, to all without substantial resources, the choice was submission or hunger for themselves and their families. Large numbers submitted.

In the interior many settlers threw down their weapons and accepted British paroles; in three areas large numbers responded by joining the British forces. Major Patrick Ferguson raised about 4,000 loyalists in Ninety Six District, enough to exercise real control in the area, and a sufficient number in Orangeburg and the area around the Little Pee Dee to maintain local order for a short time.[44]

The pacific attitude of Carolinians gave the British great expectations. Wisely governed, with civil government quickly restored, as Admiral Arbuthnot, James Simpson, and William Bull hoped, the state might remain peaceful. But the British jeopardized their success by their subsequent actions. Not content that "the majority" of interior settlers, "tho' ill disposed to us," had put down their arms, the military commanders declared neutrality unacceptable.[45] The British had premised their entire campaign, even the continuance of the war in America, on their ability to raise large number of loyalist troops. They soon realized their error. General Clinton was forced to note not only the Carolinians' willingness to acknowledge British rule but also their "scruple about carrying arms against the Congress." The attempt to organize a loyal militia in Georgetown and Charleston was handicapped by the "discountenance" of the leading men. And if one was formed, discipline and order had to be imposed with great caution, one British officer wrote, "so as not to disgust the Men, or mortify unnecessarily their love of freedom."[46]

Perhaps most important, the British discovered that loyalists were outnumbered and terrified. Prevost had commented on the "severe" laws that kept "zealous" loyalists from taking up arms. Others repeated the observation. James Simpson found loyalists "not so numerous . . . as expected." Some had simply been driven from the colony. They "daily fly from South Carolina," said an officer in Georgia, many "in a truly deplorable situation."[47] Loyalists who responded, if unprotected by British troops, were in grave danger, as the loyalists defeated at Kettle Creek could testify. Only with British soldiers nearby would Carolinians brave the wrath of rebels. Clinton sadly concluded that "the revolutions fondly looked for by means of friends to the British government I must represent as visionary." Wherever the British went they would have to establish garrisons. "The accession of friends, without we occupy the country they inhabit, is but the addition of unhappy exiles to the list of pensioned refugees.''[48] That point was established when Major Archibald McArthur was called back from the Cheraws ''so suddenly that the friends of government were not apprized of it in time to concert measures for their own security.''[49]

Learning that persons of true loyal sentiment were not as numerous as Major General Robertson and other informers had said, the British began to force people into loyalist ranks. Campbell's promise of protection to people who supported the crown militarily anticipated General Henry Clinton's more famous proclamation of 3 June 1780: all prisoners on parole, except those who had been in Fort Moultrie or Charleston when the city surrendered, were freed from their paroles and required to swear allegiance to the English government or be deemed in rebellion. The oath made them liable for military service with the British. If they refused they risked punishment. Lord Rawdon jailed more than 160 people unwilling to take up arms to oppose an American army approaching Camden. Many were chained to their prison floors. Soon after the American defeat at Camden, Lord Cornwallis imprisoned those who would not turn out for service and ordered their property confiscated.[50]

Many backcountry settlers had been willing to remain neutral or inactive in the face of British force. But Clinton's policy of raising troops by treating as enemies rather than as neutrals all who would not positively aid his forces created trouble for the British. Clinton claimed that his proclamation would expose enemies and help loyalists chase them from the country; instead, it chased them to the rebel camp. Lord Rawdon, who believed that backcountrymen had not taken arms against the British, reported that after the proclamation was issued ''nine out of ten'' of those to whom he and another officer had given paroles were ''embodied on the part of the Rebels.'' He barely contained his rage, noting that the proclamation ''had very unfavorable consequences.''[51]

The consequences were evident after the Williamsburg militia sent its major to inquire of the British whether it would have to fight those who remained in rebellion. The inevitable answer spurred the raising of troops for Francis Marion's partisan brigade and that, in turn, prompted Cornwallis to declare ''the whole country between Pedee and Santee . . . in an absolute state of rebellion.''[52]

The settlers of the backcountry and Georgetown District took the field against the British, reacting, however, not only to the Clinton proclamation but, at least partly, to cruelty which was widespread and calculated. During the invasion of 1778–1779, Carolinians had been given a glance at the future when two British deserters, pressed into service in Dublin, testified that Sir James Beard, their commander, had ordered ''every man who made a prisoner'' to be deprived of his rum ration for two months. Beard himself set an example by murdering thirteen or fourteen of the surrendered enemy.[53] The brutality emerged as a policy in the summer of 1780 when twenty-six-year-old Banastre Tarleton, commander of Clinton's cavalry, chased a Virginia regiment fortunate enough not to reach Charleston in time to aid in its defense. Tarleton caught the Americans at the Waxhaws, near North Carolina, disregarded a white flag shown after the battle had commenced, and slaughtered his opponents, his men using bayonets to untangle bodies that they might get at those on the bottom who still lived. That action roused the Scots-Irish, who had as yet taken little part in the struggle. Others were roused when Tarleton burned a dissenting church at Indiantown.[54]

In August Colonel Tarleton visited the Black River region in Georgetown District to "strike terror into the inhabitants of that district" for their "breach of paroles and perfidious revolt." He would destroy all before him. "If warfare allows me I shall give these disturbers of the peace no quarter; If humanity obliges me to spare their lives; I shall carry them close prisoners to Camden." He was prepared to "destroy the Country."[55] His cruelty was most grotesque at the home of the late General Richard Richardson. In 1775 and 1776 Richardson had led the military campaigns against backcountry loyalists. He later accepted British parole only to denounce Clinton's alteration of it. Richardson was six weeks dead when Tarleton had his coffin dug up and his body exposed. Then, according to Governor Rutledge, he "exceeded his usual barbarity" and burned everything which could not be stolen.[56]

Major James Wemyss of the 63rd Regiment was little better. Faithfully executing his orders to demolish the plantations of those who concealed arms and ammunition, Wemyss invaded the area from Georgetown to Cheraw. He burned a path seventy miles long and in some parts fifteen miles wide, including in the destruction Presbyterian churches, which he thought "sedition shops," and supervised the hanging of Adam Cusack, who was convicted of breaking his parole by firing across a river at the British.[57]

Even the generally humane Lord Cornwallis, after the battle of Camden, ordered "immediately hanged" upon capture all who had returned to the enemy after serving with the British. He watched the execution of Samuel Andrews, Richard Tucker, John Miles, Josiah Gayle, Eleazer Smith, and others.[58]

"It is not," wrote Banastre Tarleton in justification of the cruelty, "the wish of Britain to be cruel or to destroy," but "Treachery, Perfidy, and Perjury will be punished with instant Fire and Sword."[59] What should have been equally obvious to the British was that their viciousness and their definition of "Treachery" — failure to join England's crusade — neither appeased nor intimidated. Four years before, the British military had, by its excesses, marred an initial success in New Jersey, where thousands had within a few weeks taken an oath of allegiance to England. Lord Rawdon, later to object to Clinton's proclamation, then approved of unleashing the British soldiers so that "these infatuated creatures may feel what a calamity war is.''[60] Almost as quickly as they had conquered the state, the British lost effective control. The pattern was often repeated. In 1778 England's Colonel Charles Stuart recognized it. He found no reason to think that brutality would ''cause these people to submit''; rather, he noted that the British army had everywhere committed ''every species of barbarity'' and thereby given birth to ''an irrecoverable hatred.''[61]

Like other Americans, Carolinians were infuriated rather than cowed. The revolution in mind and heart, the ''great & serious revolution'' in the ''temper of the people'' that ended in hatred of the English, was caused not by Parliamentary legislation, about which the interior regions had scarcely expressed themselves, but by the conquering army. Aedanus Burke called it ''outrage & cruelty . . . beyond description.'' Francis Kinloch, a reluctant rebel at best, accurately summed up the turn of events: ''Officers whom I could Name,'' he wrote former Governor Thomas Boone, had committed acts which ''would make you and every worthy Englishman blush for the degeneracy of the Nation.'' The result of British stupidity was the existence now of ''a hundred enemies'' where there had been one.[62]

British stupidity was born of ignorance about the people and history of the backcountry. The South Carolina backcountry was an area of distinct ethnic groups and religions. Violence was an unfortunate recurring fact of life. The vicious Cherokee War of 1760-61 had been followed by a terrifying crime wave and then by the Regulator-Moderator strife of the late 60s. Because settlers lacked a political voice and because there were too few local institutions in which they could operate, they had little tradition of cooperation or even communication. Theirs was a heritage of hostility. When the Revolution came, inland settlers were not united. Many could not decide whom to aid or pray for, or how to remain neutral. Rarely consulted about the Revolutionary crises and unsympathetic with the lowcountry elite which had treated the backcountry and, until recently, Georgetown like colonial dependencies, many people supported the British or kept quiet. Others, their allegiances weak, in a way that neither rebel nor British commanders understood, rode with whichever side appeared strongest from moment to moment. Some people, perhaps seeing in the war a chance to gain for themselves and their area political power, became committed rebels. The rebels prevailed first in the state, and since they did not know their opponents well enough to respect them as people, they annoyed, plundered, and oppressed them.

The British had not intended to increase the war's inhumanity. But their encouragement of loyalists and their inability to suppress the rebels helped to escalate a civil war. In January 1779, shortly after Campbell's arrival in Georgia, American rebels captured three brothers serving with Colonel Thomas Brown and sentenced them to hang. They were exchanged when Campbell built a gallows visible to the rebels and threatened to hang two Whigs for each brother. Following the loyalists' defeat at Kettle

Creek, many, considered traitors or criminals, were put on trial at Ninety Six. Twenty were sentenced to death, although, perhaps fearing retaliation, Carolinians hanged only five. The excutions, a loyalist wrote to a Georgia newspaper, "justify measures which otherwise would be condemned."[63]

The British came into a difficult situation and were inappropriately forceful. James Simpson, reporting on South Carolina loyalism, had described a people "clamorous for retributive justice" and anxious to inflict on rebels "the punishment their iniquities deserve."[64] With England controlling the state, the recently persecuted British sympathizers would seek to retaliate. Paradoxically, the British, intent first on pacifying the state, desperately needed to restrain officers like Tarleton and Wemyss and the loyalists who followed their example. Although Simpson was "convinced there are some who are deservedly so obnoxious" that they would not "escape the effects of private resentment" no matter how the British tried to protect them, the British needed to adhere strictly to the spirit of Clinton's order of May 1780, urging the head of the militia to "protect the aged, the infirm, the women and children of every denomination from insult or outrage. . . ."[65] They did not, and on all fronts the war worsened.

Loyalists sought revenge. The British, no doubt feeling the plight of loyalists, acted also out of frustration, disappointment, and hatred. They had not come to South Carolina to conquer but to liberate. The rebels headed "an arbitrary and tyrannical government."[66] They were "banditti" (hopefully Tarleton would chastise them), inflicting on loyalists "the most cruel torments and . . . the most violent oppressions." News of one British victory could not even "penetrate" east of the Santee River because "any person daring to speak of it . . . [was] threatened with instant death."[67] One rebel leader gathered supporters "partly by the terror [of] his threats and cruelty of his punishments, and partly by the promise of plunder."[68] Clearly, British presence would allow loyalists to free themselves. But the British were surprised. Despite the tyrannical behavior of their Carolina enemy, perhaps because of it, they could not find a satisfactory number of people to accept liberation.

The disappointment bred anger. So did the desertion of British troops. Lord Rawdon, stationed in the Waxhaws among immigrants from Ireland, thought his Irish troops would win over the inhabitants; instead, they deserted, prompting Rawdon, in jest he later said, to declare he would flog or exile to the West Indies anyone aiding a deserter. He offered a reward of £5 for the return of a deserter, £10 for the return of his head.[69] More and more, the British seemed to follow the advice of Josiah Martin, royal governor of North Carolina, who urged the use of methods which "have been found effectual to cure rebellion in all ages and countries."[70]

Forced to take sides against an enemy who scorned neutrality, Carolinians rose almost independently. Some quickly joined partisan bands commanded by Thomas Sumter, from the Camden area, Francis Marion, from Georgetown, and Andrew Pickens, from Ninety Six. Several of Marion's officers were from prominent families — the Allstons, the Horrys, the Waties. Small farmers along the Black and Pee Dee rivers and Scots-Irish from the Black Mingo area also led troops — Colonels Hezekiah Maham and Adam McDonald, Majors William Benison and John James, Captains Thomas Potts, John McCauley, and John Postell. Many would emerge after the war as figures of importance in state affairs. Elsewhere, surviving members of the Hampton family, devastated by an early Indian attack, took arms and assumed an importance they would not relinquish.[71]

Throughout the interior of the state men organized; they repaid fire with fire, burning the property of Tories and murdering prisoners as they and their neighbors were burned out and murdered in turn. When troops from several states trapped loyalist forces under Major Patrick Ferguson on King's Mountain in South Carolina in October 1780, shouting "Tarleton's quarters" they slaughtered their surrendering enemies. A hastily conducted court martial condemned thirty-two Tories, and nine were hanged before officers stepped in.[72] William Cunningham, a Tory from a leading backcountry family, was among the most violent partisans. Supposedly avenging the whipping to death of his lame brother by a Whig militia captain, "Bloody Bill" terrorized Ninety Six District. In one action, his 300 troops, many of them drunk, trapped 30 Whigs and killed 20 — chopping them to pieces. The "growing enormities" in the backcountry shocked the Continental army's General Nathanael Greene. "The whigs and tories," he wrote, "pursue one another with the most relentless fury killing and destroying each other whenever they meet."[73] One slaughter generated another. Greene's aide was horrified: Whigs and Tories cut "each other's throats. . . . For want of civil government the bands of society are totally disunited, and the people, by copying the manners of the British, have become perfectly savage." Cornwallis was so outraged at the "savage barbarity" of the rebels that he threatened to "retaliate on the unfortunate persons" in his power. He had already made his contribution, however, supervising the hanging of 'deserters' at Camden.[74]

By 1781 a British officer could write that the Americans had "adopted the System of murdering every man (although unarmed) who is known to be a loyalist." He exaggerated, but none could deny the war had become so vicious on both sides that people were murdered unjustly. This reciprocal fury was clear early in 1781 when Colonel Watson, a British officer, reported an exchange with some Carolinians. "After Genl. Sumter had taken some waggons on the other side of the Santee," he wrote, "and the escort of them had laid down their arms, a party of his horse who said they had not discharged their pieces came up, fired upon the prisoners and killed seven of them. A few days after we took six of his people." There was hardly need for further comment. "Enquire," Watson said, "how they were treated."[75]

The intensity of South Carolina's war can be illustrated, somewhat inadequately, by conservatively estimated casualties. Almost 66 percent of the close to 1,000 rebel battlefield deaths in 1780 occurred in South Carolina. Almost 90 percent of the roughly 2,000 wounded that year suffered their wounds in South Carolina. Although the percentages fell in 1781, the estimated two year total of 1,089 killed in South Carolina represents about 18 percent of the estimated rebel battlefield deaths in the entire Revolutionary War, while the 2,478 wounded amount to about 31 percent of the American rebels wounded.[76] And the estimates do not include the casualties in small, unknown skirmishes nor the Carolina loyalists.

The British did more than help revolutionize the temper of the people. Their scorched earth policy and the civil war between retaliating bands of Tories and rebels devastated the countryside. When General Nathanael Greene moved into Carolina to challenge the British, he was disappointed to discover that living off the land would be difficult because the British were "laying waste" the country above their posts at Ninety Six and Camden.[77] He did not mention Georgetown District, which may have been the most affected by the war. That region, prosperous before the war, was invaded three times by the British. Wemyss ended his mission by reporting that he had "burnt and laid waste about 50 houses and Plantations." When the British evacuated the town of Georgetown they set fire to forty-two houses.[78]

Camden was ruined, destroyed by the British when they withdrew. "They burnt the Court House, Gaol, & the greatest Part of the best Houses."[79] Joseph Kershaw, one of the leading backcountry merchants, found his mills and other property at Camden burned or destroyed. Part of Sumter's property was destroyed.[80] General Richardson's property was wrecked by Tarleton. Farther to the north, near the North Carolina border, Colonel William Hill's iron works were ruined. Around Fishing Creek, near the iron works, settlers "were vastly plundered and distressed." Reverend John Simpson's "property was destroyed, his house burned, not so much as a farthing's worth was left." After a depressing journey through part of the state, William Drayton wrote, "from Camden to Charleston, we could trace . . . [the British army's] last Retreat by the Stacks of Chimnies that appear'd along the road." And, moving somewhat in the opposite direction, General William Moultrie described his passage from Winyaw, on the Georgetown coast, to the Ashley River, as "the most dull, melancholy, dreary ride that any one could . . . take."[81]

Farther to the west, William Cunningham devastated part of the Saluda River region. In the Dutch Fork, plantations were laid waste. Major James Dunlap terrorized a section of Ninety Six District; when he plundered and destroyed Andrew Pickens's house, Pickens felt freed of his parole and rejoined the fight. The British burned the town of Ninety Six when they pulled out.[82]

Plunder accompanied destruction. What the British army did not destroy it tried to carry off. The loss of furniture, plate, silver, and stock, like the total destruction, cannot easily be estimated. Edward Rutledge thought that the Beaufort area alone had been robbed of property worth millions of pounds during Prevost's invasion. Fort Granby, near the center of the state was a storehouse of plunder. When Major Andrew Maxwell surrendered it in 1782 to Colonel Henry Lee, a Continental officer, the terms allowed him and his men to carry off "private property of every sort, without investigation of title," another way of saying that what they had stolen they could keep. For his own "property," Maxwell used two wagons. Leaving Charleston in 1782, one British officer confiscated St. Michael's church bells for shipment on one of the thirty vessels in the harbor that Edward Rutledge counted and found "inadequate to carry off" the spoils of the war.[83]

The rebels also sought personal gain. At Friday's Ferry, near Fort Granby, soldiers, according to Colonel Wade Hampton who fought with them, "combined in committing robberies, the most base and inhuman that ever disgraced mankind." Sumter's men, some of whom were recruited with slave bounties, seemed driven by a "thirst after plunder" which, their temporary commander, Colonel William Henderson, noted, "seems to be countenanced by too many officers," and which made "the command almost intolerable."[84]

Most valuable of the war's booty, according to Carolinians, were the slaves, 12,000 of whom, Ralph Izard charged, including 170 of his own, were collected by the British in Charleston. In March 1782 General Alexander Leslie sent troops from Charleston to gather in "all the slaves, who belong to those in arms against the British government."[85] In December 1782, 5,000 Negroes were evacuated from the city, partly because "every department, and every officer" tried to leave with newly acquired slaves. Each regiment took a bonus of 10 slaves. The army stole some out of greed, some to replace those the rebels had taken from loyalists, and some as compensation for the more general confiscation of loyalist property begun in 1782 by the Carolina legislature.[86]

Altogether South Carolina slaveowners may have lost between 20,000 and 25,000 slaves during the war.[87] But not all were stolen — certainly not all by the British — and not all left the state. The Americans contributed to the forced movement of the black population. When they invaded British-held Georgia in 1779, they came away with slaves indiscriminately taken from friend and foe alike, perhaps thereby encouraging General Thomas Sumter's unusual bounty system. In the state's civil war it was a horse for a horse, even a Negro for a Negro. Because of "circumstances and the necessity of the case," Sumter adopted the "disagreeable" plan of using slaves plundered from Tories, ostensibly, to raise troops. Under his "law," which helped him raise 1,100 men, a colonel received three and a half slaves a year, a major, three; the "law" was scaled down so that a private got one slave for a ten-month enlistment. It was necessary to distinguish enemies from friends, said Sumter, sounding much like Tarleton, and treat the former "as their baseness and perfidy authorize."[88]

But the number stolen by both sides during the war was probably not as great as the number of slaves who simply ran away, "coveting," James Madison said, the liberty we "have proclaimed so often to be the right, & worthy pursuit of every human being."[89] The flight started early. In 1775 so many slaves fled to Sullivan Island that the Council of Safety ordered their encampment destroyed. William Moultrie and his men took prisoners and killed fifty blacks who would not surrender.[90] Although some Carolinians, like Henry Laurens and William Moultrie, claimed their slaves were so well treated that none deserted, others lost large numbers. "Today came thirteen Negroes fleeing from Young's plantation on Wadmalaw Island," an officer entered in his diary on 8 March 1780. That year William Hazzard Wigg lost ninety-six slaves and Rawlins Lowndes seventy-five, some no doubt running to the British, for whose victory, Governor Rutledge said, slaves prayed.[91]

Wherever the British army went it attracted slaves, many of whom, perhaps on the verge of freedom, tragically died. David Ramsay accused General Prevost's men, who were unable to transport all the Negroes who had fled their owners, of preventing the blacks from holding on to the British boats by chopping off "the fingers of some," and keeping others "at proper distances" with "cutlasses and bayonets."[92] Large numbers died unavoidably or through neglect. Too many to be cared for, crowded together around British lines, slaves became victims of smallpox and "camp-fever." Around Camden, the British blamed smallpox, which killed many black laborers, for their inability to complete more quickly their military defenses. "Great numbers of them died, and were left unburied in the woods," Ramsay wrote, reporting also that "infants were found in unfrequented retreats drawing the breasts of their deceased parent. . . ."[93]

The war would have been even more destructive, more brutal, and more costly in lives had the British armed the slaves, but their intent in moving south to find loyalist support had been to take advantage of the blacks and unnerve the enemy, disrupt the economy, and make the war more painful, psychologically and financially, to people who would see their mobile property disappear. The British could not arm slaves and retain the support of slave-owning loyalists, so they used the blacks much as the rebels did, as laborers, sometimes as skilled mariners. Only occasionally were they sent into battle. Thomas Sumter thought their use on sallies in 1781 earned "the resentment and detestation of every American who possesses common feelings." The next year Charles Cotesworth Pinckney denounced the British-armed blacks who were "daily committing the most horrible depredations and murder in the defenceless parts of our Country."[94]

American complaints against the British were somewhat inappropriate since blacks could have ventured out on their own, emulating either side, but encouraged by none. If they seemed threatening and capable of resistance before the war, they were capable of unaided aggressiveness during it. Former governor William Bull thought that slaves became "ungovernable" when their masters were called away; it was then difficult to enforce the laws needed to control them. Eliza Pinckney thought no one could stop her slaves from joining the British, "for they all do now as they please everywhere." She could not sell her slaves because they "behaved so infamously" and were "so Insolent" that no one would buy them.[95] Traveling with the British, a few blacks banded together undoubtedly terrified many whom they encountered. It was bad enough for Eliza Wilkinson to face "the inhuman Britons" who arrived at her house, but what "augmented it," was that "they had several armed negroes with them, who," she said, "threatened and abused us greatly."[96]

When Reverend Archibald Simpson returned to his home in the lowcountry near Georgia in November 1783, he described what others saw and many felt. "All was desolation," he wrote. "Every field, every plantation, showed marks of ruin and devastation." The British army had come to plunder and not to "conquer" or "conciliate" Carolinians.[97] He was wrong about their intent, but in a real sense right about their actions. What Simpson and most other returning Carolinians did not do, however, was to distribute the blame, placing some on their warring countrymen.

The revolution in mind, heart, and country came to a large section of South Carolina after the British occupied the state in 1780. Strangely, while many in the lowcountry who had done most to bring on the war were ingratiating themselves with the British, people in the backcountry were entering the battle and fighting to preserve complete independence. Strangely also, the lowcountry area around Charleston was less affected by the war than the backcountry, where the fighting may have been bloodier and more cruel than anywhere else in America.

Certainly there was considerable property damage in the Charleston area. A fire in Charleston destroyed 250 houses in January 1778.[98] Part of this lowcountry territory was plundered by Prevost on the initial march into the state. Undoubtedly most of the slaves lost during the war came from the lowcountry area around Charleston.

But the devastation of the parishes around Charleston and even of those in Beaufort District was of a different kind from that in the rest of the state; it was not as total, not as widespread, not as cruel. For the most part, the war was not fought there. There were 137 battles during the war in South Carolina. Seventy-eight were fought in the backcountry. More than half of the remaining battles were fought in the immediate vicinity of Charleston. The numbers do not include the small hit and run opera-

Ruins of Sheldon Church, by Charles Fraser. Courtesy, Carolina Art Association/Gibbes Art Gallery

tions or the unrecorded fights that characterized the backcountry civil war. Four important battles took place in the coastal area; more than fourteen were fought in the interior. In the lowcountry war, land did not pass from hand to hand as often, houses were not so frequently attacked, Tories and rebels did not so violently prey upon one another. Although there was looting, destruction, and depredation, "the houses of the planters were seldom burnt," David Ramsay wrote soon after the war.[99] When the British came Eliza Wilkinson watched her trunks split open, her buckles pulled from her shoes, and wax pins taken from her hair. In a second visit, the enemy destroyed furniture and took doors and window shutters. But the house remained standing. In August 1782 the new South Carolina governor, John Mathews, told Arthur Middleton that their plantations were "among those that have suffered most." But he went on to describe not the destruction of his house but the "distress" caused by his having only "fourteen acres of rice standing out of 100, & not an acre of any kind of provisions." He told Middleton also that the British had burned the houses of William Somersall and his (Middleton's) father. He soon passed on the information that he had been misinformed: "it was not the houses I have mentioned but the barns that were burnt. . . ."[100]

The British did sequester some lowcountry Carolina estates, running them for the benefit of the British forces. Sequestration denied some owners the enjoyment of their property, but a proportion of the annual product of the estates was supposed to be set aside for the families who had formerly possessed the property. And, even if the British did loot the estates they occupied, their use of the property guaranteed at least some maintenance of the plantations.[101]

The best picture of the effect of the war was Colonel Henry Lee's. When in November 1781, one and a half years after the capture of Charleston, he and his troops moved into the "country settled by the original emigrants into Carolina," they saw "spacious edifices, rich and elegant gardens, with luxuriant and extensive rice plantations." It was an amazing contrast to what they had come through. "Never before had we been solaced with the prospect of so much comfort." And even, "to crown our bliss, the fair sex shone in its brightest lustre."[102]

For individuals in the Charleston District also, the war was not as harsh as it was for others. The reign of terror that prevailed in the backcountry and parts of Georgetown scarcely touched the lowcountry. For a number of reasons Charleston and the aristocratically dominated parishes which surrounded it escaped the worst consequences of the war. The white population was small and relatively united. In 1790 fewer than 3,000 free white males over sixteen lived in the eleven parishes outside the city. Always in political power, they had worked together, communicated, compromised, and presented a united front to the overwhelming number of blacks. Although people might oppose one another over the advantages of independence, they were not driven by hatreds or hardened by lives of violence. To the loyalists, the rebels, and the British, the risks of unrestrained violence during the war were too great to be dared. So lowcountry settlers did not war on each other.

Neither did the British prey upon them. Lowcountry rebels were friendlier and more recognizable. Many were Anglican and many had been educated in England. They and their families traveled there; merchants had business associates there. They had friends in the British army. When Thomas Pinckney was wounded, an English army officer persuaded British surgeons to look after him, and they saved his leg. Pinckney had been to school in England with the officer's brother, who, after being captured at sea, had asked to be released into Pinckney's custody. Alexander Garden, a Carolina officer, wrote of British officers, "all old Westminsters, [who] were faithful to old friendships."[103] Charles Cotesworth Pinckney was separated from his town house and family, and lost a son to smallpox, but he was on parole at a relative's plantation and was allowed a slave to run his errands. He had the inclination and the time to help guide his nephew's education. His condition may have worsened, however, when he and other officers not exchanged were sent to Philadelphia.[104]

Many state leaders were seized by the British, in an effort to prevent trouble, and exiled to St. Augustine. It seemed a cruel fate, but for most it was not unbearable. The exiles could take servants with them. They could rent houses and live comfortably as long as money arrived from home. Christopher Gadsden, because of his character, suffered most. So unyielding in his principles was he that he refused a parole and was kept in a dungeon for forty-two weeks.[105]

One lowcountry officer was executed. Isaac Hayne, a prominent resident of St. Paul's parish and a member of the state Senate from 1778 to 1780, his wife and children seriously ill, had under protest taken British protection. In 1781, after his wife died, and after being threatened with imprisonment unless he joined the British army, Hayne considered himself released from his parole and rejoined the American forces. He was quickly recaptured in July and sentenced to death, partly as an example to other Carolinians breaking their paroles, and partly out of anger over the American execution of John André. Despite the pleas of prominent Tories, including William Bull, the sentence was carried out, after a short delay to allow a farewell to his surviving children.[106]

Tragic as the execution was, however, its importance rests on the name of the condemned man. Many more were executed in the backcountry with no surviving pleas or protests. Had Hayne been a backcountry soldier, he might well never have lived to see a British camp. Abel Kolb, like Hayne a member of the South Carolina legislature, was surprised in his house by Tories and shot after surrendering; his house was plundered and destroyed.[107]

Lowcountry women were better off also, although they too suffered the mental anguish of separation from husbands, fathers, and sons. When the British came to her home, Eliza Wilkinson was terrified. "The whole world appeared" to her like "a theatre, . . . where neither age nor sex escaped the horrors of injustice and violence. . . ." Her house was plundered, she lost some pins and shoe buckles, she was apparently insulted. But no one harmed her or anyone close to her; no one, if her story is told in full, even touched her.[108]

Backcountry women lived in the midst of the civil war and shared its horrors. Some, like the wife of one Captain McKoy, were tortured for information. Many, like the wife of Colonel Kolb, along with their children, watched as their husbands were summarily executed. When Wemyss hanged Adam Cusack, only the intervention of a young British officer stopped him from trampling Cusack's pleading family as it lay before his horse. Some women, if they were lucky, watched in terror as their husbands fled to temporary shelter in Carolina's woods. When warring parties descended on an area they left families in misery. Reverend Simpson reported not only the loss of his property but also that his "family were turned out all but naked." Joseph Kershaw complained that "hardest of all" for him to bear was Lord Rawdon's "turning my wife & children out of the only Room they posessed on the Inclement first day of January 1781." After viewing Tarleton's work, Francis Marion was appalled "to see women and children sitting in the open air around a fire, without a blanket, or any clothing but what they had on."[109] There was so much horror, so much death and brutality, there might well have been a corresponding amount of rape, which men accepted as a necessary, and enjoyable part of war. In 1776 Lord Rawdon had noted "most entertaining courts-martial" brought on by complaining northern women. In contrast, women "to the southward . . . behaved much better," Rawdon wrote, having heard of one woman who had accepted her fate with the proper resignation.[110]

In the year and a half that followed the British invasion, the people of backcountry South Carolina faced the destructiveness of war. But the inhabitants of the lowcountry, who first had borne the brunt of the onslaught of British troops in the attack on Charleston in 1776, Prevost's invasion in 1779, and finally, Clinton's and Arbuthnot's occupation in 1780, fared better. They escaped first-hand acquaintance with the viciousness of the civil war.[111]

After May 1780 the British fanned out from Charleston to secure and occupy the inland country and to enlist support of loyalist troops. Aroused Carolinians joined groups forming around partisan commanders Sumter, Marion, and Pickens. British posts began to fall to the combined pressure of Carolinians and Continentals. Soon, the British army was forced to retrace its steps and hole up in and around Charleston.

The initial intervention of the Continental army in South Carolina's efforts to expel the invaders was disastrous. Congress had sent south General Horatio Gates, hero of Saratoga. His army, weakened by a long march and the purgative effects of the molasses it had received in place of the usual rum, met Lord Cornwallis near Camden and was routed, with Gates himself fleeing back to North Carolina. Flushed with success, Cornwallis marched into North Carolina, followed in the south and west by Major Patrick Ferguson and his loyalist troops.

Backcountry settlers from Virginia, North Carolina, South Carolina, and present-day Tennessee, pursued Ferguson, pinned him on King's Mountain, killed and wounded almost 400 men, some after surrender, and took more than 700 prisoners. Cornwallis hastened back from North Carolina with the new Continental commander, Nathanael Greene, close behind. Part of Greene's force, led by Virginia's Daniel Morgan, defeated the hated Tarleton at Cowpens. Greene, moving strategically, then pulled his entire army back to North Carolina, drawing Cornwallis after him. They met at Guilford Courthouse in March 1781. Though Greene gave up the battlefield, Cornwallis lost men he could ill spare. And he found himself hundreds of miles from his supplies.

By April 1781 Greene was back in South Carolina. One by one the British posts fell. While Greene and the Continental army occupied the main British force, Sumter, Marion, and Pickens struck at the posts. In May Sumter took Orangeburg; a day later Marion captured Fort Motte. Pickens, with Colonel Henry Lee from Greene's army, followed with Augusta, Georgia, in June. In July Ninety Six was evacuated. Two months later, Greene, now joined by the three partisan bands, fought the British at Eutaw Springs, in the lowcountry south of the Santee. They lost more men than the British but drove the enemy from the field. There was no place for the British but the Charleston area, and there they remained for a year.[112]

Meanwhile, the Carolinians prepared to resume the government of their state. In the few years since independence, they had fought among themselves for political power and for the chance to direct the Revolution. Their freedom to engage in political battles had been interrupted by military campaigns now virtually ended. The new problems they had to face were serious, their ability to deal with them unknown.

FOUR
Reconciliation, Revenge, and the Re-establishment of Civil Government

> The people at large wanton in the first exercise of sovereign power . . . feel the same cruel joy in robbing the helpless families of those whom they can oppress with impunity, that an infant does in torturing an insect that falls within it's [*sic*] reach.
>
> Francis Kinloch, 27 June 1783.

> Our People were very moderate; their Provocations have been excessive, their losses immense, & I did expect their Resentments would have been in proportion to their sufferings.
>
> Edward Rutledge, 26 February 1782.

ITH South Carolina almost entirely in American hands, Governor John Rutledge returned from North Carolina in the summer of 1781. He acted quickly to re-establish civil government. Encouraged by General Nathanael Greene, Rutledge moved to end the bitter civil war by offering to almost all British adherents a full and free pardon if they appeared before a brigadier or colonel of the militia within thirty days and served six months in the militia. Persons who had held civil or military commissions under the British government and were still with the enemy, and those who had already refused pardon under proclamations issued in 1778 and 1779, were not eligible. Nor were those whose conduct had been so infamous that they could not be allowed the privileges of America. The Addressors of Clinton and Arbuthnot, men to Rutledge guilty of behaving "in the most criminal manner," were also excluded, although they had done little more than reassert ideas Rutledge himself had used when vetoing the constitution of 1778.[1]

General Greene, a Quaker expelled by his Meeting for participating in the war, explained the conciliatory policy of 1781 and 1782. Appalled by "the daily scenes of the most horrid plundering and murder," he acknowledged that "vengeance would dictate one universal slaughter," but forgiveness would save those who might otherwise die avenging their slain countrymen. It was advisable, therefore, "to encourage the return of the Tories."[2] General Francis Marion also approved of Rutledge's leniency. In June 1782 Marion and Major Micajah Gainey, the leader of the loyalists settled between the Great Pee Dee River and North Carolina, negotiated a truce by which the Tories agreed to restore plundered property where

General Marion entertaining a British officer in his swamp. *Courtesy, Carolina Art Association/Gibbes Art Gallery*

possible, behave peaceably, and sign an oath of allegiance to South Carolina and the United States. More than 500 of them put down their arms, Gainey and some of his men subsequently serving six months with the rebel militia. Together, they fought British-armed Black Dragoons. Thomas Sumter also encouraged Tories to give up the fight. Forty in the Orangeburg area took advantage of the pardon by 13 December. By the 22nd, 300 loyalists had come in, and Sumter enrolled about 100 in the militia. Cooperation went so far in one area that Tories and Whigs agreed to a truce to allow the cultivation of crops.[3]

The lenient policy was successful. Aedanus Burke, a South Carolina judge and member of the legislature, showed clearly how it saved lives. In May 1782 he reported that the country had been "ravaged by small armed parties" which murder "in Cold blood." They had no reason to stop. But finally the governor authorized a truce, and "these very murderers," Burke wrote, no doubt too optimistically, "are at last received on terms of pardon & reconciliation & now live at home."[4]

Yet many Carolinians opposed conciliatory measures. Sumter thought that "nothing but the sword will reclaim" the Tories. William Clay Snipes was violent in calling for blood; and the men in Marion's camp, incensed that their general was negotiating with the Pee Dee region's notorious Jeff Butler, let everyone know their intention of killing him no matter what was promised. "To defend such a wretch is an insult to humanity," they said, forcing Marion to sneak him away during the night. Gainey, his six months in the militia behind him, fled to North Carolina for safety.[5] Colonel Lemuel Benton, commander of the Cheraw militia, protested that men who had plundered and burned and murdered their prisoners of war were "restored to equal privileges with the men who have suffered every thing by them that was in their power & savage disposition to inflict."[6] Many who could see "nothing but the mournful widow and the fatherless child" thirsted for punishment rather than conciliation.[7] Angry Carolinians could not accept former enemies as equals, as citizens with power to influence the course of future legislative action.

Many also found Rutledge's full and free pardon harder to accept than Lowndes's proclamation had been in 1778. Then, before full-scale war had reached South Carolina, some men, perhaps with Edward Rutledge's help, had denounced Lowndes for allowing Tories more time to rejoin the ranks. But John Rutledge escaped serious trouble because the British still occupied Charleston. Had they not possessed the city, Rutledge would have faced popular disturbances similar to those which had confronted Lowndes and would confront later governors. But Rutledge may have avoided censure by catering in other ways to those who sought revenge when the legislature met in January 1782.

In November 1781 Governor Rutledge called for the election of a new legislature. Elections for representatives of parishes in British hands were to be held as close as possible to those parishes so that the greatest number of qualified persons could attend. Carolinians who had taken protection and had not rejoined the Americans under the terms of Rutledge's proclamation were not eligible to vote. Aedanus Burke, one of those elected to the lower house, was convinced that "the number thus excluded were considerable in some parishes, and," he wrote, "they murmured exceedingly for a few days." Though Burke was to change his mind in little more than a year, he then favored excluding some from political participation. It was "madness to allow men to influence our Elections who had born[e] arms against us."[8]

The election was sparsely attended, even for a state once accustomed to small turnouts. The exclusion of numerous Tories, the absence of citizens in the army, and the necessity to hold elections for Charleston and St. Andrew outside the boundaries of those parishes, kept down the number of voters. So also did the desire of Carolinians who could "live as easy under one Government as another" not to commit themselves.[9] In the election for St. Andrew's members, held in St. John Berkeley, four voters chose six representatives and one senator, as did St. Peter's thirteen voters. The fifteen Charleston voters who ventured out of the city or returned from other parts of the state were even more powerful, electing thirty representatives and two senators. No election was held for St. John Colleton, also in British hands.[10]

Shortly before the election, Edward Rutledge was apprehensive. ''Between Friends,'' he wrote, ''I fear there will be damned strange works when once the Assembly get together.'' Little more than a month later, however, Rutledge changed his mind. ''I like the Competent Appearance of the House very much,'' wrote the Charleston representative. ''We have the Flower of the Country.'' Aedanus Burke agreed. The Assembly was ''composed of very respectable good men.''[11]

The ''Flower of the Country'' were mostly Continental or state army officers and Charlestonians who had been exiled by the British to St. Augustine. The exiles included Christopher Gadsden, Thomas Ferguson, Edward Rutledge, Hugh Rutledge, and David Ramsay. Five other exiles sat in the legislature. The generals, colonels, majors, and captains were more numerous. Colonels John Laurens and James Postell represented Charleston. Prince Frederick sent Colonel John Baxter, Major John James, Captain John McCauley, and Captain Thomas Potts, a surgeon with Marion. The Hampton brothers, Colonels Wade and Richard, whose parents had been killed by Cherokees in 1776, represented Saxe-Gotha. The three partisan generals were there, Pickens in the lower house, Sumter and Marion in the Senate, where the strength of the military was readily apparent.[12] Nineteen of the twenty-eight elected senators appeared; ten of the nineteen held the rank of captain or higher.

The Senate was dominated by the military, and, just as significantly, for the first time by the backcountry and lowcountry parishes outside the Charleston District, even though those areas were still inadequately represented. Seven senators attending the 1782 legislature were from the Charleston District, twelve from the rest of the state.[13] Much the same geographical alignment existed in the lower house. The lowcountry parishes around Charleston had lost the opportunity to control the legislature at the polls. Voting by habit, voters repeatedly elected absentees to office. The fifteen Charleston voters chose only sixteen representatives who would attend. Henry Laurens, captured by the British in 1780 while on a diplomatic mission, was still in England when Charlestonians elected him. He returned to South Carolina in 1784. Charles Cotesworth Pinckney, elected by two parishes, was a prisoner on parole in Philadelphia and did not return to the state until the Assembly had adjourned. Thomas Bee, a delegate to the Confederation Congress, was chosen by both Charleston and St. Paul's parish. He did not appear, nor did thirty other representatives elected by the lowcountry parishes of the Charleston District. All told, with no election in St. John Colleton, Charleston District was short thirty-nine representatives. Only twenty-six from the rest of the state stayed away, giving those regions eighty representatives to the Charleston area's fifty-seven.

The legislators who gathered in January 1782 at Jacksonborough, a little village about thirty-five miles from Charleston, remembered the viciousness and destruction that had visited the state since the last assembly had met in 1780; many had themselves been brutal, and some had suffered from the destruction. Feelings ran high. One member displayed on his pistol a tally of victims: "The notches amount[ed] to twenty-five." Another had "killed his fourteen."[14] Five of the ten representatives allowed the District Eastward of the Wateree River attended, and at least three had reasons to seek revenge. James Bradley, harshly handled by Tarleton, still had marks of iron on his wrists. Joseph Kershaw was but recently returned from exile in Bermuda, his brother Ely having died of typhus dysentery on the voyage. Richard Richardson's wife had been thrown out of her house by Tarleton, taunted with recitals of punishments to be inflicted on him when captured, and had seen his father's body exhumed. Outside the legislature, too, the war had "excited in the breasts of our Citizens" an "inveterate hatred & spirit of Vengeance" not confined to one sex. "The very females talk as familiarly of sheding blood & destroying the Tories as the men do," wrote Judge Aedanus Burke.[15] Little wonder, then, that Edward Rutledge feared "damned strange works."

Edward Rutledge also might worry because the dominant legislators, however competent in appearance and respectable, were too new to be taken for granted. Their unknown philosophies caused uncertainties seldom felt in pre-Revolution legislatures. When John Laurens appeared at the Jacksonborough Assembly with another plan to arm and free slaves, Rutledge feared that he himself would possibly "be the only Speaker on the right side of the Question." The defeat of the plan by a vote he remembered as about 15 to 100 satisfied him, but that he could be worried by a proposal so overwhelmingly unpopular showed his ignorance of his fellow legislators.[16] Close votes must have been more disquieting to him.

Rutledge's original fears no doubt increased after his brother greeted the new legislature. Despite his earlier lenience, John Rutledge's opening words were hardly designed to smooth over differences or promote forgiveness. The governor congratulated the legislators on the recent American victories, noted that General Greene was entitled to "honourable and singular marks of . . . approbation and gratitude," and warned the British that Americans were resolved "never to return to a domination which, near six years ago, they unanimously and justly renounced." But then, after his introductory remarks, Rutledge went on to stimulate rather than dull the desire for revenge. He described in general terms what legislators had lived through: "prisoners of war . . . killed in cold blood," others "delivered up to savages," churches "consumed in flames." He reminded the legislators of the homes of the widowed, the aged, the infirm, that were destroyed when "neither the tears of mothers, nor the cries of infants, could excite in their breasts pity or compassion." And, speaking of the remaining Tories, he noted that "justice and policy forbid their free admission to the rights and privileges of citizens." It was hard to reconcile Rutledge's speech, his vivid picture of the war, with his proclamation of pardon.[17] He was not asking the legislature to show restraint.

The legislature turned first to the election of public officials. Christopher Gadsden was elected governor, by two votes Aedanus Burke thought, but declined the office, according to Burke again, in "the most illustrious action of his Life." But Gadsden probably felt about his election in 1782 the same way he had felt about his election as lieutenant governor in 1778: that he had been "honored" in an effort to get him out of the way.[18] In the end, John Mathews became governor, Richard Hutson, lieutenant governor. New delegates to Congress and new privy councilors were elected.

Then, following Rutledge's suggestions, acts were passed for the better regulation of the militia and for procuring recruits and preventing desertion. General Greene was rewarded with an estate worth 10,000 guineas. At the same time, the legislature turned down Laurens's plan to raise Negro troops. Although the legislature repealed an act making paper currency legal tender, it did nothing to fix a scale of depreciation or to determine how old contracts were to be paid. The lack of any legal tender or specie in the state led the legislature to forbid suits for the recovery of debts until ten days after the next meeting of the General Assembly.[19] Knowing Congress needed revenue, the legislature approved the impost, an *ad valorem* tax of 5 percent on imported goods that would go into effect when all states made similar grants to the central government.[20] None of the acts to strengthen the military and economic condition of the state and nation was motivated by "inveterate hatred" or the "spirit of vengeance." Other legislation was.

Legislators had no need of Rutledge's graphic reminder to remember the murder, arson, and robbery of the war. To punish at least some wartime criminals, the legislature decided to open the Courts of Oyer and Terminer. Aedanus Burke, a legislator and one of the judges who would be forced into action by the opening of the courts, strongly condemned what he thought an absurd act. So many crimes had been committed, some even "from necessity," that the civil courts "w[oul]d not be able to settle them in twenty years." Besides, Burke was convinced that strict enforcement would not allow "one thousand men . . . [to] escape the Gallows." Judge John Faucheraud Grimké advised mercy in 1783 because to secure justice Carolinians would have to "wade" through a "field of blood."[21] Burke exaggerated the number of required hangings, but thousands of Carolinians, rebels and loyalists, would have been affected. Rebels might ease the burden on the courts, however, by prosecuting only Tories. Burke feared that he was to be "a tool to gratify the fierce revenge of the people." That some wanted revenge rather than justice he learned when backcountry people warned him not to let lawyers defend Tories; further, he was told to "be cautious how . . . [he] adjudged any point in their favor."[22]

Fortunately for Burke, whose reluctance to be turned into a hanging judge, "a *Jefferies,*" made him decide to hold courts without trials and then resign, the courts did not sit. Judge Henry Pendleton was captured by the British, and a "Cornet of Dragoons" impressed Burke's horses. Thus, Burke told the governor that he had to be excused from opening the courts.[23]

The legislature's most serious attack on loyalists and British sympathizers did not involve the judiciary. Referring in his opening address to those citizens who had avowed their allegiance to the British, Rutledge told the legislators that they had to decide whether the loyalists' property should be seized. The Jacksonborough legislature responded by confiscating or amercing the property of many who had not supported the American cause. The amercement act provided for a 12 percent tax on the appraised value of the property specified. Most of the people listed in the confiscation act were also banished from the state.[24] These acts of 1782 differed markedly from, but logically extended, earlier acts or expressions of legislative intent which had been aimed at potential loyalists, for these were designed not to prevent future desertions to the enemy by Carolinians as yet unknown, but to punish those who had already taken actions considered inimical to the state. A confiscation act of 1776 had provided for the execution of people who joined or aided the British and for the sale of their property. In 1779 the legislature defeated a bill with a ringing clause denouncing those who "shamefully abandon a cause the most favorable to the rights of humanity that ever any people were engaged in," but passed an ordinance allowing the sale of property belonging to Carolinians who joined the enemy and failed to return when summoned by a proclamation. Neither act was much enforced, the first being applied to the estates of three people out of reach of the state government.[25] But the acts of the Jacksonborough Assembly, vehemently debated by a few representatives and senators, were passed with enforcement in mind.

Primarily the legislation of 1782 was legislation of revenge. The legislators' desire to raise revenue for a financially destitute state, and the prospect for speculation in confiscated lands, were not inconsistent with the dominant motive. Edward Rutledge, who first drafted the bill confiscating estates, thought the act necessary because the state could not "raise a Tax." Francis Marion expected confiscation and amercement to yield at least a million pounds sterling. Without the bill troops could not be raised. "Two regiments are to be raised as our Continental quota," Marion wrote, "giving each man a negro per year . . . taken from the confiscated estates."[26]

Burke, again reacting strongly and with the same attitude that had led him two years earlier to support ill-used militia men, objected to the confiscation of estates "so a few Land Jobbers or Speculators . . . [could] engross them." The law was "so framed that a man who wants land has no chance to get any"; only a man with "land enough already" could give the security required.[27] Christopher Gadsden, only recently returned from St. Augustine, where he had refused the more lenient treatment offered other exiles, also lashed out at "land jobbers who were very eager . . . to gratify their voracious appetites." To counteract the speculators, Gadsden introduced, and saw incorporated in the final bill, a clause to prevent monopolization of the land by a few. All confiscated lands and plantations were to be divided into tracts containing from 200 to 500 acres. Where it could be done without "great and manifest prejudice to the sale," no tract was to exceed 500 acres. According to Gadsden, this clause "met with general approbation," being "oppos'd only by . . . the greatest land jobber in the State."[28]

Confusingly, Gadsden was entertaining two ideas not easily reconcilable. He believed speculators "were very eager" for the confiscation act to pass, while at the same time he found only one who opposed the clause specifically devised by him to foil their plans. The lack of more substantial opposition should have made Gadsden wary. The people primarily interested in speculation or monopolization of land must have realized that the limitation on the size of the tracts did not threaten them. The sale of lands in small tracts allowed Carolinians with small holdings to add several hundred acres to their possessions, but it did not prevent large purchases by the more affluent or more ambitious. Nowhere did the act limit the number of tracts that each person could buy. Benjamin Reynolds purchased eighteen tracts, all formerly the property of John Bailey, and presumably adjoining one another, a total of 5,723 acres. Thomas Ferguson, a member of the Jacksonborough Assembly and Gadsden's son-in-law, besides securing other property, bought four more tracts of Bailey's confiscated property, amounting to more than 1,400 acres. All told, 14,529 acres of John Bailey's land were sold on 15 August 1782. His property went to seventeen purchasers, nine of whom bought single tracts; four of the purchasers acquired a total of 9,310 acres. The Wadboo barony, on the Cooper River, belonging to a descendant of one of the original proprietors of the colony, Sir John Colleton, went to even fewer purchasers. In June 1783, 12,724 acres were sold in twenty-seven tracts to eight individuals, only one of whom bought less than 700 acres. One man, Maurice Simons, bought 5,208 acres, while Peter Fayssoux bought 2,292.[29] When property in Georgetown was sold, the largest tract was purchased by William Allston, and when eighty-two slaves were sold on 7 May 1783, Joseph Allston bought half of them. People who bought were already substantial property owners.[30] Gadsden notwithstanding, and the intent of the legislature aside, a few people capitalized on the confiscation act and purchased large quantities of property.

But in spite of the obvious need to raise money, and the equally obvious and not surprising desire of some people to acquire as much confiscated property as possible, the most compelling motive for the passage of the confiscation and amercement acts was revenge. "We shall certainly go into the matter of Confiscation," wrote Edward Rutledge. "I hope they will be lenient, but as I said before, I fear.'' Although he favored the principle of confiscation, Rutledge tried ''to restrain the tempers of the impetuous.'' ''I do assure you,'' he wrote Arthur Middleton, ''the passions of some People run very high.''[31] Aedanus Burke referred to ''the rage & violence of some ag[ains]t such as took protection.'' Burke, who saw nothing truly contemptible in the actions of the Carolinians who had lived under the British after 1780, acknowledged, nevertheless, the emotional intensity of the Jacksonborough legislators by adding that he would have his ''throat cut for saying this in publick.'' In a way, Burke had been through the experience before, tempted by and then resistant to the idea of revenge. He had been present when the British troops surrendered and marched out of their garrison at Yorktown. When he saw the ''miserable melancholy plight'' of the British, he at least temporarily got over his ''Love of Revenge.'' Four months later, in Jacksonborough, Burke favored an act of oblivion with ''some exceptions to satisfy publick justice.''[32]

Gadsden, too, condemned the harsh actions of the legislature, noting that legislators had a responsibility ''to be without passion''; their task was to correct ''the rash impetuosity of the people.'' Perhaps Gadsden was referring to John Rutledge when he commented that some people, ''for a momentary dirty popularity, gave way to . . . every whim and violent caprice no matter where they lead to.'' Like Burke, Gadsden aroused the ire of ''the violent confiscation men.'' Even his friends concluded, on the basis of his attitude toward this legislation, that he had been badly affected by his confinement while in exile.[33]

After the war, Johann David Schoepf, traveling through America, attributed to ''the lower and rougher class'' the desire for revenge. Their reasons for opposing the conciliation others preached were ''neither sufficient nor seemly.''[34] After the war, also, Pierce Butler, an Irishman who had lived in South Carolina for more than a decade and had served in the legislature since 1778, tried to locate the ''bitterness of vengeance.'' Butler pointed not to a class but to a region, the backcountry, trying to convince the area's legislators ''that mercy and forgiveness are Godlike virtues.'' He thought others might consider his ideas seriously because they came from one who had lost not only property but a favorite son during the war.[35]

Both Schoepf and Butler were partly right. In 1787, five years after the Jacksonborough Assembly, a motion was made in the lower house to repeal the confiscation and amercement acts. It was soundly defeated by a vote of 61 to 97. Lowcountry parishes in the Charleston area favored repeal by an almost two to one margin, 49 to 25. Their representatives, however, were overwhelmed by a union of representatives from the other parishes and districts who voted against repeal by a six to one margin, 72 to 12.[36] In 1787, neither a desire for state revenue nor speculation motivated the legislature. Undoubtedly the same areas most strenuously supported the acts when they were originally passed.

But Schoepf was hopelessly wrong in writing that the opponents of forgiveness had insuffient reasons for their stubbornness, for the back-country districts and the distant lowcountry parishes that dominated the 1782 legislature were the areas which had suffered most from the war. Prevost had plundered the lowcountry parishes near Georgia; Wemyss had marched through the Pee Dee region committing atrocities and destroying property. Tarleton had devastated the Camden area. Others had spread the violence into Ninety Six and other backcountry regions. In these desolated regions, for reasons which were adequate and understandable, contemporaries found "passions . . . run[ning] very high."[37]

In 1783 inhabitants of the upper part of Prince George Parish petitioned the House of Representatives to put the confiscation act into strict effect. Three days later their pleas were repeated by inhabitants of Prince Frederick Parish, slightly to the west of Prince George. The grand jury of Beaufort District, sitting before Judge Aedanus Burke, complained of the continued residence in the district of persons who "have hitherto behaved as enemies to their country." They singled out for special consideration one "William Kelsale, a man so well known for his infamous and violent practices to the good citizens of this District during the late war."[38] In 1783, the year after Burke had been warned by backcountry members not to treat Tories fairly, the foreman of the Goergetown Grand Jury publicly stated that Tories were not to be granted impartial treatment.[39]

There was no need, however, for the representatives and senators from the distant parishes and districts to push the confiscation and amercement legislation through the Jacksonborough Assembly. The heart of the lowcountry did not make a determined stand for any act of oblivion. Alexander Garden, "on the spot" in 1782, years later reported that no more than twelve legislators spoke or voted against confiscation.[40] Aedanus Burke found only two, presumably not including himself, opposed. And, he reported, no one joined him in opposition to the amercement act.[41]

Gadsden wrote a long, detailed explanation of his fight against the "unjust, impolitic, cruel, premature" confiscation act. He opposed it and the motives of those he believed responsible for it. He attacked not only the land jobbers, but also lawyers who, he thought, "will palm immense sums on this melancholy occasion." A person whose name appeared on the confiscation lists might pay handsomely to have a persuasive lawyer in the legislature attempt to get him relieved. Indeed, Gadsden was suspicious that the law had been passed to stimulate legal business.[42]

Gadsden thought the bill unjust because it seized the property of people who had signed congratulatory addresses to the British commanders. What else could they have done, he asked, "when visibly under the power and restraint of a known cruel, oppressive and tyrannical enemy?" Furthermore, Gadsden thought the bill remarkably unwise because the British still occupied Charleston, and passage of the bill might persuade them to prolong their stay. The legislature should not "sell the bear skin before they catched the bear.'' Having failed to convince many, he declared dramatically that he would amputate his hands before voting for so bad a bill.[43]

Aedanus Burke delved more deeply into the problem. Not only did he hold people blameless for submitting to the cruel British, but he believed that they had every right to accept protection. Their army was ruined, ''Law & Gov[ernmen]t extinct, the Gov[erno]r & his Council having provided for themselves'' by escaping to North Carolina. According to the judge, who soon went to Puffendorf, Vattel, and Hobbes for support, people could lawfully ''shift for themselves'' when their government is ''usurped by an invader, who has an army at command.'' Although he agreed with others that some Tories had behaved so oppressively toward Carolinians that they merited banishment and the confiscation of their property, he continued his opposition to the principle of the bill. He broadened his argument by citing a clause of the Massachusetts constitution. Laws which punished people for acts which had not been crimes when committed were ''dangerous, arbitrary, & contrary to the principles of free Gov[ernmen]t.'' As always, aware that legislative actions affected real people, Burke denounced the confiscation bill for the ''beggary & ruin'' it would bring. Lastly, he pointed out that the confiscation and amercement acts, by condemning men without hearings, established ''a Precedent of a most pernicious nature'' which might one day work against the descendants of the propertied men who favored the bill.[44]

Neither Burke's lofty ideas nor Gadsden's assaults on land jobbers and lawyers won significant support, although the final version of the bill called for efforts to maintain the support of the widows and children of those whose property was seized. Few people opposed the principles of confiscation. But even with fundamental agreement, there was still room for considerable debate, for the legislators had to select victims; they had to determine whose estates to confiscate and whose to amerce. Superficially, judging from the form of the confiscation and amercement acts, the decisions were easy. The confiscation act divided British sympathizers into six classes roughly corresponding to the divisions made by Governor Rutledge when he issued his proclamation of pardon in September 1781. The first list in the act of 1782 consisted of the names of British subjects, as well as of persons who had left the state in 1777 and 1778 to escape taking oaths of allegiance to the state but who had returned during the occupation of Charleston. The list also included names of Carolinians who had joined the British and had not surrendered to a magistrate when called on by a proclamation of 1779. The second list of names consisted of Addressors of Clinton and Arbuthnot, the third of people petitioning to be embodied as militia in the British service. The fourth class consisted of people who had signed a congratulatory address to Lord Cornwallis. Those holding civil or military commissions under British rule, also singled out by Rutledge's proclamation, had their estates confiscated in the fifth list, and

AN

ADDRESS

TO THE

FREEMEN

OF THE

STATE of SOUTH-CAROLINA.

Containing Political Obſervations on the following Subjects, viz.

I. On the Citizens making a temporary Submiſſion to the Britiſh Arms, after the reduction of Charleſtown in 1780.

II. On Governor Rutledge's Proclamation of the 27th of September, 1781.

III. On the Mode of conducting the Election, for the Aſſembly at Jackſonborough.

IV. On the EXCLUSION ACT, which cuts off the Citizens from the Rights of Election.

V. On the Confiſcation Act. VI. On the Amercement Act.

VII. The Concluſion, with Remarks to prove the Neceſſity of an Amneſty, or Act of Oblivion.

BY CASSIUS.

Suppoſed to be written by ÆDANUS BURKE, Eſquire, one of the Chief Juſtices of the State of South-Carolina.

Who with the gen'rous ruſtics Sate,
On Uri's rock, in cloſe Divan,
And wing'd that arrow ſure as Fate,
Which aſcertain'd, THE SACRED RIGHTS OF MAN.

PHILADELPHIA:
PRINTED and SOLD by ROBERT BELL, in Third-Street.

Price one third of a Dollar.—M DCC LXXXIII.

Courtesy, Massachusetts Historical Society

finally, persons who had not voluntarily avowed their allegiance to Great Britain, but who had manifested attachment to British government by the tenor of their conduct, were included in the sixth class. The amercement act taxed the estates of Carolinians who, although they had withdrawn from the American cause, had not behaved as infamously as those mentioned in the confiscation act.[45]

The proposal to confiscate the property of the six classes only superficially determined what names were to be included in the bill. Fifty-three estates were mentioned in lists two and four, lists of Addressors of Clinton and Arbuthnot and Congratulators of Cornwallis. Yet the documents sent to the British military commanders had been signed by over 350 people. In fact, the confiscation act specifically seized only 237 estates; no names were given of those who had left the state in 1778 and 1779 and had returned when the British occupied Charleston, or of those who had not surrendered to a magistrate in 1779. The unnamed may have numbered about 140.[46]

Some Carolinians escaped punishment for committing the same acts which condemned others. Henry Middleton, former president of the Continental Congress, had taken British protection, but his property was not seized by the Jacksonborough Assembly because Arthur Middleton, his son, had remained active on the rebel side throughout the war. Rawlins Lowndes, the former governor, "wrote up a long canting Letter, and he was forgiven," though he, too, had accepted British rule.[47] But Colonel Charles Pinckney was not so fortunate. Pinckney, the first president of the colony's Provincial Congress and a member of the Council in 1780, had fled the state with Rutledge but had then returned to accept British rule. For his action in returning, after being out of the enemy's reach, Pinckney's estate was amerced. Only the virtues of other Pinckneys, Edward Rutledge wrote, saved his estate from confiscation.[48] Daniel Horry, a brother-in-law of Charles Cotesworth and Thomas Pinckney, found his estate amerced also because he, too, had returned to Charleston to accept British protection.

William Blake was treated much the same as Pinckney. Blake, "a Man of the first Fortune in this Country," lived in Europe while his Carolina plantation continued to produce rice for sale. He was, according to Edward Rutledge, "a thousand Times better off than any one Man on our Side of the Question." Nevertheless, Rutledge and Ralph Izard exerted their considerable influence to save Blake's estate from confiscation. The Senate finally agreed instead to place his name in the amercement act.[49]

Friendships and animosities were sometimes crucial in determining individuals' fates. Everyone, Aedanus Burke said, "gives in a List of his own and the State's Enemies." An "idle story, an old grudge, revenge, or malice," were substituted for trial by jury. If Burke can be believed, at least once personal friendship was carried to inordinate lengths. In 1783 he charged that one member of the assembly was saved from banishment and confiscation by a friend who "secreted the slip of paper on which his name was inserted."[50]

Despite the truth of some of Burke's remarks, the acts of confiscation and amercement were not extreme. Edward Rutledge expected that the people's "Resentments would have been in proportion to their sufferings." Instead the people acted moderately.[51] Only 237 estates were specifically confiscated, only 47 amerced 12 percent of their appraised value. About 140 additional unnamed estates were confiscated and another 47 amerced. Originally a committee of the House of Representatives had made out a list of about 700 persons to be punished. It was reduced to 119. Over 200 names were added by the Senate when it considered the bill. On that day, 13 February, ten senators from the backcountry and distant lowcountry parishes were present and only six from the Charleston area. The people they added to the bill were mostly "insignificant Characters," Addressors of Clinton. To some of the changes the lower house agreed.

The confiscation act seized the real and personal property of the persons named. It did not touch the debts owed to the owners of the estates. When General Leslie, the British commander in South Carolina, objected to the act and threatened retaliatory plundering, Governor Mathews quickly pointed out that he could deprive those whose estates had been confiscated of the debts due them.[52] His words were echoed by John Laurens. "There is a considerable value in English Debts which we have in our power," Laurens wrote, implying that the legislature could easily confiscate those debts if the British acted rashly.[53]

Confiscation and amercement were aimed primarily at the lowcountry. Of the 47 persons whose estates were amerced, 21 lived in Charleston. Of the 237 whose property was confiscated, 135 were from Charleston, and not many more than 10 from the backcountry.[54] The legislature, dominated by the non-Charleston areas, temporarily shied away from any action that might rekindle backcountry fires. Many of the Tories in the inland region may have protected themselves and saved their property by accepting Rutledge's full and free pardon. Perhaps the legislature was simply striking out in resentment against an area not as hard hit by the war as the non-Charleston area and at some people not faced daily with difficult choices — a few could use their wealth in England and Europe while others could take protection and remain secure in parishes the British effectively controlled. "Wealth was too frequently regarded as an indication of crime," Alexander Garden wrote years later. Garden, present at Jacksonborough but not a member of the legislature, described committee meetings punctuated by a repeated cry: "'a fat sheep — a fat sheep — prick him! prick him!'"[55] Whatever the reasons, the Jacksonborough Assembly passed legislation punishing lowcountry British sympathizers, some of whom were men of means, like Colonel Charles Pinckney, William Blake, and John Deas, Jr. But the legislation also affected many relatively innocent artisans and mechanics who had signed addresses to the British in order to keep working and eating. Their plight was brought to the attention of the legislature in 1783, when it would also consider the activities of the backcountry Tories, those who had been far more active in the war than their coastal counterparts.

The action of the Jacksonborough Assembly in confiscating and amercing estates was, on an individual level, harsh. Yet the acts were not radical. They were limited in application. They were also a logical outcome of the conduct of the war. By the time the legislature met, the fighting and plundering had laid waste a large section of the state and had ruined countless lives. Against such a background, Gadsden and Burke could not prevent retaliatory legislation.

But however mild the acts, in the postwar years they became a battleground on which representatives from Charleston District fought those from the backcountry and Georgetown and Beaufort districts. Lowcountry legislators attempted to amend the acts, to remove the sentence of banishment, confiscation, and amercement from old friends or relatives. Other legislators, more radical in their desire for legislative punishment, opposed striking any name from any list. Occasionally, people outside the legislature joined the fights.

FIVE
A Temporary Return to Prewar 'Normalcy'

> Several persons, formerly citizens, who left this place with the English, have returned. . . . I am in hopes they will be ordered back, to live under their *blessed king and good father* George the Tyrant.
>
> *Gazette of the State of South-Carolina,* 8 April 1784.

> Our legislature have likewise shewn themslves remarkably moderate towards the Refugees. The confiscation and amercement laws are in a great measure done away. . . . Would to God I could say that tranquility was perfectly restored to this state.
>
> Ralph Izard, 27 April 1784.

SOUTH Carolina's full-scale warfare ended in 1781, before the meeting of the Jacksonborough Assembly. After the summer of 1781, British, Tories, and rebellious Americans fought minor battles, deadly for some, but no threat to American control of the state. The British could make no great strategic move, no major thrust into the country; they ventured out of the Charleston area only to gather provisions and ''all the slaves who belong to those in arms against the British government.''[1]

By taking slaves in response to the confiscation of loyalists' property, the British hoped to induce a more just line of conduct on the part of the Americans. But Governor John Mathews returned threat for threat, warning that future seizures of slaves would be met, not with an easier confiscation policy, but with a far stiffer one. Estates reserved by marriage settlements and debts due to confiscated estates would also be confiscated if the British continued their slave-gathering raids.[2]

During one enemy foray twenty-seven year-old John Laurens was killed. As a humanitarian obsessed by the evils of slavery, Laurens was rare among Carolinians. He sought not to ameliorate the conditions under which slaves lived, but to abolish slavery completely. He deplored ''the bloody wars excited in Africa to furnish America with slaves.'' He was moved by ''the groans of despairing multitudes, toiling for the luxuries of merciless tyrants.'' To the objection that blacks preferred slavery to ''the untasted sweets of liberty,'' Laurens confessed that ''the minds of this unhappy species must be debased by a servitude from which they can hope for no relief but death.'' But, he added, pointing out what other Carolinians either did not see or did not admit, blacks were not ''insensible that a better life exists.'' They were aware of ''the galling comparison between themselves and their masters.''[3] Abolition, Laurens realized, was impossible, so he urged that slaves be allowed to fight for the state's freedom and their own, all the while undoubtedly acknowledging the justice of his father's criticism: if one believed the blacks truly free one should ''then address them in the language of a recruiting Officer to any other free men'' and accept as ''very extraordinary'' a favorable response of ''four in forty.'' Laurens persevered despite ''that monstrous popular prejudice, open-mouthed against me.''[4] Wealthy, talented, and assured of a leading place in South Carolina law and politics, Laurens might not, indeed would not, have accomplished any of his humanitarian goals had he lived to try, but, taking heart even when losing by a vote of about 100 to 15 because ''truth and philosophy had gained some ground, the suffrages in favor of the measure being twice as numerous as on a former occasion,'' his efforts would have been magnificent attempts to awaken a conscience in his fellow Carolinians. After he died no one took up his fight. ''You have . . . reason to say,'' John Adams wrote Henry Laurens, '' 'I would not exchange my dead son for any living son in the world.' ''[5]

As the war dragged to a close, South Carolina's prewar ruling class attempted to reassert its power and return to the 'normalcy' of governing in the old manner, with its own interests not only understandably paramount but virtually unchallenged. That ''vulgar'' lower orders would soon begin to ''inveigh against generous and exalted souls'' did not seem to disturb or even occur to the old governing elite.[6]

Working through the executive when the legislature was not in session, South Carolina aristocrats reasserted their power and influence in 1782. Governor John Mathews concluded two agreements with the British which protected the interests of the slave-owning planters while sacrificing the emotional and material well-being of their fellow Carolinians. One little-known agreement fell through, but not before eliciting a private denunciation from Christopher Gadsden. The more famous pact ignited a political fire that lasted over a year and touched off something new for South Carolina: strong, vitriolic, and open criticism of ''*the conduct of* [elected] *public officers*.''[7]

In August 1782, knowing that the British would soon evacuate Charleston, Mathews again warned General Leslie that his government would react to any further theft of Carolina slaves with a new and tougher confiscation policy. The general proposed a negotiation of differences, out of which came, on 10 October, a ''Treaty Respecting Slaves within British Lines, British Debts, [and] Property Secured by Family Settlements.''

For many Carolinians, this state treaty was far better than the later Treaty of Paris which ended the war. Negotiated by Northerners not fully appreciative of the problem caused by the huge Southern debt owed British creditors, the Treaty of Paris caused economic hardship and bitter political fighting by providing that creditors should meet no "lawful Impediment" in recovering bona fide debts.[8] British creditors, therefore, were immediately entitled to press their American debtors (Carolinians owed £412,000 sterling in prewar debts), many of whom had been so hard hit by the war that they could not begin to pay. But because the negotiators of South Carolina's treaty, Edward Rutledge and Benjamin Guerard, were members of the Jacksonborough Assembly, they were aware that the state's exhausted financial condition had made necessary a law preventing suits for the recovery of debts; they secured protection for indebted Carolinians. Their agreement wisely allowed British creditors only the same power to sue debtors as the "citizens of the state may at any time be entitled unto." If conditions warranted further legislation preventing debt collections, the British would have no legal grounds for complaint provided they were not discriminated against.[9]

The provision regarding slaves, however, more clearly indicated how the treaty favored the lowcountry elite. All slaves within British lines were to be restored to their former owners, "as far as is practicable," except for those promised freedom by the British or those whose behavior in adhering to the British had rendered them obnoxious to the Americans and likely to suffer severe punishment if returned. The state was prohibited from punishing returned slaves, and masters were urged to forget the past, humane provisions that could hardly be enforced. Slaves not returned were to be valued and paid for.

Over this provision in particular Gadsden erupted. His outspoken oral and written objections to the whole agreement were partly inspired by the governor's lack of consultation with him and other members of the Privy Council. But he complained of more than Mathews's snubbing of "the natural council appointed by the State" in favor of "certain lawyers" (who as individuals and as a class aroused Gadsden's hatred) from whom the governor sought and received advice. Gadsden's major complaint was that the agreement, the heart of which he thought the slave clause, was expressly written to save and serve an aristocratic minority not worthy of special consideration. The treaty was not for him, as it was for David Ramsay, "a benevolent scheme . . . calculated for mitigating the calamities of war"; it was an act of self-interest.[10]

Rutledge and Guerard had agreed that debts owed to British merchants or to those whose estates had been confiscated, or property secured by family settlements, would not be withheld by the governor. They had agreed also that the governor should be urged to use his "whole power and influence" to prevent any future act confiscating those protected debts and properties from passing the legislature.[11] For whom, Gadsden asked, had the state given up its hold on this British property? Who besides the British benefited? "The great negro owners. . . . The inhabitants near the sea," he said. They were the ones "principally concerned in negroes."[12] Carolinians could easily see how slaveowners had been considered above others. The British had stolen not only blacks but vast quantities of other property — plate, silver, furniture — and not all of it from the lowcountry areas that had been robbed of slaves, yet nothing in the treaty effectually provided for its return. A postscript pledged the British to return such items when practicable, but when it was not, no effort was to be made to value and pay for them. Unreturned slaves, however, were to be "bought" by the British from their former owners.

Carolinians affected by this provision may have argued that slaves were the most valuable, most identifiable, and least troublesome to return of all stolen property; that since arrangements could not be made for all property, it would be foolish to reject the return of some. Such reasoning would have been reminiscent of 1775, when South Carolina delegates had agreed with others in the Continental Congress that rice, but not indigo, could be exported from the colonies. When challenged, however, the plan was modified in South Carolina so that rice planters had to share their bounty with others. In 1782, when negotiators were unable to secure promise of payments for all stolen property, Carolinians could have considered plans to divide the money received for slaves not returned among all who could prove that the British had robbed them. Nor would it have been unreasonable to suggest that planters whose slaves were restored contribute to a common fund. But no plans along those or similar lines were formed. Agreeing to the treaty, Rutledge conveniently ignored an argument he had used in 1774 when opposing a plan that allowed people to continue their legal exportations of wheat and flour while closing other colonial trade: "It was said," Rutledge wrote, that if the wheat growers "were in an advantageous situation, why not allow the use of it? The answer is ready: because equality is the basis of public virtue."[13] The argument should still have applied. Carolinians needed their slaves, but to raise up some slave owners through a negotiated treaty would be to put them in a better position to get ahead, and to keep getting ahead, while others labored without returned blacks, without horses, mules, or other stolen property.

By definition, according to Gadsden, the treaty was partial to the class which had done least to expel the British from the state. In some areas, slaveowners had refused to turn out when the British appeared, and some even prolonged the state's difficulties by selling food to the confined and poorly supplied enemy in Charleston.[14] In March 1782 Governor Mathews issued a proclamation forbidding the carrying of provisions into enemy lines. Five months later he was entreating General Marion to form some plan to stop the extensive trade with the city. To do so, Marion replied, would necessitate making prisoners of "every person adjacent to town."[15] Gadsden, who thought anyone named in the confiscation act a saint compared to those "damnable provisions supplie[r]s," wanted them prosecuted under a sedition act. His dissatisfaction over the failure to stop the trade fed his discontent with the terms of the treaty. Trade and treaty were inextricably merged. Never on an individual level, but always in general terms, Gadsden identified the slaveowners, those benefiting from the treaty in the protection of their property, as the very people who had hindered the conduct of the war and sold food to the British.[16] Little wonder that he disapproved of the pact and the lawyers who had advised the governor.

But the treaty was broken before the British evacuated the state, before the legislature met, and before Gadsden could find public allies. Otherwise there would have been a public fight over it. The two Carolinians aiding in the restoration of slaves were allowed to examine the British fleet bound for St. Augustine but not the vessels bearing the king's pendant. They claimed 136 Negroes, received only 73, and then were denied the opportunity to ship those outside British lines until General Nathanael Greene returned three captured British soldiers. On 19 October Governor Mathews notified General Leslie that the agreement was "dissolved." Although David Ramsay thought the treaty fell through because "the prospects of gain, from the sale of plundered negroes, were too seducing to be resisted" by the British, Leslie may have been moved more by England's promise of freedom to those blacks who had joined them, a promise General Carleton told Leslie had to be kept. "In justice," Leslie agreed, the slaves could not be "abandoned to the merciless resentment of their former masters."[17]

Gadsden had no time to find allies for his fight against the treaty, but he had sufficient time and nearly enough allies to fight successfully the agreement made with the British merchants, for this lasting agreement antagonized many citizens hard hit by the war. Despite the many people who, as the British prepared to withdraw, "breathed nothing but the bitterness of vengeance, and would hear of no forgiveness," the governor and the legislature began to behave as though there had been no war, no violence, no brutality, and as though "religion and piety, [and] love and charity" for all, had suddenly appeared in South Carolina.[18]

After the occupation of Charleston in May 1780, the British had denied American prisoners on parole the "Liberty" of working.[19] As a result, many Carolina merchants and mechanics, struggling to support families or simply taking advantage of conditions, accepted British rule, for which some later lost their estates by confiscation. As a result also, opportunistic British merchants flocked to the Carolina port. When their army prepared to depart in 1782, the English merchants sought security for themselves and their goods. They requested permission from Governor Mathews to remain in the city for eighteen months with full freedom to sell their merchandise and collect debts. They asked that they be considered neutrals, exempt from military or public service, duties, and imposts, and that cargoes in transit be exempt from capture for six months after the departure of the British army.[20]

Edward Rutledge, a close associate of Governor Mathews, thought little of the merchants' proposals. At least one request was "the very Essence of Impudence." Since Carolinians were to grant everything and receive nothing, Rutledge expected Mathews to give the British "a trimming Answer."[21] But Mathews disappointed him. The governor agreed to allow the merchants six months to sell whatever stock they had and to collect debts, although he refused to grant them the right to commence court actions for the money owed them, since the act prohibiting suits for the recovery of debts was still in force. Mathews agreed that during the time the merchants remained they should be considered neutrals, exempt from public service and duties, but he asserted that South Carolina had no authority to guarantee freedom from seizure for vessels carrying goods.[22]

Many of the merchants thought the terms unsatisfactory, but about fifty, after unsuccessfully asking the governor to extend their allotted time past six months, decided to stay. With goods valued at £500,000 sterling on hand, they had much to gain.[23]

The well-stocked British merchants knew that Carolinians who wanted to rebuild and re-equip their plantations or other property would be forced to turn to them. South Carolina merchants who had not taken British "protection" had been exiled or denied the right to trade; they could not re-establish their mercantile houses in time to supply anxious planters. The virtual monopoly gave the remaining British merchants great expectations. Charles Cotesworth Pinckney was only one of many Carolinians ready to make purchases "at a very extravagant price." He needed several kinds of wine, "the older the better," cheese, and "some negroe cloth & blankets," and he would pay an "extravagant price," because, in his words, "it is necessary I should have them." Pinckney and others kept the British busy; the £500,000 of goods were sold on credit "at an amazing advance" and brought the merchants, at least on paper, about £1,000,000.[24]

The fight over the agreement with the merchants began in January 1783, about a month after the departure of the British army. In succession, Mathews laid the agreement with the merchants before the Assembly, some Charlestonians urged that it be strictly adhered to and ended at the earliest moment, and the British merchants petitioned that the time allowed them be extended, because they could not, within the remaining four months, sell their stock, find vessels to ship produce, and collect debts. And, their petition said, many of them ardently wished to become Carolina citizens.

Led by William Logan, a Charleston merchant whom the British had exiled to St. Augustine, "a Number of Inhabitants" petitioned the legislature, complaining not about their major grievance, the very presence of the competing and better-prepared British, but about current British actions. After the end of their physical suffering and oppression, their "happiness . . . [was] lessoned on their arriveal in Charles Town" by the behavior of the British merchants who had "infringed upon the Spirit" of their agreement by refusing to sell their merchandise at the same prices it had sold for while under the British government, by refusing to take produce in payment, thereby collecting all the specie in the state, and by purchasing additional stock at public sales.[25] Technically only the last objection was legitimate, as perhaps the petitioners knew, since they pointed out that the British had violated not the agreement, but its "Spirit." The merchants had been given freedom to dispose of their goods in any manner they chose, but they had not been given permission to augment their stock by purchasing anew. The petitioning Charlestonians asked that the agreement be strictly adhered to but ended as soon as possible.

At first, it seemed they might succeed. On 19 February a five-man Senate committee, consisting of two artisans, two backcountry senators, and one senator from St. Helena, in Beaufort District, recommended only slight alteration of the agreement. Seventeen of the fifty British merchants, they reported, had considerable merchandise still on hand and many debts outstanding. But the committee decided that the previously allotted time for the sale of those goods was sufficient and need not be extended; it was willing, however, to grant the seventeen merchants named in the report additional time for purchasing produce and collecting debts.[26]

The petitioners' success was shortlived; the next day the Senate granted all fifty merchants until 1 January 1784 to dispose of goods, ship produce, and collect debts. Less than one week later the lower house added two more months to the agreement. The Senate hastily concurred.[27]

The extension suited planters, who, without specie, could purchase goods only on the credit of their forthcoming crop. That crop's value would depend not simply on its size, or on world markets, but also on the number of vessels in port and the number of merchants accepting produce in payment of debts. When the lower house extended the time from 1 January to 1 March it wisely included the months during which most of the crop would be shipped from Charleston.

The climate for agricultural business was made healthier, and the opponents of the British more miserable, by other legislative actions. Because it was "conducive to the happiness and commercial interests of this State," the General Assembly granted alien friends resident in the state extraordinary rights in the state courts. In cases involving South Carolina citizens and foreigners, half the jury had to be aliens, preferably of the same nation as the alien concerned in the trial. By September 1783 at least three trials with British subjects as jurors had been held. The results, a Pennsylvania newspaper reported vaguely, gave general satisfaction.[28]

True to their claims, many British merchants asked to become citizens. The legislature recommended that the requests of most be granted and authorized the governor and Privy Council to admit as citizens all those whose petitions had been favorably reported on by committees of either house. Over the consistent opposition of Alexander Gillon, who emerged in 1783 as the leader of the Charleston radicals, the governor and council granted citizenship to 67 of 104 who applied. Others, besides those signing the agreement with Mathews, had requested citizenship.[29]

The acts dealing with British merchants and aliens guaranteed, as much as any actions could, the existence of a large mercantile class to import necessities and export crops. Hoping to ensure low import and high export prices, as well as low freight rates, the planters wanted to attract and keep foreign merchants, most of whom would be British. They succeeded so well that the postwar period became "the sunshine harvest of British commerce, policy, and influence."[30] As late as 1787, members of a Charleston trading firm noted that people in the city might think themselves "in the Highlands of Scotland" because of the names and speech of Charleston merchants.[31]

Native merchants were swamped by the competition. Some of the £300,000 of merchandise imported by South Carolina merchants in 1783 was shipped to British merchants who had stayed when the army left and probably a great deal went to British and other foreign merchants who had come to the state after the war. In addition, the British already had on hand and ready for sale merchandise valued at £500,000. In 1784 the alien share of importations totaled at least 40 percent of the more than £1,000,000 worth that entered the state.[32]

The legislation which benefited the planters came at the material expense of the South Carolina merchants who had expected to recoup their fortunes or improve their economic status, and at the emotional expense of those who had come to hate the British enemy as a result of wartime atrocities. Although the government's actions might aid consumers and speed recovery from the war, to some the policies were a tremendous blow, an immediate and long-range disaster. Their position, too, had a rational defense. Like the planters, native merchants and mechanics had suffered from the war and felt entitled to reap the rewards of peace. These rewards were threatened when British merchants and mechanics (who also stayed behind the departing army) got a foothold and cornered the tremendous postwar trade. The native merchants and mechanics thought it far better that the planters should suffer a little longer so that all could recover from the war together.

To other citizens the agreements and legislation made no sense. Why should the British be jurors? Why should they become citizens? Why should the war be forgotten before it was officially over? Those who hated the British wanted vengeance; others wanted to be free from British economic competition, which threatened to become economic domination. Together, they certainly did not want the British to participate in, and profit from, the reconstruction of that which British soldiers had helped destroy.

Christopher Gadsden led the fight against the British merchants. It was one of his last fights against the policies of the old elite. Early in 1776 he had urged independence before the prewar rulers were ready for it; in 1778 he had worked for a new constitution. In 1782 he was busy attacking the slaveowners for being overly friendly with the enemy, the treaty with the British, and the lawyers, who "may be said to be *the aristocratical number*" governing the state.[33] And in 1783 he continued his almost relentless attack: "the Rutledges & Gadsden oppose each other," a Georgia merchant reported, not adding that such opposition was longstanding.[34] Not only did Gadsden then propose further amendments to the constitution, but he worked to raise the taxes of the slave-owning planters. And, supported by other spokesmen for merchants and mechanics, and by some backcountry representatives, Gadsden time and again opposed any extension of the agreement with the British merchants, at one time marshalling forty-one votes to the other side's fifty-three.[35] Despite his efforts, Gadsden failed to secure strict adherence to the original agreement with the British merchants. Having tried and failed, he dropped the issue. But others, more radical, perhaps more needy, carried the battle into the streets of Charleston.

Gadsden's lack of success precipitated a violent attack on the legislature and the aristocrats. Public protestors took to the streets to merge their attack on the British merchants with one on Tories that appealed to the backcountry as well as to some lowcountry areas; this connection alienated Gadsden. However much he detested the aristocracy — or at least the Rutledge faction, the lawyers, and some lowcountry planters — Gadsden consistently pleaded the cause of the Carolina loyalists. By 1784, therefore, Gadsden was denouncing some former allies as a "set of *self-created* bullying censors."[36]

Alexander Gillon, a member of the lower house, took Gadsden's place as the leading attacker of "*aristocratical principles.*" Gillon had arrived in Charleston in the 1760s, amassed a fortune in a few years from his mercantile business, served in the provincial congresses, and become commodore of South Carolina's paper navy in 1778. While the British occupied Charleston, his estate was sequestered, his wife expelled, and his stepson sent as a prisoner to St. Augustine.[37]

Gillon and his followers found an issue far more emotional, intense, and complex than the new agreement with the British merchants when the legislature began to modify the confiscation and amercement acts. As soon as the legislature met in 1783, it received petitions about the loyalists and those who had taken protection. Inhabitants of the upper part of Prince George Parish urged that the confiscation act be strictly enforced, an appeal repeated shortly by settlers of Prince Frederick Parish. At the same time, men named in the acts requested leniency. "I bear with resignation whatever situation my countrymen" put me in, James Lynah wrote, while working to have that situation altered. "With a contrite heart for . . . [his] past error," he threw himself on the mercy of the General Assembly.[38]

In response to the flood of petitions for relief, the General Assembly postponed the banishment of over sixty persons and halted the sale of seventy-one confiscated estates pending final determination of "the merits of their said petitions." In 1784 thirty-five estates were restored and ninety-five others transferred from the confiscated to the amerced list. Ramsay thought the restored property was worth £500,000 sterling. Thirty-three specifically named persons, however, and any others of those amerced who had held commissions under the British were not permitted to hold public office for seven years.[39]

Although some members of the lowcountry elite were disappointed with the leniency shown by the legislature in 1783, thinking it did not go far or fast enough, most probably agreed with Ralph Izard that the legislature had been "remarkably moderate towards the Refugees." "The confiscation and amercement laws are in a great measure done away," he wrote.[40] Izard was pleased with the changes because, as he wrote Thomas Jefferson, he thought that most people took British protection out of "compulsion, and believing the cause desperate, and almost totally lost." Concerned primarily with the confiscation and amercement of lowcountry property, he may also have seen in the leniency a way to strengthen aristocratic influence in the state by allowing for the return of some prewar conservatives.[41]

Jefferson, however, could have been misled by Izard's correspondence, for the Carolinian had not disclosed the legislature's passage of a new confiscation act, by which all the estates, real and personal, of former citizens who had "joined the enemies" of the state were vested in the commissioners of confiscated estates for sale. This sweeping act contained no names, no lists. The commanding officers of the militia regiments were required to make up returns of those former Carolinians when asked to by the commissioners.[42] The act avoided one of the features that had caused Judge Aedanus Burke anxiety in 1782 — condemnation without provisions for hearings or trials. All persons who had withdrawn were allowed six months from the end of the legislature's session to return for trial.

Fewer than 300 persons had originally been affected by the acts of the Jacksonborough Assembly, and in 1783 and 1784 the legislature lessened the punishment inflicted on 130 of them. Following the directions of the confiscation act of 1783, militia commanders drew up lists of British ad herents no longer in the state: 51 for Orangeburg, 214 for Camden, and 413 for Ninety Six District.[43] In these returns alone, the only ones existing, 678 persons were named. Their property was vested in the commissioners of confiscated estates for sale. There are no returns for any coastal regions; possibly the returns are lost, or it may well be that none were drawn up.

The confiscation act of 1783 was passed to satisfy the needs, emotional and perhaps economic, of backcountry settlers. It may have been the price that lowcountry planters were willing to pay to secure leniency for friends and relatives.

After the legislature's adjournment in March 1783, the more vehement opponents of the British merchants and reinstated Tories turned to the newspapers and streets of Charleston to mobilize their allies. The intense propaganda was probably designed to bring about a political and economic alliance between backcountry farmers — and some from the lowcountry — and the mercantile followers of Alexander Gillon and William Logan. In December 1783 members of Gillon's Marine Anti-Britannic Society, gathered to celebrate the first anniversary of the British evacuation of Charleston, toasted a "speedy restoration to *our Chamber of Commerce,* solely consisting of true American merchants, patriotic planters, and the trading Whig-subjects of our Allies." They drank also to the hope that Americans would despise "the Cruelties and Manufactures of Great Britain."[44] In the *South Carolina Weekly Gazette* "A COLUMBIAN" reminded Carolinians that "the voracious commanding Officers of the British army, . . . whose bowels yearn'd as beagles thirsting after human blood," had murdered their relatives. Would you, he asked, "suffer" the men who "perpetrated those horrid deeds," or people aiding them, "or those cowards who dare not have faced" them, "to return and enjoy the blessing of this free land?"[45]

Perhaps incited by the literature, some Charlestonians responded as expected or hoped. On 21 July 1783 Edward Weyman, first president of the Fellowship Society, a prewar mechanics' group, presided over a general meeting which asked the governor to investigate actions of the British merchants and which also resolved to petition the legislature respecting the continued residence in the state of former citizens who had acted inimically to the cause of America.[46]

Supporters of Gillon and the Marine Anti-Britannic Society probably expected little satisfaction from the government; their only real recourse lay in making life in Carolina physically and economically unprofitable for the British merchants and the not-quite-banished Tories or protection takers. "The old inhabitants of the town are becoming very uneasy respecting the admission of such a number of British merchants," wrote one Charlestonian. The unease led to "riots." A Pennsylvania newspaper described Charlestonians determined to drive away "traitors and cowards"; they forced "a certain Hugh Rose, who had formerly taken a British commission," out of the city and hourly sought others "equally obnoxious."[47]

The disorders were taken seriously. ''A spirit has gone forth among the lower class of people to drive away certain persons whom they are pleased to call Tories,'' wrote David Ramsay, unhappily predicting at the same time that ''the licentiousness of the people'' would not disappear for half a century. Nathanael Greene, still in Charleston, likened the city, with its ''spirit of mobing,'' to Philadelphia, where mutineers had threatened the Continental Congress.[48]

After renewed demonstrations in 1784, a defender of the legislature charged the opposition with simple economic greed. "They have tasted of the sweets of confiscation'' and have also purchased on credit large quantities of other goods. They hoped by their rioting, their critic wrote, to force the legislature to make depreciated treasury certificates legal tender. Then they would defraud their creditors with worthless paper money.[49] His particular economic interpretation, however, made little sense. Treasury certificates were already acceptable to the government for purchases of confiscated estates. If they became legal tender their value would rise, forcing troublemakers like Gillon to pay more for the ''sweets of confiscation.'' In June 1783 Gillon had bought an assemblage of lots, buildings, and tracts of land, for which he was supposed to pay over £23,000 currency.[50]

Not greed, but an economic fear other than that caused by the British merchants could have contributed to the unrest. In purchasing confiscated estates, people might take advantage of a law they favored for nonmaterial reasons, thinking that the British and their sympathizers deserved to be punished. Having acquired property, however, they could well become anxious over the return of the banished. Perhaps purchasers feared that if they failed to pay the treasurer promptly, their new possessions would be restored to the former owners.

But the turmoil in Charleston had many causes. Focusing on British merchants and returning loyalists, Gillon could appeal to Charlestonians upset by other troubles. The disappointment felt by native merchants facing an established and wellstocked competition was experienced also by local artisans and mechanics, who found not only the British on the scene but also skilled slaves. Negroes, a visitor in 1784 wrote, carry on almost all trades ''at the smallest possible price or for nothing almost.'' The observation had been made before: white shipwrights complained as early as 1744 that blacks were driving them out of their trade, and in 1747 a weaver was warned not to move from Philadelphia because ''white people have difficulty earning their bread'' in Charleston. Their problem unresolved before or during the war, house carpenters and bricklayers protested to the legislature in February 1783.[51]

Committees in both houses, dominated by artisans and close associates, reported favorably on the petition, but the city's workers were denied satisfaction by the legislature, which simply went back to prewar plans and prohibited slaveowners from hiring out their property without first acquiring licenses. Advertisements in city newspapers ("WANTED to hire, SIX good NEGROE CARPENTERS, for six or twelve months") were constant reminders of political failure.[52]

The slaves were more than an economic threat. The propaganda of revolution had given many notions of freedom, association with the British army reinforced the idea that the war was changing their lives, and the absence of their owners had, as former Governor Bull wrote, made many "ungovernable." White Charlestonians sought to calm their fears and control blacks who seemed insolent, sullen, or uncooperative with an ordinance passed in late 1783 which limited the number of male slaves who could gather together, the times parties could last, and which required that all free Negroes, mulattoes, and mestizos had to register and wear badges, thereby making it easier to identify individuals and regulate slaves.[53]

Charlestonians faced other troubles. The rapid resumption of trade, even before the formal close of the war, the return of people from war or exile, and the desire to rebuild made Charleston not only a busy port, but also a dangerous one. Imports from England, Holland, France, and from American states, came in ships that mingled international crews on Charleston streets. The taunts and challenges from groups commonly considered rough and almost ungovernable under normal conditions probably came as fast in 1783, when residents and sailors found themselves facing recent enemies, as they had five years earlier when conflict between the allied French and American sailors had precipitated a riot.

Although the extensive trade lowered the price of imports, Charleston was not an inexpensive place to live immediately after the war. The competition among shipowners and captains for cargo brought high prices for anything exportable. Food, or at least some staples, probably cost more than some people could manage. In March flour brought a high price. Butter too was expensive. "The poor people will not buy it . . . just now," wrote one newspaper correspondent, although "they must soon, for what is given for the Use of the dancing Ladies and Gentlemen will establish the Price, and that, not only with Butter, but every Thing else we please." And if people behaved as they had in the past, then the price of fuel might be high as a result of engrossers forcing prices up through their oft-created "artificial dearth[s]."[54]

Many people, then, lived troubled lives in Charleston — and during those days of excited feelings, anti-British and loyalist sentiment, and hard conditions, including "excessive heat and billious fevers," at least four men were slain in the city.[55]

The defiant protests against legislative policy challenged the government. Meeting in the summer of 1783, a small number of legislators, representing the area with most at stake, acted quickly to quiet Charleston, not by considering complaints, redressing grievances, or repealing laws, but by incorporating the city, thereby creating the machinery to crack down on the demonstrators. The Charleston District was even more powerful than usual at this poorly attended session. On no recorded issue did more than seventy-seven members of the lower house vote. Forty-six of the sixty-six members who can be placed at the meetings were from Charleston District.[56] Because it was the first summer after the close of a war which had destroyed or altered much of the countryside, few people far from Charleston could afford the time to attend. Only twenty men represented the areas most likely to give a sympathetic hearing to the likes of the Marine Anti-Britannic Society.

The legislature was now too busy with "weighty and important matters," the act of incorporation said, to "devise, consider, deliberate on, and determine" laws for the government of Charleston. So the state government delegated power to a corporation elected by the people of the city. The thirteen wardens and one intendant forming the corporation were given arbitrary powers to deal with "tumults or riots," or their "appearance or probability." On those vaguely described occasions the intendant was to summon wardens, constables, and other city officers, and take the necessary steps to maintain order.[57] Two years later, a critic of the Charleston government pointed out that people injured as a result of an intendant's actions "would have no redress" even if a grand jury decided there had been no riot, because city officials had unrestrained power at "the *appearance* of a tumult or riot, which they are the sole judges of."[58]

The act of incorporation divided the city into thirteen wards, each electing one warden. All city voters chose one intendant from among the thirteen wardens, after which another warden was elected to fill the place vacated by the intendant. The governing body was given the power to make bylaws, rules, and ordinances respecting the harbor, streets, buildings, and any other regulation "necessary for the security, welfare and conveniency of the said city, or for preserving peace, order and good government within the same." The wardens also received the power to sit as a court to recover fines from those persons convicted of breaking city regulations.[59]

By incorporating the city, the legislature reversed one of its longstanding policies. As early as 1762 a grand jury had demanded incorporation to enable the city to meet its municipal problems. Year after frustrating year, grand juries repeated the demand and just as frequently the legislature refused to act. Critics of government by the legislature found that the exercise of authority by nonresident commissioners resulted in lax enforcement of laws.[60] But despite the voices of Gadsden, the mechanics' Fellowship Society, and the grand juries, the planter-dominated legislature continued to rule the Carolina port in its own ineffectual fashion.

In March 1783, however, the new governor, Benjamin Guerard, suggested the incorporation of Charleston, partly "to check the Cruel havock of conflagration" — the city had been devastated by fire in 1778. Guerard

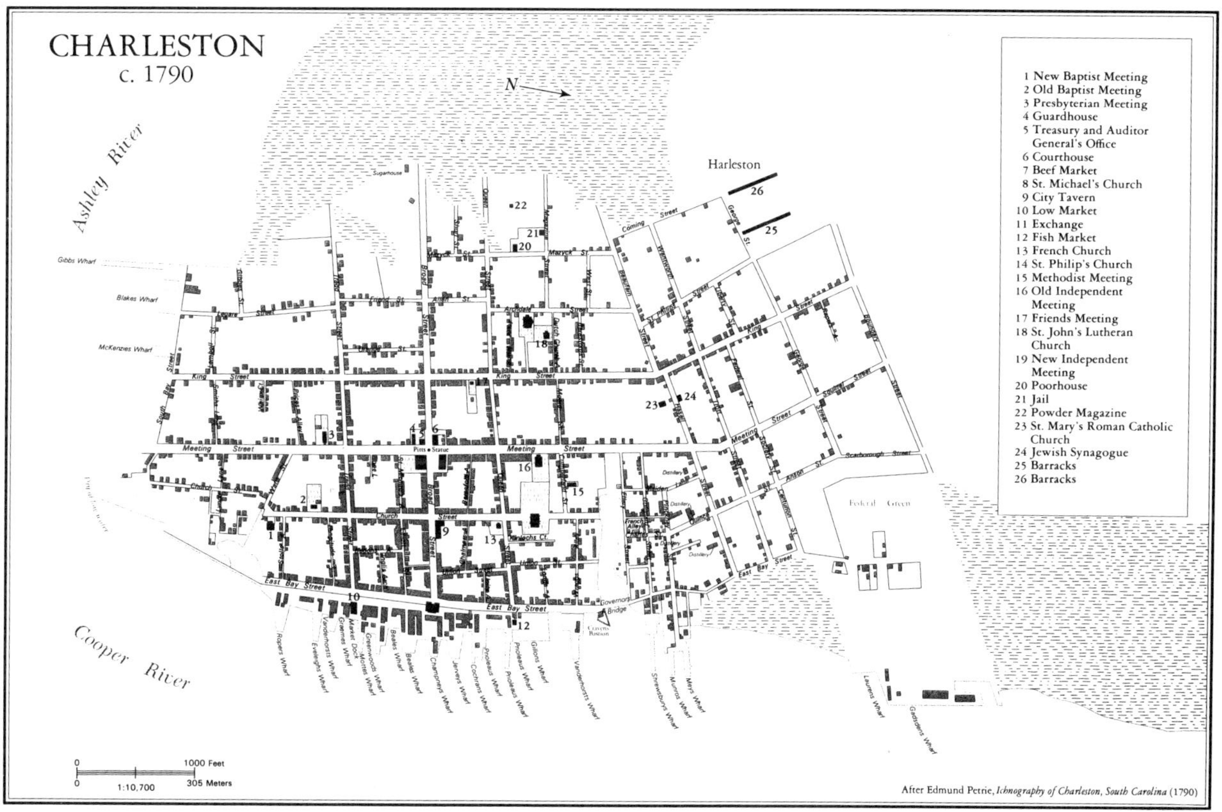

Adapted by permission, Princeton University Press

apparently felt that a local government could more effectively prevent people from bringing tar, pitch, and other dangerous materials into town; he may also have thought such a government could more readily control the residents. The danger of fires was obvious, he said, adding a reminder "that we have all Sorts of People amongst us." The legislature appointed a committee to form a plan during the coming recess.[61] After the riots the legislature realized the danger in not having a permanent government with enough power to meet emergencies. The General Assembly had passed legislation that encouraged the importation of merchandise and the exportation of agricultural produce. If Charleston continued to be torn by dissensions, the legislation could prove ineffectual. "We hear with concern," wrote a resentful country gentleman to a newspaper, "of Mobs and riots prevailing." Country people, he said, would turn out by the thousands to preserve peace, significantly reminding newspaper readers of the advantages of free trade, by which he meant "the more merchants the freer the trade."[62]

In the same paper "A PATRIOT" concentrated more openly on the relation between riots and commerce, noting that commerce "is the mistress of wealth." The "PATRIOT" did not specifically applaud the legislature's decision to keep trade as open as possible, but he did argue that neither an individual nor a "small circle of merchants" — in other words, neither Gillon nor the Marine Anti-Britannic Society — should be allowed to determine the size of the mercantile class.[63]

By incorporating Charleston, which few people could really object to, and by giving to the ruling body broad, undefined powers to deal with mass disturbances, or even the threat of mass disturbances, the legislature rounded out a consistent policy of welcoming, encouraging, and protecting alien merchants, as well as some protection takers and Tories.

The Charleston government acted quickly, passing ordinances to restrain potential troublemakers and enforce a moral code. Negroes were closely controlled in some obvious ways, by requiring licenses for their employment in some occupations and by regulating the size and hours of their gatherings, and through one unusual method. Free blacks were given special badges which they were to wear "suspended by a string or ribband, and exposed to view" on their breasts. Failure to comply resulted in a £5 fine or corporal punishment, not extending to life or limb, if the fine were not paid. Slaves who wore any similar badges were to be whipped.[64]

Whites were also restricted, mariners and seamen receiving special attention. No one was to extend more than 5s. credit, loan, or trust to any mariner under pain of losing all such money or goods and forfeiting twice the sum involved; no one was to entertain any mariner or seaman more than one hour in twenty-four or sell him more than 2s. worth of liquor in that hour. Retailers who violated that provision were subject to a 40s. fine for every offense or, on non-payment of the fine, up to thirty days hard labor. Any mariner or seaman without discharge papers was to be arrested and held until his master claimed him or, if his vessel had sailed, until turned over to any master willing to pay his costs. All mariners and seamen were to return to their vessels within one hour after sunset. If found on shore after the curfew, a mariner or seaman was to be held over night, fined up to 20s. or, for non-payment, committed to the house of corrections for up to ten days.[65]

Because theatrical entertainments might corrupt youths, apprentices, or servants, or encourage idleness, disorder, or riots, performers or exhibitors who failed to get the city's permission for presenting their entertainments were fined £10.[66]

More positively, the City Council tried to substitute religion for drink and entertainment. The Lord's Day was to be faithfully observed. No one was permitted to perform any kind of worldly labor. There were to be no sports and no exhibitions. And, church wardens, together with one or more constables, were to walk through the city each Sunday during divine services "to observe and suppress any riotous, indecent, or disorderly conduct," if necessary even entering any "public house, dram-shop, or other house, or inclosure . . . for the purpose of suppressing the same." Incredibly, church wardens on their tours of duty were authorized to stop people walking or riding through the streets and insist on their attending church until the service was over. On refusal, such people could be fined 2s. 4d.[67]

Perhaps with the incorporation of the city and the city's early legislation, lowcountry legislators and planters and some Charleston residents rested easier, believing that they had come close to returning to a prewar 'normalcy' which allowed them to live and perhaps rule without fear and without contradiction. After the adjournment of the Jacksonborough Assembly, lowcountry planters and lawyers were able to reassert their authority through the executive and the legislature. The treaty for the return of stolen or escaped slaves, the agreement with the British merchants, and the subsequent extension of that agreement by both houses of the legislature, were important to planters eager to regain, as quickly as possible, their prewar economic prosperity.

A few people, however, might have noticed in the 'normalcy' something decidedly abnormal: the rise of an opposition in the lowcountry. There was substantial protest against the executive agreements of 1782 and the legislative program of 1783, ranging from Gadsden to Gillon, some returned exiles, and others who in 1783 took their battles into the streets of Charleston rather than meekly accept acts which aided others by hurting them. If lowcountry leaders wanted to be proud of the leniency they had shown to those whose estates had been confiscated, they had to ignore the far-reaching confiscation act affecting the backcountry and perhaps passed to appease the areas which had suffered during the war.

Perhaps, when the ''clamour of the worthless, or the ingratitude of the foolish part'' began in 1783 and continued into 1784, manifested first in popular demonstrations and then in vicious newspaper attacks on lawyers and others in the aristocracy, prewar rulers remembered why some among them had hesitated to declare independence years before.[68]

SIX
The Charleston Opposition

There appears to be a swell of insolence and sinister design in many of the *leading men* of this state, which plainly indicates *a settled plan of ruling by a few, with a rod of iron.* . . .
Gazette of the State of South-Carolina, 19 August 1784.

'Tis as natural for the vulgar to inveigh against generous and exalted souls, as for dogs to bark at the moon, yet that planet appears impassible, and not being moved at the snarls of invidious animals, keeps on her heavenly course in majesty and silence.
South Carolina Gazette & General Advertiser, 9 September 1784.

BEFORE the Revolution South Carolina's government had been among the most aristocratic in America. Representatives, almost all chosen by Charleston District inhabitants, were more than financially comfortable: in 1765 over two-thirds of the members of the lower house owned property worth £5,000 sterling or more, while the remaining members were worth at least £2,000 each. That was as it should be, the rulers thought, for "in every well-regulated government upon earth, the men of family, fortune, and education, are looked upon as the natural guardians of the state. . . ."[1]

After the war lowcountry residents elected a few more men of moderate means than in the past but otherwise scarcely changed their political behavior. Almost all elections in lowcountry parishes outside Charleston were sparsely attended, dull, and uncontested. Voters behaved 'responsibly.' Throughout the 1780s voters in St. Thomas and St. Dennis presented a united front. In 1783, 17 of 22 voters made Joseph Atkinson senator for the parish. Two years later 19 voters elected 3 representatives, each receiving 17 votes while other candidates got a total of 5. In 1786, 24 voters cast senatorial ballots for John Huger while 3 voted for someone else. Near unanimity extended to other parishes, too. In 1789, 26 voters in Christ Church, voting almost as one, chose 7 men for the state's forthcoming constitutional convention. Probably at least 100 were eligible to vote. Both Charles Pinckney and John Rutledge received 26 votes, the others between 20 and 24 votes. The 41 who appeared at the parish election in 1794 gave 3 winning candidates 40, 36, and 35 votes, the losers 8, 1, and 1. There was no unanimity in St. James Goose Creek in 1783, but a special election to fill a vacancy in the House of Representatives attracted only 8 voters. Thomas Middleton, with 4 votes, won, but he declined to serve.[2]

But in the legislature there was a new political world. The enlargement of the lower house and the extension of representation to the backcountry introduced a new, less wealthy element into the legislature and led to close, troublesome divisions. The increase of Charleston's representation to thirty gave artisans and mechanics the chance to elect members of their own fraternity. In 1785 William Johnson, blacksmith, Anthony Toomer, builder, Michael Kaltieson, wagonmaster, and Daniel Cannon, housewright, and one who in 1783 joined others in petitioning the legislature to relieve them of the burden of Negro competition, sat for Charleston, along with a few nonmechanics, like Alexander Gillon, closely associated with them. Although by no means poor (Cannon before the war owned a plantation near the city), these representatives were not "the men of family, fortune, and education" who had previously governed. Nor were those who sat for the interior regions of the state, even if they were among the more prosperous members of their communities.[3]

The unavoidable entrance of new men into government upset the 'lordly.' Christopher Gadsden's idea that "honest men of good plain common understanding" could run the government was not popular among prewar rulers. Henry Laurens had complained in 1775 that the frontier representatives thought business could be completed "with no more words than are necessary in the bargain and sale of a cow."[4] After a war he saw no part of, having been in England when it started and then filling a diplomatic post in Europe, Ralph Izard lamented that while men realized handicraftsmen had to serve apprenticeships before learning their business, "our back countrymen are of [the] opinion that a politician may be born such. . . ." Izard was probably annoyed that his enemies had described him, the wartime minister to Tuscany, as an "Ambassador to the *Heronites* who abound with oil." Edward Rutledge added that many who had assumed importance "whilst the enemy were in the country" refused, when peace came, "to fall back in the ranks" where they belonged.[5]

Relative novices not only appeared but stayed, gained confidence, and eventually made themselves heard. In the years immediately following the war, according to Johann David Schoepf, Charleston's eloquent representatives, sometimes employing "a little intrigue," consistently defeated backcountry legislators, but occasionally, the backcountry members, without "courage or eloquence enough" to speak, won. Schoepf did not remain long enough in South Carolina to witness what developed. That backcountry senators and representatives might at first have been overly impressed by a display of eloquence that would honor "the senate of ancient Rome" was understandable.[6] But experience gave them courage, and men like Arthur Simkins, James Knox, and Robert Anderson, backcountry legislators throughout the Confederation period, soon did more than silently oppose the old leadership.

In 1788 Arthur Bryan, an unimportant Charleston merchant, sensed the political change, even though his explanation was insufficiently detailed, his results exaggerated, and his analysis based solely on events in Charleston. "The great people had an entire sway" before 1784, he wrote, but then "a violent opposition" in the city almost "totally ruin[ed] the Aristocracy, for if they now carry any thing in the assembly it is by deception."[7]

The Revolution brought new men, new ideas, and a new spirit into state affairs. Prewar rulers came face to face with serious opposition. After the departure of the British, Charleston dissidents, backcountry settlers, and inhabitants of lowcountry parishes far from Charleston joined to fight the legislature's policies and to denounce as well some of the legislators. They were sufficiently loud, effective, and consistent to be recognized and condemned by the state's "natural" rulers. It seemed almost unthinkable to John Lloyd, President of the Senate, that in 1784 "gentlemen of property" should be forced to exert themselves to prevent the "Malcontented party" from electing representatives "from the lower class." So distasteful to the aristocrats was this opposition from people they called "worthless" and "foolish," that there was, according to Edward Rutledge, considerable talk of abandoning the field to the malcontented; but, wrote Lloyd, a fear of "anarchy and confusion" prevented such surrender. Still, the *Charleston Morning Post and Daily Advertiser* lamented that recent events had caused "many leading members" to withdraw from the next election. The paper tried to counter the trend by arguing that "every man is public property. His time and talents . . . nay more — life, all belong to his country."[8]

Ironically, the idea that men were public property was the very idea causing some people to consider resigning from political life. Because they were property, that one paper argued, they were obliged to serve the state. But because they were public property, their critics wrote, their actions ought to be dissected and examined for corruption, conspiracy, and intrigue. "It is the first feature of a free government," wrote Alexander Gillon, that all officers were "public property," to be watched with an "ever wakeful vigilance."[9] Thus members of the Charleston city government were attacked for not giving account of how they spent the revenue they raised. And a newspaper asked whether the City Corporation had not "sold to its *own members,* friends and *favorites,*" lots which were to be improved with public monies.[10] The simple assertion that the government was run by gentlemen who, "notwithstanding the pressing calls of their private affairs, sit in that capacity without fee or reward," was now answered contemptuously. "Enormous wealth," wrote one commentator, "is seldom the associate of *pure* and *disinterested virtue,*" while another asked whether calling city councilors men of rank meant that some were "*rank cowards,* others *rank tories,* several *rank upstarts, rank pettifoggers, rank idio[t]s,* . . . &c." And "OLD HOMESPUN" sarcastically asked: "if *they* are the best men living, . . . ought we not to be alarmed on account of their successors . . . ?"[11]

To attack public servants and make them account for their behavior, the dissidents used the city's presses. Because of newspapers, they said, "ladies cannot paint or bare their bosoms," "old virgins cannot marry young batchelors," nor gentlemen "seduce innocence," and, more seriously, "magistrates cannot oppress the poor" nor "senators . . . betray their trust."[12] In their denunciations of the government, critics rejected the doctrine of seditious libel, which protected incumbents by asserting that the constitutionally-guaranteed liberty of the press meant only the "liberty to insert any thing that does not tend to disturb the peace of the government," and not the liberty to print the truth if it would "undermine and in the end destroy all peace and good order."[13] No one could respect, and some might not obey, the government described by "RUSTICUS SCRIBLERUS," for "men of despicable abilities" had been elected to the legislature "by bribery and corruption."[14] It was clearly not Blackstone's *Commentaries* which set the tone of the 1780s, but Gillon's "vigilance." Liberty of the press was of no use if truth, no matter how unpleasant, could not be printed for all to read. Gillon's followers brushed Blackstone aside: "if truth be a libel," they argued, "what must falsehood" be? One writer went so far as to suggest that it would be dangerous to check "the enormities of private slander," for "the breach of innovation once made, widens every moment, and . . . there is no saying where it might end."[15]

By their need, the opponents of the aristocracy helped to create a free and expanded press. In the late 1760s, South Carolinians read about and argued over England's experimental policies in two weekly newspapers. Three papers, two weeklies and one semiweekly, carried stories of the conflict forward from 1770 to 1775. The war interfered with individual newspaper businesses, but shortly after it ended, printers were again at work. Between 1783 and 1789 three and often four newspapers appeared at the same time, their names constantly changing as their publishers died and as partnerships were formed and dissolved. From late 1784 to October 1786, there were four papers, two of them, the *Charleston Morning Post and Daily Advertiser* and the *Charleston Evening Gazette,* dailies reporting at length the debates in the state legislature, the evening summaries apparently printed just hours after the debates occurred.[16]

The newspapers were generally one-sided, and the critics of the government, despite complaining that John Miller's *South Carolina Gazette & General Advertiser* was closed to them, were almost unchallenged in the *South Carolina Gazette & Public Advertiser* (for a short period called the *South Carolina Weekly Gazette*), the *Columbian Herald,* and the *Gazette of the State of South-Carolina,* which was printed by Ann Timothy, a widow of the politically-active Peter Timothy, who had printed the paper before and during the war. Using these newspapers, the postwar opposition attacked aristocrats and undermined the government by "*animadverting on the conduct of public officers, the measures of Government,* and *the exposing mal-administration of men in power or public trust.*"[17]

Unawed by the popular unrest precipitated by the temporary postponement of the sale of some confiscated estates in 1783 and by the continued presence of the British merchants, the legislature touched off further trouble by restoring thirty-five estates in 1784 and transferring ninety-five others from the confiscation to the amercement list. Such leniency irritated people already hard pressed by Negro competition, high prices, and a scarcity of provisions which necessitated a government ban on the exportation of corn in the summer of 1784.[18] In response to the legislature, a crowd assembled, hanged in effigy James Cook, one of those removed from the confiscation list, carted the effigy through town, and burned it at Gadsden's wharf as an act of protest against Gadsden's support of leniency. Furthermore, "a secret Committee" ordered thirteen persons out of the state within ten days.[19] Governor Guerard, with the unanimous advice of his Privy Council, offered a $1,000 reward for evidence that led to the conviction of the troublemakers.[20]

In July there were new disturbances, "riots" the government called them. According to one witness, a few people entered John Wagner's home, assaulted him and some friends, and destroyed much of his property. Shortly afterward, "ANOTHER PATRIOT" claimed that a few "artful, designing and turbulent men" hired poor sailors, gave them "pure *spirit,*" and then sent them into battle.[21]

The most detailed accounts were written by the supposed rioters. According to them, Intendant Richard Hutson formed a volunteer corps of horse "with a view of attacking unawares (under the pretext of quelling riots)" Whig citizens who supported "*Democracy* and the Revolution" and held in contempt "*Tories* and *Aristocrats.*" On 8 July Hutson's armed band of "*Whigs, Tories,* and *British Merchants,*" broke up a group of not more than twenty unarmed sailors and citizens parading with American colors. Hutson then ordered "Capt. James Johnston, Mr. M'Farlow, Messrs. Cudworth and Waller, Mr. Joseph Bee, Capt. Thompson and others" brought before him for refusing to take up arms against the "rioters."[22] And there apparently the disturbances ended.

Some nondemonstrators thought the protest understandable, perhaps even justifiable. John Lewis Gervais, a respected merchant and member of the lower house, and president of the Senate in 1782, told Henry Laurens that the legislature had provoked trouble by allowing the return of people whom many would find it "irksome . . . to live with."[23] Although the legislature's leniency was in many cases warranted, it frequently was not. James Cook, whose effigy had been so roughly handled, and Gilbert Chambers, for example, had not been mere protection-takers. They had circulated a petition to the commandant of Charleston during the occupation suggesting that prisoners on parole be prohibited from working. William Rees's return provoked serious retaliation from backcountry settlers. Rees had been an officer in the loyal militia and had captured three rebels, one of whom was hanged after being turned over to the British. Other rebels swore revenge. When Rees came back to the state after the war, "sons of Liberty" visited him and laid on fifty stripes, promising more if he did not depart the state within three weeks. They then openly published an account of their action and listed their names. Rees stuck it out, but despite the wishes of the legislature, neither Cook nor Chambers felt secure enough to settle again in Charleston.[24]

But despite reports of mob actions, the city's demonstrations never amounted to more than a relatively peaceful public protest against the acts of the legislature, as one Charleston witness admitted when describing the "Riots" caused by the leniency shown the Tories and protection takers. The riots, such as they were, had done "little or no damage."[25] That all persons tried as a result of the July events were apparently acquitted also indicates that the popular protests had been largely vocal and symbolic rather than physical and violent.[26]

Indeed, given the frustrations created by some unavoidable postwar problems, to which the legislature was adding, what is surprising is the absence of more substantial violence in Charleston. In 1783 and 1784 the crime and brutality widespread in the backcountry repeatedly shocked the state's judges, but they understandably attributed it to the effects of war, which had taught all men to live and die by violence. Charleston not only had its discharged veterans, but also slaves, who seemed despite the laws to be roaming the city at will. Often, too, there were hundreds of sailors, who were sometimes treated violently and from whom violence was usually expected, as the Charleston grand jury made clear in 1784 and 1785 when it complained of the consequences that invevitably followed when sailors were not separated from the "tipling houses" on the wharfs and returned to their vessels when the evening gun was fired.[27]

But violent or not, the conflict between the government and the supporters of "*Democracy* and the Revolution" continued long after the original act of provocation receded into the background. The propaganda which followed for the next few years was sometimes inaccurate, contradictory, and exaggerated; publicists painted in black and white, considering no middle grounds, no extenuating circumstances when judging men's motives or behavior. But there was, too, a broadening and maturing of the opposition's arguments. Propaganda changed from anti-Tory to anti-aristocracy, from attacks on legislation to attacks on legislators. And, ultimately, within the propaganda contemporaries could find a political philosophy common in the eighteenth century but hitherto largely unspoken or unemphasized in South Carolina. The conflicts and rhetoric contributed to a democratization of state government.

Almost always the biting, often sarcastic, diatribes were directed in general terms against the aristocracy and the legislature. One critic wrote about the "*mal-administration of men in power or public trust,*" and "DEMOCRATIC GENTLE-TOUCH" aimed his barbs at the "Nabob Phalanx in the legislature." Its behavior indicated "a *settled plan of ruling by a few, with a rod of iron.*" With a humorous disguise of his attack, "BRUTUS" censured "the people at large, for not taking care to make a better choice the last election."[28] "AMICUS," true to his name, was milder in speech than the other anonymous writers, but he was alarmed by the "*aristocratic* influence (both IN and OUT of the legislature). And "OLD HOMESPUN" denounced the plans of some wealthy, "designing, men" who, with the danger of war behind them, wanted lifetime appointments which they could hand down to their children.[29] "OLD HOMESPUN" was the most farfetched of the writers, yet when John Lloyd could be dismayed that "gentlemen of property" occasionally had to work for election, and when Elizabeth Rutledge could tell her son John that he was only twenty-two and so would have to wait another few years before the state could send him to the new Congress, then perhaps his fears were not so much imaginary as slightly exaggerated.[30]

Newspaper correspondents lashed out in particular at one group in the aristocracy. "Shun all lawyers," "AMICUS" warned, "as they are more liable to corruption than other men." Time and again the "double tongued," "double fee" lawyers were condemned as greedy enemies of the state. "We ought not longer to be *led by the nose by corrupt, avaricious lawyers,* but honest men (NOT LAWYERS). . . ."[31] Lawyers deliberately enacted confusing legislation to increase their business. "Without a *blush,*" lawyers took money "to prevent" justice. So the newspapers warned citizens not to elect any member of "that double tongued race of men, who are bred up to chicanery and deceit."[32]

The aristocracy's opponents were wise to attack lawyers. The actions of the legal class in sponsoring "the obnoxious and contrary" were easily exploitable in Charleston and in the backcountry where anti-Tory feeling was still high. Not long after the whipping of William Rees, a newspaper noted that "the Champions of the town are . . . probably to strike some notable stroke for the admiration of their Country Party. . . ."[33]

Polemics aimed at lawyers were doubly effective. Backcountry settlers not only resented modification of the Jacksonborough legislation but also harbored long-standing grievances against the Charleston bar. In 1767 the

Regulators complained of expensive and oppressive, deliberately drawn out, court cases. They demanded a limit on the number of lawyers allowed to sit in the Commons.[34] Sixteen years later, the grand jury for Ninety Six District presented as "a source of enormous hardships & oppression" the fact that lawyers' fees were not "sufficiently ascertained by known laws." And in 1788, ninety-two petitioners from Clarendon County in Camden District denounced in stronger words the "set of men" who prosper on "the follies and distress of the people which it becomes their interest to promote."[35]

The Regulators, some of whom blamed lawyers for the failure to set up a county court system, also charged that they were being deliberately enslaved by not being shown copies of laws passed by the legislature, an evaluation other commentators agreed with.[36] And in 1782, in the midst of his protest over the 'treaty' respecting slaves, Christopher Gadsden attributed the lawyers' importance to "the infinite number of our laws" and their "perplexity and confusion." Gadsden thought the necessary laws could be put in one octavo volume. The legislature's lame prewar defense was that since 1734 the clerks of the House and Council had been making full copies of all laws.[37]

After the war, the legal secrecy diminished. Perhaps because of the attacks on the lawyers, Governor Guerard in 1784 recommended that the legislature take steps to "digest, collate, consolidate & print" South Carolina's laws, "*which you all too well know the want of for me to enlarge on.*" When *The Public Laws of South-Carolina* finally appeared in 1790, Judge John Faucheraud Grimké sounded like a Regulator: no longer was a Carolinian "degraded into the condition of a slave, by a total ignorance of what was the law of his country."[38]

The specific attacks on lawyers were reasonable as well as politically expedient. Lawyers, politically and economically powerful, were few in number, there being only twenty-four practicing attorneys in 1771.[39] Many people thought the number small by design. Benjamin West complained that he could not share the wealth of the Charleston attorneys because the colony's lawyers had rules which "excluded all their brethren on the continent." Before the Revolution the chief justice and his brother judges set the qualifications for admission to the bar. No one who had not studied five years in Carolina, or three in Carolina and two abroad, could qualify.[40]

Those regulations were changed after the war. To qualify as a lawyer in 1784, citizens had to study for four years in a South Carolina law office or in a foreign nation so as to qualify for that nation's bar. The next year, when the creation of a county court system encouraged lawyers to settle outside Charleston, the legislature eased the requirements somewhat by allowing citizens resident in any state for four years to qualify for the bar by examination before the judges of the Court of Common Pleas. Persons serving clerkships and those studying abroad were also required to pass examinations.[41]

Lawyers were important in the state government. Christopher Gadsden, overlooking his own election as governor, thought that the governor would always be a lawyer because of the "number and confusion" of the state's laws. "The QUERIST" supported Gadsden while trying to defend the loyalty and pariotism of the lawyers. Three of the four governors since 1776 had been lawyers, and the fourth a judge. (The next four would also be lawyers.) Lawyers had also served in high military posts during the war, one commanding the state's first regiment.[42]

Critics of the legislature's amendments to the Jacksonborough legislation only made explicit what had angered Gadsden in 1782. Gadsden, not later involved in the newspaper denunciations, had then urged "honest men" to join together in opposition to the legal profession. If they did not, they would "be more abjectly at the feet of the lawyers than ever our forefathers were at those of the Priesthood," and he, at least, would "not be surprised" if lawyers soon demanded "that their *wished for* Chancellor the Pope of the Law pageantry should have perhaps his ____ kissed."[43] (The reference had to be to John Rutledge's ____.)

Attacks on the lawyers and aristocracy are joined in accounts of the trifling Thompson-Rutledge affair in 1784. On St. Patrick's day Captain William Thompson refused to permit one of John Rutledge's slaves to view from his tavern's second floor some artillery demonstrations. Interpreting the affront to his slave as an insult to himself, Rutledge summoned Thompson to his house; several days later Thompson demanded satisfaction of Rutledge for the accusations made against him. Rutledge, as usual a member of the legislature, sought refuge by referring Thompson's challenge to the lower house.

The Assembly ordered Thompson not only, in his words, "*to apologize to the House for a breach of privilege,* but *also to solicit pardon of my enemy.*" On refusing to agree to the second half of the order, Thompson was "conducted by a *great number* of *respectable* citizens" to jail. According to tavernkeeper Thompson, who thought himself singled out "to deter others from ever *rebelling* again against their *petty Majesties,*" not only had his rights been impaired, but so also had the rights of all those who "go at this day under the opprobrious appellation of the *Lower Orders of Men.*" Thomas Bee, a lawyer, was trying to have him banished, he said, while at the same time exerting his whole industry "to recall from banishhment the *most atrocious proscribed traitors* of the Commonwealth."[44]

Still in those hard and fast terms which divided the people into the good and the bad, the high and the low, reports of the Thompson-Rutledge dispute epitomized the new political spirit of the 1780s. Casting their story and arguments in biblical terms, Thompson's supporters mocked an overly sensitive Rutledge, who "laid him[self] down *upon his bed,* and turned away his face, and would not eat bread,'' and charged that his ''*brethren,* and T______s, the Scribe, and R____h who holdeth it as an abomination *that the people should bear rule,*'' referring to Edward and Hugh Rutledge, Thomas Bee, and Ralph Izard (the only nonlawyer), ''said unto J__n, Hast thou not been ruler over this land?'' Against the ''NABOB *Tribe,*'' said the spokesman for the ''*lower orders,*'' it might be necesssary for every man to ''hold a tool and . . . a weapon.''[45]

No one seriously argued that arms were necessary to defend the freedoms won by the Revolution. But time and again newspapers urged less extreme defensive measures. ''A perpetual *jealousy,* respecting *liberty,* is absolutely necessary,'' said ''AMICUS,'' while another writer warned that ''*slavery* is ever preceded by *sleep.* . . .'' Judge Aedanus Burke, writing as ''Cassius,'' argued that the loss of ''public liberty commence[s] in all republics with plausible pretences of promoting some public good, or remedying some evil.'' He gave the more common reason when he reminded readers that ''supreme authority . . . [was] intoxicating to human nature. . . .''[46] ''OLD HOMESPUN'' repeated the theme in his 1785 argument with the Charleston magistrates, who, he complained, had too much power, including the power to act however they saw fit when there was only an ''*appearance* of a tumult or riot''; such ''unlimited power . . . [was] intoxicating. . . .'' The City Corporation, in the person of Intendant Richard Hutson, known to his enemies as Richard the First because of his harsh actions during the disturbances of July 1784, was again denounced when the imaginative ''FLOATING BATTERY'' stated that Hutson was ''drunk'' with power.[47]

Because the unrestrained exercise of power led to tyranny, Carolinians had written into their constitution of 1778 procedures for the impeachment of government officers and the principle of rotation, which required that governors and sheriffs be automatically retired after two years in office and commissioners of the treasury after four. If their retirement did not precede their corruption, at least their evil would be limited in time. With the attack on the aristocracy and the legislature after the war, the same fear of power led people to demand closer control over representatives and senators. Voters should, they said, take more care in electing legislators. They ought not to be awed by ''enormous wealth''; they should ''shun all lawyers,'' for they were more corruptible than other men.[48]

There were more positive injunctions. Legislators were warned not to forget that they were dependent on and responsible to ''the collective body of the people.'' And voters, in turn, were urged to examine candidates' beliefs and not to vote for any man who refused to abide by his constituents' directions.[49]

Only occasionally were there hints of extralegal activity. One writer warned that if the legislature continued to ''disregard the unanimous voice of the *uninfluenced Whig citizens,*" then "the alternative . . . to be adopted by *freemen* may be easily comprehended. . . ." And "IGNORAMUS," who claimed not to understand one of the city ordinances, questioned the idea that citizens ought to obey implicitly all ordinances, right or wrong. So did Benjamin Waller, who was involved in legal difficulties with the city government. "A *subordination* to the laws," he wrote, "is always the cant word to enslave the people."[50]

The defenders of the government only partly joined the debate. They attacked the men of the opposition, their motives, and some of their ideas, frequently commenting on the proposition that some laws could justifiably be set aside by individuals. They denounced "riot and faction" and supported law and order and the admirable work the City Corporation had done in making the streets safe once more. One correspondent, in terms which could not have been more exaggerated, described the September 1784 contest between Alexander Gillon and Richard Hutson for Intendant as an election which will decide, "perhaps irreversibly," whether Carolinians would "bask in the sun-shine of Freedom," or whether "the Demon of Anarchy" would "stalk your streets with gigantic and destructive strides, uncurbed and uncontrouled."[51] In less extreme fashion "AN AMERICAN WHIG" called for "a mild subordination to the laws of our country," and still another writer argued that "where the law is not omnipotent, liberty cannot possibly exist. . . ."[52]

Christopher Gadsden, defending his support of leniency toward those who had weakened in the face of the British, was the most persistent, identifiable opponent of Gillon and his "set of *self-created* upstart bullying censors." No one had done more than he, he argued, to oppose, "in the *proper* place, *every* appearance of *Aristocracy,*" but he did not think the legislature's policies should be protested by mobs in the streets. And, as "A STEADY and OPEN REPUBLICAN," he warned the demonstrators in the headline of one of his newspaper essays that "Cunning, the Offspring of Knavery and Folly, Seldom Fails, Sooner or Later to Outcunning Herself, And Then She is Quite Undone."[53]

Both sides professed a fear of tyranny, Gillon and his followers the tyranny of an aristocracy, and the government's defenders the tyranny of "three or four artful, designing and turbulent men" who were attempting to seize "the powers of the state." Quoting "the Great Washington," "HORATIO" supported quick punishment of "the internal enemies of our constitution," lest there be a " 'natural progression from the extreme of anarchy to that of tyranny.' "[54] Frequently the leaders of the opposition were damned as mere demagogues who stirred up trouble "by poisoning the minds" of the people. Bolingbroke was quoted: "Nothing is easier than for a few designing, inflammatory demagogues to persuade the lower class of people that they are in danger of being oppressed by their rulers."[55]

SOUTH CAROLINA GAZETTE, AND

GENERAL ADVERTISER

Vol. II.] From Thursday, September 9, to Saturday, September 11, 1784. (Numb. 20[illegible]

CHARLESTON: Printed for J. MILLER, Printer to the STATE, Church-street.

To the Public in general, and to Commodore GILLON IN PARTICULAR.

CUNNING, THE OFFSPRING OF KNAVERY AND FOLLY, SELDOM FAILS, SOONER OR LATER TO OUTCUNNING HERSELF, AND THEN SHE IS QUITE UNDONE.—ANON.

THO' your Honor's performance in Mrs. Timothy's last paper came out so late on Thursday evening, that I had scarce time to run it over before I went to bed, yet, as I do not see A SINGLE TITTLE IN IT to the MAIN point, the following strictures thereon I hope will be thought FULLY sufficient; indeed, were it not for the public, I should pass it over altogether with that UNNOTICED CONTEMPT it deserves. My duty to the community alone has called me out on this occasion. I shall make my observations, for the ease of the reader, in the same manner I did on the Commodore's last "BAG OF FEATHERS," just as any rise WORTH remarking on. Reasoning and facts I shall take notice of; bullying nonsense, infamous and notorious falsities, mischief making hints, "LICK-SPITTLE" cringings, and artful attempts to make me the peace offering of reconciliation to men you have so OFTEN and POINTEDLY abused, or caused to be so, (even in that VERY paper you have not yet cleared yourself from,) I shall leave just as they stand, to SUIT the SIZE of such understandings as you seem to have CALCULATED them for. The candid and considerate public will be at no loss to see the drift of all this. You say, "I did and do now tell you "that I have proof UNEQUIVOCALLY DECLA-"RATIVE who IS the AUTHOR of all the "Gentle Touches you have had, and that I "neither *directly nor indirectly* had any thing to do "with them." In my opinion, Sir, and that of numbers of others, the only proof hitherto produced (Mr. Hornby's oath) does not by any means support this assertion, or prevent your being still thought to have a finger in the pie with regard to that paper I PINN'D YOU TO, printed in Mrs. Timothy's Gazette, No. 2202; for even by Mr. Hornby's own account, there were more than one concerned; and from good authority I can say there were not LESS than four. The deponent "excepts two or three lines which" (he says) "was added by ANOTHER "HAND after he sent the piece to the press." Does not this make TWO, Sir? Does he say you were not the author of THESE lines? Does it not then require ANOTHER oath, sir, to explain this matter? Some *very intimate* friend this person must *certainly* be to take *such liberties*; and would he do it without knowing *whose* he made this addition to? and could not this person (supposing it was not your Honor) acquaint you with the contents of the whole?

AT ALL EVENTS, Sir, you ought to have contradicted the many falsities and scurrilities that paper contained relative to the public trust you were honoured with; your plain duty to the public required it—but have you yet done any thing like it? *On the contrary,* are you not supporting and encouraging this Mr. Gen[illegible] Truth in his insults on the public? Many more [illegible] remarks might be made on Mr. Hornby's extraordinary deposition, which time will not now permit [illegible].

It is well known I could not take my seat in the [illegible] at Jacksonborough, till the day the stone of [illegible] ended, antecedent to which the names of [illegible] had been in possession of the House, and [illegible] the [illegible] gentleman alluded to amongst the rest. I have not been the means of a *single* man's [illegible] you on any list, but of *many* being transferred [illegible] confiscation to the 12 per cent. list, when nothing better could be done for them, or got off entirely. [illegible] my little abilities for every body, *foreign or* [illegible] when I could *excuse* at the least circumstance in [illegible]. I seem to carry favour, or your and hand [illegible] attempts to do on this paper) [illegible] or friendly whatever. I always was of opinion [illegible], to make a few examples, the fewer the [illegible] distinguish who had been entrusted, and in the highest offices; my political game on such occasions ran always *high*; witness your Honor's GREAT SELF at the present moment; most of your tools I pity, your *maxims* I laugh at—but this gentleman is gone, peace to his *ashes*! I with pleasure voted for his name being taken off the 12 per cent. list. In the affair at Jacksonborough, by a proper use of his name, numbers were entirely got off, and others removed from the confiscation to the 12 per cent. list. His "delinquency was not the *mere acceptance* of protection," I wish to say no more, and hope shall not be obliged to it.

Too much has been said of Gen. W. Is it not YOU, sir, and not I that "*you persecute him*"? While his affair was pending, I acted as my conscience directed, and am well pleased and satisfied with the determination of the House; that gentleman himself could not wish more earnestly than I did for his honorable acquittal. I was very glad to see the General stigmatized as "*a cut off*" in that *most seditious* paper dropt in the last riot; it weighed with me, as I told several of my friends, much to his honor, and was the occasion of my hint about the tête a tête. You may publish and *keep* your INTIMIDATING doomsday records if you please; for my part, on account of the public *at large*, and for posterity's sake, and not to favour *any particular*, relative or not relative, I wish that all these matters were *forgotten*. If a man is to be answerable for the misconduct of any relative or friend, how must your Honor's relatives and friends BLUSH for your conduct on the present occasion? but [illegible] are with us, and such another European Puff as lately appeared (and I predicted weeks before) may be easily manufactured *here* (as I believe that was) and sent to Europe, to ease the sensibility of your relations who are there.

Your random with regard to Col. L.'s house, is a random indeed; have you not been *already* told I was absent on public business (at New York) when that happened, and never heard or knew a syllable of it till my return; does not half the state know this? Just such another is your insinuation with regard to Col. Grant in 1761. I never, to the best of my recollection, was ever in his company but on Col. Middleton's affair.—What pity, after such great labour, not to be able to occasion the mischief you wish for!

'Tis not possible for Falshood herself to invent a greater untruth than that "I wished an act to be passed that *no bird of passage* should hold any office of property or honour in this commonwealth." Your Honor *well knows* my meaning of "birds of passage" is confined to *merchants as merchants*, in contradistinction to planters and farmers, and this takes in all merchants whatever, as well *natives* of this state as any others, [illegible] many *natives* of this state, *as merchants*, after having acquired good fortunes here, have gone and settled in other countries they liked better, and why not? Is a man to be fixed to a spot like a pine? Did ever any reasonable man blame them for doing so? I say, and it has been always said, that the greatest dependance of a country is on the cultivators of its *soil*; that these are *fixed*; merchants are not so, but still extremely useful and honorable members of any society while they stay, and very properly admissible, *such* as are qualified, to hold any offices they may be appointed to. I have always endeavoured to act as a citizen *of* the world, and wherever located, have strove to add to the stock of human happiness in that spot all I could.

This fly manoeuvre, Commodore, is easily seen thro'. I flatter myself that I have as many friends amongst the citizens, whose ancestors came from Holland, Germany, *Ireland*, and other parts of Europe, as your Honor. They know I wish them well, and have always promoted their interest in common with all others. We are all, (or ought to be so) AMERICANS here, and the mentioning Dutch, German, *Irish*, &c. citizens, is at least *improper*, and often done *with design* to create and foment *invidious distinctions*. I thought your Honor was "a little skilled in the genealogy of the Nabobs of this state," (on which cash you or your tools have blamed me); if so you would have known I have some Irish blood in me, and that my grandfather, by my mother's side, whom I am named after, was of that nation; so that according to your honor's narrow *national* ideas, I should hardly be "*unnaturally against*" them. My scribbling, sir, I am *ever unfavorable* [illegible], very rarely any person [illegible] a single [illegible] of it till printed.

The resignation of my commission was not, and *could not*, at the time be attended with any inconvenience to the community; whether my country took it amiss, may be judged from the many honourable stations I have been [illegible] in since, and the still more honourable that have been offered me, which the knowledge of my own weak abilities, and sincere affection for them, obliged me to decline—I never asked any man, *directly or indirectly*, for his vote in any trust whatever I have been honoured with; and never was concerned, or [illegible] supposed to be concerned in any cabal whatever. The honours I have received from my fellow citizens have been always *unsolicited*; I am the more obliged to them, and sensible of their favour. Was this the case with your Honor, for Commodore, *for* Privy Council, and particularly for *Warden*. [illegible] *all do with* Gen. M[illegible] has been long since [illegible], and the public know all about it, however I have no objection to your *authentic record*, from whence you say you took it, being reprinted, together with another true and authentic record I have lately seen, entitled "the Cat let out of the Bag," for the complete amusement of the public.

I could not with propriety give my hand to the gentleman hinted at, till I knew what reception he had received from the Governour, whose quarters I was then at. My reflection was harsh I confess, and blamed myself for it presently after; but this very gentleman I have had the pleasure since to give my vote to have his fine taken off. This, and the two other instances your Honour has started, shew the old proverb verifyed in me, that, better one man steal a sheep than another look over the hedge. That I should be *pointedly* censured—*more than any man in the State* for severity, for endeavouring to save any man during these unhappy times, must appear *strange*, I am certain, to every gentleman besides your Honour, that has served with me. *No Partiality*, to be sure, in your Honour, in thus *singling* me out for such remarks! You and your tools seem to think they have a right to act as who chuse this way, and are jealous of the least interference in their *favourite* [illegible]. I am sometimes with your Honour [illegible] *at all*, at others I am, as it were, the Fac [illegible], as for instance, "that for every year I attended the House of Representatives I put the State to the expence of 9000 dollars." I declare I do not understand what is meant here, unless that all the Members I have served with for near thirty years have been mere cyphers, and suffered me to lead them by the nose, and do what I please. If because I gave my vote, or spoke in favour of a matter, am I therefore to [illegible] account [illegible]? If so, I confess I did vote for your Honour's being sent on the *[illegible]* Service you were sent, which I believe the whole State have re[illegible] ever since but this at thirty years purchase, a[illegible] per annum, will not amount to what *the [illegible]* cost us. The affair of the tobacco [illegible] I never bought up, nor either of my sons, a single cask, nor have any intentions upon any account [illegible]. I think the Members of Assembly have no right to grant favours; I have often told them so in the House; if my wharf is an *improper* place for the inspection of the tobacco let it be removed, and in the next House your Honor may move for it if you think proper; neither myself or mine will petition against it.

Boundary-street is the widest, and may be made one of the finest streets in Charleston, and has been for MANY YEARS established by law, and was ruined during the siege, when the owners of lands at this end of the town, suffered in their estates at least THIRTY times more than the gentlemen at the other end of the town, are they, after suffering so much, to be payers of taxes for streets, and receive no benefit from the most essential to them? That street was impassable to carriages of any sort for near a year after the evacuation, before any stir was made about it, and what has been done now? only forty feet repaired, when they have a right to seventy. That street is not on my land, nor did I give an inch of ground, as *some think*, towards it; it is as necessary, and will be when properly repaired, as frequented a street as any in town, whether the tobacco warehouse is or is not continued at my wharf.

Salt I have never bought a bushel for sale since I began my wharf, but perhaps may by and by, and why not?

Why more of the bridge? Con what I said in my last, I shall say no more here.

Whatever service I may have done, in any capacity the country called me to, I leave the State to judge, my fellow citizens know I have been always at their service, that I never courted, [illegible], or *flattered* one of them, and have more than once, at [illegible], ventured to oppose them in instances where they have been misled, and some of them have been [illegible] enough to acknowledge afterwards that I was right; and I make no doubt many well-meaning [illegible] now misled, will not think the worse of me by and by for that opposition.

When my stores since the evacuation were burnt, and my indigo lost by carelessness in [illegible] in some conversation with you I mentioned, that it could be [illegible] a thousand or 1500l. abroad, for two, or not exceeding three years, it would be acceptable; you then told me, you made no doubt you could get it for me, if I would take it for seven years, the foreigners did not choose to lend their money in general for less time. This I declined; however said I would consider of it, and some weeks thereafter, meeting you *casually* in the street, I desired you to write, provided when you received an answer it could be at my option to draw for the money, or not, as might then suit me. You told me you would write. This is all that passed. Upon reflecting that the time to keep it was too long, and the *difficulty* of remitting the money to Holland, might, *nay probably would*, be very great, I therefore neither thought, nor heard, a syllable more about it, till this *point* at [illegible] in the news paper.

††† For the conclusion—see the last page.

Besides the unrealistic charge that the Gillon supporters were striving for anarchy or even creating an anarchic situation, the specific charge most often hurled at those who might be called radicals was that their actions were motivated by a purely narrow, selfish motive. The radicals were denounced as "an assemblage of Drunken Tavern-Keepers, Mountebank Doctors, Pettifogging Attornies and necessitous Speculators, with a Jesuit Priest at their head," probably a reference to William Thompson; Dr. John Budd, who denounced the City Corporation before the legislature and who had led the protest against Governor Lowndes in 1778; Gillon, one of the largest purchasers of confiscated estates; and Dr. James Fallon, a Georgian who is known only by the remarks of his enemies.[56] Nathanael Greene called Fallon a "Jesuit and desturber of all good Government," but fortunately for society, "a great coward." According to "MENTOR," these were the men who had "tasted of the sweets of confiscation," and the public disturbances, the anarchy, were somehow designed to facilitate the payment of their debts. They were going to force the legislature to issue paper money as a legal tender.[57] In fact, however, only Gillon among the leaders of the opposition had purchased a large amount of confiscated property, and the drive for the issuance of a paper currency was led by lowcountry planters rather than by Charleston radicals.

The government's defenders chose to remain silent about the return of the banished and the presence of the British merchants, the problem which caused the dissenters both economic and emotional distress. Instead, at times, they distorted the aims of their opponents. The protestors sought neither to overturn the government nor to fundamentally alter its foundation, no one even attempting to introduce new groups in public life through the abolition of property requirements for office holding or voting, although an exchange between "JULIA" and "CORNELIA" in the Charleston newspapers did suggest that it was "high time for the women to try their skill in politics," since they might "do better than the men" and could not "do worse."[58] The leaders of the opposition — two merchants; a lawyer; two doctors, one virtually unknown; and a tavern keeper — tried to interest the existing electorate in influencing or controlling their government by more closely supervising those who ran for office and those who were elected. "The rights of election . . . are invaded," said "ARISTIDES," "by an appeal to the electors to form an unconstitutional combination and to dictate terms to the elected. . . ."[59] But "ARISTIDES" was wrong; although there was nothing in the constitution binding legislators to instructions, neither was there anything to prohibit people from withholding votes from those who would not consult or follow the wishes of their constituents.

When Edward Rutledge attacked "the clamour of the worthless," he summed up the beliefs of many advocates of law and order. The people, he said, have become "the dupes of a word. 'Liberty' is the motto; [and]

every attempt to restrain licentiousness or give efficacy to Government is charged audaciously on the real advocates for Freedom as an attack upon Liberty."[60] He was partly right. Positions had become so polarized that government actions were denounced in terms that sometimes bore no relation to the insignificance of particular policies. Thus, the jailing of William Thompson for challenging John Rutledge was not a sufficient reason to say that "the *grand hierarchy* of the State were not to be controuled, at least [not] by any of the *lower orders. . . .*" Thompson had, after all, challenged a member of the House of Representatives to a duel while the House was in session. Christopher Gadsden pointed out that Thompson could very simply have waited until the session ended.[61]

But similarly, men like Edward Rutledge were too quick to denounce the opposition as advocates of anarchy and disturbers of society. They ignored the justice of some of the complaints. Although there was no proof, whatever "AMICUS," "OLD HOMESPUN," "BRUTUS," or "DEMOCRATIC GENTLE-TOUCH" said, that any of the rulers were intent on establishing an oppressive government or one which was ruled by only a few, there was reason to argue that they were interested in and worked for a government controlled by as few as possible. John Rutledge thought the people did not want "a simple democracy, or . . . [a government] verging toward it." Ralph Izard, who had expressed his dissatisfaction with backcountry representatives for their "opinion that a politician may be born such," opposed schemes to move the government inland, where most of the people lived, because that "would strengthen the country interest in a proportion of four to one."[62] Nor was the country interest to be strengthened by substantially increased representation. The constitution of 1778 called for reapportionament in 1785, but the legislature took no general action then or in later years, although in 1789 it created two new backcountry counties. The inaction did not represent tyranny, but it did indicate an aversion to letting the people rule.

When the radicals began to attack the members of the Charleston city government in 1784 their language was harsh and their arguments telling. They complained that the vague act of incorporation gave magistrates too much power to act when they sensed a tumult in the air. On the floor of the lower house in 1787, Dr. John Budd stretched the argument to its utmost, maintaining that should the corporation imagine a riot in the making it could legally massacre the citizens and burn the town.[63]

More effective attacks on the City Corporation perhaps unexpectedly followed the September 1784 election, that fiercely contested race between Hutson and Gillon — between "Law and Liberty" and "Anarchy and Tyranny." The July disturbances, "riots," some called them, produced a bitter election fight. "The great, the important day comes on apace, Big with the Fate of Charleston," wrote an opponent of "PECULATORS, SPECULATORS, And FRANCISCAN PRIESTS." "AN AMERICAN

WHIG'' warned citizens not to be misled by the agents of faction. The election, he said, would decide whether they would enjoy ''the blessings of peace, resulting from a mild subordination to the laws . . . or whether we are to be enslaved by riot and faction.'' ''SENEX,'' claiming to be an old man nearly ruined by the war, more calmly urged the election of consistent ''*advocates for a democratic equality.*''[64]

Both sides made tremendous efforts, and on election day the turnout was large. The year before, Hutson had won the intendant's position at an election attended by fewer than 250 voters. In 1786 John Faucheraud Grimké was elected with 174 votes to his opponents' 101, and two years later Rawlins Lowndes received 279 of the less than 425 votes cast. But the election of 1784 was heated enough so that 647 people voted. [65] The 647 may have represented about 50 percent of Charleston's eligible elctorate; and they reflected both the influence of resolutions passed by the City Council to explain the property requirement for voting and the government's lenient policy of 1783. One week before the election, to enlist the support of lowcountry planters who lived part of the year in Charleston, the wardens declared eligible to vote any person who met the requirements for citizenship (basically one had to be a free white, resident for one year in the state); paid a tax the previous year of three shillings sterling; and kept a house in the city for his own use or resided in the city for three months in the year before the election.[66] Nothing in the wording of the law or resolutions seems to have excluded women, but it is unlikely that any voted. Although the alien act of 1784 made citizens of those living in the state for a year while denying them the right to vote for another two, that act did not apply to the sixty-seven merchants and others who had been admitted by the governor and privy council in 1783. The planters and British merchants undoubtedly contributed heavily to Hutson's 387 votes. Gillon, in his losing cause, was favored by 260 votes. And that, said one of Hutson's supporters, was the end of opposition; it was ''laid . . . prostrate and panting on the ground.''[67]

But, in fact the opposition continued active. And, forming around a new issue, the supposedly unconstitutional and oppressive treatment of Benjamin Waller, the opposition launched a newspaper war somewhat less exciting than the trouble of 1783 and 1784 but constitutionally more significant. The defense of Waller involved protection of individual rights. The cry for liberty, although used to stimulate further opposition to the existing authority, was not a demand for licentiousness.

Benjamin Waller and Benjamin Cudworth were vendue masters in Charleston. They sold at public auctions secondhand goods belonging to persons attempting to raise cash quickly, property owned by people involved in bankruptcy proceedings, and property ordered sold by the court of chancery. Auctioneers were required by the government to secure licenses, give bonded security, and pay a tax of 2½ percent, one-half their commission, on almost all the goods they sold. In 1784 the City Corporation limited vendues to Tuesdays and Thursdays — the legislature had first regulated their frequency in 1750 — and also prohibited vendue masters from holding their sales in the streets. According to Waller, who claimed that he and Cudworth lost upwards of 1,000 guineas by that "manoeuvre," the City Corporation forbade street sales because it had "imprudently rented out the cellars under the Exchange to Auctioneers, by which means," because of the passage of the auctioneers' customers, "the lower end of Broad-Street became almost impassable."[68]

Apparently to escape legislative taxation and restrictions imposed by the city government, Cudworth and Waller retired from the vendue business and opened what they called a "Chalking Office" for the sale of goods every Monday and Friday. There was, Waller insisted, "no act in existence" against such an office. Nevertheless, Waller, and for a shorter time Cudworth, was imprisoned by the City Corporation, which took the position that a "Chalking Office" differed from a vendue business in name only.[69]

The Corporation's prosecution of Waller intensified criticism of the powers granted the city government by the incorporation act of 1783 and a subsequent act of 1784. In 1783 the city corporation received whatever judicial power was exercised in the state by the justices of the peace. An act of 1784, which the wardens had requested, extended the city's judicial power to cases which did not exceed £20.[70] Some inhabitants realized that the acts were in at least two instances faulty and dangerous to individual freedom.

Waller's remarks, offered in his own behalf, exposed one threat by focusing on the unbalanced nature of the government. The act of incorporation "blended together" the powers of the legislative, judicial, and executive branches. The wardens enacted laws, appointed the officials who enforced them, and tried the violators of those laws. "It is an alarming circumstance," Benjamin Waller wrote, "that the *Prosecutor* sits judge." At his trial, Waller found his accusing enemies "set as jurymen and judges of a *Law enacted by themselves.*" The same self-interested people were informers, legislators, prosecutors, and judges. That confusion of people and offices, another critic wrote, was "contrary to the letter and spirit of the *Constitution,* which keeps each department separate from the other."[71] The charge itself was inaccurate, however, since judges and legal officers were allowed to sit in the legislature if they were chosen by their constituents after their appointment by the legislature.

The other feature of the city government thought dangerous to freedom and unconstitutional was the absence of jury trials. There was no jury when the wardens decided to throw Waller in jail. His supporters cited the forty-first article of the state constitution, which guaranteed one a trial "by the judgment of his peers or by the law of the land." "Judgment of his peers" meant trial by jury; "law of the land" meant something equally specific, they said. When the constitution of 1778 was written, "OLD HOMESPUN" stated, the legislature was given the power to decide the fate of any "great and atrocious villain" whose influence was such "that he could not be proceeded against in the common manner." But such power to proceed without a jury could not be delegated to a court of wardens. In general, "AMICUS" argued, no legislature of a democracy could "*subdelegate* what to themselves is *only delegated.*"[72]

The forthright criticisms of the aristocracy, the act of incorporation, and the city government produced some immediate effects. Both John Budd and Benjamin Waller won special elections to the legislature from Charleston in January and February 1786. (Gillon was already a member.) Complaints over Negro competition led to an ordinance limiting the number of slaves city dwellers could hire out for work. Adverse comments over unsupervised spending by the wardens forced them to publish the city's receipts and expenditures in the fall of 1786. That Budd could criticize the published financial statement, or that some people expressed confusion over the meaning of the ordinance regulating slave labor did not detract from the fact that the city government had been forced to respond positively to public protests.[73] And the absence of serious, sustained criticisms in 1786 possibly indicates that the wardens were behaving more circumspectly by then.

But Gillon, Budd, Waller, and their supporters never became strong enough to control the city or dominate elections to the legislature. Their goals and arguments certainly guaranteed them the opposition of the wealthy. Their rhetoric, which played down their own middle-class background and divided the opposing forces into the rich and the poor, antagonized those who expected to rise into the upper-class and those who feared the lower orders more than they worried about British merchants or aristocratic tendencies, especially when the Council could be made to respond. That members of the legislature were not deaf to protest either and incorporated artisan societies also undercut the appeal of critics.[74]

More importantly, the Charleston opposition may have failed to produce more immediate results because in its attacks on the aristocracy and government and in defense of some freedoms and rights it was both too radical for some and not radical enough for others. At a time when many people feared disorder, worried about riots and crime, Budd and others stood forward and spoke up on behalf of sailors, men who could do them little political good, except to participate in demonstrations, because they were either citizens of other states or too often gone from home to be counted on. The wardens had reacted to the grand juries' suggestions that the safety of the citizens might be enhanced by restraining seamen. But "OLD HOMESPUN" called the Council's actions "the cloven foot of tyranny." Jailing sailors for being out after the evening gun, confining them in a small jail during "the extreme hot season," was dangerous to debtors and criminals locked up with them, to the whole city, and should have been "reprobated by every man of humanity."[75] According to one "seafaring man," the persecution was continual. After a hard day's work, one was allowed little time on shore. If a sailor violated the curfew, he was fined a month's wages or "flogged unmercifully." Budd was embarrassed as well as upset: "Tell it not in Gath, publish it not in Askelon," he told the legislature, "that this has happened in one of the United States." The defense of the sailors, however, could have been no more popular than the attack on the city ordinance allowing any two magistrates to commit apprentices and servants to the workhouse on the complaints of their masters. "ARGUS" argued that the magistrates might have the power to confine them, but not the claimed authority to impose punishments of moderate whipping and the placing of shackles on them.[76]

But while identifying those problems, and sometimes acting as spokesmen for the poor, as when "OLD HOMESPUN" attacked the stallage rates and a heavier duty on fish which "distressed the poor" and sent many to seek relief from the parish, the Charleston opposition never suggested anything more radical than giving the lower orders a different set of rulers.[77] They never challenged the property qualification for voting, payment of a three shilling sterling tax in the year preceding the election, or the requirement that no one could serve as warden unless he met the property qualifications set for representatives, ownership of a "settled" plantation and ten slaves or property valued at £1,000 currency, free of debt, a requirement which excluded the lower class entirely from the legislature and the City Council. And, perhaps for that reason, the critics could not mobilize their most likely supporters.

Hammering constantly on certain arguments, however, Gillon and others did have a long-range influence on some principles of government. By stressing that men in government could become corrupt and use their offices for selfish ends, they furthered the idea that officeholders needed laws to free them from temptation. In 1787 the legislature prohibited the surveyor general, secretary of state, commissioners of locations, and related clerks from taking up any lapsed grants of land, either directly or indirectly, because by the nature of their jobs they had "great advantages over their fellow citizens."[78] In 1787 also the legislature provided that none of its members could hold the office of escheator. Escheators, appointed for each district by the joint ballot of house and senate, were responsible for reporting all lands and estates not claimed by legal representatives of deceased owners. Such property was to be advertised and sold by the escheators, who received a 2½ percent commission of the total amount of money they paid into the treasury. The next year, legislators were denied the opportunity to serve as tax collectors. The most sweeping legislative restraint was the 1787 act establishing the civil list and forbidding any elected state official with a salary above £150 to hold other paying offices under the government of the state or of the United States.[79] And that principle was even more widely applied in 1790. Specifying only a few exceptions, the state's new constitution excluded from the legislature people who filled offices "of profit or trust" under the state or national government.

The arguments of the Charleston opposition also affected court decisions. When, in 1794, the wardens fined a tallow-chandler £100 for keeping a shop within the bounds of the city, their decision was overruled by a superior court which adopted some of the arguments of the 1780s. Thomas Waties declared that the state court would have ruled the same way even had the fine been less than £20. Waties saw only two ways of interpreting the act of 1784 which had enlarged the powers of the wardens by allowing them the same powers exercised by the Courts of Common Pleas and Admiralty in cases up to £20. And no matter which way he viewed the act, the court of wardens lost its cause. The judges of the Court of Common Pleas could try cases without a jury, Waties noted, but only subject to "the right of either party in a suit to demand a jury if he chooses." No jury was empanelled when the wardens tried cases; no one, then, could receive a jury trial if he requested it.[80]

On the other hand, Waties ruled, if the legislature in 1784 had meant to grant the Charleston government the power to try cases involving sums under £20 without a jury, then it had passed a law violating the constitution and "therefore void." Though Waties construed the "law of the land" in a broader manner than had Waller and his friends, recognizing that admiralty courts, courts-martial, and courts of the justice of the peace had from necessity and custom acquired the rights to function without juries, he did not believe that the legislature could constitutionally create a new court that functioned without a jury.[81]

Waties ended his decision like a newspaper contributor in 1785, by denouncing the very nature of the act of incorporation. "There surely could not be contrived by the most ingenious tyrant a more complete instrument for all the purposes of oppression," he wrote, adding, however, that he did not yet think it had "been employed in doing mischief." He objected strenuously to the "unnatural combination of the legislative, the executive and judicial powers." In free governments those powers were separated. In despotic governments they were joined.[82] Waties did not mention it, but on a state level the new constitution of 1790 prohibited judges from sitting in the legislature.

When Alexander Gillon and his supporters attacked the city government in 1784 and 1785 they did not accuse the wardens of exceeding their authority, for they knew that the wardens were exercising, however unwisely and harshly, only the power granted them by the legislature. But given the nature of man and the nature of power they had argued that there was danger that the wardens might stretch their powers beyond legal bounds and become harsher and less wise; unless they were constantly vigilant the wardens would seize greater authority.

Future events proved the critics right. In 1787 the court of wardens imprisoned a seller of liquors for nonpayment of a £50 fine. Their decision was overruled by a state court which accepted the arguments of the dealer's lawyer. The corporation was confined to suing and recovering amounts under £20, and the attempt to collect more was an attempt to "grasp" new power.[83] Undaunted, the City Council in 1794 fined the tallow-chandler £100 for breaking one of its ordinances. In the ensuing case, Judges Thomas Waties and Aedanus Burke sanctioned some of the ideas of the Charleston government's early critics, Burke by talking about power and corruption. The action of the council in fining someone £100 when it could legally recover only £20 served "to illustrate upon a small scale," Burke said, "the intruding, usurping nature of power."[84] Starting with little judicial power in 1783, the wardens had asked for and received more in 1784 and had then sought by themselves to extend that power even further.

Many dissatisfactions emerged in the years after the war. Unhappy with the policies of the legislature, people protested with demonstrations, propaganda, and political action. Their propaganda was sometimes exaggerated, but, given the attitudes of many old rulers, founded in truth. Arguments in defense of a free press, for choosing men responsive to their constituents, and against the government created for Charleston, gave evidence of a concern for democratic rights. The old rulers, who had known little opposition before independence, were, by their own admission, alarmed and uncomfortable. They still came to office almost unopposed in their own lowcountry parishes, but now they faced "the snarls of invidious animals." In 1784, 1785, and 1786, their outspoken opponents could not be overlooked. To make matters worse for the Rutledges, the Pinckneys, and others whose families had been accustomed to govern, the backcountry began a forceful attack after 1785.

SEVEN
The Awakening of the Interior

> The Intendant rose and said . . . [as] this new town was to be erected . . . where the laws were laughed at and despised, . . . he meant to move that this town should be called the
> Town of Refuge.
>
> Col. Gervais said he had no objection to its being a town of refuge, but not in an opprobrious way; he hoped that in this town we should find refuge under the wings of
> Columbia. . . .
>
> Senate debate on moving the government, 9 March 1786, *Charleston Morning Post and Daily Advertiser,* 11 March 1786.

HILE dissidents from the city annoyed legislators from Charleston and the surrounding area with denunciations of their policies and motives, settlers in the backcountry and Georgetown and Beaufort districts were silent. Occasionally in 1783 and 1784 they spoke up, but only to list their problems. In 1783 the grand jury of Orangeburg District cited as grievances the lack of a minister and a seminary of learning, the practice of fire hunting, the neglect of patrol duty, and the use of firearms by Negroes. The grand jury of Ninety Six objected to the ease with which criminals escaped punishment and the fees of lawyers. The next year Georgetown's grand jury complained that gamblers from other states infested their area; and, also in 1784, the grand juries of Beaufort and Ninety Six districts objected to the continued presence of men who had supported the British in an infamous manner.[1] Such complaints hardly challenged the status quo.

But the threat of opposition from people who had in the past opposed some governmental policies was great, and lowcountry leaders recognized it. The Charleston opposition was loud and had access to newspapers, but the backcountry and the distant lowcountry parishes, with 106 representatives and sixteen senators, had far greater political power.

Perhaps twice in 1783 and 1784 the areas given voice by the revolutionary constitutions had substantial influence on the legislature. When in 1783 the legislature began to modify the confiscation and amercement acts, it passed another confiscation act seizing the estates of those who had fled the state or those who had died in the British service. The act was probably passed to appease the legislators of the non-Charleston areas. And in 1784, the same areas may have been responsible for the passage of a new plan of taxation.

Many people had disliked the old tax. Before the war backcountry petitioners had informed the legislature that they were "discourage[d] and dishearten[ed]" by the "unequal and grievous Taxation" which subjected their own relatively poor land to the same taxes "laid upon the best Lands below." Their proposed solution was simple and logical: a graduated tax to place heavier burdens on more valuable rice and indigo plantation land.[2] But the system was not changed then. In 1783 Christopher Gadsden tried to increase the burdens of the plantation owners by proposing to double the tax on slaves. That move failed; so also did his mild and not very far-reaching proposal to raise the land tax paid by persons owning more than 20,000 acres.[3] The act finally passed in 1783 placed a tax of one dollar on every 100 acres of land, good or bad, valuable or valueless, and a tax of one dollar on each slave in the state.

The desired change came in 1784. It was obvious by then that the state desperately needed revenue to meet its normal expenses and its war-time obligations, which had been increased in 1783 when the state agreed to pay the federal government's debt to South Carolinians. According to Johann David Schoepf, the representatives from "the remoter and poorer districts" who usually sat quiet obstinately and "strongly opposed" an attempt to raise the land tax "equally over the entire state." They successfully demanded that the increase be based on the land's "quality and yield" rather than on its "extent." William Hornby, the newspaper's "DEMOCRATIC GENTLE-TOUCH," also found "the more numerous, and NOW more clearsighted" backcountry legislators "determined to oppose all attempts to filch the money out of their pockets, to ease the *rich Rice* and Indigo planters."[4] The act of 1784 placed a tax of 1 percent on the value of all land. In the Charleston area, land was valued from six pounds an acre down to five shillings. Backcountry land was valued as low as one shilling an acre. The law also doubled the tax on slaves. For each slave a master now paid 9s. 4p.

The effect of the change was soon apparent. In 1783 the planters of St. Paul's parish paid a tax of £163.7.5 on 70,018 acres of land. In 1787, the next year for which an itemized account exists, the planters paid taxes on 97,640 acres. At the old rate their land tax would have amounted to £227.16.4. Instead it totaled £537.13.2. In 1788 Christ Church's planters paid £402.19.8½ on 68,549 acres. For the same land they would have paid only £159.18.9 in 1783. But while the land tax apparently doubled for many in the lowcountry parishes, it decreased substantially for backcountry settlers on poorer lands. In 1788 settlers in Lexington County paid taxes on 165,148½ acres. In 1783 they would have paid over £385, or almost what the planters of St. Paul and Christ Church combined would have paid at the same rate in 1787 and 1788. In 1788, however, Lexington County's land tax amounted to only £189.16.2, less than half of what it would have been in 1783. The tax on 35,652 acres of land in one district between the Edisto and Savannah rivers amounted in 1787 to a little more than £22. It would have been over £83 in 1783. The change could scarcely have been more drastic. The new law, in the words of one backcountry representative, levied "certainly the most equal [tax] that can be laid, because the rich must pay the chief of the same."[5]

The tax law of 1784 had a political as well as an economic side. Although the representatives Schoepf singled out worked for change, possibly aided by some Charleston radicals, they were not strong enough to push their desires through the legislature. The planters were too well represented. If the rich were now to begin paying the "chief" of the tax, it was because they agreed to pay it. The political side of the issue could have determined the nature of the tax act. The constitution of 1778 required that the Carolina legislature be reapportioned in 1785, "Regard being . . . had to the Number of white Inhabitants and . . . taxable Property." Since the backcountry's population far outnumbered the lowcountry's, and since the inland settlers occupied and farmed a much greater acreage, the planters stood in grave danger of losing control of the legislature if reapportionment was undertaken. Increased taxation was the price planters agreed to pay to justify their political dominance.

However it was achieved, the changed system of taxation represented the only substantial legislative advance made by the non-Charleston areas in 1783 and 1784. Before 1785 backcountry settlers, as well as many in Georgetown and Beaufort districts, were unable to rise above their immediate pressing circumstances to demand other changes. The war left many interior regions physically desolated; many inhabitants were demoralized and probably incapable of considering broad or long-range issues. The burning of houses, the plundering, the often wanton destruction, "so reduced" some people, wrote Patrick Calhoun, a backcountry legislator and tax collector, that they could not "procure even the necessarys of life." William Drayton, traveling in 1784 near the Little Saluda River in the backcountry, described the "miserable dwellings" along the road. In them lived "half naked Beings, almost every one with out shoe or stocking, & amongst them great numbers of children." The year before, Reverend Archibald Simpson had poignantly contrasted the lowcountry region near Georgia with Charleston, where the people "appear to be more happy." In the country, Simpson wrote, "a dark melancholy gloom appears everywhere," and on "almost every countenance" one could see "poverty, want, and hardship." Indeed, he reported, "all society seems to be at an end."[6] Certainly many of the people pictured by Calhoun, Drayton, and Simpson, concerned with living from day to day, could not manage political and constitutional debate or the luxury of protest.

But more than physical needs held back some people and areas. When Simpson described the gloom and end of society, he pointed not only to the distresses caused by the British army as a source of postwar grief but also to the lingering problems caused by a lawless element which "peeled, pillaged, and plundered" the people who had survived the war.[7] Criminal operations in 1783 and 1784 were serious, similar to those described by the Reverend Charles Woodmason after the French and Indian War. William Bratton complained in 1784 that thieves near North Carolina were robbing people "in open daylight" and that they could not be suppressed. Conditions were so bad, he wrote Governor Benjamin Guerard, that "we labour under nearly as much difficulty as when Cornwallis was amongst us." Close by, in Ninety Six District, settlers faced the same marauding. On his trip, William Drayton avoided the fork of the Broad and Saluda rivers because of what he heard about horse thieves. In December 1784 Judge Aedanus Burke was horrified to discover the poor people "half ruined by a sett of horse thieves & an outlying Banditti." The effects were such that "the wretched people are precluded from improving their Estates"; if a man set out on the road with a wagon and a good horse he had little chance to reach Charleston; if he made it to the market, he would be intercepted on the way back. There was no "security for life or property there," Burke wrote, then concluding, painfully, that for the time being he would have no mercy for horse thieves.[8]

Burke thought the crime a direct consequence of the war. War not only inspired men to noble deeds and sentiments but it gave birth also to "a contempt for laws and civil order, a love of pleasure and dissipation." His experiences in the backcountry seemed to justify his fear that man "may be so brutalised as to relish human blood the more he shed of it." Others agreed. Drayton met a landlord who had killed two neighbors and was ready to kill again. "He talk'd as cooly tho' as pleasantly of having murder'd these two," noted Drayton, "as if they had been Bucks or wolves." Such callousness he, too, traced to the war, which "inur'd men to the wanton shedding of Blood & dissolved not only the ties of Friendship & Neighbourhood, but even of Humanity!"[9] Judge John Faucheraud Grimké found people confused by the war; robbery then was considered "justifiable & commendable."[10]

To support their ideas about crime and war, Burke and Grimké told tragic stories. Burke wrote about two criminals. James Booth, sentenced to be hanged for robbery, was "not now twenty years of age." His father and brother had been killed by the enemy. "He himself was an active soldier, behaved well as such & never joined the British." But since 1781 he had been "the terror of the southern parts of this state by his enormities." The jury recommended mercy, "on condition that he would be banished the continent forever." Burke recommended mercy for Samuel Wiggins, who was to hang for horse stealing. He was sixteen, his mother poor, his father dead. Burke believed that the boy had been "debauched into his present unhappy condition'' by the ''disadvantages of extreme poverty'' and a ''family connection'' with the ''Banditti.''[11] Grimké recommended mercy for Robert Lewis, who had ''scarcely attained the age of manhood.'' Lewis, ''a brave & gallant soldier'' who had defended his country, was to be executed for stealing Negroes; his accuser was a man ''who did not favour our Cause.''[12]

Cruelly, the war also made criminals of blacks. Some slaves who had escaped to the British lines and served with them chose at the close of the war not to depart with the British but to stay in what was for many their native land. They had no choice but to live like previous fugitives, as maroons, in fixed communities hidden along the Savannah River, from where they plagued people in two states. Other blacks had not only had a similar taste of freedom but an introduction to warfare and a life of crime like that whites had grown used to. They had ventured out on their own or had been used by the British in raids which frightened and angered Carolinians. Thomas Bee described the work of fifty to one hundred ''Black Dragoons.'' For ten days they had been ''plundering & robbing.'' From the plantation of Mrs. Godins they ''carried off everything they could . . . all her Cattle, Sheep, Hogs [and] Horses.'' For years after the war the ex-slaves continued the thieving, maintaining an isolated but free existence. One black encampment, half a mile long, contained twenty-one houses and land which was farmed.[13] But little is known about the black fugitives. No Burke sketched their lives to win sympathy or mercy for them. No one, however, could doubt stories as sad and as tragic as those told about Lewis, Booth, and Wiggins.

The criminals singled out by Grimké and Burke were young. The crimes they and others committed affected a young population. Precisely what effect the war had had on the population cannot be known because of the lack of adequate prewar and postwar population statistics, but the bitter fighting waged in the backcountry between 1780 and 1782 had taken many lives. Ninety Six District alone, according to one estimate, contained 1,400 widows and orphans at the end of the war. Whether the result of the war, or frontier conditions, there was a sharp contrast between the composition of the backcountry population and that of the lowcountry. In St. Thomas parish in 1790 there were 67 white males under age sixteen and 145 over sixteen. In St. Andrew there were 71 white males under sixteen and 125 over, in St. Stephen 45 under and 81 over sixteen. In no parish in the Charleston District did the males under sixteen outnumber those over sixteen. For the district as a whole, the figures were 5,060 over sixteen and 3,177 under.

In the backcountry, those proportions were reversed. Every county in Camden and Ninety Six districts had more males under sixteen than over. There were 2,535 males under sixteen in Pendleton County and only 2,007 over sixteen. In Laurens County there were 2,270 under sixteen and 1,969 over. In all of Ninety Six District there were 17,165 males under

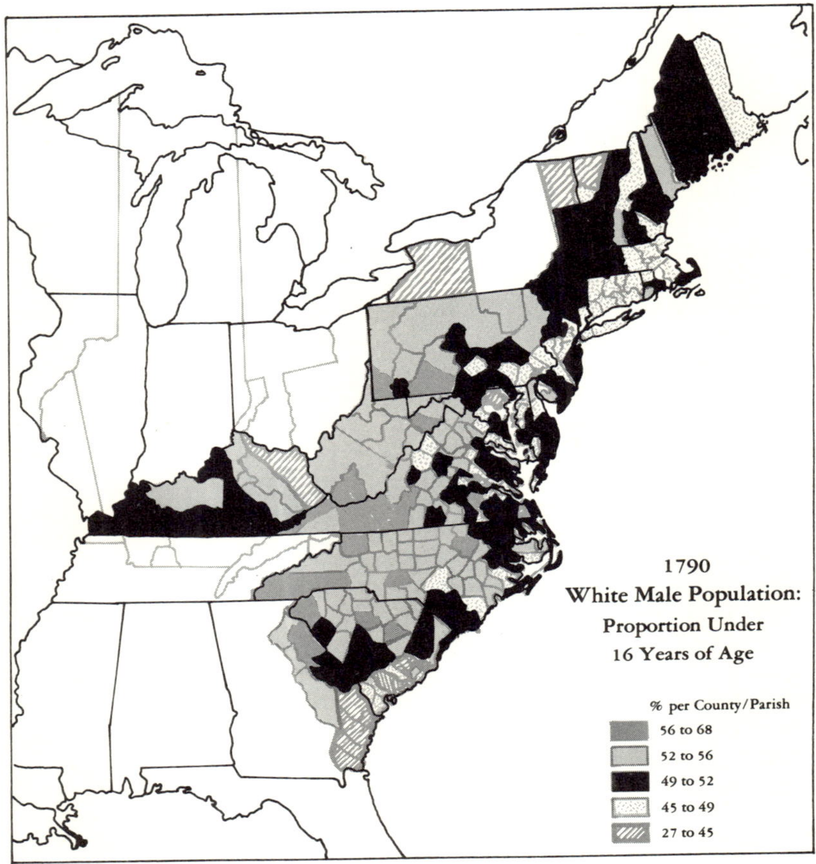

Adapted by permission, Princeton University Press

sixteen. If the proportion of young to old had been the same in Ninety Six as it was in Charleston District, there would have been more than 27,000 males over sixteen instead of the 14,973 who appeared on the census.[14] Perhaps some of the children were useful in the attempt to rebuild, but undoubtedly many in the wartorn regions could neither be adequately provided for nor controlled.

South Carolina's partisan war may have affected its survivors another way. Obviously not all those whose lives had been wrecked turned to crime, not even all those with real needs. But neither did everyone, even those with the opportunity, resume what might be called productive lives. They may have been disheartened and dispirited, perhaps confused or searching in ways they thought best for meaning in life. Or perhaps some had decided that work was unrewarded and idleness was best. Whatever their reasons and whoever they were, and many were undoubtedly new immigrants from other states, they seemed to be standing still and retarding the recovery of the countryside. Faced with similar problems after the French and Indian War, Regulators had taken direct action, whipping lower class people whose morals and lack of industry irritated them. They forced the idle to work. In April 1784 Georgetown's grand jury, fearing the "idle and dissolute" who endanged "the public peace" and by their "pernicious example" corrupted youth, suggested that "the ancient statute laws with respect to idle persons, sturdy beggars, and others of that class" be put in force that they may be whipped publicly, and then sent to their homes "if strangers" or compelled "to labour, if residents." Seven months later Beaufort's grand jury complained about "persons who have no visible means of support."[15]

The physical destruction, the crime, and "the great loss of . . . inhabitants in the late War" produced in some that "dark melancholy gloom" that Reverend Simpson observed. And though Simpson found also "a general discontent, dissatisfaction, and distrust of . . . present rulers," it was an unhappiness which left people too busy, too despairing, or too resigned to challenge their rulers.[16]

But settlers struggled on, and in some places conditions improved. The government tried to deal with the supposed idlers in 1785 by providing for the erection of whipping posts, stocks, and pillories in every county and in 1787 by passing "An act for the promotion of industry, and for the suppression of vagrants and other idle and disorderly persons." Declaring that undesirables had become "such a grievance . . . as to require an immediate remedy," legislators subjected vagrants who could not pay court costs or give one year's security for good behavior to a year's labor, or if no one purchased their services at public auctions, to between ten and thirty-nine lashes and banishment from the county or district. And, to better achieve order and establish a mode of behavior which suited the government and, probably, the more propertied residents, the legislature defined "vagrant" more broadly than in the past. The new definition included not only "all idle, lewd, disorderly men, who have no habitations or settled place of abode, or no visible lawful way or means of maintaining themselves and their families, all sturdy beggars, and all strolling or straggling persons," but also all unlicensed peddlers, all "suspicious persons" who traveled around bartering horses or Negroes without certificates of their good characters, all those who lived by gambling or horse racing, all those who owned land but did not cultivate the quantity officials thought "necessary for the maintenance" of them and their families, all fortune tellers "for fee or reward," all suspicious characters unable to produce certificates of good behavior from officials in counties they had previously resided in, and all persons who earned money by performing on stage.[17]

The state also worked to end lawlessness. Several units of specially raised troops hunted criminals. Troops guarded backcountry jails and at least once were used to prevent trouble when a court was in session. Aedanus Burke wrote in December 1784 that Orangeburg District was "as quiet & secure perhaps as any part of this country," a welcome change from 1778 when Governor Lowndes had pictured "a general panick" there from the actions of "some very desperate villains."[18]

But while Burke described the calm in Orangeburg, Ninety Six District was in turmoil, and people demanded that criminals be dealt with harshly. In 1784 the legislature raised the punishment for those convicted the first time of horse stealing from whipping to death. The change coincided with a request of Ninety Six's grand jury in 1780, but it was not what state constitution writers had in mind in 1778 when they suggested reform of the penal laws and punishments "in some cases, less sanguinary, and, in general more proportionate to the Crime."[19] Between November 1783 and November 1784 juries in Ninety Six sentenced eight people to hang.

All told, between June 1783 and November 1784 courts outside the Charleston area sentenced at least fifteen men to be hanged. But taking into account the youth of the offenders and the conditions which drove them to crime, judges and juries recommended eight to the governor's mercy, sometimes suggesting banishment as a substitute punishment. Six of the eight condemned prisoners in Ninety Six were executed.[20] In most cases, the governor seems to have spared those he was asked to, including Booth, Wiggins, and Lewis. A few were sent off. John McDonald, for example, sentenced to hang for robbery, was shipped to New Providence.[21]

Although there are few extant complaints about criminal activities after 1784, the problem was still serious. In Camden District between November 1786 and November 1789, twelve people were sentenced to hang, seven of them in 1789. Juries, however, recommended seven for the governor's pardon.[22] Ninety Six's continuing troubles were indicated in 1785 when the people around the Little River petitioned for bounties on the heads of criminals.[23]

Runaway slaves were also attacked. Carolina soldiers, with men from Georgia, found and dispersed some blacks along the Savannah River in 1786. But the next year armed Negroes were still raiding the southern part of the state. The government turned to a party of Catawba Indians led by a white officer, and a promise of a £10 sterling reward for each Negro killed or taken, in the fight against the runaways. Apparently no blacks were captured — the reward was for killing or taking — but six were killed, four by the Indians.[24]

New settlers moved into the backcountry also, and perhaps in some areas their numbers and closer settlements discouraged criminals. Virginia's Richard Henry Lee wrote about "alarming" and "powerful emigrations" from Virginia to North and South Carolina and Georgia. The emigrants, he thought, had two wants: "the desire of removing from heavy taxes and the search after land."[25] Land they could certainly get in South Carolina. In 1784 the legislature provided for the sale of old Indian lands in the northwestern part of the state at £10 sterling per 100 acres and of all other state lands at $10 per 100 acres, at the same time stipulating that no person could directly or indirectly buy more than 640 acres. In 1785 the legislature put all lands on sale for $10 per 100 acres; although it later allowed speculators greater opportunities by abolishing the limit of 640 acres, land was still readily available. Between 16 July 1784, when the state began to sell land again, and 1 January 1787, 3,490,645½ acres were granted, a large amount (more than 5,000 square miles) compared to the 2,590,765 acres that Carolinians possessed in 1769.[26]

In 1786 Judge Henry Pendleton told the lower house that the districts of Camden and Ninety Six in particular had become more populous. By 1788 it was estimated that 1,600 people had settled between the old and new boundary line in the northwestern part of the state. In 1789 there were more than enough new people in the western section of the state to justify the creation of two new counties, with representation in the legislature. Greenville and Pendleton counties then contained close to 15,000 white settlers.[27]

Many of the newcomers were poor, and large numbers of them, like many of the older settlers, were unschooled. It was not easy to acquire formal education in the interior. In the early years of the Revolution, when South Carolina was free of fighting, the legislature had tried to encourage the establishment of schools in the backcountry. But the war destroyed those plans and after 1783 there was little money for educational purposes. Educational opportunities were better in Charleston, where newspapers were published, where the educated gathered, and where individuals opened schools to teach a large variety of subjects — one teacher advertised he would offer arithmetic, trigonometry, and navigation — sometimes in the evening.[28]

The backcountry settlers' awkwardness with language and their lack of schooling were often revealed in petitions. In 1787 the inhabitants of Chesterfield and Lancaster counties complained of large surveys of land which "distress[ed] many poor honest families" and which seemed "much more like bondage than fredom and the effects seems like producing a thin settled country and the disadvantage of our stocks loosing our pasturage of lands fit for nothing else." Unable to sign their names, many of the petitioners made their marks. Petitioners from York County "begg[ed] leave to inform your Honours that wee at the earlyest our of the last war with great Brittin wee entred the field of defence of our country where wee plunged throug maney defucultys at the expence of a number of the lives of our brethering & our familys left in a distressed satuation by the enemy. . . ."[29]

Some of these new immigrants, poor and uneducated, seemed idle and dissolute to the more established settlers. The legislature dealt with the real or imaginary threat they posed not only with laws defining vagrancy but also with new voting regulations which, although perhaps not much enforced, were nonetheless usable to curb whatever challenging tendencies newcomers displayed. Disregarding the constitution of 1778, which enfranchised propertied white males resident for one year in the state, the legislature in 1784 increased the residency requirement to three years, although still declaring the new settlers citizens after one year. In 1786 the law was again changed. After one year people became citizens, but the right to vote was not granted until settlers were naturalized by special act of the legislature.[30]

The exercise of force and the judicious use of mercy were probably inadequate by themselves to reduce the numbers of inland criminals and vagrants or to bring hope to backcountry settlers. Perhaps ultimately more important was that after the war the backcountry began to experience an enormous expansion of profitable agricultural activity. Tobacco cultivation, which had been concentrated in Virginia, Maryland, and North Carolina, spread into South Carolina and Georgia. Several Georgians reported in 1781 that tobacco had been cultivated with "the utmost astonishing success" by emigrants from Virginia, an observation supported by Richard Henry Lee. Lee complained that settlers fleeing Virginia's heavy taxes were "unfortunately" spreading "the Cultivation of Tobacco." The Georgians explained that their state's climate and soil were better for tobacco than Virginia's. The longer season and faster growth allowed planters "to produce two good crops in the year."[31] Conditions were similar in South Carolina.

People were excited by the new crop. Thomas Singleton, experienced in the tobacco business, wrote that Carolina tobacco had recently brought a better price in Europe than tobacco from Virginia and concluded that tobacco was "the first staple of this State" or would be "in a short time." Governor William Moultrie was more honest but almost as optimistic when he told the legislature in February 1785 that tobacco would "in a few years be one of our first staples."[32]

By 1786 tobacco, grown extensively in the backcountry, was a major Carolina export. In 1769 the colony had exported 160 hogsheads of tobacco, in 1773, 536 hogsheads. Between November 1783 and December 1784, 2,680 hogsheads were exported; the next year 2,303 hogsheads were shipped out. In 1786, 3,929 hogsheads of tobacco were sent to foreign markets, in 1787, 5,493, and in 1788, tobacco exports totalled 5,993 hogsheads.[33]

Tobacco's importance was indicated by legislative attempts to facilitate the exportation of a quality crop by erecting public inspection warehouses and improving or building roads, clearing rivers, and constructing canals. In 1783 the legislature revived an act of 1771 which had called for the erection of warehouses, where bad tobacco was to be destroyed, at the ports, Charleston, Georgetown, and Beaufort, and on the Savannah River, the Pee Dee River, and near Camden. The next year warehouses were called for at Cheraw Hill, in the north of the state, and at Friday's Ferry on the Congaree, the approximate center of the state. In 1785 Winnsboro was designated as the place for one warehouse, as was each fork of the Edisto River. Still more were provided for in 1786 and 1789, so that a line of warehouses extended across the center of the state from the northeast to the southwest. To bring the warehouses into closer contact with the east an extensive series of internal improvements was planned. The Great Pee Dee River was to be made navigable as far as the North Carolina line, the Wateree as far as Camden, and both forks of the Edisto River as far as was practicable. A road was to be laid out from a ferry on the Congaree to join another road leading to Winnsboro. Companies were incorporated for the building of canals between the Edisto and Ashley rivers and the Santee and Cooper rivers.[34]

As tobacco spread, so did slavery and the plantation system. By 1790 there were 29,094 slaves in the backcountry. The lowcountry contained 78,000 slaves. Twenty-five percent of the backcountry's families owned slaves, an average of 5.93 slaves per slaveholding family. The blacks were not owned just by thousands of small farmers. Twenty percent of the slaves, 6,095, were the property of planters who owned at least thirty slaves each, and over 50 percent, 15,767 slaves, belonged to planters owning ten or more slaves.[35] Tobacco brought slavery and hope to the whites in many sections of the backcountry. It provided settlers with a new source of revenue, and it undoubtedly allowed many to acquire the "necessarys of life."

As backcountry conditions changed, some residents became more demanding. In 1783 and 1784 neither they nor their representatives, some of whom were undoubtedly embarrassed to speak out before the educated residents of the lowcountry, seriously protested legislative policies. In 1785, however, the people around the Little River in Ninety Six District demonstrated a new attitude when, in one petition, they suggested revising the constitution for the people's welfare, moving the seat of the government inland, reapportioning the legislature, since property was "larger represented than the free white inhabitants," recording votes in the legislature, establishing counties, reducing the fees and salaries of the officers on the civil list, and granting rewards for the heads of outlaws ravaging the frontier.[36] As settlers began to speak out, so also did their representatives. Whatever the combination of causes — confidence based on a burgeoning population, inspiration from the widely-reported activities of protesting Charlestonians, a degree of economic recovery, experience — there was a political awakening among the interior's settlers.

One request was quickly fulfilled. In 1785 the state was divided into counties, and county courts, demanded earlier by the Regulators, were established. The constitution of 1778 had called also for creation of such divisions and courts. Justices of the peace, appointed by the legislature, were given several responsiblities: judicial power generally over cases not involving more than £20, jurisdiction over roads, the power to license tavern keepers, and other administrative duties.[37]

The earliest and probably the most important demand was to move the government out of Charleston. In February 1783 a backcountry representative proposed to shift the government to a more central part of the state. Judge Henry Pendleton, representing Saxe-Gotha, agreed, arguing that the government should be fixed where the population was greatest.[38] The proposal was defeated, but the issue came up again in 1785 and 1786.

Removal of the government was partly a matter of convenience for country members, many of whom lived more than 100 miles from Charleston. The trip was uncomfortable, the time away from home potentially ruinous to their economic affairs. Colonel William Hill, who came down from an area bordering North Carolina, complained that gentlemen from inland regions could not afford to spend two or three months early every year in Charleston when they had to be home "to manage . . . rural concerns." If the legislature were to meet in the center of the state, he said, all could attend without such inconvenience.[39]

Lowcountry senators and representatives could not deny the validity of Hill's position, but many probably told themselves, as Edward Rutledge told the lower house, that it was better for country members than town members to be troubled. Rutledge betrayed an air of superiority, hinting that backcountry members would not know when to feel uncomfortable. Since they were accustomed to traveling, "the additional fatigue or trouble of riding 50 or 60 miles farther was not an object worthy of consideration."[40]

What was really at stake was power, and Ralph Izard focused attention on that when he opposed moving to the center of the state, where "the country interest" would be strengthened "in a proportion of four to one." Since changing the seat of government involved no reapportionment, it was clear people knew that the government's location was one factor in determining who exercised power. To an individual forced to decide whether to attend the legislature or not, the discomforts of a trip and sojourn at the capital might have been determining factors; to a section, the sum of all the individual decisions meant power or impotency. Old backcountry settlers may have remembered the Regulators' charge that the lowcountry had defeated a county court bill simply by waiting for country members to tire of Charleston and go home. Charleston area representatives had little trouble attending the legislature. Sometimes, too, their normal advantages of place were enhanced by the calling of special sessions. In 1783 and 1785 "thin" assemblies dominated by the lowcountry met in Charleston to consider vital matters.[41]

Legislators who did appear were influenced by their surroundings. In 1788 Aedanus Burke would charge that "the principle cause" for ratification of the federal Constitution was that the convention met in Charleston, where everyone supported it. Furthermore "the merchants and leading men" kept "open houses" for members of the convention.[42]

In 1785 and 1786 lowcountry representatives and senators defeated attempts to move the Assembly inland. Their arguments ranged from the sound and reasonable to the ridiculous. If one newspaper account can be believed, John Rutledge ran through all kinds, outdoing "his usual outdoings." Rutledge argued once that the lower house could not adjourn to meet anywhere but in Charleston since the Senate had already resolved to hold its next session in the city. The governor and Privy Council would have to take their places someplace in between. How would messages pass back and forth? But other points were more serious. Where would the members reside — and Rutledge might have noted that there were 202 members in the lower house alone — if the Assembly moved inland? Where would the public records be stored?

Ralph Izard's impolitic objections probably reinforced the opinions of backcountry settlers. Izard not only argued that the country interest would be increased but that the move would hurt the legislature by weakening the influence of the lawyers. "It would be neither grateful [n]or just to compel those gentlemen to travel 140 miles," he told the lower house, some of whose members represented people who disliked lawyers almost as much as they disliked Tories.[43]

Rutledge's objection to the lack of facilities was also voiced by Thomas Bee, who worried that sea captains would have to travel inland to pay duties, and Jacob Read, who feared that in the center of the state he could not consult the books he needed to guide his legislative acts. But Rutledge and others not only opposed backcountry demands for an immediate move but also any proposal to prepare for a future removal. If there were no buildings to house the officials, some people thought the legislature should have them built. Rutledge and Bee argued that could not be done until the state was out of debt, when its finances were in order.[44]

In the Senate, John Lewis Gervais, a Charleston merchant concerned with the Indian trade and a representative of the backcountry where he owned land, finally devised a scheme to satisfy the demands for withdrawing from Charleston and yet avoiding the financial objections raised by other members. Gervais shifted the burden of moving onto the people. Commissioners were to divide 640 acres near Friday's Ferry into half-acre lots. Only after money from the sale of one-quarter of these lots came due were the commissioners to contract for the building of a state house. If no one bought the land, the government would remain in Charleston. The bill passed the Senate by a vote of eleven to seven, with the Intendant, Colonel Arnoldus VanderHorst, proposing the name "Town of Refuge," since being situated beyond the pale of justice, men of desperate fortunes would fly to it for asylum. Gervais proposed the name "Columbia," which was adopted.[45]

In the lower house there was some opposition to the location of the town. Thomas Sumter thought the place not high enough in the country (he owned land higher up, in Camden); Edward Rutledge, perhaps reconciled to some ultimate move, recommended a more southerly and easterly spot, the confluence of the Congaree and Wateree. But ultimately, the lower house went along with the Senate. Commissioners were appointed, and work on the town apparently began quickly.[46] Backcountry members at last had won acceptance of the idea that the government should be removed from Charleston and located closer to the people. But the capital was not established at Columbia until after the state adopted a new constitution in 1790.

Simultaneously with suggestions and demands to move the capital, record votes in the legislature, and, as some Charlestonians were arguing, to elect only those who would bind themselves to follow instructions, came another threat to established rulers. Time and again backcountry districts petitioned for a convention of the people to write a new constitution. The pressure in part stemmed from the idea that the state had no real, fixed plan of government. The constitution of 1778, "being only an act of the legislature," was not "founded on proper authority." It was "a temporary fabrication"[47] The reformers rejected David Ramsay's argument that the people had sanctioned the plan of 1778 by their choice of legislators. The need for a convention, they thought, was apparent, because the constitution was repeatedly "set aside" by the General Assembly. It was "too subject to fluctuation," since "the power that creates can at any time annihilate and totally destroy."[48]

Aedanus Burke supplied proof. Pleading for a new alien bill in February 1786, he brushed aside objections that it would be unconstitutional with the curt remark that if it was, it would not mark the first time the Assembly had "broken into" the constitution.[49] The alien bill passed, and proponents of a convention quickly seized on it, and the alien act of 1784, as proof of their contention. "VOX," writing in a Charleston newspaper, stated the obvious: if an act could alter the constitution, then there was no constitution at all.[50]

Other writers, also, argued that the legislature, having altered one part of the constitution, would continue to change other parts. Where then, "EUGENIUS" asked, is our protection "against the *prevalence of the rankest aristocracy?*" Security would lie in a constitution drawn up and ratified "by the people in *full* and *free* convention, solely and for that purpose assembled."[51] Strangely, apparently few people mentioned that the legislature had not been reapportioned in 1785 as the constitution directed.

The first call for a state convention was rejected by the legislature in 1784. In 1785 backcountry forces were better prepared and organized than they had ever been. Inhabitants of the region between the Broad and Catawba rivers requested a revision of the constitution and removal of the government from Charleston. In separate petitions settlers from the Spartan District, York County, the Little River region, and the area between the Broad and Saluda rivers joined in asking for a convention of the people. The lower house responded favorably. It recommended that the people qualified to vote for legislators elect delegates in June 1785 and that the following December the delegates meet to debate means of making the constitution "more consistent with pure republican principles and the equal rights of mankind and fixing it on a more solid and permanent foundation." Any plan evolved by the convention was to be published and circulated among the people, and after six months the delegates were to reconvene and vote on its adoption. In voting, delegates were to adhere strictly to the instructions of their constituents, indicating perhaps that newspaper arguments in favor of binding representatives had made some impression. The Senate, however, defeated the plan.[52]

Year after year, in 1784, 1785, and 1787, backcountry demands were defeated by the upper house, some of whose members feared that their legislative sanctuary would be abolished. The lower house handled that fear in 1785 by recommending "*in the strongest terms,* that the Delegates be not empowered to vote for the abolition of either branch of the Legislature."[53]

But the Senate's opposition stemmed not only from its fear of a one-house legislature but also from a fear of the backcountry. The vote on calling the convention was sectional. In 1787, 11 senators, 8 from the backcountry, 2 from the Charleston area, and 1 from a distant lowcountry parish, favored a meeting of a constitutional convention. They were defeated by one vote. Aligned against them were 9 senators from the lowcountry, 2 from parishes some distance from the Charleston area, and 1 from the backcountry. The vote in the lower house, not nearly as sectional in nature, also indicated where the major force for the convention lay. The backcountry supported the convention by a vote of 56 to 7, the distant lowcountry parishes by a vote of 12 to 6. Representatives from the Charleston area were opposed by a vote of 39 to 25.[54]

Legislators in both houses knew that reapportionment, avoided in 1785, would be a necessary consideration of any convention. In 1786, Judge Henry Pendleton, of Saxe-Gotha, introduced the subject. He proposed changing the basis of representation because "alterations had taken place in this state — both with regard to actual property, and number of inhabitants." Though Camden and Ninety Six had grown substantially, "their representation is still the same."[55] Pendleton's plan to divide the entire state into counties of equal size, each, except for Charleston, to elect one senator and three representatives, and Charleston to elect two and six, would have given the large backcountry control of the General Assembly. "It was due in justice to the citizens," said Pendleton. "They had been promised it by the constitution."

Pendleton's motion touched off an angry debate, which by itself indicated the apprehension of the legislators. Irritated that Charles Cotesworth Pinckney, Judge Thomas Heyward, and Jacob Read were using a technicality of the constitution, according to which alterations could not be made "without a Notice of Ninety Days being previously given," Pendleton urged them not to "shrink" from his proposition. He reminded legislators that his alteration, or one like it, was called for by the constitution.[56]

The constitution notwithstanding, representation was not substantially altered before 1790, when the new state constitution was written. Other legislators agreed with Pinckney that Pendleton's bill unwisely threw elections "into the hands of proprietors of barren acres, instead of persons possessed of real property."[57] Many coastal leaders probably believed not only that property ought to be represented as a matter of self-interest but also that, since superiority was unitary — the wealthy were wise — it was to the state's advantage to grant greater representation to the slave-owning planters of the lowcountry.[58] There was a feeling, too, in 1786 that the legislature should not attempt reapportionment if a constitutional convention was to meet.

Unfortunately for Pendleton, no one could guarantee overcoming Senate opposition to such a meeting. All that remained if the Senate continued its obstruction was something terrible to contemplate, "a sort of convention that he never wished to see, a convention by the people," apparently meaning a convention called without the consent of the existing government.[59]

Aside from sentiment for removal of the capital, reapportionment, a constitution written by a specially called convention and not subject to change by any legislature, and some feeling for a one-house legislature, there was only one other publicized demand. Dr. Thomas Tudor Tucker, writing in 1784 as "PHILODEMUS," objected to the "blending" of the "legislative, judiciary, and executive powers of government in the same individuals." Two years later, "EUGENIUS" noted that neither Massachusetts, New York, New Jersey, Pennsylvania, Delaware, Maryland, Virginia, North Carolina, nor Georgia allowed the same mixing of powers as South Carolina did. Permitting judges to sit in the Assembly, as they had before the Revolution, gave to one person, or class of citizens, too much power, "EUGENIUS" thought. In their capacity as judges, individuals might decide issues arising from laws they had helped to pass or from laws they had fought against.[60] Neither Tucker nor "EUGENIUS," however, described how important judges were. During the 1780s Judge Aedanus Burke was prominent in the legislature. So were judges Henry Pendleton, John Rutledge, John Faucheraud Grimké, Thomas Heyward, Jr., Richard Hutson, and John Mathews. Even Alexander Moultrie, the attorney general, sat in the lower house.

There was considerable support for a stricter separation of the branches of government. Christopher Gadsden thought that "permitting our Judges to sit in the Assembly . . . [had] a natural Tendency to introduce a Confusion of Departments." He complained also that the legislature had "interfer'd too much in the judicial Department."[61] Arguments for separation were stressed most frequently by the Charleston radicals when they complained that city wardens passed laws, enforced them, and tried those accused of violating them. Finally, the constitution adopted by the state in 1790 did provide that no person holding an office or trust from the state or from the United States, with a few exceptions, could be eligible to a seat in the General Assembly.

Outside the legislature and unmentioned by the newspapers, which were most accessible to Charlestonians, there may have been more radical demands. The report of Henry Pendleton's speech did not sufficiently explain his fear of a people's convention except to state that he thought "such an assembly" would be attended by "consequent horrors" and that "another revolution might be expected to follow." Pendleton may have worried that attempts would be made to abolish the Senate since his proposal called only for enlarging the upper house so that "an equal part of the government" would no longer be in "the hands of so small a number of men."[62] But another backcountry representative, Patrick Calhoun, was also apprehensive, because "the general mass of the people were so much bent for a democratical government, that . . . a convention . . . would do more harm than good."[63] Possibly Pendleton and Calhoun, and others who opposed or only reluctantly supported a constitutional convention, were reacting to the harsh rhetoric in the Charleston newspapers in 1784 and 1785, reading in radical proposals where none were made. But perhaps to Pendleton and Calhoun more was implicit in backcountry calls for a new constitution written by a new body. Backcountry representatives were asking only for changes that would have altered the balance of power between east and west, leaving, however, most of the same people in office. New settlers might have pushed for more. Many had come from Pennsylvania or Virginia, states with more democratic provisions for voting and officeholding, only to find themselves first without the right to vote for three years and then disenfranchised until the legislature saw fit to declare them full citizens of South Carolina. They might well have sought to abolish or lower the property qualifications for voting and officeholding, as well as the residency requirement for officeholding. Probably few were disenfranchised by the fifty-acre property requirement for voters, but all were affected by the provision that no man could be a senator unless he had been resident in the state for five years or a representative unless in the state for three. And most people were removed from consideration by the provisions that representatives had to own "settled" plantations and ten slaves each or property worth £2,000.

Although the backcountry did not force many changes through the legislature in the 1780s, there were important developments. No matter where the votes came from, the new tax system of 1784 was a gain for the interior. So was the creation of counties and county courts in 1785. Just as important was the victory of 1786, which, although not immediately followed up, secured legislative approval for moving the government inland. The meaning of that decision was emphasized the next year when the Senate voted against calling a constitutional convention. Only two of Charleston District's thirteen senators were absent when the vote was taken. Those present voted nine to two against the proposal. Four senators from the backcountry and distant lowcountry parishes were missing. Nine of the twelve present favored the convention.[64] A move to the interior would almost certainly affect future votes.

In general, the future seemed promising to some of the inland settlers. Recovering from the effects of the war, many inhabitants of the area began to make serious requests. They petitioned the legislature, presented their grievances when meeting in grand juries, and elected representatives and senators whose willingness to speak out seemed to increase with their experience. The Charleston area managed to retain control without making too many concessions or bowing too frequently to outside pressure. But that it could do so forever was doubtful. Not only were there vocal opponents in Charleston, in addition to those inland, but there was an economic crisis which threatened their power. The backcountry was growing populous and developing an important crop, while the lowcountry was growing poor. The combination was full of hope for some and despair for others.

EIGHT
The Triumph of British Commerce

> Much do I fear that the early pages of our history will be sullied by an unbecoming greediness for property, — that property that, as a great and generous people, we should disdain to touch.
>
> Pierce Butler, 4 February 1784.

> When instead of unanimity prevailing, . . . planters and merchants are endeavoring to get rich at the ruin of the other, how can this or any other country so situated, expect to prosper. . . .
>
> *Charleston Morning Post and Daily Advertiser,* 21 August 1786.

ITH enthusiasm and energy, many citizens of the state began in 1783 to erase the scars of battle. Ralph Izard, told that his house was "in a very ruinous condition," planned to import a carpenter and builder from London, to have the bricks of his house "rubbed from the top . . . to the bottom," the "interstices new pointed," and "to have a Piazza in each Front, & an Area sunk." "All ranks of men think of little else than repairing their losses," wrote Pierce Butler, impressed by the "bustle and activity" at Charleston's wharves. To another Charlestonian it seemed that Carolinians had completely turned their thoughts "from war to commerce." Every day people formed "schemes of business & partnerships for extending commerce."[1]

Many people, released so recently from the hardships and deprivations of war, turned their thoughts not only to money-making, nor to plans for repairing the physical damage visible in town and country, but also to rebuilding the lighter, more social side of their lives.[2] They sought familiar pleasures and luxuries. Before the break with England, the prosperous Carolinians had filled their leisure time with entertainment and sports. Subscription balls, concerts, and the "New Theatre" had provided public entertainment; clubs and private societies — there were more in Charleston before the war than in any other American city — brought together people with similar interests. Numerous dancing instructors shared pupils with music teachers. Horse racing was popular, the Carolina Jockey Club, founded in 1758, running three races, with purses as high as £1,000.[3]

Though the war and its aftermath inevitably forced Carolinians to curtail their social activities — even exchanging family visits was made more difficult in some areas by the destruction or disappearance of horses and carriages — people did not lose their acquired tastes, their desire for culture, sport, and an active social life. As quickly as possible after regaining Charleston, Carolinians began again their entertainments. In May 1783 the Charleston theater reopened with Thomas Otway's *The Orphan; or the Unhappy Marriage,* the play which had opened the theater in 1735.[4] The St. George's Hunting Club, which included such stalwart members of the upper class as Ralph and Walter Izard, William Moultrie, and William Blake, met on the first Saturday of every month to enjoy barbecued lamb or shoat, beef, ham, turkey, fowls, and wine, rum and brandy, as well as "Pipes & Tobacco or 100 Segars."[5]

Horse racing was not immediately reintroduced — perhaps the war had destroyed the state's best horses — but by the beginning of 1785 the Newmarket races were being run. In 1786 many of the members of the St. George's Hunting Club formed a Jockey Club "for the encouragement of a good breed of Horses in this State." The Club intended to race members' horses every December. Individuals not connected with any club but interested in improving breeds could learn from newspapers that Brilliant, or Prisont, or some equally fine horse, was covering that season at only seven guineas a mare.[6]

With considerable wonder, postwar visitors to South Carolina frequently commented on the excessive drinking. Timothy Ford, a native of New Jersey who made a new home in South Carolina, after granting that the gentlemen of the state were as sociable as any he had ever met, nevertheless remarked that they were "generally very dissipated." In 1784, a year before Ford arrived, Johann David Schoepf noticed the many young, rich widows whose late husbands, because of their "incautious use of spiritous drinks," had died "in the bloom of their years."[7] That year Carolinians imported 38,561 gallons of Spanish wine, 153,558 gallons of Jamaican rum, 44,314 gallons of gin, 1,968 barrels of porter, 36,297 gallons of Portuguese wine, 17,424 gallons of brandy, and 24,841 gallons of French wine. Some of it they drank at the "Musical and Dancing Assemblies, . . . Smoking Clubs, Ugly Clubs, and Rabbit Societies" described by one critic, and at the "Evening Entertainments in the State House" mentioned by another critic, who denounced the growth of luxury and dissipation.[8]

Carolinians impressed numerous observers with their extravagance and conspicuous consumption. "Luxury in Carolina has made the greatest advance," wrote Schoepf, and "everything denotes a higher degree of taste and love of show, and less frugality than in northern provinces." In 1788 Reverend Thomas Reese, who had lived in South Carolina before the war, concluded that Carolinians were "seized with a general emulation to surpass each other in every article of expence." That "love of show" was frowned on by Timothy Ford, who found people of "the higher classes" unable to "act or move without an attending servant."[9]

Resuming their prewar life styles, Carolinians with cash or credit imported luxury items to replace those lost during the fighting and plundering. But more than luxuries entered the port. Slaves, dry goods, merchandise of all kinds came. Imports in 1783 were relatively low in value, probably because of the large amount of goods the remaining British merchants had on hand and also because other merchants had yet to receive orders from England. That year imports were worth approximately £300,000. But in 1784 trade in general increased. Incredibly the value of the merchandise and slaves entering the port between 1 January and 31 December 1784 totaled over £1,000,000 and may even have amounted to as much as £1,500,000 sterling. The slaves, 4,922 of them, at an average value of £50 each, were worth £246,100. Some merchandise — dry goods and some luxury items — paid a 2½ percent duty when shipped into South Carolina, and, on the basis of duties noted in the Treasury books, it was estimated a few years later that that merchandise of 1784 had a value of £718,931.1.8. The tea, coffee, pimento, Dutch and British refined sugar, liquor, wine, playing cards, and all other items not paying a flat 2½ percent duty were valued at £103,983. In addition to this £1,069,014 worth of imports, goods grown, produced, or manufactured in other American states entered South Carolina duty-free and hence in untotaled amounts.[10]
amounts.[10]

After the banner year of 1784 importations decreased steadily, in 1785 to about £600,000 and in 1786 to less than £400,000.[11] Nevertheless, between 1783 and the end of 1786, the imports probably totaled more than £2,500,000.

Satisfying the state's needy and conspicuous consumers promised to be profitable for merchants, manufacturers, and shippers, a commercial group potentially larger and geographically more widespread in 1783 and 1784 than it had been in prewar years. No longer had Americans to import goods only in British or colonial ships; no longer was it illegal to receive manufactured products directly from continental Europe. South Carolina's trade was open to the world.

The world, however, remained largely uninterested or incapable of capitalizing on the opportunity. Trade continued mostly in the hands of the English merchants and shippers who had controlled it when the independent state had been a dependent colony. So completely did the British dominate the state's commerce immediately after the war that Aedanus Burke called those postwar days "the sunshine harvest of British commerce, policy, and influence." The British had planted "a standing army" of traders "who out-manoeuvre, under-sell, and frighten away the French and Dutch."[12] In 1785 "A RISING CLOUD" charged that some seamen, probably British, boarded Dutch vessels and beat, insulted, and reviled the captains for "daring to trade amongst us." Two years later, Charleston merchants despairingly reported that British merchants were so

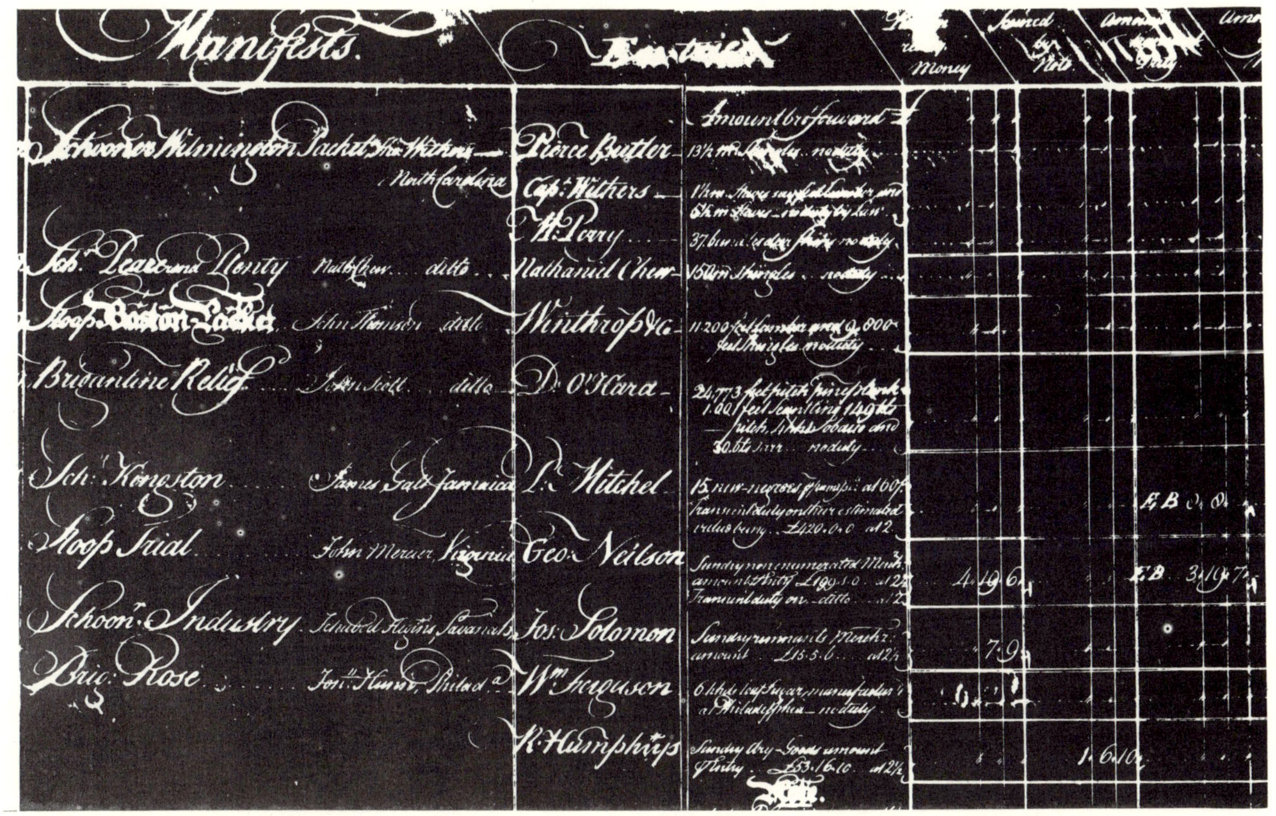

From a page of manifests and entries, 24 May 1784. *Courtesy, South Carolina Department of Archives and History.*

numerous that one might think oneself in Scotland. And, they thought, the British merchants dominating the state's trade would tighten their hold and push ahead, leaving "no means unessayed to Continue and confirm our Bondage."[13]

In the absence of legal Parliamentary restrictions, financial arrangements, knowledge, habit, and the policies of other nations confined the state's trade to old channels. South Carolina's trade, like that of other agricultural states, depended on credit. Planters pledged the coming season's crops for the merchandise they bought. Under this system their debts could, and frequently did, mount up to huge sums. In 1776 Carolinians owed British merchants over £400,000 sterling.[14] But the rice and indigo crops were of such potential value that merchants risked losing bad debts in the hopes of reaping substantial profits.

In 1783, to an even greater extent than in prewar years, Carolina planters needed credit. "When the war ended," wrote David Ramsay, "planters found desolate plantations and very few laborers." So they were "compelled to contract debts." Great Britain's Lord Sheffield, not referring to South Carolina in particular, put the case more forcefully. Whereas, he thought, before the war four-fifths of the importations from Europe had been made upon credit, "undoubtedly the States are in greater want of credit at this time than at former periods."[15] He was right. In debt from years past, planters had not been able to market substantial crops during the war. And before they could look forward to ample crops, they had to purchase the slaves and necessities to repair their plantations.

Despite the sizable colonial debt and its accumulating interest, English merchants rushed in after the war. They capitalized on their ability and willingness to supply Americans with large amounts of credit. More than any other factor, the extended credit made certain England's dominance of South Carolina's commerce.[16] Dutch businessmen gave credit on a far more restricted scale. They screened their applicants more carefully than the English and favored only reliable individuals. Pierce Butler put his finances in order by negotiating, in person, a private loan in Holland. Alexander Gillon offered to secure such a loan for Christopher Gadsden, presumably at a time when they had friendly words for each other. But it was simply "not the custom of the Dutch to give credit," Lord Sheffield reminded his readers, except "on the best security." And the French, Lord Sheffield added, who had given Americans credit during the war, "are all bankrupt."[17] The extended hands of the British merchants gathered in the trade.

That their customers were creatures of habit helped the English. Because of "prejudices . . . imbibed with our Milk," Carolinians continued to look first to British manufactures.[18] One newspaper writer, however, thought that "the taste of prejudice" for English goods was overrated, because England itself imported the merchandise it sold in South Carolina. So, believing that it was "not an *English store,* but a *cheap store* that is most frequented," he listed those goods which could be imported less expensively from Portugal, France, Germany, and Holland than from England.[19] But he neglected to mention that Carolinians needed not a cheap store but one that sold on credit.

The English benefited, too, from their own long experience in the Carolina trade. It was true, Collector George Abbott Hall wrote in December 1784, that "the United Netherlands, Hamburgh and Sweden have had several ships here," but from ignorance they had shipped goods that could not be sold.[20] To lack of knowledge about the Carolina trade, French competitors of Great Britain added another handicap—sheer folly. Not one respectable French house had been established in the state. The French had conducted their business through a set of "needy Adventurers" who imported the "refuse" of French manufacturers.[21]

The traffic in people, in Ramsay's words, "the infamous African trade," typified South Carolina's postwar trade. Slaves were both conspicuous luxuries and necessities. Stationed around the dinner table "like a cohort of black guards" to be called "upon the slightest occasion," they identified gentlemen.[22] But for most, slaves were more than signs of wealth; they obviously created wealth, working swampy rice plantations and more healthy indigo lands. Not only had the plantations been hurt by the war, but the slaves had been thinned out. Large importations were needed to replace the "upwards of 20,000" lost. Not until those Negroes were replaced, wrote George Abbott Hall, would "the produce of this Country . . . be equal to what it was formerly."[23] The pace of the slave trade quickened after 1783, when only 1,100 Negroes were imported. Close to 5,000 slaves were imported in 1784, and, sold at an average of £50 each, they cost Carolinians almost £250,000.[24]

Lord Sheffield predicted the course of the African trade. Though northern states would attempt to supply slaves, Great Britain's "decided superiority" in obtaining them "one sixth cheaper" would be one determining factor throwing the lucrative business to British merchants.[25] Another factor would be the ever-present credit. Hall traced all the Africans back to the British, apparently forgetting to note one French slaver. In 1785 and 1786 the British faced mild competition from other countries. A few "American Guineamen," including one captained by Robert Champlin of Newport, Rhode Island, who had delivered cargoes of Negroes to Charleston before the Revolution, and some Dutch vessels new to the American slave trade, arrived with blacks.[26] Nevertheless, the British maintained their dominance of the trade.

Soon after the departure of the British troops, Charleston became a buyer's marketplace. British merchants at first could advance prices considerably by the immediate sale of their stock, since needy Carolinians "made purchases at any price on credit." The merchants, Timothy Ford wrote, "failed not to take advantage . . . and advance[d] upon them from 50 to 75 pr. Cent.''[27] But their initial advantage was quickly lost. By May 1783, just five months after the evacuation, prices had fallen. ''Vessels from almost every quarter are daily droping in, two & three of a day,'' Pierce Butler wrote, so that merchandise was ''as cheap as . . . ten years ago.'' Josiah Smith, a partner of a prewar Charleston firm, and again in business, confirmed Butler's observations. He complained of ''a great glut'' of goods, ''by which very loosing sales will be made.'' In July, Smith reported that imports were sold at ''a great loss,'' and conditions were getting worse, for ''within these 20 days we have had about a dozen sail of vessels from Holland, London, Bristol & Hav[re]. . . .''[28]

If conditions were bad in 1783 for merchants, they were probably worse in 1784, when the quantity and value of the state's imports increased rapidly. Merchants then must have had more goods on hand than in May 1785, when, after importations had begun to decrease in volume and value, a Charleston merchant reported that business was ''very dull indeed.'' Merchants were ''much overstocked with all kinds of Manufactured Goods.''[29]

The slave trade shared the fate of all South Carolina's commerce. Slaves had sold for £90 each in 1783, but by 1785 the price had fallen sharply to between £25 and £30 cash, or £60 on a credit of twelve months.[30]

The enormous demand created by years of war and destruction gave the merchants great hopes for financial success; but their wished-for gains did not immediately materialize. They partly defeated themselves. Probably no merchant wanted to reduce his importations drastically unless guaranteed that other merchants would similarly cut theirs. It was a vicious cycle which forced prices down.

The fate of the merchants, however, was not all of their own making. The legislature had fostered competition among merchants by extending the time allowed the British to remain in the state and by granting many of them the rights of citizenship. And it had also generously decided that court cases involving aliens should be tried with juries that included equal numbers of citizens and aliens. The planters knew what they were doing.

When the admission of British merchants precipitated demonstrations in 1783, ''A PATRIOT'' denounced the mob action because it would hurt commerce, and because no one, or no group, was ''to say what person, and how many, shall be permitted to trade in the State.'' The people, through the legislature, would determine ''for whose advantage, and not that of an individual, or small circle of merchants, trade is to be encouraged and accomodated.'' Christopher Gadsden, ''A STEADY AND OPEN REPUBLICAN,'' although originally siding with native merchants, said more briefly what ''A PATRIOT'' meant when he censured the disorders of 1784. Let foreigners import as much as they wanted to, said Gadsden, for the more they imported the cheaper goods would be.[31]

The earlier experience of the planters and merchants demonstrated the truth of Gadsden's argument. In 1765 Robert Wells, a Charleston printer, had noted that planters were getting rich but merchants were complaining, mostly, he thought, because of "the too great number of Traders." Competition in the slave trade benefited the planters. In June 1773 the market was glutted with Guineamen, "no less than sixteen sail now in port." If planters waited a few weeks, wrote Josiah Smith, they would be able to "pick & choose the prime men at £50 stg. & perhaps less."[32]

Along with low import prices, planters received high prices for their crops. When Gadsden spoke in favor of allowing foreign merchants a share of Carolina's commerce, he examined both sides of the state's trade. Not only did a large number of merchants almost certainly guarantee large quantities of imports and low prices, but it guaranteed also competition for the purchase of the planters' crops. Pierce Butler had seen the connection. Imports were low in price because of the daily arrival of vessels, and "produce [was] in consequence very high." Again Butler was supported by Josiah Smith: "our country produce continues very high, while that of other countries are parted with to a great loss. . . ." The price paid for Carolina's crops, agreed Jacob Read in the state's lower house, to a great degree depended on the availability of shipping.[33]

The value of rice, South Carolina's most valuable crop, at least partially substantiated the beliefs of planters and merchants. Between 1761 and 1770 the average annual price for a hundredweight of rice had ranged from 4.8 shillings to 9.3 shillings. The prewar high was 11.7 shillings in 1772, the only year in which the price had exceeded 10 shillings. In 1783 Pierce Butler, after commenting on the number of vessels in port, noted that rice "is in great demand here at 13s. & from that to 14s. cash, paid even before delivery." In 1784, the year of the great importation, which brought ship after ship to South Carolina, rice sold at an average price of 15.4 shillings, the highest price in the staple's long history.[34]

The cost of freighting the crop to market also fluctuated partly in relation to the amount of shipping available. The greater the number of vessels in port, the lower shipping costs tended to be. During the Stamp Act crisis, clearance papers could not legally be issued and ships massed in the harbor. When Governor Bull was finally persuaded to open the port with permits instead of stamps, freight rates declined to unheard of figures; so low were they that Henry Laurens thought the rice planters had "gained a vast ascendant over the British owners and fairly turned the edge of the stamp tax upon them." The planters' awareness of the relationship between ships and freight prices was apparent in the 1780s. They feared then that if the Confederation Congress were given the power to pass navigation acts by a simple majority vote, New Englanders would raise freight rates by excluding British ships from the American carrying trade. They could also offer less for the crops.[35]

Unexpectedly, but fortunately for the planters, the attraction of hundreds of vessels to Charleston had one more beneficial effect: it made less serious a disadvantage in the marketing of crops which the planters, in the months immediately after the war, did not foresee — the disadvantage caused by the partial loss of the West Indian market and the total loss of the Portuguese market.

The number of vessels available to Carolinians depended not only on how much merchandise the colony imported, but also on the possibilities of marketing rice in Europe and the West Indies. Before the war, usually more than half of Carolina's rice crop was shipped to Great Britain, and then reshipped to ports in northern Europe. Some rice went directly to Portugal and other areas of southern Europe, and a large amount went to the British West Indies. In 1771, 130,000 tierces of rice had been exported, 73,000 tierces to England and then to northern Europe, 27,000 to southern Europe, the foreign West Indies, and some North American ports, and the remainder, 30,000 tierces, to the British West Indies.[36] Both the British West Indies and Portugal, the largest market in southern Europe for Carolina's rice, were valuable markets for the colony's exports.

The West Indian market in particular seemed important to Carolinians. Josiah Smith reported in 1772 that West Indian traders had pushed the price of rice too high for European shippers to bid. And the next year, too, Smith wrote that the continuance of rice at the same high price depended entirely on the West Indies, "as no European market will support such a heavy purchase."[37]

The state's trade with the British West Indies and Portugal changed drastically after the close of the Revolutionary War. On 2 July 1783 the British closed their islands to American shipping except during periods declared to be emergencies by the governors of the islands. The West Indies could import Carolina rice but only in British ships. Before the war vessels from the American colonies had been the major suppliers of the West Indies because, as one British merchant explained, Americans "time things better than we and go to markett cheaper."[38]

After July 1783 shipments of rice from Carolina to the West Indies decreased rapidly. Between January and November 1783, when the limited crop of 1782 was exported, only 2,494½ barrels of rice out of a total of 24,224½ barrels went to the islands. Not much more was shipped there the next year. Of the 61,974 barrels exported in 1784, only 2,678½ barrels, less than one-twentieth of the crop, was destined for the islands. In 1771 more than one-fifth of the rice crop had been shipped there.[39]

The planters suffered another loss in 1783 when Portugal prohibited the importation of Carolina rice. Distressed, Pierce Butler, claimed to be unsurprised: Portugal was "little better than a province of Britain." Besides, he thought it to Portugal's interest to encourage the culture of rice in Brazil. Four years later Ralph Izard was urging Thomas Jefferson to secure a commercial agreement with Portugal since "Lisbon used to take from us annually 20,000 barrels, and now there is none sent there, which is a considerable disadvantage to us."[40]

Although independence cost the Carolinians much of their market in the West Indies, and all of it in Portugal, it freed merchants from pre-Revolutionary shackles and allowed them to trade directly with the countries of northern Europe. While British ships after the war continued to transport rice to Europe via England, the state's direct trade with northern Europe became increasingly important. In 1783, 8,783 barrels of rice went to England and about 4,600 barrels were shipped from the state to northern European countries. England received 25,417 barrels in 1784, but more than 18,000 barrels were shipped directly to northern Europe.[41]

It took time, however, before Carolinians could take full advantage of their freedom. They had to find new markets and competent foreign traders to handle their crops. The biggest immediate disappointment was the failure to make a sizable inroad in the French market, either in the West Indies or in France. In 1784 the French West Indies took only 2,583 barrels. Like England, France placed restrictions on trade with her islands.[42] George Abbott Hall, the Charleston collector, reported in 1784 that France had "as yet had little or no Trade with this State." Brailsford and Morris, the Charleston business firm, thought France a better market for South Carolina's rice and tobacco than England but complained that because "the greater part of our Shopkeepers" were natives of Great Britain, and because the British merchant allowed more liberal advances than the French, England got 1,000 barrels of produce for every 100 sent to France.[43] By 1789, when more exports were sent to France than in any previous year, trade between the countries seemed to be firmly established. In March Brailsford and Morris reported that "no less than thirteen sail of Vessels" had left for France, and they expected "as many more will follow before the shipping Season is over." They were pleased with "this turn of our Trade," as they were also with the shipment of "considerable Exports to the German, Holland, and Spanish Markets."[44]

It mattered little, however, in the two years after the evacuation of Charleston, what new areas were open to Carolina's trade, for planters, because of small crops, did not have enough to export. Consequently, they found themselves deep in debt. In 1783 and 1784 goods valued at more than £1,500,000 sterling were imported. Exports for those years were worth approximately £640,000, leaving Carolinians with a sizable deficit of at least £860,000. In any reckoning of their debt, Carolinians had to include more than £400,000 owed from prewar days with its interest as well as the debt they contracted by purchasing goods from British merchants remaining in Charleston. John Lewis Gervais, President of the Charleston Chamber of Commerce, maintained that those goods sold "at an amazing advance," creating an additional debt of about £1,000,000.[45]

Though few people in 1785 agreed on the specific amount owed merchants, most thought that their fellow citizens were in serious financial difficulties. The country, wrote John Lloyd, "is in a very alarming situation."[46] For more than two years the state had presented to visitors an outward appearance of enormous prosperity: vessels daily crowded the wharves of the South's greatest port; merchants imported fantastic amounts of goods. The tonnage of ships leaving Charleston increased steadily. Between November 1783 and November 1784, 50,961 tons of shipping left Charleston. During the next twelve months, 56,162 tons of shipping cleared the port. Compared with prewar years, Charleston looked impressively active. Between 1768 and 1772 the average yearly clearance had amounted to only 31,000 tons.[47]

The bustle and activity were misleading. By 1785 it was clear that merchants had overextended credit, and that the debt of the Carolinians to them, amounting at least to £2,000,000 sterling, could not be paid off within any reasonable time. Governor William Moultrie therefore summoned a special session of the legislature for September 1785. He placed before the legislators "such matters as . . . have become oppressive and tend[ed] to opperate against the happiness and the very being of the People." The "matters" were economic: the want of a circulating medium and the "situation between Creditor and debtor," a situation which, the governor declared, would lead inevitably to the transfer of "the whole property of a large part of your own Citizens, into the hands of Aliens," unless they could "alleviate the Evil." Moultrie's address was an obvious demand for legislation to protect the state's debtors. "Ruin is now pendent over the heads of hundreds."[48]

The legislature was not surprised by the governor's bleak address. Forecasts of gloomy days had begun as early as 1784. "For God's sake," one Englishman had pleaded, "check the career of that ruinous credit which . . . will ultimately bring down the destruction of the planters!" In July 1785, a London resident warned a Carolina relation to be on guard against bills of exchange drawn by Carolinians, for many had been "Protested of late." Ominously he added, "the Credit of Carolina is very bad indeed."[49] Henry Laurens, no less pessimistic, believed that the country, "already overwhelmed with debt, will sink deeper and deeper by excessive importations."[50] Though not everyone agreed with Laurens's vision of the future, few denied the accuracy of his portrayal of South Carolina in 1785. It was truly a state "overwhelmed with debt."

Despite the gloom which a knowledge of economic facts imposed on some, the planters were not in immediate danger. Though they were liable for enormous debts, many managed to continue to live comfortably, enjoying the luxuries they had known. But for their comfort after 1785, these Carolinians depended on their senators and representatives. They sought the protection of their legislature and they were not to be disappointed. Indeed, their actions justified the remark of one sarcastic newspaper writer. Without reference to export or import figures or estimates of debt or to the almost equally bad conditions in other states, he described the state's condition in 1785: "If we are undone," he wrote, "we are the most splendidly ruined of any nation in the universe. . . ."[51]

NINE
Debtor Legislation

> The advantage that men of rank, dignity, and wealth take . . . to avoid paying . . . their debts is in the highest degree scandalous. . . .
>
> John Lloyd, 15 April 1786.

> By this Law you have been defrauded of your Just due — Defendants in all Cases availing themselves of this most unjust Act of our Interested Men in Power, who are determined on keeping their Possessions at every Hazard. . . .
>
> Joshua Ward, 28 March 1787.

ALLED to "alleviate the Evil" oppressing the state in September 1785, the special session of the legislature faced a breakdown of law, order, and the rules of commerce. In May people of Camden District prevented the judge of the Court of Common Pleas from conducting trials for the recovery of debts. Months before, in September 1784, Colonel Hezekiah Maham temporarily solved his own financial trouble with the initiative that had won him fame and honor during the Revolutionary War. Taking "wrath" when a sheriff's deputy served him legal processes, he gave "the deputy the alternative of eating four copies of the Writs or of being instantly put to death." The deputy ate the writs, "the entreaties of bystanders" earning the "poor man something liquid to help him to swallow." Judge Aedanus Burke blamed Maham for spreading "rapidly the confusion" in the state and charged him also with establishing the "mischievous precedent" that the "Laws and Government may be set at defiance by a powerful citizen. . . ."[1] Others, too, saw a precedent, wondering now where a writ could "be served or an execution . . . levied but in Charleston," or worrying, as Judge Henry Pendleton did, that opposition to civil law would soon "poison the fountain of criminal jurisdiction, which would be a complete overthrow of the government."[2]

Like Maham, many citizens had serious economic problems. One lowcountry legislator, having promised to pay part of his debt in 1785, lost "all thoughts of payment," his creditor's agent wrote, "as he had lost the whole of his last year's crop."[3] Crop failures or unexpectedly small crops were common in 1783 and 1784. Some difficulties might have been anticipated as a result of the war. Plantations had to be rebuilt and laborers found. During the war, for example, the planters of St. John Berkeley lost almost half the 1,400 slaves they had owned in 1774. Everyone knew that the slaves lost—20,000 according to George Abbott Hall's estimate—had to be replaced before agricultural production could return to prewar levels. Carolinians, however, imported fewer than 10,000 slaves between 1783 and 1786.[4]

And, unpredictably, the weather disappointed planters. "Misfortunes love a train," wrote David Ramsay. "Unfavorable seasons and . . . desolating freshets" disappointed Carolinians. In 1784 first a drought and then heavy rains affected crops; in 1785 someone reported that there had been "no crops last year from our planters, and very little hopes this year." Even after the special session met, disasters continued. In September "great Rains and high Winds" ruined crops. In 1786 heavy rains swept away bridges, destroyed indigo vats, and left the area around the Santee River in a "melancholy" state.[5]

For a few years after the war crops were only half the size they had been in the 1770s. In 1783, when the crop of 1782 was marketed, only 24,225 barrels of rice were exported. The next year, the first full year of production, 61,973 barrels were shipped out, in 1785, 63,713 barrels, and in 1786, 65,858 barrels. In 1773 and 1774 the exports of rice had averaged 129,000 barrels a year. Crops as consistently small as those after the Revolution had not been marketed since the 1740s. Indigo suffered a similar fate. The crops of 1783 and 1784 together were less than the crop shipped out of the colony in 1775. "For two years running," wrote the Charleston firm of Gervais and Owen, "the crops of indigo [had] failed. . . ."[6]

Usually, the failure of one season's crop bothered planters little, because merchants continued to extend credit. In a strange way, indebtedness sometimes benefited planters by assuring them of ready purchasers for their crops. Josiah Smith reported that Carolina merchants were often forced to purchase crops on bad terms, paying planters "a great part in cash, that they may thus secure their past year's debt." If merchants offered too little, debtors would deal elsewhere, "for tis now a common thing," wrote Smith before the war, for our planters to trade "only where they are most humour'd."[7]

Planters and merchants sometimes complained of the use or misuse of credit, but everyone understood that only its extension allowed trade to be carried on in South Carolina. Continued crop failures, and large importations throughout America, however, disrupted the normal commercial arrangements. In 1785 English newspapers reported that Americans would need at least four years to pay for the goods imported since the end of the war. By the summer of 1784 some British suppliers who had overextended credit could not extricate themselves from financial difficulties. On one day in August 1784 "five great American houses" in London fell, one losing £140,000 sterling. From 1 January 1785 to the last day in December there were 509 bankruptcies in London.[8]

Carolinians, who had amassed a postwar debt of more than £1,500,000 and had not paid off their prewar debts, contributed to England's economic woe; they were, in turn, affected. Threatened English houses pressured the merchants whom they had supplied, and the merchants passed the pressure on to their debtors. Trade suffered, and merchants and planters found themselves at odds, frequently in court.

Governor William Moultrie greeted legislators in September 1785 with a plea that they not allow "the power of the Law" to operate, for if it did the property of a large number of Carolinians would pass to aliens. Disaster, he said, "has become General. It is not confined to one or two families, but exists throughout the State, a few, very few excepted." Legislators agreed. John Julius Pringle, speaker of the lower house, spoke of the necessity of preserving "the majority of the state"; Aedanus Burke remarked simply that "the people would not suffer" creditors to sue debtors. Outside the legislature Henry Laurens wrote that "debtors are here the great majority. . . ."[9]

Only Thomas Bee and Richard Hutson dissented from those descriptions, Bee questioning at least part of the state-wide catastrophe. He was not convinced that money was scarce.[10] Bee's skepticism notwithstanding, economic distress of one sort or another was widespread. Backcountry tax collectors reported that it was "out of the power of man to collect the tax," and that some of "the poorer, distressed sort of people . . . seem[ed] willing to pay" but had no circulating medium.[11] Making payments between 1784 and the beginning of 1787, for example, settlers in the District Eastward of the Wateree paid £1,252 on their 1784 tax but only £127 on their 1785 tax. People between the Broad and Catawba paid £979 for 1784 and £175 for 1785.[12] But the reduced payments probably reflected more than a lack of currency. Some backcountry residents had purchased more than they could pay for. Indigo was grown in part of the territory east of the Wateree, and the indigo crops had failed. Tobacco was grown there also, and some planters may have been optimistic enough about the crop's future to buy slaves on credit, only to be caught in the general financial crisis. Many backcountry settlers, however, probably owed little to private creditors because their ability to borrow or buy on credit was limited.

Yet the urgency of the financial situation, the unanimity of lowcountry legislators not known for their sympathies with backcountry settlers, stemmed from the seriousness of the lowcountry problem. The distress of the lowcountry planters was apparent in their tax returns. Between 1785 and 1787 Christ Church's planters paid about £394 on their 1785 tax. They should have paid more than £1,200. Planters of St. James Santee paid £188 instead of £1,200, those of St. John Berkely £136 instead of £2,500. Between 1785 and 1787 no entry was made for St. Paul, which should have paid about £3,600 or for St. George Dorchester, which should have paid over £1,400, or St. James Goose Creek, which should have paid about £1,600. Together, all the lowcountry parishes, excluding those in the city of Charleston, should have paid approximately £37,700 and instead put into the state treasury only £7,100.[13]

Large sums were owed by parishes with few white residents. The 1790 census listed 243 heads of families in St. George Dorchester, a number probably close to the number of taxpayers in 1785. There were 118 heads of families in St. James Goose Creek and only 76 in St. Paul. The parishes in Charleston district, again excluding those in the city, contained 1,935 heads of families in 1790, paid only about £2,500 between 1785 and 1787 on their 1785 tax, and owed at least £22,500. Many of the planters who owed taxes undoubtedly had substantial private debts they could not pay because of bad crops, and it was probably to them and their possessions that Governor Moultrie was referring when he spoke of the danger that people would lose their property to aliens.

The planters' need to protect themselves and save their world was heightened by chaos which was not economic. Criminals were disrupting too many lives. Politics, especially for those in the Charleston district, was changing drastically. In 1784 there were vicious newspaper denunciations of the government and the aristocracy, as well as a highly contested election between Alexander Gillon and Richard Hutson, "Anarchy and Tyranny" and "Law and Liberty." Just a short time before the special session of the legislature Benjamin Waller's dispute with the City Corporation erupted, and defenders of the city government trumpeted the idea that "where the law is not omnipotent, liberty cannot possibly exist. . . ."[14] Lawlessness, criticism, "anarchy," and economic ruin converged.

If principle were involved, the attitude of the government and its supporters should have been clear. Only nineteen days before the special session met, a defender of the city government had predicted the early "political annihilation" of the state if punishment was not meted out to those who introduced "anarchy and confusion by flagrantly violating the rights of justice and the law of the land." As a general sentiment, the idea was agreeable to legislators. The legislature had reacted to the popular protest against the returning loyalists and British merchants by incorporating Charleston, creating the force to assert authority. Opponents of the aristocracy and the city government were denounced as demagogues "poisoning the minds" of the people and as "designing and turbulent men" trying to seize "the powers of the state."[15] The *law* was and had to be omnipotent.

But in September 1785, presented with well-known evidence of overt opposition to judicial and legal power, the governor called not for enforcement of laws, but for their modification. He beseeched the legislature to prevent the operation of existing laws against debtors, some of whom were apparently prepared to protect their property by any means possible.

"Necessity . . . obliges an interposition of the Legislature in private Contracts," he asserted. Others joined in. In 1787, when the legislature again rescued debtors, John Julius Pringle, a lawyer and speaker of the lower house, justified legislative interference with an extraordinary statement. "There is no general principle or maxim that may not admit of relaxation and exception under extraordinary circumstances," he declared. In a remarkable assertion of legislative and individual power, Pringle went on: "If in a shipwreck a man being on a plank with another and finding it incapable of saving both, casts off the other, who will condemn him for the deed?" If individuals, in the case of "extreme necessity," could violate the laws of God and justly commit murder, said Pringle, then, in cases of equal importance, the South Carolina legislature could act as it saw fit. "The safety of the people is the law paramount, to which every other must yield."[16]

Aedanus Burke, arguing that the people would not allow suits for debt, thought that since not even an army "could enforce obedience to the Common Pleas," the legislature had to act to avoid disorder. A newspaper writer echoed Burke. He compared South Carolina with Massachusetts, where "the government refused . . . a temporary departure from the maxims of justice . . . [and] exerted its whole strength to enforce the operation of the laws." The consequences were serious. "An armed force" shut the courts and now "threatens the existence of the government."[17]

The legislature was ready to act, but in a manner strikingly partial to the state's 'wealthier' debtors, perhaps partly because it, like prewar assemblies, was overwhelmingly dominated by the areas of greatest per capita wealth. At least 112 representatives were present in the lower house: of the 76 whose names are known, 58 sat for the lowcountry, 47 of them from Charleston District, and only 18 for the backcountry. But perhaps more backcountry representatives would have made little difference since the state constitution dictated the election of propertied senators and representatives. In adopting legislation the legislators gave ample testimony that South Carolina was truly a "rich man's refuge," and that the defense of law and order was partial, depending on the men and issues involved. After the legislature had finished its business Francis Kinloch noted the success of "the selfish & iniquitous views of a majority in the Assembly," and John Lloyd, who was President of the Senate in 1785, had to ask his nephew not to make known the contents of a letter, since it did not "become" him "to censure in severe terms the conduct of the Legislature."[18] When the 'right' people were hurt by legislation, the legislation was changed.

Beginning in 1782 the legislature had passed yearly acts postponing the payment of some debts. On 26 February 1782 the Jacksonborough Assembly, taking into account the "small quantity of specie" in circulation, prohibited suits for debts until ten days after the next meeting of the General Assembly. In 1783 the Assembly delayed suits for debts contracted before 1 January 1782 "until the expiration of twelve months after the passing of this act, and from thence to the end of the next sitting of the General Assembly." The act sought to prevent the hardships that would result from attempts to collect both the prewar debts and the debts contracted by Carolinians during the war years. With future economic conditions unknown, and with misplaced confidence that the citizens of the state would refrain "from contracting . . . extravagant, or great debts, than may be discharged from their incomes," the legislators allowed suits for debts arising after 26 February 1782.[19]

The legal power of a state to legislate on debts contracted before 1782 was challenged by Article IV of the Treaty of Paris. It stated clearly that creditors would "meet with no lawful impediment to the recovery of . . . all bona fide debts heretofore contracted." To many Carolinians, that article was a tragic blunder both economically unwise and morally unjust. John Lewis Gervais predicted "ruinous" consequences in some states if debtors were immediately pressed for payments. To Thomas Jefferson, Ralph Izard argued that the proper clause would have provided only that the recovery of British debts would meet with "no *greater* obstruction . . . *than those of the citizens of America.*" Izard did not mention it, but a clause to precisely that effect had been included in the more favorable pact negotiated in Carolina in 1782 by Edward Rutledge and Benjamin Guerard.[20]

The South Carolina government first rescued debtors by ignoring the peace treaty. The legislature, having acted in 1782 and again in 1783, before news of the signing of the preliminary peace treaty, interfered with the collection of debts again in 1784. On 26 March the legislature prohibited suits for the recovery of debts contracted before 26 February 1782. After 1 January 1785 creditors might sue for the interest that had accrued since 1 January 1780. But not before 1 January 1786 could they sue for any part of the principal, and then for only one-fourth. The act postponed final payment of prewar debts until 1789 and clearly violated the peace treaty.

Governor Moultrie justified the legislation by arguing that it merely continued the laws passed in 1782 before the treaty had been signed, and by pointing out that in recovering their debts British subjects "encountered no other difficulties or impediments" than American citizens. He made it sound as though the Rutledge and Guerard agreement was still operative, although it had been dissolved in 1782 and superseded in 1783.[21]

When Moultrie summoned the legislators in 1785 the laws dealing with debts no longer met the needs of South Carolina's debtors. Creditors were still free to initiate court action on debts contracted after 26 February 1782. They were forced to sue because of the breakdown in credit arrangements. Some Carolinians, outspoken where Moultrie was reticent, rationalized tampering with recent debts by blaming overseas merchants for the economic distress. Aedanus Burke hesitated not a moment in condemning the British for subtly tempting "us into a debt which their depredations a little before, and our want and distresses, . . . seduced us to contract." Burke's attitude was too common to suit Timothy Ford, who was displeased that the British merchants were pictured as "harpies preying" on "misfortunes."[22] Few people blamed the Carolinians for yielding to temptation.

Ford thought the arguments attacking British merchants, and other arguments appealing to the "passions & the interests" of the legislators, disposed the government to intervene in behalf of debtors.[23] That interposition would come was understood; legislators, however, debated its form. Some people, for reasons which differed, urged caution. No "reasonable, honest, and industrious man" would wish to suspend the law totally, "HORATIO" wrote. Stopping the courts would "totally ruin the Credit of our Country," advised Thomas Farr. When William Loughton Smith spoke in favor of temporarily suspending laws until 1 January 1786, both David Ramsay and Henry Pendleton protested, Pendleton arguing that such action would make a bad impression on the rest of the world. Similarly, John Julius Pringle thought that shutting the courts would bring national bankruptcy, a complete annihilation of government.[24] Yet both Pendleton and Pringle sought ways to protect debtors. Making fine distinctions, what many legislators wanted was an act which protected debtors but pictured Carolinians as "honest." Some people were sincerely interested in fairness, others only in appearance.

The legislature debated three important measures to relieve the state's economic ills, two of them specifically to aid debtors: prohibiting the slave trade, valuing property sold at public auctions, and issuing paper money. Each measure attacked a different aspect of the economic problem; each affected debtors and creditors differently.

Ralph Izard, supported by other members of the lowcountry aristocracy, worked to prohibit the importation of slaves for three years. Henry Pendleton, from the backcountry, joined him. Financial distress was nothing new, Edward Rutledge pointed out. Law officers had been opposed before, and schemes for protecting debtors by valuing property were proposed before the Revolution. But the legislature had responded to economic problems in 1739 and again in the 1760s by prohibiting the importation of slaves for a limited time, thereby throwing the balance of trade in the colony's favor. David Ramsay, who was probably the only public figure in South Carolina to speak against slavery, likewise felt that the balance of trade would be righted if the motion were adopted. The importation of 9,000 Negroes since the evacuation, he told the legislators, had been the cause of the citizens' debt. Prohibit the trade, and they would become rich.[25]

The opponents of prohibition were also from the lowcountry. John Rutledge thought that the Negroes imported had cost the planters only

£400,000 sterling, a sum not sufficient to have caused the "national calamities," and trifling when compared to what had been spent for dry goods. Charles Cotesworth Pinckney, like John Julius Pringle and others, thought slaves necessary "raw materials." Without them the state could not prosper.[26]

Motions to prohibit the slave trade for three years were defeated twice, once by a close vote.[27] Debtors had no reason to mourn. Prohibition of the slave trade might have restored a favorable balance of trade to the state, something desirable for the future but of no value to debtors attempting to escape legal action in 1785. Merchants, however, probably regretted the votes because prohibition might have indicated that planters were decreasing their expenses in order to pay their debts. Planters had no such intention. When other legislation was considered in October 1785, the Intendant of Charleston, Colonel Arnoldus VanderHorst, and merchant Daniel Desaussure, argued that no one who accumulated additional debts by purchasing Negroes or land should be permitted to benefit from legislation protecting debtors. They lost their argument.[28] The legislature was unwilling to distinguish between what were in merchants' eyes responsible and irresponsible debtors.

For the debtors the legislature evolved a more appropriate scheme that allowed them to enjoy property they had not paid for without formally closing the courts. On 29 September Henry Pendleton recommended a valuation bill for the relief of debtors. Ramsay supported him: the proposal was undeniably unjust but had the virtue of being less unjust than other proposals he had heard of and less unjust than issuing paper money. He thought the bill would force debtors to pay something and would show "the world that our intentions were good." The recommendation called for regulating forced property sales, by an undisclosed method, "and obliging the creditor to take it at two-thirds of the valuation."[29]

Ostensibly, the valuation bill dealt with an economic problem resulting from a lack of circulating medium in the state. The people of Camden had halted judicial proceedings because money was so scarce in their area that property did not fetch a fourth of "its real value" when sold at execution.[30] A valuation bill, people argued, would alleviate some of the economic chaos by ensuring that property would not be parted with for less than a given percentage of its real worth. In fact, however, as Pendleton admitted a few months later, the valuation act would not work that way. "It never was expected that much property could be tendered," he said, "because debtors had an option to tender what property they pleased."[31] The intent of the act was simple: creditors would refuse the property offered, and debtors would receive an extension of credit.

During the confusing and busy days of the special session, the legislators discussed several measures at each meeting. It postponed Pendleton's valuation bill, and, on the same day, debated the issuance of £400,000 of paper money that would be a legal tender in all cases except for duties paid at the treasury, one-third of which had to be paid in specie. Former governor Benjamin Guerard's paper money proposal met with the instant disapproval of many able speakers. Thomas Pinckney opposed it. Edward Rutledge called it "inexpedient," "contrary to national justice," and an infringement of the peace treaty, which provided for the payment of foreign debts in specie. David Ramsay agreed that the plan infringed on the treaty and thought it desperate and unnecessary. Charles Cotesworth Pinckney wished the idea of paper money "knocked on the head at once." The motion was defeated.[32]

On 1 October, two days after the defeat of Guerard's proposal, Henry Pendleton introduced a more detailed paper money scheme which received long and thoughtful consideration. Pendleton suggested the establishment of a loan office to put in circulation £100,000 of paper money backed by property. The money was to be lent for five years at 7 percent annual interest to individuals who mortgaged property valued three times more than the amount they borrowed. No one was to borrow more than £250. If anyone could not repay the loan or meet interest payments, his property would be sold.[33]

In response to one objection that the money would give only partial relief, since no more than 400 people could borrow from the loan office (actually 400 was the minimum number of borrowers), Pendleton and Thomas Pinckney argued that circulation and not the number of borrowers was important. Pinckney maintained that £1,000 passed from hand to hand could pay £10,000 of debts.[34]

In less than two weeks the bill was read three times in the lower house and Senate and became a law. Its final form was almost identical to Pendleton's original proposal. The state would lend between £30 and £250 to individuals who mortgaged land worth three times, or gold or silver plate worth twice, the amount borrowed. The money would be used to pay duties and taxes. One clause of the act not in the original proposal tied it closely to another act considered at the same time and passed on the same day. Article seven provided that no debtor could "avail himself of the Act for regulating sheriffs' sales" if his creditor demanded payment in paper money.[35]

The bill regulating sheriffs' sales was a complicated piece of legislation designed to close the courts to suits for debt. Because, the act began, citizens were "threatened with total ruin by having their property seized for debt and sold very considerably below its real value," no property could thereafter be sold for less than three-fourths its appraised value. Three men selected by the creditor and debtors, or, if they refused to choose, by men selected by a magistrate, determined the property's value, "estimating the same as if sold on a credit of six months." And, the act continued, to discourage suits "at this time of public distress," no creditor could sue a debtor before asking him, in writing, for payment. Incredibly, the act provided that if the creditor refused to accept a debtor's property at three-fourths its valuation, choosing instead to take the debtor to court, he would have to accept it at full value if he won the suit.[36]

The valuation act saved some debtors from ruin by preventing sales of their property at prices so low they could not repay their debts, but, not guaranteeing creditors any return at all, it hardly did them justice. Because of the way property was valued, debtors would often be unfairly favored. Creditors and debtors both chose as appraisers residents of the county or parish where the property to be valued was located, and the two appraisers chose a third, or if they could not agree a magistrate chose a third. In small lowcountry parishes where planters knew one another, creditors would have a difficult time finding sympathetic appraisers, and the property offered them would be valued too high. Fifty years earlier creditors had for a similar reason fought the creation of county courts for the coastal areas away from Charleston, fearing that juries would protect local debtors.[37] Perhaps in 1785 the legislature could find no completely fair method, yet merchants might at least have benefited from the right to choose appraisers from anywhere in the state. The legislature knew the importance of property valuation. It set up a more elaborate scheme for the valuation of property mortgaged for the purpose of borrowing money. That property was to be valued by "three disinterested freeholders," and their results were to be approved by two or more justices of the counties or parishes where the property was located. And finally, the commissioners of the loan office were still responsible for accepting or rejecting the valuation. The state was careful to protect its own rights and unconcerned about creditors' rights.

Opponents of the sheriffs' sale act quickly pointed out a more serious objection. About a month after the act was passed, "MONTALTO" launched an attack against it. "*The rulers of the land, in their great wisdom,*" he sneered, have left it to the "*defendant*" to offer what he thought "proper." For that reason, another critic wrote, the act became known as the "pine barren" act: the planter, "to avoid paying his debts," tendered the merchant pine barren, "which is a species of land producing hardly any thing else than pine trees."[38] According to a British official, a debtor unfortunate enough not to possess this suddenly valuable but intrinsically valueless land "applys to some one that has [it], of whom he purchases or procures a grant of a certain Quantity sufficient to pay the Debt." Another opponent of the act wrote that a debtor could assemble "a parcel of hay, fodder, cows, calves, pigs, boots, staves, fence rails, &c.," have them valued "2 or 300 miles from a sea port, and then . . . [say] to the foreign merchants, sir, now take these things, they are valued to the amount of your debt." Far from the coast, the hay, fodder, and assorted items would be worth little to the merchant. Only "ideots and madmen," he wrote, "will trust such a people" in the future. The act, wrote someone else, was the "most infamous of all the most infamous laws to be met with in the history of mankind."[39]

Courts continued to sit after the valuation act was passed, but they were so useless to many creditors that people indicated simply that they had closed down. Nathaniel Russell, who had sold a cargo of slaves in 1784, reported in 1786 that the legislature had "shut up the Courts until January next" so that he had no hopes of "compel[ling] people to do justice." Francis Kinloch described the "selfish & iniquitous views of a majority in the Assembly" who had shut "up the courts of justice," and John Lloyd, President of the Senate, denouncing the use of the law by "men of rank, dignity, and wealth," complained that creditors would not receive payments "until the Courts are open."[40]

Some legislators were apparently surprised by the act's effect. Both Thomas Bee and Charles Cotesworth Pinckney soon protested that people were offering pine barren, and Pinckney thought that the law was abused so much that a "check had become absolutely necessary." Most representatives and senators present at the special session, however, had probably known what to expect. No one could have imagined that much property would change hands.[41]

Perhaps more people were genuinely surprised by another development. According to "RUSTICUS," legislators had intimated that when the paper money began to circulate, they would work to repeal the law "which made property a tender."[42] The valuation act and the loan office act were intended to operate successively. The valuation act prevented sales when there was no money in circulation. After currency was issued, creditors would demand it, or, if they did not, and property was put up for sale, then people would have more money and be able to bid more at auctions. The sheriffs' sale act was not actually to be repealed, as "RUSTICUS" said, but it would be less important once the money was in circulation.

But the legislature did not follow through with that scheme. Instead of placing less emphasis on the valuation act, it made the loan office act less important. From the merchants' and creditors' view, the legislature repealed the only acceptable feature of the debtor legislation by amending the loan office act in March 1786, over Pendleton's objections, so that, until 1 January 1787, debtors could offer property at three-fourths its assessed value, even though the creditor requested payment in loan-office bills. Nathaniel Russell subsequently wrote that he had "but little prospect of getting even paper money" for the debts due him.[43] Many debtors were now completely freed of pressure.

Responding to the governor's message that they address a state-wide crisis, legislators secured some debtors from their creditors' demands. Their interference in private contracts was understandable and at least partially defensible under principles set forth by Burke, Pringle, and others. "The safety of the people" was "the law paramount, to which every other must yield," although merchants might have argued that debtors could be protected and at the same time forced to make payments on their debts or prevented from purchasing more slaves and lands.

But the legislature was inconsistent, and the principles it followed too narrowly applied. Governor Moultrie had described an economic crisis "become General," one "not confined to one or two families," but existing "throughout the State, a few, very few excepted."[44] Hardly anyone challenged the description. The legislature's program of debtor relief, however, benefited almost exclusively only the debtor with substantial amounts of property and left less propertied debtors, in the backcountry and lowcountry, still threatened by "the power of the Law."

The loan office act clearly illustrated the preferential treatment granted those with large amounts of property. Originally the justification for issuing paper money was to allow, perhaps to force, people to repay their debts and to raise prices at sheriffs' sales. To borrow the minimum sum of £30, however, individuals had to mortgage land worth £90 or deposit gold or silver plate worth £60. Buildings on the land mortgaged or fashions on the plate were not included in the valuation.

Most settlers could not meet the requirements. At least for tax purposes backcountry land had little value. Of the 156,918 acres for which taxes were paid in Lexington County in 1788, over 123,000 acres were valued at one shilling an acre, only 14,380 acres were valued at five shillings an acre, and only 762 acres at £3 an acre. At those rates one needed 360 acres of five-shilling land or 1,800 acres of one-shilling land to meet the mortgage requirements. Most backcountry farmers owned less than 200 acres. In Clarendon County, where taxes were paid on 109,907 acres in 1788, over 85,000 acres were valued at the one-shilling rate. On the basis of that land tax, only 37 of the 145 listed on the return, slightly more than 25 percent, could have borrowed £30. And Clarendon County was a well-developed backcountry region, located near the lowcountry, along the Santee, Congaree, and Black rivers. The 145 people owned 1,210 slaves, an average of 9 each. Although about half the tax was paid by 10 people, only 16 apparently paid no land tax, and only 23 owned no slaves. In other backcountry regions far fewer were eligible to borrow. One return for a small number of the people between the Broad and Catawba rivers listed 43 people with 200 acres of land or less, and 21 with more than 200 acres. The tax valuations would have enabled only 13 people, slightly more than 20 percent, to borrow money. And, because of the sale of inexpensive new lands, backcountry land values were probably low for other than tax purposes. Between 16 July 1784 and 1 January 1787, the state sold over 3,000,000 acres of land at a price of £2.6.8 per 100 acres.[45]

A greater percentage of qualified property owners resided in the lowcountry, particularly in Charleston District. Of the 124 people listed on a tax return for Christ Church in 1788, 78, over 63 percent, would have qualified for loans.[46] And, since the loan office was located close by, in

Charleston, these people had a far easier trip than the potential borrowers from the backcountry or other parts of the lowcountry.

Perhaps because of the bank's location, or perhaps because news of the bank's existence may not have penetrated all areas, the loan office appealed only to people with far more than the necessary amounts of property. Only 9 of about 450 borrowers borrowed £50 or less. No one borrowed £30. But 254 people borrowed £250 each, for which each one mortgaged either £750 worth of land or deposited £500 worth of plate.[47] Obviously, for the poor, or for those with moderate amounts of property, 200 or 300 acres of land, and for some of those too who met the requirements, the bank and its paper currency were useless.

The legislature's effort to distribute the money throughout the state was also inadequate and added to the hardships of many. The loan office was to lend £25,000 to residents of Charleston District, which in 1790 had fewer than 16,000 whites, and £12,500 to each of the six other districts, where in 1790 more than 124,000 whites lived, although many had moved in after 1785. In fact, because all of the other districts did not borrow their full amounts, about 150 people from Charleston received a little more than £32,000, while the remainder went to about 300 people from other districts. Perhaps the settlers outside Charleston District might have taken more advantage of the loan office had the legislature in its special session of 1785 made it easier for them. In 1783 when the legislature adopted a plan for the auditing of Revolutionary accounts, it appointed district auditors who moved through the state, notice of their coming preceding them.[48] The legislature similarly might have set up temporary locations for the bank outside Charleston. Those relatively few who traveled from the more populous interior to the bank probably carried little money back with them, and what they did bring home soon must have found its way to Charleston in the normal course of trade, leaving their areas again without currency.

The sheriffs' sale act was of little more use to the poor, although some people who could not borrow money may have benefited from it. The act served as a stay law for debtors with enough diversified property that they could offer creditors worthless pine barren valued too high. But those without different kinds of property had to offer creditors something of value, at least to them. Valuation of the poorer debtors' property was probably also more favorable to the creditor. Especially in the more populous regions far from Charleston, debtors had less familiarity with magistrates and less ability to influence the choice of some appraisers, while local merchants were more likely than lowcountry merchants to find sympathetic residents to serve for them. Those people without property they wanted to offer creditors might still have their possessions seized, valued, and sold at auction, although that property could not be sold for less than three-fourths its value.

Some of the poor, again especially those far from Charleston, may have escaped their creditors by opposing law officers and preventing them from serving writs or conducting sales. Alexander Gillon remarked in 1787 that sheriffs could not perform their duties thirty miles from Charleston.[49] But if that was true, the burden was still placed on the poorer debtors to oppose the law and officials, while the wealthier enjoyed the new laws and beat off their creditors legally.

In one other way the legislators showed their partiality toward Carolinians with resources, whether they were debtors or not. In 1784 the legislature had encouraged settlement by placing the state's vacant lands on sale for either £10 or $10 per hundred acres, depending on the land's location. Early in 1785 it standardized the price at $10 for a hundred acres. The legislature was careful, however, to guarantee as best it could that the vast amount of land not be gobbled up by speculators, stipulating that no one could acquire more than 640 acres and that whatever was purchased had to be settled or cultivated within two years or at least twelve months before it could be sold. But in the summer of 1785, the small session which met to consider matters between debtors and creditors decided to change the state's land policy by abolishing the 640-acre limit and repealing the clause requiring cultivation before the land could be sold again.[50] Three years before, the legislature had similarly pleased large purchasers with its confiscation act, which, although apparently encouraging people to buy small amounts of land through inclusion of Christopher Gadsden's suggestion that land be sold in tracts of 200 to 500 acres, failed to limit the number of tracts an individual could buy.

Before long the effects of the new policy were felt. In 1787 some settlers of Orangeburg complained about a grant of 55,000 acres to Thomas Aikins. Later that year people from Lancaster and Chesterfield counties said they were greatly oppressed by large surveys of land, sometimes made with "no other view but to make gain and distress the poor." Further, they were upset about "those verry exceeding large surveys which seems much more like bondage then fredom and the effects seems like producing a thin settled country. . . ."[51]

In October 1788, at a time when debtor legislation was again a troublesome issue, David Ramsay denounced another version of a valuation bill as "the rich man's refuge and the poor man's ruin."[52] What he said then applied even more to the legislation passed in October 1785 by a legislature dominated to an even greater extent than usual by the lowcountry, particularly the Charleston District.

Lowcountry debtors could not rest with their victory of 1785. When the legislature met early in 1786 two major controversies developed. On 17 February Senator John Barnwell sought an explanation of the clause which continued the valuation act in force until the end of the next session of the legislature. Some people believed that a "session" included all meetings in the two years between elections. Others argued that "session" was interchangeable with "meeting" or "sitting." The constitution prohibited rejected bills from being reintroduced during the session in which they were defeated, but allowed them to be brought forward at the next session. In practice, bills were often reintroduced at the next meeting. Therefore, the opponents of the "pine barren" act said "session" and "meeting" were the same and the sheriffs' sale act expired when the Assembly adjourned in March 1786 and not in 1787.[53]

Instead of defining terms the Senate proposed to repeal the act. Opposition to the valuation act arose also in the lower house. John Rutledge, who according to one agent would not pay his own debts, thought the act destroyed the honor and welfare of the state and argued that "indiscreet" people who contracted "debts beyond their ability to discharge" ought to suffer.[54] Pierce Butler, who was absent from South Carolina when the act passed, wanted to know why an act which invited injustice and oppression should be continued. Thomas Bee denounced it also. But despite the opposition, the lower house defeated attempts to repeal the valuation act.[55]

The legislature's intent was clearly to continue the sheriffs' sale act, but not for its full term. It rejected repeal and amended the loan office act so that people could offer creditors property at three-fourths its valuation until 1 January 1787, stipulating no new procedures for valuing property.

In January 1787, however, the Court of Common Pleas decided that the sheriffs' sale act was inoperative. Daniel Desaussure, Jr., a lawyer from a mercantile family, cited the constitution and the practice of reintroducing defeated bills at subsequent meetings of the legislature to prove that "session" meant "meeting." Judge Henry Pendleton, a member of the legislature and a leading force in the passing of the disputed act, admitted an ignorance of the constitution when he acknowledged that he had not remembered that part of it before. He and Judge Aedanus Burke declared the act "null and void to all intents and purposes."[56] Not everyone accepted the court's decision. Senator Barnwell, sounding much like Hezekiah Maham, warned sheriffs that they would seize his property at the risk of their lives. Another senator, William Hill, of the northwestern New Acquisition District, remarked that regardless of what the judges had said in Charleston, the judges of other courts were of a different opinion.[57] The decision was meaningless, anyway, and cost the judges nothing. Both Burke and Pendleton were members of the new legislature which was about to reconsider debtor legislation.

The other conflict in 1786 concerned an attempt to alleviate some of the distresses the valuation act caused merchants. Although unable to initiate suits for the recovery of debts, merchants remained liable for duties owed the treasury. The paper money issued by the loan office was receivable at the treasury in payment of duties, but it was not available for circulation until May 1786. The treasurers decided, cleverly they thought, not to wait. They "hastily sued the Merchants," who "determined" to resist.[58] John and Edward Rutledge, Pierce Butler, William Loughton Smith, and Alexander Gillon pleaded the merchants' cause in the lower house. Smith claimed he knew of a commercial house owing £6,000 in duties but unable to pay because it could not collect debts. Gillon suggested that merchants be allowed to offer pine-barren to the treasurers. Nevertheless, every measure proposed for the relief of the merchants was defeated by either the lower house or the Senate. Henry Pendleton seems to have expressed the fears of the majority: if merchants did not pay duties the wheels of government could be clogged.[59]

Merchants contined to protest after the legislature adjourned. "We apply to the Generosity of our Debtors," said John and Thomas Manson, picking up Pendleton's phrase, "for their Assistance to enable us to grease the Wheels of Government, to prevent their rusting on the Axle." Merchant determination not to pay forced the treasury to adopt a new position. Whenever 5 percent of the duties owed was paid, the treasurers would grant several months for the payment of the remainder.[60] By that time the paper money would be in circulation.

When the legislature met in January 1787 the best one could say about the state's economic condition was that it had not worsened since 1785. In 1785 and 1786 Carolina planters reversed the trend of the two previous years and exported more than they imported. But the difference was slight and probably reflected not new-found financial honesty or wisdom but the effects of the already huge debt. A newspaper reported in 1786 that England's trade with America was "entirely at a stand" because the British merchants were "determined not to give the smallest credit in [the] future." In 1785 imports declined in value to about £600,000 and the next year to about half that. The combined imports for 1785 and 1786 amounted to less than what Carolinians had imported in 1784 alone. The estimated value of the exports for those years was £930,140.[61]

South Carolina's paper money, which depreciated despite merchant and planter agreements to accept it "equal to gold and silver, making no distinction," probably facilitated dealings between merchants and planters, but it could not solve the debtors' problems.[62] Although Ramsay, Thomas Pinckney, and others had expressed great faith in the circulation of money as a means of wiping out debts, they discovered, if they had not already known, that no matter how brisk the circulation the money could not balance accounts between Carolinians and their British creditors.[63]

While the legislature considered long-range solutions to the problem of rescuing, in Gillon's words, "the honest debtor" from the suspect intentions of the "unrelenting creditor," it also acted quickly to give debtors new, temporary protection. The temporary acts gave the poor, for the first time, the same protection the more fortunate received. Once in February and again in March the legislature passed ordinances suspending sales by execution for twenty days. The General Assembly was then free to give unhurried attention to the demands of creditors and debtors, although according to Ramsay, the lack of haste was not to ensure wisdom: "More time" was spent writing a law "than was employed in building the world, & yet," he wrote, "it cannot be said that all of it is very good."[64]

On 16 February Gillon moved that debts be paid in installments, since "the full operation" of the law "would be ruinous and oppressive." Ramsay explained his intention of moving a contrary resolution. His arguments were not drawn "from the situation and circumstances of the country." They were constitutional. Arguing that citizens had a right to be protected in their property, he denied that the legislature could interfere in private contracts. "The power of all legislative bodies was limited by the eternal laws of justice and reason." The legislature, he said, could not "secure debtors in the quiet possession of their creditors' property."[65]

It was a little late for a debate on the principle involved, but John Julius Pringle defended the extraordinary power of states and individuals in emergencies: "The interest of individuals must be sacrificed when such sacrifice is absolutely necessary for the preservation of the society." The state's duty was to protect the majority of its citizens.[66]

Gillon's motion was approved, and the legislature soon passed a law that provided for paying debts in installments. One such act, dealing with prewar debts, had been passed in 1784, but its operation had been suspended by the "pine barren" act. The installment act of 28 March 1787 postponed final payment of all debts contracted before 1 January 1787 until March 1790. Beginning in March 1788 debtors would make three annual payments to their creditors.

Unlike the earlier legislation, the installment act met with at least the partial approval of creditors. Although some continued to oppose legislative interference as an "unjust Act of our Interested Men in Power," many were pleased that they were promised partial payment.[67] One clause gave particular pleasure. Ralph Izard, Edward Rutledge, and David Ramsay saw their efforts to prohibit the slave trade succeed. For economic and not humanitarian reasons, the importation of Negroes was prohibited for three years. George Miller, an agent of the English government who arrived in July 1787, thought the installment act "would be satisfactory to the Merchants of Britain," for the temporary end of the slave trade seemed "to indicate a serious wish to rescue the Credit of the Country from the disgrace into which it is fallen." Christopher Gadsden agreed. The decision to stop the slave trade, he wrote, showed we were "coming to our Senses."[68]

The decision was also sectional and gave no particular pleasure to those who were beginning to prosper and advance into the higher levels of South Carolina society. The lowcountry favored prohibition of the slave trade by a vote of forty to twenty-two; the backcountry opposed by a vote of thirty-one to eighteen.[69] Perhaps in addition to correcting the balance of trade, some lowcountry planters were beginning to think of selling a few of their Negroes to tobacco farmers in the interior.

Agent George Miller had only one qualification regarding South Carolina's action, but it was important. There was unfortunately, he wrote, "no security" that the installment act "would not be followed" by another act "to screen the private Debtor."[70] Miller and everyone else knew that the South Carolina legislature would re-evaluate debtors' problems whenever it was necessary. Installments could always be postponed.

Most of the recorded opposition came naturally enough from Charlestonians, from merchants and the lawyers frequently associated with them. John Rutledge had reservations about the "pine barren" act. So did Edward Rutledge, Charles Cotesworth Pinckney, and Thomas Bee, all lawyers, all, by any standards, high in the aristocracy.[71] In 1787 the lawyers supported the installment act, another indication that it was more favorable to the interests of the creditors than previous legislation had been.

Another group, a small one, was concerned with the new debtor legislation. Remembering Hezekiah Maham's action and John Barnwell's threat, the legislature somewhat comically but seriously included in the installment act a clause which provided that any person who assaulted or opposed a sheriff or sheriff's officer would, "on conviction, be thereafter rendered incapable of being employed by, or serving the State, in any office, civil or military."[72]

About one week after the legislature adjourned in March 1787 David Ramsay wrote to Thomas Jefferson. "I do not pretend to justify it," he said of the installment act, although he thought that postwar conditions "in some degree palliate this interference of the legislature." Because Carolina, and other Southern states, he said, had refused "legal protection to the prosecution of the just rights of creditors," the Southern governments were "much more quiet" than the Northern. It was not, however, for him, a time for looking back to talk of what might have been. It was, rather, a time to look forward and beyond South Carolina. "Our eyes now are all fixed on the continental convention to be held in Philad[elphi]a in May."[73] What happened there would interest all Carolinians, debtors and creditors alike.

TEN
South Carolina and the Federal Constitution

What have you been contending for these ten years past? Liberty! What is Liberty? The power of governing yourselves. If you adopt this Constitution, have you this power? No.
James Lincoln, 18 January 1788.

I hope the Friends of Federal Government may be as successful in New York as they have been in South Carolina. We had a tedious but trifling opposition to contend with.
Edward Rutledge, 20 June 1788.

OLLOWING passage of the new debtor legislation in 1787, and partly because of it, many merchants and lawyers looked with "anxious expectation" to Philadelphia, hoping "Heaven" would "favor" the work of the Constitutional Convention. But because the convention was meeting officially to revise the Articles of Confederation, a great many other Carolinians who had in the past favored strengthening the union were also interested.[1]

By 1787 men as different in philosophy and activity as Alexander Gillon and William Logan, popular leaders in Charleston, and John and Edward Rutledge, Ralph Izard, and Thomas Bee, the spearheads of the "Nabob Phalanx," agreed that the central government's inability to regulate foreign trade was serious — even fatal, some of them thought. Restriction of American trade by foreign nations unafraid of the weak Confederation Congress angered them. Carolina rice could no longer be shipped to Portugal; rice and other American products could be exported to the British West Indies only in British ships. Henry Laurens was not alone in wishing America to do to other nations, Great Britain in particular, "whatsoever they do unto you in their commercial regulations." South Carolina did not again "*cut off the use of British manufactures,*" nor did it agree in 1784 to give the Confederation Congress power to pass navigation acts. Instead, the state approved a Virginia proposal authorizing Congress to prohibit ships owned or partly owned by British subjects from carrying West Indian products to America.[2]

Quickly, people realized the inadequacies of the 1784 act. Daniel Desaussure, a merchant, John Lewis Gervais, President of the Chamber of Commerce, Dr. John Budd, William Logan, and a few others, responded with a memorial signed by upwards of 300 that suggested Congress be allowed to regulate trade with countries having no commercial treaties with America. If Congress passed a navigation act, it would give the British "a tenfold sickness at the stomach one day or other," and it might compel England to alter its mercantilistic West Indian policy.[3]

In February 1786 a committee chaired by John Rutledge drafted a bill to give Congress control of foreign trade for fifteen years. Jacob Read, for many years a state representative to Congress, argued that only Congress could threaten England. The "Nabob Phalanx" and the popular leaders rushed to Read's side. Ralph Izard and Dr. John Budd spoke for the bill. Judge Henry Pendleton, now "compleatly informed" about Great Britain's attitude toward America, joined Edward Rutledge in support of the bill. Camden District contributed a petition favoring a bill like the one introduced, at the same time showing its political ideas by requesting a convention to revise the state's constitution. After Alexander Gillon added his voice to the harmonious, monotonous chorus, Thomas Bee was moved to refer to the unanimity which pervaded the lower house. "It was," he said, "a pleasing alteration. . . ."[4]

The harmony was partly the result of economic interest. Some merchants, like John Lewis Gervais, thought a stronger Congress might "rescue the commercial interests of the United States from impending ruin." "Our commerce," wrote Brailsford and Morris in 1787, will "experience the fruits of Order and Energy. . . ." Rice planters hoped to recapture markets and to attract even more vessels to Charleston, and all planters might hope that a central government with the power to control the country's trade could force the British to pay for the slaves taken away at the end of the war. Artisans and mechanics wanted to restrict the importation of competitive goods.[5]

Vengeance, too, played a role in the grant of commercial powers. Gillon and other popular leaders, having fought the return of British merchants, wanted to retaliate against England. In 1784 members of the Marine Anti-Britannic Society, led by Gillon, agreed not to import British goods when goods of equal value could be obtained from Americans or from the subjects of allies.[6] Backcountry settlers opposed to the return of loyalists probably supported the grant because it could be used against wartime opponents they had not yet forgiven.

Few people opposed the extension of congressional power. Although Carolinians spoke of the need to "sacrifice some local advantages for the general good," the state carefully protected its own interests by prohibiting Congress from passing trade legislation without the approval of nine states, a limitation designed to prevent the Eastern, commercial states from exploiting the South. And, because of the "well known . . . prejudices of the Eastern States," the central government was to have no power over the slave trade.[7]

The unanimity which pleased Thomas Bee in 1786 was gone by 1787 and 1788, when the work of the Philadelphia Convention became known. Although John Rutledge at one time reminded delegates in Philadelphia that capturing the West Indian trade "was the great object" of their work, he and the other delegates knew that "the great object" was not expressed by a single, detailed power but by the fulfillment of a resolution adopted shortly after the Convention began its deliberations. "It is the opinion of this committee," Edmund Randolph of Virginia had said, "that a national government ought to be established consisting of a supreme Legislative, Judiciary, and Executive."[8] The members of the convention ceased then to think of revising the old Articles and began to write a new constitution, to create a new order.

South Carolina's delegates supported the sweeping changes. John Rutledge, Charles Cotesworth Pinckney, Charles Pinckney, and Pierce Butler possessed ideas based on experiences and reactions shared by many, but not most, Carolinians. Because of their backgrounds and positions, their thoughts were not confined by Carolina's boundaries. Their worlds went beyond their plantations, their law offices, even beyond the cultured society that developed where the Ashley and Cooper rivers flowed together in Charleston. But their thoughts also were formed by South Carolina's recent political history.

Both Rutledge and Charles Cotesworth Pinckney, English-trained lawyers, had entered the South Carolina Commons before the Revolution, Rutledge in 1761, Pinckney eight years later. When the war ended, they returned to the lower house, Rutledge continuing to sit after being appointed Chancellor, the state's hightest judicial officer, in 1784. Pinckney resumed his extremely profitable law practice.[9]

Charles Pinckney, like Rutledge and his cousin, was a lawyer, but the Revolution had prevented him from studying abroad. His father, a wealthy planter and the first president of the Provincial Congress, returned to Charleston after the British captured it and swore allegiance to the crown. During the war Charles Pinckney was captured by the British. Although he was only twenty-nine when the Convention met, his political experience was already broad. He had been a Privy Councilor and was a member of the lower house. From 1784 to 1787 he was a representative from South Carolina in the Confederation Congress.[10]

Pierce Butler was as worldly as Rutledge and the elder Pinckney, but he had traveled in a different direction. An Irishman, the son of a member of Parliament, he became a major in the British army. He was in Boston at the time of the Boston Massacre. Sent to South Carolina, he resigned his commission in 1773 after marrying a daughter of Thomas Middleton of Prince William parish. In 1779 he became adjutant-general of the state.

He served in the lower house throughout most of the Confederation period. He traveled abroad in 1784, leaving his six-year-old son in England for schooling (it lasted at least until 1795) and continuing on himself to Holland to negotiate a loan that would carry him through the difficult postwar years.[11]

In their knowledge of and concern for external events, their contacts with people outside the state, these four lowcountry delegates had much in common with merchants who naturally dealt with non-Carolinians and with planters who traveled abroad or to the north. In the summer of 1786 alone, Francis Kinloch and his wife sailed north, as did Edward Rutledge, Thomas Pinckney, William Loughton Smith and their wives, Walter Izard, Mrs. Ralph Izard, and Thomas Bee. The impressions they received seemed all bad. From Newport, Rhode Island, Kinloch wrote that the Northern and Eastern states had been ruined by the Revolution. "Boston is going fast to decay, & the ruin'd wharves of Newport imply a melancholy truth." All of the travelers were greeted with news of Shays's Rebellion. Thomas Pinckney noted that Massachusetts's officials were "at present in some confusion on account of an opposition to their government." Edward Rutledge returned to South Carolina with information about the spirit of faction prevalent in other states. With these men the delegates shared a horror of what America had become.[12]

Charles Pinckney's experience was extreme, and his reactions predictable. As a member of Congress he saw the weakness and inefficiency of the national government which resulted in part from the deliberately weak Articles of Confederation, in part from an apparent lack of concern. On only ten days in December 1785 did Congress have a quorum of representatives from seven states. Throughout January 1786 no more than seven states were represented. Shortly afterwards attendance improved, but in the meantime New Jersey challenged the government by resolving in February that it would meet no more Congressional requisitions of money until the national government was granted the right to levy an impost. New Jersey's action, wrote Nathaniel Gorham of Massachusetts, meant "the end of all federal Government." To prevent disaster Congress sent Gorham, William Grayson of Virginia, and Pinckney to New Jersey. Their pleas convinced the legislature to rescind its resolution, but the event made a lasting impression on Pinckney and others. In May Pinckney asked for the creation of a committee to consider the affairs of the nation.[13]

In 1787 Pinckney drew a distressing picture of America. "Our government is despised — our laws are robbed of their respected terrors — their inaction is a subject of ridicule. . . ."[14] The next year, leading off a discussion of the Constitution in South Carolina, he returned to the same theme: the "total want of government, the destruction of commerce, of public credit, private confidence, and national character." Charles Cotesworth Pinckney, too, worried about the Confederation government. Could it "secure us tranquility at home or respect abroad?" Pierce Butler thought that only a new constitution could "rescue the States from . . . foreign contempt" and sustain a "Union." And Edward Rutledge feared that without a new constitution "the sun of American independence would indeed soon set — never to rise again."[15]

Relations with other nations, their lack of respect for America, scared, embarrassed, and humiliated the Pinckneys, Rutledges, and others whose contacts spread throughout America. But most of these same people were frightened more by the anarchy, "or rather worse than anarchy," they saw within individual states, South Carolina included. Charles Cotesworth Pinckney found "a disregard for law" in every state. In Rhode Island, Charles Pinckney said, "licentiousness" prevailed, and the people were oppressed "by laws the most infamous that have ever disgraced a civilized nation." In Massachusetts "similar attempts" to oppress were "rendered abortive [only] by the zeal and activity" of the government.[16]

For the delegates, and for many who sent them to Philadelphia, the Revolution had gone too far and stimulated too much change. To John Rutledge the constitution of 1778 seemed too democratic: the people had won the right to elect senators and the governor had lost his veto. Where would the disorder end? In 1785 backcountry spokesmen had begun to demand reapportionment, which Charles Cotesworth Pinckney thought would "sap . . . our present mode of representation."[19] The spirit was new also. No longer were the wealthy necessarily considered natural rulers. "Enormous wealth is seldom the associate of *pure* and *disinterested virtue,*" one of the new men wrote. There was now an "ever wakeful vigilance" over men in power. John Rutledge himself had been attacked in terms that could hardly have been harsher: he who had once "been ruler over this land," and his "*brethren,*" thought it "an abomination *that the people should . . . rule,*" and so they oppressed the "*Lower Orders of Men.*"[18] Such disorders in other states were irritating; 'anarchy' in South Carolina was unacceptable.

Some of the people who agreed with the delegates' political analysis of postwar America had not always thought all the supporting evidence appropriate, for some of it concerned the interference by state governments with the collection of debts. The two Pinckneys and Rutledge were lawyers, although they had plantation interests as well, and in South Carolina they had sided often with the merchants and against the indebted planters. So had Pierce Butler. John Rutledge and Charles Cotesworth Pinckney had fought the debtor legislation. Pierce Butler had denounced the "pine barren" act. After the Constitution was written, however, Charles Pinckney's denunciation of debtor legislation was strongest. "No more shall paper money, no more shall tender-laws . . . darken the American name in every country where it is known." "Honor and virtue," he said, "shall be again known and countenanced among us."[19] But some lowcountry planters, worried not only about the future of the state and country, but also about their own economic problems, had disagreed with the delegates. Government intervention in private contracts was not a sign of chaos but an indication of genuine concern.

By 1787 and 1788, however, the different attitudes of delegates and those they represented toward debtor legislation was no longer important. The debtor legislation was a matter of record. All could react to the political disturbances. Somehow the convention to revise the Articles of Confederation, the convention that would in fact produce a new frame of government, would solve the problems caused by a too revolutionary Revolution.

At the Constitutional Convention, Butler, Rutledge, and the Pinckneys sought to decrease the role of the people in the proposed government. On 7 June Charles Pinckney spoke against the popular election of senators. All of them rejected the plan to have the people choose representatives. Butler, declaring such an election "impracticable," argued for election of representatives by state legislatures. Charles Pinckney agreed, "contending that the people were less fit Judges." Rutledge joined in. The members of the Convention, he said, were "proper characters" precisely because they had been elected by legislatures and not "by the people at large." Charles Cotesworth Pinckney pronounced popular elections inconvenient because the people were too "scattered," particularly in South Carolina. Better representatives would come from elections in the state legislatures, for their members "had some sense of character."[20]

Failing to convince the Convention that state legislatures should choose representatives, Charles Cotesworth Pinckney proposed that each state legislature fix its own method to elect representatives. To the few who may have needed the intent pointed out, Alexander Hamilton explained that the motion was designed to remove "the people" from the process. It was defeated.[21]

The South Carolina delegation tried to minimize the evils of popular elections by voting against James Madison's proposal to give representatives liberal and fixed salaries so they would not have "an improper dependence" on state legislatures. The same issue arose over the payment of senators. Butler argued that senators would "lose sight of their Constituents unless dependent on them for their support." Twice more, however, the Carolinians were on the losing side.[22]

Although they failed to tie Congressmen closely to the state legislatures, they at least succeeded in amending one clause of the proposed plan which would have rendered national legislators ineligible to hold offices in their own states. "The ablest men," Charles Cotesworth Pinckney argued, with the support of his cousin and Pierce Butler, might be "discourage[d] . . . from going into the Senate" if they could not at the same time hold state office. Or, should they choose to serve the central government, the states would lose their valuable services. The objectionable clause was removed.[23]

Disliking the weakness of the Confederation government and the behavior of state legislatures, the Carolinians worked for a strong central government — to levy taxes and exercise some control over the states and trade. Their problem was to see that the control was exercised by responsible people. Ultimately the South Carolina delegates, like other supporters of the Constitution, were persuaded that good Congressmen could be elected by the people voting in large districts, where "the little demagogue" would discover "his intrigues useless." The larger the election district the more likely that men with broad, noble vision would be chosen.[24] But at Philadelphia, the delegates placed their faith in the state legislatures. The lowcountry aristocracy of South Carolina still dominated the state government, although with constantly decreasing majorities. But even if the people elected demagogues to represent them, the demagogues were to be propertied according to the state constitution, and, somehow, the delegates at Philadelphia believed, no matter how radical and unjust the legislation they passed, the state legislators always chose able men for higher positions. The governors elected since independence showed that.

The first Congressional election proved that the people of South Carolina were not to be trusted. Aedanus Burke and Thomas Sumter, two strong opponents of the new Constitution, were elected to the House of Representatives, as was Dr. Thomas Tudor Tucker, who had fought a duel with Ralph Izard a few years before and had defeated one of Izard's cousins in a race for the state legislature. And Tucker had early supported a state constitutional convention to form a government based on the consent of the people, and unalterable by the legislature. According to John Faucheraud Grimké, Tucker was antifederal, against the new government. All Charles Pinckney would write was that he was "unacquainted" with Tucker's sentiments, a damning enough comment. The two others elected to the lower house were William Loughton Smith, a Federalist, and Daniel Huger, to Pinckney a Federalist and to Grimké, doubtful. Grimké's remark summed up the popular election. "What a black list," he wrote, adding that "we must endeavor to mend it by our election of Senators. . . ." And the legislature did act "responsibly," choosing Pierce Butler and Ralph Izard, "both strong federalists" in Pinckney's opinion.[25]

Partly because South Carolina had supported Congressional demands for increased powers, and partly because the lowcountry areas that abhorred the politics of the 1780s were overrepresented in the government, there was little doubt that the state would ratify the Constitution. David Ramsay thought the constitution would be "accepted by a very great majority." Henry William Desaussure was optimistic because of "the temper of the people, and . . . the unanimity of the Leading Men.'' Pierce Butler had ''scarce a doubt.''[26]

Their expectations were realized. When the Constitution was discussed in the lower house, Rawlins Lowndes, old *Ralinus postponatur,* a political foe of the Rutledges and former governor, ''was the only man who made direct formal opposition to it.'' And even he joined in the unanimous vote to call a ratifying convention.[27] A month after the convention met and ratified the Constitution, Edward Rutledge summed up the Federalists' success: ''We had a tedious but trifling opposition to contend with.''[28] The opposition, without the services of Lowndes, who was not elected to the convention, mustered only 73 votes, while those supporting ratification swept all before them with 143.

Tedious and trifling to Rutledge, the nonetheless intelligent opposition represented the views of a majority of Carolinians. Antifederalist Aedanus Burke thought the Constitution had been ratified ''notwithstanding 4/5 of the people do from their souls detest it.'' One North Carolina Federalist agreed that a majority of South Carolinians had opposed the Constitution.[29]

Because each parish and district sent to the ratifying convention the same number of delegates as it sent legislators to the General Assembly, the coastal areas easily dominated. Charleston, Georgetown, and Beaufort, with 28,644 white inhabitants in 1790, were allowed 143 delegates, the backcountry, with 111,534 whites, almost four times the number in the lowcountry, received only 93, about two-thirds of the east's number. And the vote to ratify was divided unmistakably along sectional lines. Federalist strength radiated out from the coastal centers of the three lowcountry districts. The parishes around Beaufort favored the Constitution by a vote of 14 to 0, those around Georgetown by 12 to 1, and Charleston and the six parishes surrounding it by a vote of 73 to 0. In six other lowcountry parishes the vote was 22 to 15 in favor of the Constitution. The lowcountry supported the proposed government by 121 to 16.[30] Six delegates were absent.

The backcountry vote was 57 to 28 against ratification. Eight were absent. Seventeen of the 28 backcountry votes for ratification, and only 1 of the 57 opposition votes, came from four election units bordering lowcountry parishes. Two of those units, St. David and St. Matthew, had been organized before 1770, while a third, Orange Parish, had been formed out of St. Matthew.

As closely as can be determined the delegates opposed to the Constitution represented about 52 percent of the population, those supporting it represented 39 percent of the people, while those not voting represented almost 9 percent.[31]

Backcountry antifederalism was more adequately shown by Thomas Sumter's motion to adjourn the Convention until October. The interior supported adjournment 72 to 15, 9 notes for and 9 votes against coming

THE

COLUMBIAN HERALD,

OR THE

INDEPENDENT COURIER OF NORTH-AMERICA.

EXTRAORDINARY.

TUESDAY, *October*, 2, 1787.

Fœderal Conſtitution.

Publiſhed by Authority.

WE the People of the United States, in order to form a more perfect union, eſtabliſh juſtice, inſure domeſtic tranquility, provide for the common defence, promote the general welfare, and ſecure the bleſſings of liberty to ourſelves and our poſterity, do ordain and eſtabliſh this Conſtitution for the United States of America.

Article I.

Sect. 1. ALL legiſlative powers herein granted ſhall be veſted in a Congreſs of the United States, which ſhall conſiſt of a Senate and Houſe of Repreſentatives.

Sect. 2. The Houſe of Repreſentatives ſhall be compoſed of members choſen every ſecond year by the people of the ſeveral ſtates, and the electors in each ſtate ſhall have the qualifications requiſite for electors of the moſt numerous branch of the ſtate legiſlature.

No perſon ſhall be a Repreſentative who ſhall not have attained to the age of twenty-five years, and been ſeven years a citizen of the United States, and who ſhall not, when elected, be an inhabitant of that ſtate in which he ſhall be choſen.

Repreſentatives and direct taxes ſhall be apportioned among the ſeveral ſtates, which may be included within this union, according to their reſpective numbers, which ſhall be determined by adding to the whole number of free perſons, including thoſe bound to ſervice for a term of years, and excluding Indians not taxed, three-fifths of all other perſons. The actual enumeration ſhall be made within three years after the firſt meeting of the Congreſs of the United States, and within every ſubſequent term of ten years, in ſuch manner as they ſhall by law direct. The number of Repreſentatives ſhall not exceed one for every thirty thouſand, but each ſtate ſhall have at leaſt one Repreſentative; and until ſuch enumeration ſhall be made, the ſtate of New-Hampſhire ſhall be entitled to chuſe three, Maſſachuſetts eight, Rhode-Iſland and Providence Plantations one, Connecticut five, New-York ſix, New-Jerſey four; Pennſylvania eight, Delaware one, Maryland ſix, Virginia ten, North-Carolina five, South-Carolina five, and Georgia three.

When vacancies happen in the repreſentation from any ſtate, the executive authority thereof ſhall iſſue writs of election to fill ſuch vacancies.

The Houſe of Repreſentatives ſhall chuſe their ſpeaker, and other officers; and ſhall have the ſole power of impeachment

Sect. 3. The Senate of the United States ſhall be compoſed of two ſenators from each ſtate, choſen by the legiſlature thereof, for ſix years; and each ſenator ſhall have one vote.

Immediately after they ſhall be aſſembled in conſequence of the firſt election, they ſhall be divided as equally as may be into three claſſes. The ſeats of the ſenators of the firſt claſs ſhall be vacated at the expiration of the ſecond year, of the ſecond claſs at the expiration of the fourth year, and of the third claſs at the expiration of the ſixth year, ſo that one-third may be choſen every ſecond year; and if vacancies happen by reſignation, or otherwiſe, during the receſs of the legiſlature of any ſtate, the executive thereof may make temporary appointments until the next meeting of the legiſlature, which ſhall then fill ſuch vacancies.

No perſon ſhall be a ſenator who ſhall not have attained to the age of thirty years, and been nine years a citizen of the United States, and who ſhall not, when elected, be an inhabitant of that ſtate for which he ſhall be choſen.

The Vice-Preſident of the United States ſhall be Preſident of the ſenate, but ſhall have no vote, unleſs they be equally divided.

The Senate ſhall chuſe their other officers, and alſo a Preſident pro tempore, in the abſence of the Vice-Preſident, or when he ſhall exerciſe the office of Preſident of the United States.

The Senate ſhall have the ſole power to try all impeachments. When ſitting for that purpoſe, they ſhall be on oath or affirmation. When the Preſident of the United States is tried, the Chief Juſtice ſhall preſide: And no perſon ſhall be convicted without the concurrence of two-thirds of the members preſent.

Judgment in caſes of impeachment ſhall not extend further than to removal from office, and diſqualification to hold and enjoy any office of honor, truſt or profit under the United States; but the party convicted ſhall nevertheleſs be liable and ſubject to indictment, trial, judgment and puniſhment, according to law.

Sect. 4. The times, places and manner of holding elections for ſenators and repreſentatives, ſhall be preſcribed in each ſtate by the legiſlature thereof; but the Congreſs may at any time by law make or alter ſuch regulations, except as to the places of chuſing ſenators.

The Congreſs ſhall aſſemble at leaſt once in every year, and ſuch meeting ſhall be on the firſt Monday in December, unleſs they ſhall by law appoint a different day.

Sect. 5. Each houſe ſhall be the judge of the elections, returns and qualifications of its own members, and a majority of each ſhall conſtitute a quorum to do buſineſs; but a ſmaller number may adjourn from day to day, and may be authoriſed to compel the attendance of abſent members, in ſuch manner and under ſuch penalties as each houſe may provide.

Each houſe may determine the rules of its proceedings, puniſh its members for diſorderly behaviour, and, with the concurrence of two thirds, expel a member.

Each houſe ſhall keep a journal of its proceedings, and from time to time publiſh the ſame, excepting ſuch parts as may in their judgment require ſecrecy; and the yeas and nays of the members of either houſe, on any queſtion, ſhall, at the deſire of one-fifth of thoſe preſent, be entered on the journal.

Neither houſe, during the ſeſſion of Congreſs, ſhall, without the conſent of the other, adjourn for more than three days, nor to any other place than that in which the two houſes ſhall be ſitting.

Sect. 6. The Senators and Repreſentatives ſhall receive a compenſation for their ſervices, to be aſcertained by law, and paid out of the treaſury of the United States. They ſhall in all caſes, except treaſon, felony and breach of the peace, be privileged from arreſt during their attendance at the ſeſſion of their reſpective houſes, and in going to and returning from the ſame; and for any ſpeech or debate in either houſe, they ſhall not be queſtioned in any other place.

No ſenator or repreſentative ſhall, during the time for which he was elected, be appointed to any civil office under the authority of the United States, which ſhall have been created, or the emoluments whereof ſhall have been encreaſed during ſuch time; and no perſon holding any office under the United States, ſhall be a member of either houſe during his continuance in office.

Sect. 7. All bills for raiſing revenue ſhall originate in the houſe of repreſentatives; but the ſenate may propoſe or concur with amendments as on other bills.

Every bill which ſhall have paſſed the houſe of repreſentatives and the ſenate, ſhall, before it becomes a law, be preſented to the preſident of the United States; if he approve he ſhall ſign it, but if not he ſhall return it, with his objections, to that houſe in which it ſhall have originated, who ſhall enter the objections at large on their journal, and proceed to reconſider it. If after ſuch reconſideration, two-thirds of that houſe ſhall agree to paſs the bill, it ſhall be ſent, together with the objections, to the other houſe, by which it ſhall likewiſe be reconſidered, and if approved by two thirds of that houſe, it ſhall become a law. But in all ſuch caſes the votes of both houſes ſhall be determined by yeas and nays, and the names of the perſons voting for and againſt the bill ſhall be entered on the journal of each houſe reſpectively. If any bill ſhall not be returned by the preſident within ten days (Sundays excepted) after it ſhall have been preſented to him, the ſame ſhall be a law, in like manner as if he had ſigned it, unleſs the Congreſs by their adjournment prevent its return, in which caſe it ſhall not be a law.

Every order, reſolution, or vote to which the concurrence of the Senate and Houſe of Repreſentatives may be neceſſary (except on a queſtion of adjournment) ſhall be preſented to the Preſident of the United States; and before the ſame ſhall take effect, ſhall be approved by him, or, being diſapproved by him, ſhall be repaſſed by two-thirds of the Senate and Houſe of Repreſentatives, according to the rules and limitations preſcribed in the caſe of a bill.

Sect. 8. The Congreſs ſhall have power—

To lay and collect taxes, duties, impoſts and exciſes, to pay the debts and provide for the common defence and general welfare of the United States; but all duties, impoſts and exciſes ſhall be uniform throughout the United States;

To borrow money on the credit of the United States;

To regulate commerce with foreign nations, and among the ſeveral ſtates, and with the Indian tribes;

To eſtabliſh an uniform rule of naturalization, and uniform laws on the ſubject of bankruptcies throughout the United States;

To coin money, regulate the value thereof and of foreign coin, and fix the ſtandard of weights and meaſures;

To provide for the puniſhment of counterfeiting the ſecurities and current coin of the United States;

To eſtabliſh poſt offices and poſt roads;

To promote the progreſs of ſcience and uſeful arts, by ſecuring for limited times to authors and inventors, the excluſive right to their reſpective writings and diſcoveries;

To conſtitute tribunals inferior to the ſupreme court;

To define and puniſh piracies and felonies committed on the high ſeas, and offences againſt the law of nations;

To declare war, grant letters of marque and repriſal, and make rules concerning captures on land and water;

To raiſe and ſupport armies, but no appropriation of money to that uſe ſhall be for a longer term than two years;

To provide and maintain a navy;

To make rules for the government and regulation of the land and naval forces;

To provide for calling forth the militia to execute the laws of the union, ſuppreſs inſurrections and repel invaſions;

To provide for organizing, arming, and diſciplining, the militia, and for governing ſuch part of them as may be employed in the ſervice of the United States; reſerving to the States reſpectively, the appointment of the officers, and the authority of training the militia according to the diſcipline preſcribed by Congreſs;

To exerciſe excluſive legiſlation in all caſes whatſoever, over ſuch diſtrict (not exceeding ten miles ſquare) as may, by ceſſion of particular ſtates and the acceptance of Congreſs, become the ſeat of the government of the United States, and to exerciſe like authority over all places purchaſed by the conſent of the legiſlature of the ſtate in which the ſame ſhall be, for the erection of forts, magazines, arſenals, dock-yards, and other needful buildings;—And

To make all laws which ſhall be neceſſary and proper for carrying into execution the foregoing powers, and all other powers veſted by this conſtitution in the government of the United States, or in any department or office thereof.

Sect. 9. The migration or importation of ſuch perſons as any of the ſtates now exiſting ſhall think proper to admit, ſhall not be prohibited by the Congreſs prior to the year one thouſand eight hundred and eight, but a tax or duty may be impoſed on ſuch importation, not exceeding ten dollars for each perſon.

The privilege of the writ of habeas corpus ſhall not be ſuſpended, unleſs when in caſes of rebellion or invaſion, the public ſafety may require it.

No bill of attainder or ex poſt facto law ſhall be paſſed.

No capitation, or other direct tax ſhall be laid, unleſs in proportion to the cenſus or enumeration herein before directed to be taken.

No tax or duty ſhall be laid on articles exported from any ſtate. No preference ſhall be given by any regulation of commerce or revenue to the ports of one ſtate over thoſe of another; nor ſhall veſſels, bound to, or from one ſtate, be obliged to enter, clear, or pay duties in another.

No money ſhall be drawn from the treaſury, but in conſequence of appropriations made by law; and a regular ſtatement and account of the receipts and expenditures of all public money ſhall be publiſhed from time to time.

No title of Nobility ſhall be granted by the United States:—And no perſon holding any office of profit or truſt under them, ſhall, without the conſent of the Congreſs, accept of any preſent, emolument, office, or title, of any kind whatever, from any king, prince, or foreign ſtate.

Sect. 10. No ſtate ſhall enter into any treaty, alliance, or confederation; grant letters of marque and repriſal; coin money; emit bills of credit; make any thing but gold and ſilver coin a tender in payment of debts; paſs any bill of attainder, ex poſt facto law, or law impairing the obligation of contracts, or grant any title of nobility.

No ſtate ſhall, without the conſent of the Congreſs, lay any impoſts or duties on imports or exports, except what may be abſolutely neceſſary for executing its inſpection laws; and the net produce of all duties and impoſts, laid by any ſtate on imports or exports, ſhall be for the uſe of the treaſury of the United States; and all ſuch laws ſhall be ſubject to the reviſion and controul of the congreſs. No ſtate ſhall, without the conſent of congreſs, lay any duty of tonnage, keep troops, or ſhips of war in time of peace, enter into any agreement or compact with another ſtate, or with a foreign power, or engage in war, unleſs actually invaded, or in ſuch imminent danger as will not admit of delay.

II.

Sect. 1. The executive power ſhall be veſted in a Preſident of the United States of America. He ſhall hold his office during the term of four years, and, together with the Vice-Preſident, choſen for the ſame term, be elected as follows:

Each ſtate ſhall appoint, in ſuch manner as the legiſlature thereof may direct, a number of electors, equal to the whole number of ſenators and repreſentatives to which the ſtate may be entitled in the congreſs: but no ſenator or repreſentative, or perſon holding an office of truſt or profit under the United States, ſhall be appointed an elector.

The electors ſhall meet in their reſpective ſtates, and vote by ballot for two perſons, of whom one at leaſt ſhall not be an inhabitant of the ſame ſtate with themſelves. And they ſhall make a liſt of all the perſons voted for, and of the number of votes for each; which liſt they ſhall ſign and certify, and tranſmit, ſealed, to the ſeat of the government of the United States, directed to the preſident of the ſenate. The preſident of the ſenate ſhall, in the preſence of the ſenate and houſe of repreſentatives, open all the certificates, and the votes ſhall then be counted. The perſon having the greateſt number of votes ſhall be the Preſident, if ſuch number be a majority of the whole number of electors appointed; and if there be more than one who have ſuch majority, and have an equal number of votes, then the houſe of repreſentatives ſhall immediately chuſe by ballot, one of them for preſident; and if no perſon have a majority, then from the five higheſt on the liſt, the ſaid houſe ſhall in like manner chuſe the preſident. But in chuſing the preſident, the votes ſhall be taken by ſtates, the repreſentation from each ſtate having one vote; a quorum for this purpoſe ſhall conſiſt of a member or members from two thirds of the ſtates; and from the backcountry areas which two days later supported the Constitution 17 to 1. The lowcountry opposed adjournment 120 to 17, making the total 135 to 89 against prematurely closing the convention.[32] Undoubtedly some backcountry delegates, moderate in their dislike of the Constitution, decided that since further opposition was useless, they might join the winning side.

Antifederalism was stronger in the state at large than the ratification vote and probably the vote to adjourn indicated. Reverend Francis Cummins was chosen as a delegate to the convention because his constituents thought he opposed the Constitution. In fact, he favored amendments, including the insertion of a religious test. Only Cummins of ten New Acquisition delegates voted to ratify.[33] There must have been others whose views conflicted with those of their constituents. Some may have been persuaded by Federalist oratory unheard by the people. Others were simply pressured. Aedanus Burke later wrote that "the principle cause" of ratification was the unity of Charleston. Ratification was supported by "the merchants, mechanicks, the Populace, and mob of Charleston." In the entire city, according to Burke, "there are not fifty Inhabitants" unfriendly to the new government. "The whole weight and influence of the Press" was actively for ratification. And, in addition, perhaps most irresistible (Burke did not say that), "the merchants and leading men kept open houses for the back and low country members during the whole time the Convention sat."[34] Flattered, cajoled, wooed, some yielded. Opponents of the Constitution had known beforehand of Charleston's adverse influence, which explained why the motion to hold the ratifying convention in the city had passed the lower house in January by only a 76 to 75 vote, the backcountry voting 57 to 2 for the losing side.[35]

The geographic division between Federalists and Antifederalists reflected an economic and social conflict. The old, ostentatiously wealthy and educated lowcountry settlers supported the Constitution. The leading practising lawyers were Federalists: Charles Cotesworth Pinckney, his partner Edward Rutledge, and his cousin Charles Pinckney, John Julius Pringle, and Jacob Read. Eleven other Federalists were lawyers, including John Rutledge, the Chancellor. Only three Antifederalists were: James G. Hunt and Samuel Lowry, both representing the New Acquisition, had been admitted to the Charleston bar in 1786. Aedanus Burke, who had studied law in Virginia, had been a judge since 1778. Leading merchants like Josiah Smith, Daniel Desaussure, Edward Darrell, and Nathaniel Russell were Federalists. There were, however, two important Antifederalist merchants: John Lewis Gervais, who had backcountry ties, and Keating Simons.[36]

Federalists were wealthier than Antifederalists. A greater percentage of Antifederalists owned public securities (68.5 percent to 41.6 percent), but the Federalists owned larger amounts. Eighteen Federalists, or slightly over 12 percent, owned more than $5,000 each worth of securities compared to only four, or 5.5 percent, of the Antifederalists. Among those whose property holdings are known, the slaveholding and land-owning patterns were equally well-defined. Federalists owned an average of 66 slaves each, Antifederalists 34. Thirty-five Federalists, almost 24 percent, owned more than 100 slaves each. Only four Antifederalists, 5.5 percent, owned so many. Eighty-seven Federalists, 59 percent, were large planters, while only thirty-one Antifederalists, 41.7 percent, could be so classified. But twenty-seven Antifederalists, 34.2 percent, were small planters and farmers compared to fifteen Federalists, 10.7 percent.

There was too an enormous gulf between the large Federalist planters and the large Antifederalist planters. Those large planters supporting the Constitution owned an average of 90 slaves each, those opposed, 49. In the lowcountry alone, large Federalist planters owned an average of 95 slaves each, large Antifederalist planters, 66. In the backcountry large Federalist planters owned an average of over 48 slaves each and large Antifederalist planters, 37.[37]

There was, therefore, an economic division between the opposing sides at the ratifying convention. In simplest terms, the more valuable the property a delegate owned the more likely he was to be a Federalist. And the gulf between Federalists and Antifederalists was even greater outside the convention. Backcountry settlers invariably sent to the convention the same people they sent to the legislature, and no one was supposed to sit in the lower house unless he had a freehold estate worth £1,000 currency clear of debt or 500 acres and ten slaves, or in the Senate without a freehold estate worth £2,000 currency. While the same qualifications applied throughout the state, a greater percentage of lowcountry settlers could legally be elected to the legislature. Scattered tax returns indicated that few in the interior could fill even the much lower qualifications for borrowing paper money from the state.[38]

In one distant lowcountry parish, Georgetown's Prince Frederick, the delegates' four to three vote for the Constitution may have been based on religious differences and personal hostilities. Presbyterians in the parish had divided into warring factions, the majority "auld lichts" drawing strength from settlers who moved in shortly before the Revolution. So intense did the feelings become that in August 1786 the minority new "lichts" with about 100 slaves destroyed their rivals' church down to its foundation and carried the pulpit three miles into the country. Brought into court, they were forced to pay damages.[39] At the ratifying convention, the four delegates who voted with the dominant lowcountry group were the sons of original settlers who came from Ireland of Scots-Irish descent in 1736, while the three who opposed them had arrived only about 1770 and were of Irish descent.

The arguments over the Constitution were neither geographic nor economic. They were political and constitutional. Environmental influences visited on many people common problems and like experiences that shaped their lives, stimulated their hopes, and formed their opinions about man and government. And it was about man and government that people argued.

Few objected to the specific powers granted to the new central government. Except for a debate on the wisdom of allowing Congress to prohibit the slave trade after 1808, there was hardly any discussion of what the Constitution would do to or for South Carolina. Rawlins Lowndes was one of the few who talked in material terms. He complained that Congress could pass navigation acts by a simple majority vote. According to David Ramsay, Lowndes thought the New Englanders a ''set of sharpers'' much ''too cunning for our honest people.''[40] But Lowndes's position was not much different from that of many Carolinians. During the 1780s the state legislation granting Congress commercial powers had required that Congress act only with the assent of two-thirds of the states. South Carolina's delegates at Philadelphia thought the restriction wise. Charles Pinckney favored a three-fourths vote because Southern states would otherwise be subject to ''oppressive regulations.''[41]

The other delegates opposed Pinckney but only to conciliate the "affections of the East[ern] States'' and achieve another goal: security for their slaves. When Southerners won a vote to distribute representation in the lower house on the basis of a population that included three-fifths of the slaves, some delegates tried to empower Congress to prohibit the slave trade. The Carolina delegates, except Charles Pinckney, compromised. They secured protection of the slave trade until 1808 and gave up on requiring more than a majority vote for navigation acts.[42] Slaveowners were further protected, Charles Cotesworth Pinckney argued, by gaining a right to recover fugitive slaves.[43] But neither the right to recover fugitives nor the right to import slaves until 1808, traded for the majority vote on navigation acts, impressed Rawlins Lowndes. He did not think the deal just.

Lowndes also attacked the Senate's treaty-making power. He thought two-thirds of the Senate too small a number for the ratification of treaties. But no one joined him. Carolinians, despite the scare in 1786 when John Jay had proposed to give up America's right to navigate the Mississippi for commercial concessions from Spain, seemed satisfied that the provision protected them from Northern power.[44]

The lack of detailed discussion of the specific powers granted the government testified that in most economic matters the Carolina delegates had represented fairly the interests of the state. But because in political matters they had satisfied mostly people in the lowcountry, there was opposition to the form of the new government and the political philosophy which justified it.

Both supporters and opponents of the Constitution spoke of the people's voice, the American Revolution, and liberty. ''All power of right belongs to the people,'' said Charles Pinckney, beginning a long defense of the Constitution. "It flows immediately from them, and is delegated to their officers for the public good." It was "indispensable, in a republic, that all authority should flow from the people." David Ramsay, a strong advocate of the Constitution, had written six months earlier that the origin of the new plan was "the voice & its end the good of the people."[45] Echoing ideas about the importance of the people, Patrick Dollard mentioned "an old saying, and I believe a very true one, that the general voice of the people is the voice of God." The people spoke differently to Dollard than to Ramsay and Pinckney, however. They would not accept the Constitution, he thought, unless a standing army "ram it down their throats with the points of bayonets."[46]

The speakers disagreed about the relation between the Constitution and the Revolution. James Lincoln, from Ninety Six District, warned the people that they were changing a "well-formed democratic" government into an aristocratic one, and pointedly asked them what they had been "contending for these ten years past?" Liberty, "the power of governing yourselves." Adopt this Constitution, he said, and you throw away "all that human wisdom and valor could procure," sentiments echoed by a poem in the *State Gazette of South-Carolina:*

> Some alterations in our fabric we
> Calmly propos'd, and hoped at length to see—
> Ah, how deceived!—these heroes in renown
> Scheme for themselves—and pull the fabric down—
> Bid in its place Columbia's tomb-stone rise
> Inscrib'd with these sad words—*Here Freedom Lies!*[47]

Shortly after the ratifying convention Aedanus Burke explained his fear of a counterrevolution: the Antifederalists thought they were "likely to be robbed both of the honour and the fruits of . . . [liberty] by a Revolution purposely contrived for it."[48] Federalist Francis Kinloch welcomed the return to an older system because Americans did not have "virtue enough for . . . [a] free form of government." Ramsay, however, argued that the Revolution would be incomplete until the Constitution, "or something equivalent, is established." In like manner, the *City Gazette, or the Daily Advertiser* noted that with few exceptions the same men led in the drive for both the Revolution and the new Constitution.[49]

Antifederalists admitted vaguely, perhaps reluctantly, that the Articles of Confederation needed revision, for they were written, as Lincoln said, "in times of confusion and distress." Alexander Tweed, in the end a supporter of the Constitution but originally an Antifederalist, like Lincoln and Patrick Dollard, thought that the Articles needed changing. Tweed, however, challenged the most important Federalist argument, the necessity for haste. The convention had been told, he said, that without the new Constitution some "powerful despot might start up and seize the reins of government." He thought the situation not so desperate. "Are we invaded by a foreign enemy? Or are the bowels of our country torn to pieces by insurrections and intestine broils? I answer, No.''[50]

Antifederalists protested that the new government was not sufficiently responsive to the people. They complained, in almost their only expressed difference with the Federalists, about the structure of the government to be established: a two-house legislature, only one branch of which was chosen by the people, with both senators and representatives eligible for lifetime service. Not expressed, perhaps because Carolina legislators usually failed to speak in these terms, was a fear of the framers' intent. Lowndes may have come close in sarcastically noting that opponents of the Constitution were not supposed to ''be uneasy, since every thing would be managed in [the] future by great men; and great men . . . were infallible. . . .''[51] Not long after ratification Pierce Butler said about another issue being debated that ''it is the measure and not the men we are to judge.'' One should consider the ''effect'' of a measure and not ''the cause.'' If the effect were good, it was unimportant whether or not the cause was ''self-interest or any other base passion.''[52] But Antifederalists could not separate measure from men, the Constitution from the South Carolina delegation.

Regardless of how Federalists, with ''eloquence and learning,'' explained the philosophy behind each clause of the Constitution, and ignorant of the efforts South Carolina's delegates to the Constitutional Convention had made to deprive the people of the choice of representatives, backcountry Antifederalists had reason to doubt the virtues of any political system supported by Rutledge, by oppressive lawyers who welcomed back loyalists, and by the rest of the lowcountry aristocracy.[53] If Charles Pinckney favored, as the citizens knew he did, a government which had an absolute veto over all state legislation, and if he feared ''the anarchy, . . . or rather worse than anarchy of a pure democracy,'' Antifederalists could conclude that he was interested not only in increasing the powers of the central government but also in depriving Westerners of their newly-won influence.[54] Their powers decreased when state governments were weakened. Pinckney's satisfaction was cause for alarm.

The Constitution, Antifederalists said over and over, was a step toward despotism. ''Lust of dominion is natural in every soil,'' said Patrick Dollard. Aedanus Burke remained consistent with his stand in 1783 when he had argued that "anarchy or no Government is far preferable to an arbitrary one.'' He answered Federalists who held that without the Constitution the country would be thrown into a state of anarchy by saying that despotism was worse than anarchy, ''for a war must be succeeded by peace, but despotism was a monster very difficult to be got rid of.''[55]

Reminders were common that the effects of power on character made jealousy necessary. The solution to the potential, and too often real, evils of power, was also commonly known. ''The only security the people had for their liberties,'' Burke said, ''lay in their officers of government being rotationary. . . ." Dr. Peter Fayssoux objected that the absence of a limitation on terms of officeholding, combined with Congress's power to pay itself, might destroy liberty.[56]

Rotation was a fundamental principle of the Articles of Confederation, article five of which prohibited any delegate to Congress from serving more than three years in any six, and of most state constitutions, South Carolina's included. James Lincoln remarked that there was nothing to prevent a President from repeating his four-year term fourteen times. "You do not put the same check on him," Lincoln said, "that you do on your own state governor, a man born and bred among you, a man over whom you have a continual and watchful eye."[57] South Carolina's constitution of 1778 prohibited the governor from serving more than two years in a six-year period, a feature retained when the state drew up a new constitution in 1790.

Lincoln's argument was two-fold. The absence of rotation was all the more serious because the government was located far from the "continual and watchful eye" of the people. They were giving away their liberty "into the hands of a set of men who live one thousand miles distant." Aedanus Burke moved the government 100 miles closer but thought that senators would still act in darkness and might lose sight of their country's welfare, an argument some Federalists really agreed with: Jacob Read had, in fact, said in 1786 that he had been in Congress too long to know how his constituents felt about commercial legislation. More appropriately, Charles Cotesworth Pinckney had argued at Philadelphia that a senatorial term longer than four years would cause senators to "lose sight of the States they represent."[58] Even worse than the danger from ignorant senators, Burke thought, was the danger from senators who might soon learn to "consult only the dictates of inordinate ambition."[59]

Again the Antifederalists' ideas were rooted in recent experiences. In an age when transportation and communication were slow, the location of the capital was of major importance to competing interests. Regulators had attributed some of their sufferings to the meetings of the legislature in Charleston. People knew of the continuous efforts to move the state government from Charleston to the interior. The attempts had begun in 1783, but not until 1786 did the legislature agree to the building of a town where the capital would be relocated. And not until 1790 was the government moved permanently. Antifederalists stressed the importance of Charleston even when explaining the ratification of the Constitution. If backcountry settlers worried about a Charleston government, they would naturally fear a great deal more from a government 900 or more miles distant.

In the legislature Rawlins Lowndes attacked the provision by which senators were to be elected by the state legislatures rather than by the people themselves. Lowndes referred to the state's constitutional history: originally the upper house had been chosen by the lower, "which practice proved so inconvenient and oppressive,'' he said, that it was changed.[60] Vetoing the constitution of 1778 John Rutledge had specifically objected to the popular election of senators because it was less likely to produce ''persons of the greatest integrity, learning, and abilities,'' an objection much like the one he made at Philadelphia to the plan for the popular election of representatives.[61] Those Carolinians who were willing to abolish the state senate during the Confederation period were undoubtedly sympathetic to Lowndes's attack on the Senate.

None of the Antifederalists' arguments went unanswered. Point by point the Federalists supported the Constitution. In response to Lowndes, Charles Cotesworth Pinckney argued that the state legislature was not analogous to the federal. If the lower house of the state government elected the upper, there would be no balance, because the Senate would be dependent on the branch which elected it. But in the federal government the Senate was independent of the lower house by virtue of election by the state legislatures. There was no need for popular election.[62] For Pinckney balance was important; for Lowndes, at least in this case, the ''rights and privileges'' of the people mattered.

Federalists, too, talked about the responsiveness of the government to the people. Charles Pinckney opened the convention with the idea that all power belonged to the people and that the people's rulers were in fact servants, ''amenable to their will and created for their use.'' Under the new Constitution, Federalists argued, the people would be more truly represented in Congress than they had been under the Articles, when the state legislatures chose all the delegates to Congress. No one seems to have countered, but some might have thought, that it mattered little who attended the meetings of the weak Confederation Congress. But more important, the Federalists argued, thinking probably of Alexander Gillon and a few others, the new government would be a republican one without the usual accompanying evils, "dissensions, tumults, faction, the attempts of ambitious citizens to possess power.''[63]

They repeated the same argument time and again. ''Little demagogue[s],'' ''factious and designing men,'' would not be able "to infect the whole people" when the "sphere of government" was enlarged.[64] Free from the machinations of politicians who played on their emotions, fears, and hopes, the people would be able to elect the best men.

As for the doctrine of rotation, Federalists labeled it ''a political mania'' which ''operated like wild fire'' at the end of the war, causing considerable inconvenience in Congress. In effect, John Rutledge said, people with experience could not serve the government. South Carolina treasurers, and a few other state officials, like the governor, were dismissed from office when they were only beginning to know their jobs. Rotation in the army, Jacob Read said, almost ruined the country. Perhaps more seriously, rotation was seen as an insult to the man everyone knew would be the country's first President. Pierce Butler admitted, but only privately, that the President's powers were ''full great,'' greater indeed than he ''was disposed to make them,'' but that was because the convention's ''members cast their eyes toward General Washington as President,'' which meant — and the admission was still private — that Washington's ''Patriotism & Virtue, [which] contributed largely to the Emancipation of His Country, may be the Innocent means of its being, when He is lay'd low, oppressed.''[65]

The dialogue, which could have gone on indefinitely, was meaningless in the end. Federalists could permit extensive debate and not fear the consequences because backcountry representatives were neither powerful enough to win nor vicious enough to cause much discomfort. Sometimes in the past they had united with like-minded people in distant lowcountry parishes and with Charleston radicals to press their views, occasionally with success and more often with the threat of success. But no matter how many responsive and even familiar chords the Antifederalists struck with constitutional and political arguments, they could not convince their former allies. Charleston radicals, led by Alexander Gillon, had viciously attacked the political ideas of the aristocracy, calling its members ''*rank cowards, . . . rank tories, . . . rank upstarts, . . . rank idio[t]s.*'' ''DEMOCRATIC GENTLE-TOUCH'' and other anonymous writers had focused on the ''*corrupt, avaricious lawyers*'' who composed part of the aristocracy.[66] But no one came forward in 1788 to attack the lawyers who represented the state at Philadelphia. No newspaper assailed the aristocracy. The harmony, which allowed Edward Rutledge to label opposition ''tedious but trifling,'' existed apparently because Charleston radicals overlooked whatever might have been their political objections to the Constitution in order to strengthen Congress' control over trade, in order to secure tariffs against British goods. Backcountry settlers, struggling for political power within the state, found the advantages of the Constitution too slight compared with its poltical disadvantages. Had Gillon and others been actively engaged, the ratification fight would have been closer and more exciting, but, probably still, equally futile for the Antifederalists.

With but few exceptions the visible division over the Constitution in South Carolina was economic and geographic. Federalism's strength lay in the lowcountry, among planters, lawyers, and merchants, who, along with city inhabitants generally, welcomed the serious attempt to strengthen the central government. The Charleston firm of Brailsford and Morris thought other nations would stop ''view[ing] us with Contempt,'' a sentiment and hope shared by many others. Respect promised economic advantage, for foreign countries would "gladly court our rising Consequence."[67] City workers hoped to keep out some foreign importations; rice planters looked for a reopening of markets in the West Indies and Portugal.

Backcountry Antifederalists had little quarrel with those goals. Their stated objections were constitutional. Antifederalists had little faith that representatives could remain honest, committed, and responsible while serving for long periods far from home. The structure of the proposed government was less protective of the people's rights and freedoms than their own state government. Their reluctance to share authority was undoubtedly increased by their recent attainment of substantial local power and by their suspicions of some of their opponents' less visible, political motives.

There was, however, according to some contemporaries, another dimension to the economic division between Federalists and Antifederalists. Article 1, section 10, of the Constitution provided that "no State shall . . . emit Bills of Credit; make any Thing but gold and silver Coin a Tender in Payments of Debts; [or] pass any . . . Law impairing the Obligation of Contracts. . . ." In the North Carolina convention William R. Davie justified that "fundamental principle" by citing South Carolina's financial record and its meaning for the future. Legislators there might, "as they have already done, make pine-barren acts to discharge their debts." They might, he concluded, "pass the most iniquitous instalment laws, procrastinating the payment of debts due from their citizens, for some years — nay, for ages." Matthew Locke replied, defending the necessity of South Carolina's actions: the laws were passed "to save vast numbers of people from ruin."[68] But surprisingly, neither side in South Carolina talked much about the limitation on the state's financial powers. Creditors did not praise it. Debtors did not damn it.

Debtor legislation, strenuously supported by many of the same lowcountry planters who became Federalists, was a fact of the state's recent past. When the ratifying convention met in May 1788, some people, perhaps mostly Antifederalists, were silently interested in paper money bills, valuation schemes, or installment acts — in short, in a re-enactment of the legislation of 1785 and 1787 — but apparently the Federalists were no longer concerned with financial problems. With a strict economic interpretation, Charles Cotesworth Pinckney, for example, maintained that "if we were allowed to pass Installment & valuation Laws as heretofore, an antifederalist would be a rare *avis* in this state."[69] The assured statement was misleading; it neither accounted for past legislation nor anticipated sentiments and actions only a few months away. Had the ratifying convention been held in October 1788, rather than in May, Pinckney would have had a difficult time distinguishing between a Federalist and Antifederalist stand on debtor laws.

ELEVEN
"No Reason to Despair"

However unexceptionable democratic power may appear at first view, its effects have been found arbitrary, severe, and destructive.

John Rutledge, 5 March 1778.

In a Republican Government, an address by petition to an Assembly of deputies of the People must be considered a gross absurdity! Shall the people petition the people! The inhabitants of Pendleton, therefore, adopt the mode of respectful Representation!

Pendleton County, 10 July 1794.

DESPITE Patrick Dollard's prophecy that the people of Prince Frederick would reject the Constitution unless an army imposed it, opposition never became physical or violent. Aedanus Burke reported only a rumor that in some backcountry sections coffins were painted black and "solemnly buried, as an emblem of the dissolution and interment of public Liberty." If they occurred, the symbolic protests apparently satisfied the Antifederalist majority in the state, perhaps because leaders like Thomas Sumter, Burke, and even Dollard, ended the convention with assurances that they would urge people to accept the new government.[1] Resigning themselves to defeat, however, they soon made the best of a bad situation.

Federalists rejoiced, expecting increased trade, prohibitive tariffs on British goods, assumption of state debts, or the reformation of the political order. Representatives of the butchers, bakers, carpenters, tanners, and other crafts marched with gentlemen planters, merchants, judges, and legislators in a huge Charleston celebration. Even in the Camden area, where there was a "very great backwardness" regarding the Constitution, "a great many gentlemen" celebrated. A newspaper noted that the militia and many inhabitants of Prince Frederick proved Dollard a poor prophet by showing their approbation of the federal Constitution.[2]

The victors looked for action, change, and improvement. Ralph Izard hoped there would be no "idle discussions about amendments to the Constitution": rather, he urged immediate efforts to improve the country's "embarrassed and disgraceful [financial] situation." Edward Rutledge thought the Constitution would bring "all the Advantages that flow from good government." For Francis Kinloch progress would come because the powerful new government was like "the system we destroyed some years ago."[3]

Since the national government was not yet organized and functioning, however, its supporters' optimism was not unqualified. Antifederalist cooperation was pleasant but troublesome. Carolinians elected to the first Congress not only William Loughton Smith and Daniel Huger, but Aedanus Burke, Thomas Sumter, and Thomas Tudor Tucker, the men who made John Faucheraud Grimké's "black list."[4] And Federalists had to worry still about state politics and problems. Between ratification in May 1788 and Washington's inauguration in April 1789, South Carolina became once more a place of economic turmoil, forcing anew on the legislature the divisive topic of debtor legislation. Moreover, a little more than a year after the new Congress met, South Carolinians wrote their third constitution. The controversies following ratification marked a fitting close to the period of Revolution and Confederation.

Although legislators and delegates at the ratifying convention hardly mentioned the enormous private debts while arguing the merits of the Constitution, David Ramsay and Charles Cotesworth Pinckney explained opposition in simple economic terms: Antifederalists, they said, were worried debtors. Even before the convention met, Ramsay had warned people to "guard against the misrepresentations" of debtors; they might want to reject the Constitution because of the clause banning state paper money and state interference with private contracts. He feared "the numerous class of debtors more than any other." For Benjamin Rush, Ramsay summarized the Antifederalists' argument: "if we agree to the new constitution, . . . we will be obliged to pay our debts & taxes."[5] Pinckney supported that economic interpretation, believing that there would be few Antifederalists in South Carolina if states could pass debtor legislation.[6]

But both Pinckney and Ramsay knew that the link between debtors and Antifederalists was not what they tried to make it seem. They not only failed to explain recent legislative divisions but they also ignored completely the federalism of those debtors who had earlier worked for protective legislation. In October 1788 Pinckney would argue against debtor legislation and stress that in the past "gentlemen from the upper country" had agreed to legislative interference in private contracts only "in compliance with the wishes of the lower country gentlemen."[7] Both Pinckney and Ramsay had been present in 1785 when the legislature, dominated by the lowcountry, and in particular by Charleston and neighboring parishes, passed a paper money scheme and a pine barren act. They were present again in February 1788, just three months before ratification, when another valuation bill was introduced. It was defeated by a vote of ninety-two to fifty-three. The backcountry opposed it twenty-five to twenty-eight, which hardly proved that Antifederalists were against paying debts.[8]

Arthur Bryan would have been as confused by the Federalists' correspondence as he was by their actions. An unimportant Charleston merchant, Bryan could not understand "how the lower & Middle [Country] Members . . . [could] support a system whose only good quality (the payment of debts) is so repugnant to their bad intentions of keeping entire possession of all [the] property they can get."[9]

There was, in fact, little connection between a person's indebtedness and his stand on the Constitution. Federalists and their opponents spoke favorably and forcefully on debtor legislation. John Julius Pringle, speaker of South Carolina's lower house and a Federalist, made the extraordinary justification of the legislature's right to suspend private contracts when necessary to protect the community.[10] Alexander Gillon supported debtor legislation and the Constitution, and Pierce Butler, a Philadelphia delegate, attempted to prove in February 1788 a need for further intervention between debtors and creditors. On that idea Antifederalist Thomas Sumter agreed with Butler, Gillon, and Pringle.[11]

Rawlins Lowndes lent some slight support to the charge that Antifederalists favored debtor legislation. In January 1788 he told members of the lower house that Congress' power to make treaties binding on the states "did away with the instalment law." He defended South Carolina's paper money and warned that "an entire stop must be put to any more paper emissions, however great our distress may be." But it was strategy and not interest that concerned Lowndes, for he himself had opposed the installment law, and in February he strongly attacked newly proposed debtor legislation by insisting on the sacredness of contracts.[12] His intent in bringing up the subject was to win support for his Antifederalist position, which he held for reasons unrelated to the Constitution's impact on debtors. The Federalists answered his arguments by insisting, as Charles Cotesworth Pinckney and John Julius Pringle did, that ratification of the Constitution would not overturn laws already passed.[13]

Lowndes's warning that the Constitution would affect debtor legislation was apparently not considered seriously, even though early in 1788 there was sentiment, notably in the backcountry, for further action. York County petitioners begged "leave to look up to your Honours as childring to a father & prays that you in your wisdomm will fall on some meathod" to issue paper money. At the same time they expressed a dislike of the pine barren and installment acts. From Winton County, Orangeburg District, also in the backcountry, came a request for a valuation law; because there was no circulating medium, "the infant farms" in the area, which was "just immurging from the ruins & devastations of the late unnatural war," sold at executions for too little money to satisfy creditors' demands.[14] Judge Henry Pendleton, a backcountry Federalist, agreed that existing legislation was inadequate, partly because "a 40s. bill was as scarce almost in the country as an elephant." Such scarcity led Sumter to support an emission of £300,000 in paper money.[15]

Gillon and Butler most persistently demanded new legislation. Gillon, arguing that the state was poverty stricken, asked for an extension of the installment act.[16] He told the legislature that New Hampshire, New Jersey, and Maryland had already passed such legislation. "The scarcity of Money in this country is inconceivable," Butler reported; "the difficulties in this State increase." He was a Founding Father upset by the Constitution's limitation on the states' economic powers. When there was "extreme necessity" the state must protect debtors. "If that necessity does exist" — and Butler thought it did — it was "the indispensable duty of the legislature to interfere." He predicted civil war unless the legislature intervened.[17]

Neither Gillon nor Butler was persuasive enough. Lowndes upheld the inviolability of contracts and said that debtors had nothing to fear, because there were no "worthier human men than the merchants." They would not be "inexorable" if debtors were "honestly inclined to discharge their debts." Dr. Peter Fayssoux thought creditors would try to avoid the universal odium that would follow cruel actions.[18]

Most legislators sided with Antifederalists Lowndes and Fayssoux. On 18 February the Senate defeated a motion to extend the installment act by a vote of 12 to 9. Backcountry senators favored extension by a 5 to 3 vote; the four senators present from lowcountry parishes far from Charleston voted against extension, and the Charleston area senators voted 5 to 4 against extension. A few days later the lower house defeated Butler's valuation scheme by a 92 to 53 vote. The lowcountry parishes in and around Charleston opposed the plan 49 to 22; the other lowcountry parishes voted 15 to 6 against valuation, while backcountry areas opposed it 28 to 25.[19]

The legislature's failure to pass new debtor legislation reflected the tranquility of many Carolinians. Because their first installments were not due until March 1788, debtors were unaware of how pressing their creditors would be. A motion in the Senate suggested the calm attitude: since the installment act "has not yet had any operation," and since no one has complained, the legislature ought not to interfere again. The Senate, perhaps unwilling to limit future actions, defeated the motion but continued to oppose new debtor legislation.[20]

Obviously pleased, Edward Rutledge reported in March, two months before the ratifying convention met, that the South Carolina legislature had "determined to interpose no more." Probably convinced that the margin of victory over debtors was substantial enough to absorb defections in the short time remaining before the new government began functioning, Rutledge implied that the decision was irrevocable. He clearly did not envision any immediate crisis, although he recognized the "almost inextricable difficulties" of the Southern states and commented on South Carolina's "trifling" supply of circulating currency.[21]

But creditors knew that the decisions of winter were not necessarily those of the coming fall, if only because the legislature had adjourned in March, agreeing, according to David Ramsay, to "meet again in October avowedly to have a further opportunity of securing debtors." That creditors were right to anticipate trouble was clear on 21 October, five months after the ratifying convention, when the House of Representatives resolved that there was "an indispensable necessity for the further interposition of the Legislature between creditors and their debtors." The Senate had already passed a similar resolution.[22]

Legislators recognized a new economic crisis, similar in many ways to the crisis which had brought on the paper money and pine barren acts a few years before. In September 1784 Colonel Hezekiah Maham had defied the law and forced a deputy to eat four writs. The next year people in Camden District closed the courts for the recovery of debts. In 1788 some people in Cheraw District, east of Camden but still in the backcountry, who had no circulating currency, banded together to prevent every "*sale for cash,* when taken by execution, by any sheriff or constable in this district." They would treat as "an enemy to humanity" any sheriff acting contrary to their resolutions and would protect any one threatened for obeying them.[23]

Petitions to the legislature emphasized the inadequate supply of currency. There was so little, said some people in the District Eastward of the Wateree, that property sold at sheriffs' sales brought no more than one-fifth its value. Orangeburg's settlers put the sale price at one-third to one-half the "intrinsic value," while Cheraw's settlers pushed the fraction down to one-tenth.[24] In the legislature Peter Fayssoux, though an opponent of debtor legislation, noted that a Negro had recently sold for £8, and 150 acres, belonging to a man who owed £9, had sold for only £6, while Ramsay, another opponent, privately acknowledged after the Constitution was ratified that conditions were "gradually growing worse" and that the people's "sufferings . . . as to money matters . . . [were] greater than in the time of the war or just after its close." Gillon said that there was no "stronger proof of a heavy debt" and lack of currency "than that bonds of gentlemen equal in fortune to any in this state are now selling at 40 or 50 per cent." Arthur Bryan reported that John Rutledge "openly buys his own bonds at ⅓."[25]

The lack of currency was important not only because it hindered business transactions within the state but also because of a new threat from England. When English concerns extending credit to Americans failed in 1784 and 1785, pressure was put upon American debtors. English houses specializing in the linen trade began again to totter and fall in 1788, partly because of their large American trade. According to the *Gentleman's*

Magazine, "the mercantile part" of London was seized by a "general consternation." The Charleston *City Gazette* reported in July that the total failures exceeded £1,500,000; it was "the greatest failure ever known at one time."[26] Even before the failures, Ramsay had written that each of three Charleston mercantile houses "could sue bonds to a greater amount than all the circulating money in the country would pay."

England's problem almost demolished the arguments of Lowndes, Fayssoux, and Ramsay that merchants could be trusted not to press intolerably hard for what was due them. In October Alexander Gillon could argue, without direct reference to the English failures but probably with them in mind, that merchants had no alternatives. They would follow either their own interests or their orders and enforce payments. Merchants might be compelled "by their necessities to sue the planters."[29] But despite the financial crisis, creditors might temporarily be lenient because they were aware that suits could inspire new debtor legislation while restraint might see them through until the federal Constitution became operative.[28]

Despite similarities, the crisis of 1788 differed significantly from that of 1785. Serious economic unrest had spread inland. Although Pendleton said that the interior opposed legislative intervention, other backcountry representatives, supported by petitions from their constituents, indicated otherwise. Settlers in the District East of the Wateree were "impressed with the deepest concern and heart felt grief at the new and faithful reports of the many destressing scenes" throughout the state, while those in Newberry County (the Lower District between the Broad and Saluda rivers) wrote of "almost insupportable distress" worse than the "Horrors of War." People from York and Orangeburg counties complained that they still suffered from the ravages of war; York's settlers warned that "their feelings will revolt at the idea of tamely suffering themselves and families to be totally stript of the conveniences and comforts of life and to be reduced to indigence and want."[29]

One lowcountry parish sent a petition, different in style and manner, but not in basic principles, from the usually humble productions of the backcountry. St. Bartholomew's settlers wrote of the loss of crops, the scarcity of money, and the "weak state of public and almost total annihilation of private credit" which had caused large numbers of good people problems "which no human foresight could have prevented and from which no industry or means within their own power can extract them." Confidently and boldly they assured the legislature of its duty to protect "virtuous citizens." They could not imagine "that a merciless capricious creditor" would be allowed to reduce a family to "beggary."[30]

St. Bartholomew was the only lowcountry parish to request legislation, but other parishes indicated by their votes that they were again interested in intervention, even though some parishes were not as desperate as they once had been. When the lower house resolved to act, without specifying how, backcountry representatives agreed by a vote of 36 to 4, those from the lowcountry far from Charleston by 14 to 1, and representatives from parishes near Charleston by 40 to 11, while Charleston representatives stood alone in opposition, casting 21 votes against and only 5 votes for the resolution.[31]

Charles Pinckney, who had denounced paper money and the pine barren act in the ratifying convention, like Gillon and Butler sought new legislation, and he supplied a reason for the renewed interest of the distant lowcountry parishes. Pointing to the often overlooked agricultural division that had become apparent during the fight over nonexportation in 1775, Pinckney described "*the failure of indigo* as one of our staples," arguing that there was now little hope for planters with indigo on hand, because their lands were not fit for the cultivation of rice.[32] Gillon called the failure of indigo an unexpected addition to the state's troubles. The crop could not be sold to the British since they had adopted a policy of importing indigo from the East and West Indies. "What immediate use can the planters on the southern sea islands turn their lands to?" Gillon asked. He noted the effect of the crop's failure on one backcountry area by reminding legislators that indigo was grown along the Congaree, Wateree, and Santee rivers.[33]

Indigo planters had been suffering since the war ended, annually marketing crops only half the prewar size. Their exports in 1788 were more than 100,000 pounds less than those of the previous year, and their prospects were not good. In the first few years after the British departed, the rice planters, too, had sold crops half the size of those sold in the 1770s. But by 1788 they were recovering, exporting then 17,000 more barrels of rice than in 1787 and predicting another substantial increase for the following year.[34] The recovery of rice may have been the reason for the Charleston District's decreased interest in radical debtor legislation.

The backcountry was vitally interested in intervention. As Gillon pointed out, some backcountry areas produced indigo which could not be sold. But the backcountry was also growing tobacco, in crops which were increasing in size in 1787 and 1788. The entire region had seemingly become more commercial-minded; its representatives worked for improved inland navigation and in 1787 voted by a thirty-one to eighteen margin against prohibition of the slave trade.[35] Perhaps that commercial growth not only necessitated a paper money bill to facilitate trade but debtor legislation as well to protect new planters whose sights had been set too high. There were also in the backcountry, as elsewhere, many whose fortunes had in no sense started upward.

Like Fayssoux, many foes of debtor legislation admitted the seriousness of the crisis. Edward Rutledge had written in March of the scarcity of money. Lowndes, again a leading spokesman for creditors, agreed that the state did not have sufficient currency. But Lowndes, who in September was elected Intendant of Federalist Charleston despite his Antifederalism, argued that private debts amounted to less than £1,200,000 sterling and could quickly be paid off.[36] Neither he nor John Mathews, however, who estimated the debt at only £880,000, could satisfactorily explain how to repay creditors within the three years provided by the installment act of 1787 if the state's exports continued to be worth no more than £500,000 a year, while imports rarely amounted to much less than £400,000. Charles Cotesworth Pinckney acknowledged also that the distress was very great, but he, like others, adamantly opposed new legislation, arguing that "the evil must work its cure."[37]

Most of the arguments supporting intervention were unchanged from 1785. Gillon, for example, repeated that the legislature must listen to and "effect the happiness of the people." He argued also that one could not trust merchants to be compassionate.[38]

But because they had a new argument, Gillon's opponents somewhat altered their emphasis. Jacob Read, a Federalist, told the legislators that conditions had changed, that "the people from whom all power was derived" had adopted a constitution that prohibited state intervention. When New Hampshire ratified the Constitution on 21 June it became binding, Read said, on all who had previously agreed to it. William Loughton Smith attempted to prove the new government binding, although not actually in existence.[39] As usual, David Ramsay expressed his ideas clearly. If we argue that, despite ratification, we still have "a right to do wrong, the world will say that we mean to be rascals under the new government as well as under the old." Henry Pendleton agreed.[40]

Ramsay thought it logical now to seek relief from the federal government, for it could restore credit, borrow money, establish banks, and "emit federal paper, which will be a circulating medium from New Hampshire to Georgia." Likewise Charleston merchants opposed state action and said that relief would come through "'*the Uniform Law on the subject of Bankruptcy*' *to* be adopted by the New Constitution throughout the United States."[41]

The new argument was useless. Most legislators agreed that the central government was not yet functioning and that the Constitution was not yet binding. To those who stressed that the new government would alleviate distress, Gillon made the obvious rejoinder: when it did, "our own laws might easily be repealed." Besides, it was not proper to let others do for you what you could do for yourselves.[42]

The debate over whether to intervene was shorter and easier to understand than that over how to intervene. Backcountry petitioners and state legislators disagreed on the choice of remedies. The inadequacy of the circulating medium was mentioned repeatedly in petitions and in the legislature, where Charles Pinckney had said that the state needed at least £300,000 of currency.[43] But not until January 1789 did James Lincoln, an Antifederalist, suggest a paper money act. The lower house overwhelmingly rejected the proposal, perhaps partly because Lincoln, aware of who had benefited from the money lent in 1786, tried to guarantee "that the poorer class of our citizens should have equal benefit from such paper emission as the rich lately had" by prohibiting previous borrowers from borrowing again.[44]

The backcountry met with similar failure in the vote on a valuation bill, which all their petitions requested. Pierce Butler brought forward a bill providing for the sale or transfer of property to creditors at a minimum of three-fourths the value set by district appraisers. Discussions were lengthy and frequently involved comparisons between the bill and the pine barren act, under which, said Edward Rutledge, "no man received justice. . . ." The comparison was probably fair, and Butler's plan was defeated by a vote of 89 to 43, with Charleston casting a solid 27 votes against the proposal, nearby parishes 37 votes against and 12 for, parishes far from Charleston 8 against and 7 for, and the backcountry 17 against and 24 for.[45]

Having disregarded pleas for paper money and defeated the valuation bill, the legislature decided to extend the installment act by making debts payable in five annual installments beginning in March 1789. So that no one who had obeyed the installment act of 1787 would feel unfairly treated, the law provided that money paid since 28 March 1787 for debts contracted before the first day of that year would be allowed the debtor "in the payment of any instalment which shall become due under this Act." To show good faith or perhaps to increase the value of slaves already in the state, the slave trade was prohibited until 1793. William Loughton Smith, a vehement opponent of debtor legislation, attacked the scheme because some debts were already thirty years old, but he, like Edward Rutledge, accepted it as the least harmful plan introduced in the legislature.[46]

It was debtor legislation, but not the kind sought by the backcountry. Only two petitions from the backcountry had suggested extending the installment act and then only combined with a suggestion for either a paper money or a valuation act. But extension was the only request of St. Bartholomew's petitioners. The bill, which passed by a vote of 59 to 45, was pushed through by the lowcountry parishes around Charleston, which cast 30 of 37 votes for it, while representatives from Georgetown and Beaufort, the other lowcountry districts, supported the bill by a 7 to 5 vote. Strangely, Charleston, splitting its vote 12 to 7, and the backcountry, with a 21 to 15 vote, joined in opposition.[47]

While some Charleston representatives opposed debtor legislation in general, backcountry opponents of the installment act must have hoped that its defeat would unite legislators behind more desirable inflationary plans, such as a paper money or valuation act, that would raise the value of their crops and property. Lowcountry planters, however, may have feared that inflation would hurt them: as Lowndes said, "all merchandize would immediately rise two or three hundred per cent., for that merchant who did not average the sale of his property in proportion to the risque of his loss might fairly be pronounced a fool.''[48] Perhaps the planters thought an installment act might effect a reduction of their debts. William Loughton Smith reported that bonds were selling at a discount of 40 or 50 percent, and that a seven-year installment act would reduce their worth to less than 25 percent.[49] Merchants might settle for a few payments totaling less than what was due them rather than wait five years to close an account, especially when they would have to pay duties to a new central government less likely to be lenient than the state government. Perhaps for that reason Joshua Ward, a lawyer who for years had tried to collect a debt from John Rutledge, called the new installment act an ''unjust & oppressive law calculated wholly for the Rich and most dissipated part of our community.'' Henry Pendleton was equally harsh, denouncing the law as one that would aid a class of planters who ''in their avidity for wealth have engrossed more land and negroes than they can pay for.''[50]

If backcountry settlers had expected the legislature to grant them the same indulgence enjoyed by lowcountry debtors in 1785 and 1786, they were disappointed. The act of 1788 continued the program of debtor legislation begun in 1782. Most of the legislation served primarily the interests of those with substantial amounts of property, primarily those in the lowcountry. When a lowcountry-dominated legislature met to ''alleviate the Evil'' in September 1785 it had found conditions so pressing as to justify the emission of paper money and the passage of a valuation act which closed courts. Unfortunately for some of the distressed, the paper money could be borrowed only by propertied debtors. In 1788, with many of the same men still serving as legislators, the legislature no longer found paper money or valuation acts fitting. The government's behavior was again remarkably partial.

Taken by themselves, the acts showed that the old ruling group had retained substantial political power; but the history of their passage indicated that their power was not impregnable. By 1788 the old rulers were in a weakened position. The backcountry had developed a commercial interest in tobacco, which brought slavery and the plantation system inland; and, by the state constitutions, the backcountry and distant lowcountry parishes had gained representation. There was a new maturity and drive apparent by 1788. Petitions to the legislature often awkwardly, but sometimes poignantly, described inland grievances. The petitions, similar enough in wording to suggest at times an organized campaign, had to be considered seriously by the legislature. In 1784 Johann David Schoepf talked of backcountry members without the ''courage or eloquence'' to argue against proposals they thought ''undesirable or burdensome.''[51] The silent ones still appeared at the legislature, but more and more backcountry legislators gained experience and confidence. The backcountry found spokesmen, more in the October and November legislature than in the May ratifying convention. Both Pendleton and Gillon, although on different sides, spoke for Saxe-Gotha, Gillon, if newspaper reports were accurate, almost incessantly. James Lincoln and Robert Anderson spoke for Ninety Six and James Knox for the District between the Broad and Catawba. It was a small but growing group, and it appeared likely to grow faster when the government fulfilled the promise made in 1786 and moved inland.

The legislature inadvertently showed in 1788 and 1789 why the move inland, even without reapportionment, could effect further change and weaken the lowcountry more. On 21 October 1788, 132 of the lower house's 202 members voted on interposition. The Charleston District, allowed 96 representatives, cast 76 votes; the two other lowcountry districts cast 15 of their 30 votes, while the backcountry cast 41 of 76. When the installment bill was passed on 2 November, only 104 members voted, 56 from Charleston District, 12 from other lowcountry areas, and 36 from the backcountry. The Charleston District vote could easily have been larger had it been necessary, since only 19 of the city's 30 representatives voted. The small vote was understandable. Sunday, 2 November, was two days before adjournment. Some members, who saw no further chance of getting their valuation bill, left early, perhaps to prepare for forthcoming state and Congressional elections. Many members never even appeared at the fall session. The legislature had met in January, February, and March, the ratifying convention in May, and the legislature again in October and November. A new one would meet in January 1789. The inconvenience was too great for one year. Even so, the backcountry had made its wishes known and mustered a sizable vote. It did so again in 1789 when, for example, a motion to place a relatively low 4s.8d. tax on each slave passed by a vote of 80 to 68, with the Charleston area supporting it 65 to 1, the backcountry opposing 58 to 7, and Georgetown and Beaufort opposing 9 to 8.[52] Narrow margins of victory for the Charleston area showed that a move inland could be dangerous.

Little was done after 1786 to follow through on the legislature's expressed intent of moving to Columbia. If construction of the town ever began, it probably ceased almost immediately because of the economic conditions faced by the state's citizens. But accident and the federal Constitution brought the issue up again in 1788 and 1789, reawakening the lowcountry's fears. In February 1788 the General Assembly building burned down, making another meeting place necessary. A few months later Aedanus Burke blamed the Antifederalists' defeat on the choice of Charleston, which a geographically-divided legislature had picked by one vote as the site of the ratifying convention. The next year Jacob Brown, a far-sighted backcountry representative, urged the legislature to move before the new government's appointees could persuade legislators to remain permanently in the port city.[53]

In January 1789 Arthur Simkins, a representative of Ninety Six since 1782, reintroduced the subject. Pierce Butler, who had spent the summer of 1788 in the mountains of inland South Carolina marveling at the climate, the healthfulness, the freedom, repeated the usual argument that most people lived in the west and added another argument in favor of moving that Burke, Jacob Brown, and others appreciated: "the great influence and weight which the Charleston members possessed" made removal essential, said Butler, who remembered the unanimous twenty-seven votes Charleston representatives cast against his valuation bill in 1788.[54] Lowcountry members tried to block the scheme, Edward Rutledge saying that moving was proper but that there was no place to move to. He had looked for Columbia and found nothing. Nevertheless, the Senate, which had acted first in 1786, acted first again and forced through a bill for moving public records to Columbia by 1 December 1789, because it was "essential to the general interests of the state." The legislature followed its records in January 1790.[55] The move inland became permanent when the state adopted its third and last constitution of the revolutionary period.

The constitution of 1790, like those of 1776 and 1778, has been seriously misunderstood by historians, and the result is a failure to comprehend the Revolution in South Carolina. One historian, seeing little that was new, thought the constitution gave lowcountry planters "almost unlimited power to oppress the up-country people."[56] Others, although generally concluding that "to a large extent, the low country had its way," have at least described the constitution as a compromise.[57] But in only one major respect was the constitution of 1790 a triumph for the old aristocracy; in more important ways it was a victory for emerging powers.

In 1776 South Carolina adopted a constitution that satisfied most of the political figures from the Charleston area. It differed substantially from the constitutions being written in other states. Seeking no innovation in government, the provincial congress created a two-house legislature similar to what had long existed. The people elected the lower house, but the upper house was still removed from popular control, its members chosen by and from the lower house. The two houses jointly elected a governor who served a two-year term and had substantial power. Like the royal governor he had an absolute veto, but he combined that with what royal governors like Thomas Boone would have envied, a guaranteed fixed, annual salary of £9,000 currency. And he was eligible for re-election indefinitely. The Anglican Church, to which most of the Charleston District revolutionaries belonged, remained the established church, for which all were taxed.

There was some innovation. Even the poorly distributed representation, apparent in the division which gave the backcountry seventy-six representatives, Georgetown and Beaufort thirty, and the Charleston District ninety-six, was a significant advance. Not only the backcountry but also the newer areas of the lowcountry, more devoted to indigo than to rice, had been poorly represented in the colonial legislature.[58]

Two years later, the legislature wrote a constitution recognized as a democratic advance by John Rutledge, who temporarily blocked it with his veto. The plan of 1778 left representation in the lower house alone but provided for reapportionment based on population and taxable property in 1785 and every fourteen years thereafter. It raised the quorum in the 202-man lower house from 49 to 69, making domination by the Charleston area a little more difficult. Politically, it struck at the old rulers by attacking the governor's office and the upper house. The executive lost his veto, was denied a fixed salary, forced out of office after a two-year term, no man being allowed to serve as governor for more than two years in any six (other officers were also rotated out of the government), and like others was subject to impeachment. The rotation was "hardly digested by our ambitious people," the Reverend William Tennent wrote. And the constitution removed "one avenue for family intrigue" by enlarging the Senate from a body of thirteen members elected by and from the few in the lower house to one of twenty-nine elected by the people in their parishes and districts. Charleston District, which had completely dominated the old upper house, was given thirteen senators, the backcountry eleven, and Georgetown and Beaufort five, an apportionment still unjust according to population but slightly more favorable to the west than that in the lower house. The new Senate so resembled the House of Representatives that few serious disputes occurred between the two branches, and, as in the lower house, the old rulers frequently found themselves dangerously close to losing major votes. On 21 May 1787, for example, the Senate defeated by a twelve to eleven vote a resolution to call a state constitutional convention. Eight backcountry senators, two from the Charleston District, and one from Beaufort were outvoted by nine senators from the Charleston District and one each from Georgetown, Beaufort, and the backcountry. The constitution of 1778 also disestablished the Anglican Church and required that ministers of all churches be chosen by their congregations.[59]

Despite the Senate's continued opposition in the 1780s a constitutional convention finally met. Backcountry settlers and representatives had requested revision since 1783, but after the adoption of the federal Constitution in 1788 some lowcountry leaders joined them, thinking it necessary to bring the state constitution into line with the new federal plan. No longer was the state legislature to elect annually the delegates to Congress, and no longer could the governor, with the legislature's consent, declare war, make peace, or enter into any treaty. And some people thought the new government possessed a structure that the state should copy.

In March 1789 the legislature agreed that a convention should be held the following year. Although opponents of constitutional revision had argued in 1785 that writing a new frame of government would require first "a total dissolution of . . . [the] present constitution," and consequently granting to everyone "an equal right to become a party in the new compact," the law of 1789 did not grant everyone an equal share in the convention. Parishes and districts were to send the same number of delegates as they had representatives and senators. Since in March 1789 the legislature had granted the backcountry two more senators and six additional representatives, the convention would have a total membership of 239.[60] But no provision was made for submitting the convention's handiwork to the people for ratification.

The delegates met in Columbia from 10 May to 3 June. They introduced few changes, but these few, along with those in the previous constitution, gave South Carolina a government quite different from that which had existed before 1778. Property qualifications for officeholding and voting remained similar to those in 1778. No one could represent the district in which he lived unless he had a freehold estate worth £150 sterling clear of debt or 500 acres and ten slaves, or be a senator from his home district without a freehold estate worth £300 sterling. Nonresidents were to own more than three times the property. A governor's estate was to be worth at least £1,500 sterling.[61] As in 1778 a senator had to be over thirty and five years a resident of the state, a representative over twenty-one and three years a resident, and the governor ten years a resident. The constitution of 1790 specified that the governor must be over thirty, but no minimum age had been required in 1778. The governor was still elected by the legislature rather than by the people.

Voters for legislators had to own either a fifty-acre lot or a town lot, or pay a three-shilling tax to support the government, an alternative much like that provided in the 1778 constitution.[62] The constitution of 1790, however, changed the residency requirement for voters. The 1778 constitution allowed all free white males resident in the state for one year to vote, but that had twice been amended during the 1780s by simple legislative acts. In 1784 the legislature decided that free white males resident for one year in South Carolina could become citizens but could not vote for another two years. In 1786 the legislature made the residency requirement indeterminate: after one year free whites could be citizens but they could not vote until naturalized by special act. The constitution of 1790 granted the suffrage to free white male citizens who had resided for two years in the state. Another provision which could not be understood simply by comparing it with the old constitution allowed legislators compensation for their expenses while traveling to and attending the legislature. There had been no similar provision in 1778, but the legislature nonetheless had voted itself expense money.[63]

Other provisions, too, were retained and more widely applied. Again the governor was denied a veto, and again the constitution stated that no man could serve more than one two-year term as governor in any six years or be treasurer, surveyor general, or secretary of state for two consecutive four-year terms. In 1778 the limit for treasurers and others had been two two-year terms. Sheriffs were still rotated out of office, although their terms were increased from two years to four, answering the criticism of those who in the 1780s complained that sheriffs were removed just as they were beginning to learn their job.

The more experienced constitution writers of 1790 went further to protect the people from corrupt or corruptible officials than their predecessors had. Suspicious of people who monopolized positions, all of the nine other states writing constitutions in 1776 and 1777 had prohibited paid government officials from sitting in their legislatures, but South Carolina, in its first constitution, had required only that legislators elected to state posts resign their seats, allowing them to serve again if chosen by the people in the special elections held to fill their vacated places. Opportunities for multiple officeholding were narrowed in 1778 when the new constitution provided that treasurers, sheriffs, customs officials, and several other officers could not be re-elected to their seats. In 1790 South Carolina finally made the prohibition complete by excluding from the legislature all those who held offices "of profit or trust" under the state or new national government, or under any other power. The convention rejected completely the arguments both Pinckneys and Butler had used successfully to exclude from the national constitution any clause prohibiting state officials from serving the new government. Excepted from the state ban were militia officers and justices of the peace or of the county courts, while those positions received no salaries. No longer, then, would John Rutledge, Henry Pendleton, Aedanus Burke, or other state judges vote on laws they would later be called on to enforce. Nor could contractors for the army or navy of the state or the United States or their agents sit in the legislature.

In another attempt to guarantee freedom from corrupt or arbitrary rule the quorum was increased from 69 of 202 in the lower house and 13 of 29 in the upper to a majority in each, denying the Charleston area, or any area, the ability to pass self-serving legislation in poorly attended, inconvenient emergency sessions of the legislature.

The constitution of 1790 extended political rights by accepting in full the principle of religious toleration and equality. Although the Anglican Church had long been established in South Carolina, the colony had also for a long time contained a multiplicity of religions and sects, including a body of Jews significant in numbers for the colonial period. The constitution of 1776 left the Church of England as the established church to which all contributed their tax monies but said nothing about religious qualifications for civil rights. It allowed Franciş Salvador, a Jew, to continue sitting in the legislature as he had in the revolutionary Provincial Congress. Two years later, with dissenters participating actively on all levels of the Revolutionary struggle, the Anglican Church was disestablished by the new constitution, which also granted toleration to all people acknowledging one God, a future state of rewards and punishments, and a belief that God was to be publicly worshiped. Male Protestants, gathered in minimum groups of fifteen, were allowed to incorporate their churches. But the dissenters won their rights at the expense of other groups. Only Protestants could in the future become governors, privy councilors, or legislators, and only people who in addition to meeting the property qualifications believed in God and a future state of rewards and punishments could vote.

The restrictions notwithstanding, South Carolina's history, its new constitution, general climate of opinion, and opportunities not only apparently kept the state's Jews content but attracted in the 1780s some Catholics, about 200 of whom were said to live in Charleston in 1790. In 1788, in a quiet but remarkable announcement in the *City Gazette,* the Catholics informed the public of a forthcoming Sunday mass in the church opposite Charleston's synagogue.[64]

For some people, like Charles Cotesworth Pinckney who had supported disestablishment in 1778 and who in 1786 had opposed a proposed oath for new clergymen and schoolmasters, the toleration was a matter of principle. For others, among whom were those Reverend Thomas Reese denounced in 1788 for their religious ignorance or disbelief, it was a matter of indifference. Free-thinking nobles, Reese thought, were content just to restrain the "vulgar" and their own wives and daughters with ideas of future rewards and punishments.[65]

Experience, indifference, and principle joined in 1790 to overturn all religious restrictions. That year's constitution established no religious qualifications for officeholders, the new oath for officials even omitting the usual "So help me God." Ministers, however, still were not allowed to sit in the legislature. Voters were not required to believe in any creed, any God, or any future state. And, lastly, the constitution allowed "the free exercise and enjoyment of religious profession and worship," as long as the peace of the state was not disturbed.

The constitution of 1790 changed the structure of government by abolishing the useless Privy Council, established in 1776 and retained in 1778. It made future constitutional change more difficult. No new convention could be called except by a two-thirds vote of all the members of the legislature. The constitution could not be amended unless a bill to that effect was passed by a two-thirds vote of the whole membership, published three months before an election, and then passed again by two-thirds of the new legislature. The constitution altered the apportionment of representation in both branches of the legislature, although it failed to provide for future reapportionment, and moved the capital to Columbia, where it was to remain unless two-thirds of all members decided otherwise. But dual offices for the treasurers, secretary of state, and surveyor-general were established in Columbia and Charleston.

Even though William Loughton Smith thanked Edward Rutledge and his friends for inserting "such advantages for the Low Country" into a constitution which was "much better than the former one," the constitution of 1790 was not an improvement for the old rulers.[66] If lowcountry leaders expressed satisfaction, it was not because they had secured major alterations favorable to their own interests, but because they had not been forced to give up more. More than some contemporaries openly admitted, and more than historians have subsequently realized, the constitution of 1790 was a major advance for the newer areas of the state. In some ways even the absence of change was misleading. The old rulers had complained more about rotation in office than their opponents had about property qualifications for officeholding and voting. That backcountry demands for change had not included expressions of discontent with the suffrage requirements was not surprising. Probably more people were concerned that officeholding was restricted to those with substantial amounts of property, but even so, no extant petitions from an area vitally interested in putting down criminals and dealing with vagrants mentioned political inequality. Nor did the aristocracy's Charleston opposition protest. But as early as 1782 Edward Rutledge had denounced the "damned Rotation Business" which the state was "at least half a Century too early for," and his sentiments, attacked by Antifederalists in 1788, were defended by John Rutledge and Jacob Read, who referred to that "political mania." Rotation was one principle in the constitution of 1790 that William Loughton Smith disliked.[67]

Charles Cotesworth Pinckney fought hard for another change at the convention. Just as he had in 1787 opposed granting United States senators salaries, so that "the wealthy alone would undertake the service," Pinckney urged that state legislators not be paid. He trusted only those wealthy enough to serve without compensation. John Rutledge and Pierce Butler had agreed with Pinckney at Philadelphia. In 1787 also, Thomas Bee had argued in favor of reducing the expense money already allowed state legislators, but backcountry representatives countered that reduction might be tolerated by those representatives who lived within fifty miles of Charleston and could be fed by their own plantations, or might be acceptable when the legislature met at Columbia, but that some compensation was necessary because few from the backcountry would serve unless their expenses were paid. Bee in 1787 and Pinckney in 1790 lost their arguments.[68]

Christopher Gadsden was also among those disappointed at Columbia. Gadsden favored restoring to the governor a veto over legislation. In 1787, writing to John Adams, and even sounding a great deal like Adams, the former leader of the artisans and mechanics confessed his error years before in working to strip the governor of that power. Now he thought the too-powerful assembly ought to be checked by an executive veto. Few agreed with him, however, and a move to grant the governor a simple power to delay legislation for a few days lost by a large majority.[69]

But success for individuals or groups at Columbia did not depend on rotation, legislators' pay, a governor's veto, or even, perhaps surprisingly, on property qualifications for officeholders and electors. Retention of those qualifications pleased Charles Cotesworth Pinckney, Thomas Bee, and others, while hardly dampening the spirits of their opponents. Rarely in the 1780s had property qualifications been an issue; only once during the protracted newspaper onslaught against the aristocracy, the legislature, and the city corporation did the topic even come up. The impetus for change at the convention came not from people worried that they could not vote or serve, but from people who were denied their full rights because property was ''larger represented than the free white inhabitants,'' and because their legislators could not always attend the ''very inconvenient'' seat of government.[70] Apportionment and the location of the government were the ''advantages'' people fought over.

It was probably obvious in 1789 when the legislature set the rules for representation at the convention that the principle on which apportionment was based, weighing wealth as well as numbers, would not be changed. Nonetheless, delegates for the backcountry, which in 1790 had over 110,000 whites compared to approximately 29,000 in the lowcountry, went through the motions of arguing that representation be based on population. In its only real victory at Columbia, the lowcountry defeated that proposal and another basing representation on a specific plan which combined wealth and numbers, apparently fearing that soon the backcountry would be prosperous as well as populous.[71] Instead, the constitution, without mentioning property although obviously considering it, assigned the number of representatives and senators for each parish and county, making no provision for future changes. The lower house, consisting of 202 in 1778 and 208 in 1789, was cut to 124 members, of whom 54 represented the backcountry. The senate, with 29 in 1778 and 31 in 1789, was enlarged to 37, 17 representing the backcountry.

With change in size came reapportionment. In 1778 the backcountry had elected 37.9 percent of the senators and 37.6 percent of the representatives. In 1790 it elected 45.9 percent of the senators and 43.5 percent of the representatives.[72] But those figures obscured the backcountry's real strength. Politically the state was divisible into not two but three sections: the backcountry, Charleston District, and Georgetown and Beaufort districts. Although Georgetown and Beaufort were geographically part of the lowcountry, they were politically separate; their interests and experiences differed, and so, often, did their votes, as in 1787 when the lower house voted against repeal of the confiscation and amercement laws and in 1789 when it voted to levy a 4s.8d. tax on each slave. In 1787 the Charleston District favored repeal by a 49 to 26 vote, the backcountry cast 58 of 64 votes against repeal, and Georgetown and Beaufort joined the backcountry with a more balanced 14 to 6 vote against repeal. In February 1789 the Charleston area supported the slave tax 65 to 1, the backcountry opposed it 58 to 7, and Georgetown and Beaufort voted 9 to 8 against the proposed tax.[73] The reapportionment of 1790 can only be understood when the state is divided into its three political sections.

Percentages of the two houses elected by the three sections

Sections	Senate			House of Representatives		
	1778	1789*	1790	1778	1789*	1790
Charleston District	44.8	41.9	35.1	47.5	46.1	38.7
Georgetown and Beaufort	17.2	16.1	18.9	14.8	14.4	17.7
Backcountry	37.9	41.9	45.9	37.6	39.4	43.5

*In March 1789 Greenville and Pendleton, the westernmost counties, were each given the right to elect one senator and three representatives.

The backcountry emerged from the convention of 1790 as the most powerful section in both branches of the legislature. Its political power increased substantially: expressed in terms of representation, it moved in 1789 from a point almost 7 percent behind the Charleston area in the lower house to almost 5 percent ahead, and from an equality with the Charleston area in the upper house to more than 10 percent ahead. The increase in its power since 1778 was even greater.

The reapportionment took on greater meaning and importance when combined with a related change. Western petitioners had requested removal of the capital from Charleston as a matter of convenience. People knew, however, that convenience meant power, and they made the fight over location the longest and harshest of the convention. Everything at Columbia moved along smoothly for a while, reported the *City Gazette,* "but when we came to the question respecting the seat of government, all was violence and confusion."[74]

Attendance at the convention reminded people of the issue's importance. Because of "ill health," "unexpected circumstances," private affairs "deranged" by past public service, or "business," conditions that had often affected backcountry legislators, at least nineteen lowcountry delegates informed the governor they would not go to Columbia, though many had had no past trouble serving in Charleston.[75] Elections were held

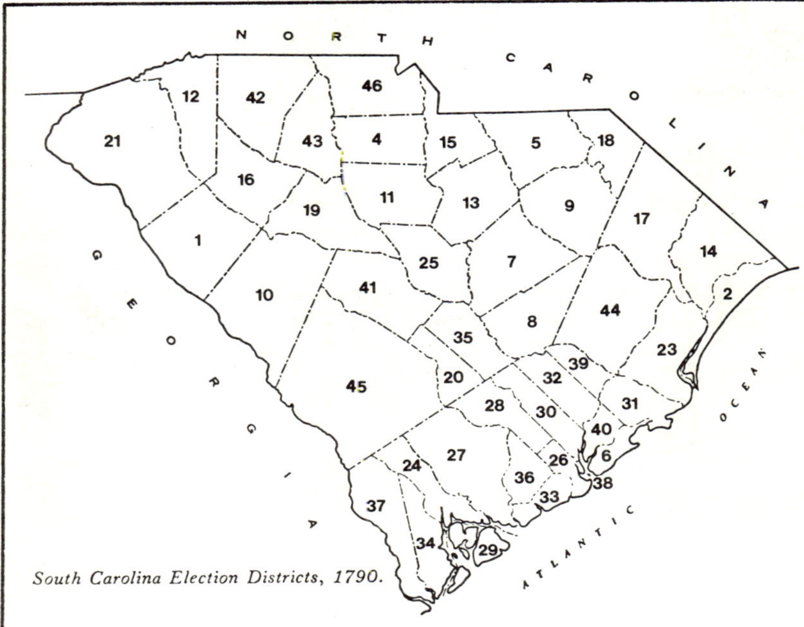

South Carolina Election Districts, 1790.

Apportionment under the Constitution of 1790

Election District	1790	Election District	1790
1. Abbeville	3	24. Prince William	3
2. All Saints	1	25. Richland	2
3. Anderson		26. St. Andrew	3
4. Chester	3	27. St. Bartholomew	3
5. Chesterfield	2	28. St. George Dorchester	3
6. Christ Church	3	29. St. Helena	3
7. Claremont (Sumter)	2	30. St. James Goose Creek	3
8. Clarendon	2	31. St. James Santee	3
9. Darlington	2	32. St. John Berkeley	3
10. Edgefield	3	33. St. John Colleton	3
11. Fairfield	2	34. St. Luke	3
12. Greenville	2	35. St. Matthew	2
13. Kershaw	2	36. St. Paul	3
14. Kingston (Horry)	2	37. St. Peter	3
15. Lancaster	2	38. St. Philip & St. Michael (Charleston)	15
16. Laurens	3	39. St. Stephen	3
17. Liberty (Marion)	2	40. St. Thomas & St. Dennis	3
18. Marlboro	2	41. Saxe Gotha (Lexington)	3
19. Newberry	3	42. Spartan	2
20. Orange	2	43. Union	2
21. Pendleton	3	44. Williamsburg	2
22. Pickens		45. Winton (Barnwell)	3
23. Prince George Winyah	3	46. York	3

Courtesy, South Carolina House of Representatives Committee on Historical Research

The State House at Columbia, 1794. From an engraving by James Aiken.

to fill the vacancies, but the resignations highlighted both what was at stake and a lowcountry problem at the convention. The lowcountry lost the first vote on moving inland by one vote, 105 to 104. Eighty-six of the 87 backcountry delegates voted in favor of moving, while 103 of the 122 lowcountry delegates opposed the motion. The outcome, however, was determined as much by those absent as by those present. Twenty-two absentees were from the lowcountry and only eight from the interior.[76] Had the convention met in Charleston the backcountry would have lost.

Lowcountry spokesmen recognized the cause of their defeat. Gadsden blamed the setback on "the Impatience and Desertion of our lower members," and emphasized the point by adding, not very optimistically, that the remaining members "will endeavor to do the best" they can. William Loughton Smith damned "the most incredible treachery of some of our low country people."[77]

One compromise made removal of the government more acceptable to the lowcountry. Columbia became the capital, but the dual offices of some state officials spared coastal residents much of the inconvenience those in the interior had faced since settlement began and had complained of since 1767. The compromise cost the backcountry little.

The new constitution neither toppled the old rulers nor gave backcountry politicians who after the war refused "to fall back in the ranks" the power to deprive men like John and Edward Rutledge, Thomas and

Charles Cotesworth Pinckney, Ralph Izard, or Thomas Bee of influence, often dominant influence.[78] But, reflecting the rise of the backcountry, it allowed westerners the opportunity to force their views on the legislature.

The effects were apparent throughout the 1790s, perhaps most startlingly in 1793 and 1794 when the legislature revised the militia law to follow some general guidelines set by the federal government. As passed, the law called for the election, by the militia men, of all officers under the rank of brigadier general. Polls would be open from 9 to 5 following at least a fifteen-day notice. Furthermore, the law established a scheme of scaled fines for non-attendance at musters. For absence from a regimental muster, a lieutenant colonel was to be fined a sum not to exceed £10 plus an amount not more than 5% of his last general tax. A non-commissioned officer or a private was to be fined not more than 14s plus no more than 5% of his last general tax. The new provisions reflected the more democratic ideas of the backcountry. When the vote on fines was taken in December 1793, the backcountry, with 72% of its representatives voting, supported the scaling 27 to 12. Charleston and the surrounding parishes, with only 52% of their representatives voting, cast 8 votes for the proposal and 17 against. Parishes in Georgetown and Beaufort, with 55% of their members participating, evenly divided 12 votes. The decision in May 1794 to elect officers was even more sectional. The 80% of the backcountry representatives voting favored the change 35 to 8. The Charleston area representatives, 58% voting, cast 27 of 28 votes against the change, while Georgetown and Beaufort districts, with 82% of their representatives voting, supported the change by a 10 to 8 vote.[79]

Important sectional votes followed. In 1796 backcountry votes defeated a move to incorporate the Bank of South Carolina; in 1807 the legislature, mostly because of backcountry support, provided for the popular election of sheriffs and court officials in place of their appointment by the legislature.[80]

And, a decade after it was adopted, the constitution of 1790 helped elect a president. "The issue of the election," wrote Thomas Jefferson in December 1800, "hangs on S. Carolina."[81] State politics had for years been complicated by national events, by Genêt, the Jay treaty, and Charles Cotesworth Pinckney's involvement in the XYZ affair. Generally, however, despite Edward Rutledge's friendship with Thomas Jefferson, Thomas Pinckney's 1796 candidacy for President or Vice-President, or his brother's similar candidacy four years later, South Carolina's political fights pitted lowcountry Federalists against backcountry Republicans.[82] In 1800, not only Jefferson, but also politicians throughout America anxiously awaited the results of the South Carolina fight over presidential electors. Federalists took heart because General Charles Cotesworth Pinckney, their candidate for Vice-President, and in some circles for President, was a Carolinian, and, as a newly-elected state senator for Charleston, a member of the body that would choose the state's electors. Republicans were relying on the strenuous efforts of one of South Carolina's United States senators, Charles Pinckney, the general's cousin, and to many contemporaries a traitor to his family, class, and lowcountry background because of his leadership of the state's Republicans. Rather than attend Congress, Charles Pinckney went to Columbia to work for Jefferson.[83]

Charles Pinckney was not an impartial witness to events at Columbia; his letters to Jefferson repeat almost endlessly the great forces combining against him and his own valiant efforts. But his descriptions nonetheless help explain the election and indicate the importance of South Carolina's political changes. Sounding not only like Aedanus Burke explaining the Antifederalist defeat in 1788, but also like Jacob Brown urging that the government move inland before the federal government could appoint influential officers who would reside in Charleston, Pinckney expressed his unbounded delight that the legislature met in Columbia, far removed from "the influence of the officers of Government and of the Banks and of the British and Mercantile Interest." The "Country Interest," he thought, was "as pure as ever." But he complained about Charleston's election, in which, he said, "several Hundred more Voted than paid taxes." Federalists supposedly extended democracy by going to the people. "*The Lame, Crippled, diseased, and blind were either led, lifted or brought in Carriages to the Poll.*"[84]

Despite Charleston the Republicans controlled the legislature. But because party lines remained weak, it took Pinckney's work and the location of the capital to defeat his popular cousin; perhaps even some who did not like the general wanted to vote for him and honor the state. Charles Pinckney spent days at Columbia unifying the Republicans, protesting the Charleston election, and apparently holding politicians in line with promises of patronage.[85] On 2 December the legislature chose eight Republican electors, including Arthur Simkins, a backcountry spokesman for about twenty years, and other backcountry leaders from the 1780s: John Hunter, Wade Hampton, Andrew Love, and Robert Anderson. The Republican electors received between eighty-two and eighty-seven votes, the Federalists between sixty-three and sixty-nine. Nine members of the lower house were absent, all from the lowcountry.[86] If the legislature had met in Charleston, more lowcountry members would have attended while some backcountry members might have stayed away. Then too the vast financial and governmental power of Charleston that Charles Pinckney feared would have been applied on behalf of the Federalists.

When the results, in the form of "alarming Accounts from General Pinckney," were known, one Massachusetts congressman despaired. "God forbid!" he said.[87] South Carolina had made Jefferson President.

A decade and more before Jefferson's election two South Carolina judges cast long looks backward to review and draw meaning from the state's postwar history. Richard Champion spoke to the Grand Jury of Lancaster County in January 1788 about "the terrible inroads which the disorders of war have created." He talked about the hostilities between neighbors and illegal and immoral behavior. Admitting that he, unlike many others, had not been through the "fiery ordeal of personal suffering" caused by the war, having made only a financial sacrifice, he nevertheless felt justified in recommending that Carolinians forget the brutality and end the squabbling between Whigs and Tories. Because in 1788 "many noisome dregs of the disorders of war still exist among us," he called on the grand jury to enforce the law rigorously, prevent crime, and strike at the "disorderly livers, such as profane swearers, drunkards, those who live in fornication or adultery, [and] lewd women having bastards."[88]

Champion, emphasizing that vigorous effort and time would check and remove the disorders he spoke of, failed to note what had already been done. Although there was a confrontation between wartime enemies at a backcountry election in 1786, when, according to the election managers, men who had "Sheathed their Swords in the Bowels of their Country . . . Set themselves up to make Law for those whom they could not Subdue," the bitterness had already largely disappeared.[89] And if Champion could focus his attention on "disorderly livers," perhaps it was because the most serious criminal disorders had been lessened, Aedanus Burke reporting by December 1784 progress in the reassertion of law and order in the backcountry.[90]

Economic trouble remained, Champion continued. He mentioned the enormous purchases of European luxuries by planters anxious to reestablish prewar standards. But "the very seed with which this poisonous vine is sown," he explained, "has in itself an antidote that will expel the poison . . . this antidote is our poverty." Champion indicated that those economic troubles were related to the war, but he did not describe the "devastations of the late unnatural war" that had caused part of the economic turmoil in the backcountry. With respect to the existing debt, he supported indulgence for debtors owing small sums, the existing paper money, and no further interference with the law.[91]

Like many Carolinians and many other Americans, Champion moved from a recitation of the state's postwar problems to a recommendation that the proposed federal Constitution be ratified. He differed, however, from those who thought they could argue for the new only by disparaging the old. Without proving or explaining what he meant, he praised the accomplishments of the past years. "We have," he said, "no reason to despair of the commonwealth. Every year has proved better than the last."[92]

Most of the old lowcountry political leaders disagreed with Champion's evaluation, at least as applied to state government. They had more reason to accept Judge John Faucheraud Grimké's interpretation of the past years. In December 1790 Grimké addressed the grand jury of Camden District. He talked about the central government and mentioned that assumption of state debts would benefit South Carolina by relieving the state of the need to tax its citizens for the debt and by putting into circulation the money that would raise prices and facilitate trade. Assumption, he thought, too, would serve "as the basis of reconciling to the federal union the minds of those honest citizens who at first were opposed to the constitution."[93]

Grimké spoke of the state's political development, a subject Champion ignored. Without specifically commenting on or describing the trouble of previous years, Grimké identified the "disorders" he thought serious by warning the grand jurors of future dangers. "Beware of the false friend," he said. "The specious mask of honesty" was too often worn by men who "trample on the good sense of the people, thro' unbecoming or selfish motives." The long dark note was not the imaginative warning of a political theorist; Grimké was a city warden in 1784 and the Intendant in 1786 when Alexander Gillon, Benjamin Waller, and the other supposedly "artful, designing and turbulent men" were attacking local government and, according to some, attempting to take over "the powers of the state."[94] Designing men or not, Gillon and his followers had made an impression on Grimké and a great many more Carolinians.

One other development had impressed Grimké. He advised the grand jury to be thankful for the new state constitution and the spirit of conciliation that had produced it, and he went on to urge the jurors to resist efforts "to render the interior country jealous of, and inimical to, the sea coast." Settlers should strive for union, avoiding actions that threatened to divide the state and create antagonisms between sections.[95] The unmistakable fear of future rupture, so readily apparent in Grimké's warnings, revealed how wide the old split was and how seriously Grimké and others took it.

By statement and by implication, Judges Champion and Grimké rehearsed much of their state's postwar experience; but neither one adequately described the change in spirit and attitude, although Grimké came close with his exaggerated attack on demagogues and their "selfish motives." Gillon's "ever wakeful vigilance," the denunciation of lawyers, the admonition not to be awed by "enormous wealth," represented a consequence of independence and Revolution that was evident immediately after the close of war.[96] So did Thomas Reese's words, which took on added importance because clergymen were not usually critics of native rulers. The state's government, Reese thought, tended toward aristocracy partly because, although offices should be rotatory, they would be in the hands of a few if the people were not educated. The consequence was "that the rich and learned *few* will rule and oppress the poor and ignorant *many*." So, to "*ride*" the poor "at pleasure," aristocrats fought against educating the "lower ranks."[97] True or not, and the legislature was at least incorporating backcountry educational societies although not contributing tax money, Reese's charges, like those of Gillon and others, were severe and unrelenting: to men who had taken their elections and their roles in government for granted, they were unwarranted, destructive words of opposition.

No one, however, could any longer convince himself, nor hope to persuade others, that the people were content to be ruled by their superiors. Backcountry settlers in particular worked persistently during the 1780s to win greater freedom, to extend their rights through a new constitution written by men gathered together for that one specific purpose.

The effect on South Carolina of the struggle with England and the war was great, although some developments after 1776 were not caused by the Revolution. The expansion, the growth of population, the spread of tobacco cultivation, all would have occurred, perhaps even faster, without war or independence. Fear of newcomers, a concern about "vagrants," probably more criminal activities inland, would then have emerged. So, too, would pressure from "outsiders" for political change.

But some of South Carolina's difficulties and some developments were connected to the break from England. The loss of life, both white and black, the destruction of property, the disappearance of slaves, some of whom were freed, the depression, the fate of indigo — these were the "disorders of war" and the consequences of independence. So were the problems caused by the hardened, inhuman criminals formed, witnesses thought, by their wartime experiences.

In the matter of government South Carolina in 1790 bore little resemblance to the colony five years or even one year before Lexington and Concord, and the speed and extent of change depended on the war, which made necessary the enlistment of widespread support and which gave new people experience and confidence. Two developments were drastic and, at least for the people and groups involved, seemed revolutionary: the extension of representation to the west and the rise of a harsh political rhetoric.

The firmly entrenched aristocrats were not thrown out wholesale, property rights were not overturned, there was no democracy for all — the poor elected others to be their rulers. But a new spirit was there, exemplified best perhaps in 1794 by the frontier people of Pendleton County. "In a Republican Government," they said, "an address by petition to an Assembly of deputies of the People must be considered a gross absurdity! Shall the people petition the people! The inhabitants of Pendleton, therefore, adopt the mode of respectful Representation!"[98] They did not politely or humbly request anything of the legislature. They described their condition and assumed simply that the people who were no better than they but who happened to sit in the legislature would act. Behind the assumption, of course, were a new maturity and a new power, a conviction that legislators must listen to them. That was the revolution.

Abbreviations

Newspapers and Journals

CEG	*Charleston Evening Gazette*
CGDA	*City Gazette, or The Daily Advertiser*
CMPDA	*Charleston Morning Post and Daily Advertiser*
CnHd	*Columbian Herald*
GSSC	*Gazette of the State of South-Carolina*
JSH	*Journal of Southern History*
PaPDA	*Pennsylvania Packet & Daily Advertiser*
PaPGA	*Pennsylvania Packet & General Advertiser*
SCG	*South Carolina Gazette*
SCGGA	*South Carolina Gazette & General Advertiser*
SCGPA	*South Carolina Gazette & Public Advertiser*
SCHM	*South Carolina Historical Magazine* and *South Carolina Historical and Genealogical Magazine*
SCSGGA	*South Carolina State Gazette and General Advertiser*
SCWG	*South Carolina Weekly Gazette*
SGSC	*State Gazette of South-Carolina*
W&MQ	*William and Mary Quarterly*

Places

BM	British Museum, London
BPRO	British Public Record Office, London
DU	Duke University, Durham, North Carolina
HSP	Historical Society of Pennsylvania, Philadelphia
LC	Library of Congress, Washington
NYHS	New-York Historical Society, New York City
NYPL	New York Public Library, New York City
SCA	South Carolina Department of Archives and History, Columbia
SCHS	South Carolina Historical Society, Charleston
UNC	University of North Carolina, Chapel Hill
USC	University of South Carolina, Columbia

NOTES
CHAPTER ONE

1. Benjamin Smith to Rev. William Smith, 16 May 1766, quoted in George C. Rogers, Jr., *Evolution of a Federalist: William Loughton Smith of Charleston (1758-1812)* (Columbia, S.C., 1962), pp. 46–47; Josiah Smith to James Poyas, 10 Jan. 1776, Josiah Smith Letterbook, UNC.

2. Bull to Lord Dartmouth, 31 July 1774, Sainsbury Transcripts, SCA (CO 5/229, BPRO). The Sainsbury Transcripts are copies of documents in the British Public Record Office relating to South Carolina. I am including the citations to the originals for the convenience of some readers.

3. Heyward to his father, 11 Feb. 1767, *Charleston Year Book,* 1886, 329–335; on changing ministries, see Robert McCulloch Weir, " 'Liberty and Property, and No Stamps': South Carolina and the Stamp Act Crisis" (Ph.D. dissertation, Western Reserve University, 1966), p. 370.

4. Bull to Lord Dartmouth, 31 July 1774, Sains. Trans., SCA (CO 5/229); the Commons resolution is quoted in Weir, " 'Liberty and Property, and No Stamps,' " p. 265.

5. Edward McCrady, *The History of South Carolina under the Royal Government, 1719-1776* (New York, 1899), pp. 621–622; W. Roy Smith, *South Carolina as a Royal Province, 1719-1776* (New York, 1903), pp. 367–368; the South Carolina resolutions of 19 Aug. 1769 are printed in Merrill Jensen, ed., *American Colonial Documents to 1776 (English Historical Documents,* ed. David C. Douglas, IX [London, 1955]) pp. 723–724; on the reaction to Boston's fate see Benjamin Woods Labaree, *The Boston Tea Party* (New York, 1964), p. 248; Laurens to John Laurens, 22 March 1774, "Letters from Hon. Henry Laurens to His Son John, 1773–1776," *SCHM* 4 (1903): 30; Smith to John Ray, Jr., 9 Aug. 1774, Josiah Smith Letterbook, UNC.

6. Jack P. Greene, *The Quest for Power: The Lower Houses of Assembly in the Southern Royal Colonies, 1689-1776* (Chapel Hill, 1963), pp. 191–194.

7. *Ibid.,* pp. 193–196.

8. Jack P. Greene, "Bridge to Revolution: The Wilkes Fund Controversy in South Carolina, 1769–1775," *JSH* 39 (1963): 27, 33, 37; for a brief treatment of Wilkes in England see Merrill Jensen, *The Founding of a Nation: A History of the American Revolution, 1763-1776* (New York, 1968), pp. 317–322.

9. David Morton Knepper, "The Political Structure of Colonial South Carolina, 1743–1776" (Ph.D. dissertation, University of Virginia, 1971), p. 36; Christopher Gadsden, "To the Gentlemen Electors of the Parish of St. Paul, Stono," *SCG,* 5 Feb. 1763, reprinted in Richard Walsh, ed., *The Writings of Christopher Gadsden, 1746-1805* (Columbia, S.C., 1966), pp. 17–50; Robert McCulloch Weir, " 'Liberty and Property, and No Stamps,' " pp. 37, 38.

10. Jackson Turner Main, *The Social Structure of Revolutionary America* (Princeton, 1965), pp. 57–60, 102–103, 112.

11. Weir, " 'Liberty and Property, and No Stamps,' " pp. 53, 60; Jackson Turner Main, "Government by the People: The American Revolution and the Democratization of the Legislatures," *W&MQ,* 3rd Ser. 23 (1966): 396.

12. On the lack of factions and the ideology of the South Carolina rulers, see Robert M. Weir, " 'The Harmony We Were Famous For': An Interpretation of Pre-Revolutionary South Carolina Politics," *W&MQ,* 3rd Ser. 26 (1969): 473–501.

13. Robert M. Weir, " 'Liberty and Property, and No Stamps,' " pp. 37, 50, 52; Manigault to Charles Alexander [Spring, 1768], quoted in Weir, " 'The Harmony We Were Famous For,' " p. 482.

14. Carl Bridenbaugh, *Myths and Realities, Societies of the Colonial South* (Baton Rouge, La., 1952), p. 79; Weir has found wills or inventories for some of the eighteen members of the Commons who served between 1762 and 1768 and who died before 1776. They owned from 3 to 279 slaves; the median was 47. " 'Liberty and Property, and No Stamps,' " p. 50.

15. Robert L. Meriwether, *The Expansion of South Carolina, 1729-1765* (Kingsport, Tenn., 1940), p. 160; Knepper, "The Political Structure of Colonial South Carolina," p. 36; Samuel Dubose, "Reminiscences of St. Stephen's Parish, Craven County, and Notices of Her Old Homesteads," in Theodore Gaillard Thomas, ed., *A Contribution to the History of the Huguenots of South Carolina* (New York, 1887), p. 40.

16. South Carolina Slave Code of 1735, quoted in Winthrop D. Jordan, *White Over Black: American Attitudes toward the Negro, 1550-1812* (Chapel Hill, 1968), p. 109; the report of the Commons committee on the Stono rebellion, quoted in John Donald Duncan, "Servitude and Slavery in Colonial South Carolina, 1670–1776" (Ph.D. dissertation, Emory University, 1971), p. 794.

17. Henry Laurens to John Laurens, 14 Aug. 1776, *The Lee Papers* (2 vols., New-York Historical Society, *Collections* 5–6 [1872–1873]), II, 218; the Georgian is quoted in Duncan, "Servitude and Slavery in Colonial South Carolina," p. 802; Laurens to Christopher Rowe, 8 Feb. 1764, quoted in Weir, " 'The Harmony We Were Famous For,' " p. 483.

18. Glen to the Board of Trade, 11 April 1756, quoted in Knepper, "The Political Structure of Colonial South Carolina," p. 37; Pinckney to the Board of Trade, 1756, quoted in Duncan, "Servitude and Slavery in Colonial South Carolina," p. 813.

19. Duncan, "Servitude and Slavery in Colonial South Carolina," pp. 819–823, 832, 837–843; Alexander Innes to [Lord Dartmouth], 16 May 1775, B.D. Bargar, ed., "Charles Town Loyalism in 1775: The Secret Reports of Alexander Innes," *SCHM* 63 (1962): 128; Henry Laurens to John Laurens, 30 July 1775, Henry Laurens Papers, LC.

20. Campbell to "My Lord," 19 Aug. 1775, quoted in George Smith McCowen, Jr., *The British Occupation of Charleston, 1780-1782* (Columbia, S.C., 1972), p. 99; Campbell to "My Lord," 31 Aug. 1775, quoted in Duncan, "Servitude and Slavery in Colonial South Carolina," p. 840.

21. Benjamin Quarles, *The Negro in the American Revolution* (Chapel Hill, 1961), p. 125; Edward Rutledge to Ralph Izard, 8 Dec. 1775, quoted in *ibid.*, p. 20n; John Rutledge's address, 11 April 1776, in William Edwin Hemphill *et al.*, eds., *Journals of the General Assembly and House of Representatives, 1776-1780* (Columbia, S.C., 1970), p. 53; McCowen, *British Occupation of Charleston,* p. 100. For the possibility that some Carolinians used the threat of slave rebellions as a means of uniting the colony, see Peter H. Wood, " 'Taking Care of Business' in Revolutionary South Carolina: Republicanism and the Slave Society," in Jeffrey J. Crow and Larry E. Tise, eds., *The Southern Experience in the American Revolution* (Chapel Hill, 1978), pp. 280–283.

22. Thomas Heyward, Jr. to his father, 11 Feb. 1767, *Charleston Year Book,* 1886, 329–335; Benjamin Smith to Rev. William Smith, 16 May 1766, quoted in Rogers, *Evolution of a Federalist,* pp. 46–47.

23. All the quotations are taken from Jack P. Greene, " 'Slavery or Independence': Some Reflections on the Relationship Among Liberty, Black Bondage, and Equality in Revolutionary South Carolina," *SCHM* 80 (1979): 195, 197, 198, 202; see also, F. Nwabueze Okoye, "Chattel Slavery as the Nightmare of the American Revolutionaries," *W&MQ,* 3rd Ser. 37 (1980): 3–28.

24. "An Advertisement," in Richard J. Hooker, ed., *The Carolina Backcountry on the Eve of the Revolution: The Journal and Other Writings of Charles Woodmason, Anglican Itinerant* (Chapel Hill, 1953), p. 258; Burke, quoted in Greene, "'Slavery or Independence,'" p. 204.

25. Jack P. Greene and Richard M. Jellison, "The Currency Act of 1764 in Imperial-Colonial Relations, 1764–1776," *W&MQ,* 3rd Ser. 18 (1961): 496; Virginia D. Harrington, *The New York Merchant on the Eve of the Revolution* (New York, 1935), p. 33. On the circumvention of the law see Jensen, *Founding of a Nation,* pp. 379–380.

26. M. Eugene Sirmans, *Colonial South Carolina: A Political History, 1663-1763* (Chapel Hill, 1966), pp. 74, 162, 167; Leila Sellers, *Charleston Business on the Eve of the American Revolution* (Chapel Hill, 1934), pp. 53, 157.

27. Sellers, *Charleston Business,* pp. 161–169; Charles Joseph Gayle, "The Nature and Volume of Exports from Charleston, 1724–1774," South Carolina Historical Association, *Proceedings,* 1937, p. 29.

28. Stuart Bruchey, ed., *The Colonial Merchant: Sources and Readings* (New York, 1966), Table 8A; George Rogers Taylor, "Wholesale Commodity Prices at Charleston, South Carolina, 1732–1791, 1796–1861," *Journal of Economic and Business History* 4 (1932): 372; Sellers, *Charleston Business,* p. 166.

29. Wells to Dear Sir, 12 Aug. 1765, South Carolina Box, Charleston folder, NYPL; Smith to George Austin, 25 Feb. 1772, Josiah Smith Letterbook, UNC.

30. Bruchey, ed., *Colonial Merchant,* Table 3C; Richard Walsh, *Charleston's Sons of Liberty: A Study of the Artisans* (Columbia, S.C., 1959), pp. 57–58.

31. Benjamin R. Baldwin, "The Debts Owed by Americans to British Creditors, 1763–1802" (Ph.D. dissertation, University of Indiana, 1932), p. 96; Emory G. Evans, "Planter Indebtedness and the Coming of the Revolution in Virginia," *W&MQ,* 3rd Ser. 19 (1962): 511.

32. David Duncan Wallace, *The Life of Henry Laurens, with a sketch of the life of Lieutenant-Colonel John Laurens* (New York, 1915), p. 204; Edward McCrady, *The History of South Carolina in the Revolution, 1775-1780* (New York, 1901), pp. 3–28; William Edwin Hemphill and Wylma Anne Wates, eds., *Extracts from the Journals of the Provincial Congresses of South Carolina, 1775-1776* (Columbia, S.C., 1960), p. xxiii.

33. Innes to Lord Dartmouth, 3 June 1775 and 3 July 1775, Bargar, ed., "Charles Town Loyalism," pp. 131, 135; Timothy to William Henry Drayton, 22 Aug. 1775, Joseph W. Barnwell, ed., "Correspondence of Hon. Arthur Middleton, Signer of the Declaration of Independence," *SCHM* 27 (1926): 131.

34. McCrady, *SC in the Revol., 1775-1780,* pp. 30–31, 88; Marvin R. Zahniser, *Charles Cotesworth Pinckney: Founding Father* (Chapel Hill, 1967), p. 31; Innes to [Lord Dartmouth], 16 May 1775, Bargar, ed., "Charles Town Loyalism," p. 128; for Lowndes's nickname, see Arthur Middleton to William Henry Drayton, 12 Aug. 1775, Barnwell, ed., "Correspondence of Arthur Middleton" (1926): 127.

35. Middleton to William Henry Drayton, 22 Aug. 1775, Barnwell, ed., "Correspondence of Arthur Middleton" (1926): 134; Innes to Lord Dartmouth, 10 June 1775, Bargar, ed., "Charles Town Loyalism," p. 134.

36. Innes to Dartmouth, 1 May 1775, and Bull to Lord Dartmouth, 28 March 1775, Sains. Trans., SCA (CO 5/229); *SCG,* 29 May 1775.

37. Laurens is quoted in Wallace, *Henry Laurens,* p. 212; on "Independancy," see Innes to Dartmouth, 1 May 1775, Sains. Trans., SCA (CO 5/229).

38. Ralph Izard to George Dempster, 1 Aug. 1775, Anne Izard Deas, *Correspondence of Mr. Ralph Izard, of South Carolina, from the year 1774 to 1804; with a short memoir*

(New York, 1844), p. 111; William M. Dabney and Marion Dargan, *William Henry Drayton & the American Revolution* (Albuquerque, N.M., 1962), pp. 116–118; Wallace, *Henry Laurens,* p. 221; Fletcher M. Green, *Constitutional Development in the South Atlantic States, 1776-1860: A Study in the Evolution of Democracy* (Chapel Hill, 1930), p. 61; McCrady, *SC in the Revol., 1775-1780,* pp. 109–110; Harriot Ravenel, *Charleston: The Place and the People* (New York, 1906), p. 225.

39. Smith to Capt. Joseph Blewer, 13 May 1775, Josiah Smith Letterbook, UNC. See also the legislature's first address to the state's new governor. Hemphill *et al.*, eds., *Journals of the General Assembly,* 1 April 1776, p. 17.

40. Quoted in Wallace, *Henry Laurens,* p. 225.

41. Innes to Lord Dartmouth, 10 June 1775, Bargar, ed., "Charles Town Loyalism," p. 133; Bull to Lord Dartmouth, 28 March 1775, Sains. Trans., SCA (CO 5/229).

42. Walsh, *Charleston's Sons of Liberty,* pp. 37–38; *SCG,* 2 June 1766, quoted in Weir, "'Liberty and Property, and No Stamps,'" p. 242; Smith to Reverend William Smith, 16 May 1766, quoted in Rogers, *Evolution of a Federalist,* pp. 46–47.

43. Walsh, *Charleston's Sons of Liberty,* pp. 17–18, 24.

44. *Ibid.,* p. 31; for the most important members of the Commons, see Weir, "'Liberty and Property, and No Stamps,'" p. 95n. John Pringle commented on the people discussing politics, but he did not indicate who was influencing decisions. John Pringle to William Tilghman, 30 July 1774, Preston Davie Collection, UNC.

45. Walsh, *Charleston's Sons of Liberty,* pp. 45–50.

46. *Ibid.,* pp. 41–44, 56–58; Arthur Meier Schlesinger, *The Colonial Merchants and the American Revolution, 1763-1776* (New York, 1918), pp. 140–143.

47. William A. Schaper, "Sectionalism and Representation in South Carolina," American Historical Association, *Annual Report,* 1900, I, 253–257; Meriwether, *Expansion of SC,* pp. 113–114.

48. Sirmans, *Colonial South Carolina,* pp. 36–37, 61–62, 77, 96–100. In 1775 all thirteen members of the Council of Safety were Anglicans. McCrady, *SC under Royal Government,* p. 797.

49. The quotation on lack of divine worship is from Bull to Lord Dartmouth, 15 May 1773, Sains. Trans., SCA (CO 5/228); on settlements see Richard M. Brown, *The South Carolina Regulators* (Cambridge, Mass., 1963), pp. 2–3; John Belton O'Neall and John A. Chapman, *The Annals of Newberry in Two Parts* (Newberry, S.C., 1892), pp. 21–25, 51, 55; Alexander Gregg, *History of the Old Cheraws* (New York, 1867), pp. 51–55, 62, 69–71; William Willis Boddie, *History of Williamsburg* (Columbia, S.C., 1923), pp. 10, 22, 25–26, 32–35; George Howe, *History of the Presbyterian Church in South Carolina* (2 vols., Columbia, S.C., 1870, 1873), I, 285–286, 341; Douglas Summers Brown, *A City without Cobwebs: A History of Rock Hill, South Carolina* (Columbia, S.C., 1953), pp. 38, 43; A.S. Salley, Jr., *The History of Orangeburg County* (Orangeburg, S.C., 1898), pp. 29–30, 35, 89–90; Meriwether, *Expansion of SC,* pp. 50, 57, 61–67, 76, 79–80, 91, 103.

50. The account of the Cherokee War is based on Brown, *Regulators,* pp. 4–12.

51. Stella H. Sutherland, *Population Distribution in Colonial America* (New York, 1936), pp. 240, 250; Sellers, *Charleston Business,* p. 29; Meriwether, *Expansion of SC,* pp. 160, 242.

52. Brown, *Regulators,* pp. 9–11, 29–36; Gregg, *Old Cheraws,* pp. 127–129; Regulators' "Remonstrance," in Hooker, ed., *Carolina Backcountry,* p. 214.

53. "SYLVANUS" [Charles Woodmason], in *South Carolina Gazette and Country Journal,* 28 March 1769, reprinted in Hooker, ed., *Carolina Backcountry,* pp. 260–263; "Remonstrance," in *ibid.,* pp. 215, 223.

54. Knepper, "The Political Structure of Colonial South Carolina," pp. 144–145, 178–179, 182, 198; "Remonstrance," Hooker, ed., *Carolina Backcountry,* pp. 225, 226.

55. "A Letter to John Rutledge," Hooker, ed., *Carolina Backcountry,* p. 277.

56. Richard Maxwell Brown, *Strain of Violence: Historical Studies of Violence and Vigilantism* (New York, 1975), pp. 72–73; Brown, *Regulators,* pp. 47–52.

57. Hooker, "The South Carolina Regulator Movement: An Introduction to the Documents," *Carolina Backcountry,* p. 168; "A Letter to John Rutledge," *ibid.,* pp. 274–275.

58. "An Advertisement," *ibid.,* p. 258.

59. "Remonstrance," *ibid.,* p. 221; see also Bull to Lord Hillsborough, 10 Sept. 1768, Sains. Trans., SCA (CO 5/379).

60. George C. Rogers, Jr., *The History of Georgetown County, South Carolina* (Columbia, S.C., 1970), pp. 62–63.

61. Knepper, "The Political Structure of Colonial South Carolina," pp. 154, 198; *SCG,* 12 Dec. 1774; Hooker, "The South Carolina Regulator Movement," *Carolina Backcountry,* p. 168.

62. Commons committee of correspondence to Charles Garth, 24 Sept. 1764, R.W. Gibbes, ed., *Documentary History of the American Revolution: Consisting of Letters and Papers relating to the Contest for Liberty, Chiefly in South Carolina* (3 vols., New York, 1853–1857), I, 5.

63. Knepper, "The Political Structure of Colonial South Carolina," p. 182.

64. "Remonstrance," "A Letter to John Rutledge," and an "Answer to Christopher Gadsden," in Hooker, ed., *Carolina Backcountry,* pp. 222, 272, 278, 266.

65. Brown, *Regulators,* pp. 76–77, 81, 96–98; Gregg, *Old Cheraws,* pp. 153–156, 186–192.

66. King in Council, 26 June 1767, Sains. Trans., SCA (CO 5/378). Since the 1730s, the British had expressed their intention of extending representation to the backcountry. But representation was to be granted by the king and not by the colonial legislature. Apparently, the governor could have created new parishes, but such action would certainly have brought howls of protest from the Carolina Commons. Other colonies were also affected by the British policy. Meriwether, *Expansion of SC,* p. 19; Benjamin Woods Labaree, *Royal Government in America: A Study of the British Colonial System before 1783* (New Haven, 1930), pp. 186–187.

67. Meriwether, *Expansion of SC,* p. 50.

68. Jensen, ed., *American Colonial Documents,* p. 593; Timothy to Benjamin Franklin, 3 Sept. 1768, Hennig Cohen, ed., "Four Letters from Peter Timothy, 1755, 1768, 1771," *SCHM* 55 (1954): 163.

69. Boone to Lords of Trade, 21 Jan. 1764, Sains. Trans., SCA (CO 5/377); Jack P. Greene, "The Gadsden Election Controversy and the Revolutionary Movement in South Carolina," *Mississippi Valley Historical Review* 46 (1959): 486.

70. Gadsden is quoted in Weir, "'Liberty and Property, and No Stamps,'" p. 203; Wallace, *Henry Laurens,* p. 111.

71. Knepper, "The Political Structure of Colonial South Carolina," p. 202n; Greene, *Quest for Power,* p. 382; Woodmason to "Sir," 26 March 1771, in Hooker, ed., *Carolina Backcountry,* pp. 194–195.

72. Middleton to William Henry Drayton, 4 Aug. 1775, Barnwell, ed. "Correspondence of Arthur Middleton" (1926): 123; Henry Laurens to John Laurens, 30 July 1775, Henry and John Laurens Papers, LC.

73. Dabney and Dargan, *William Henry Drayton,* p. 93; Brown, *Regulators,* pp. 15,

26; Sellers, *Charleston Business,* pp. 88–91; McCrady, *SC in the Revol., 1775–1780,* pp. 33–34, 39–42; Rogers, *Georgetown County,* p. 63.

74. Schaper, "Sectionalism and Representation in South Carolina," p. 362; Dabney and Dargan, *William Henry Drayton,* pp. 91–92; Anne King Gregorie, *History of Sumter County, South Carolina* (Sumter, S.C., 1954), p. 189.

75. Arthur Middleton to William Henry Drayton, 22 Aug. 1775, Barnwell, ed., "Correspondence of Arthur Middleton" (1926): 134.

76. McCrady, *SC in the Revol., 1775–1780,* pp. 86–97, 193–199; Brown, Strain of Violence, pp. 73–74.

77. Jensen, *Founding of a Nation,* pp. 505–507, 517–518.

78. Henry Laurens to John Laurens, 8 Jan. 1775, "Letters from Henry Laurens to His Son," p. 273; see also the *SCG,* 2 Jan. 1775.

79. Gadsden was joined in opposition by Rawlins Lowndes and Reverend William Tennent. Peter Force, ed., *American Archives* (Fourth Series) (6 vols., Washington, 1837–1846), I, 1111–1112.

80. [James Glen], "A Descriptive Account of South Carolina," in B.R. Carroll, ed., *Historical Collections of South Carolina* (2 vols., New York, 1836), II, 204; Rutledge to Samuel Myers, 8 Nov. 1787, Gratz Collection, Old Congress, HSP.

81. David Ramsay, *The History of South Carolina, from Its First Settlement in 1670, to the Year 1808* (Charleston, 1809), II, 278, 292; Guion Griffis Johnson, *A Social History of the Sea Islands with Special Reference to St. Helena Island, South Carolina* (Chapel Hill, 1930), pp. 21, 35, 105; Dubose, "Reminiscences of St. Stephen's Parish," pp. 37–40, 61.

82. Salley, *Orangeburg, SC,* p. 381; Gregorie, *Sumter, SC,* p. 20; Edwin L. Green, *A History of Richland County* (Columbia, S.C., 1932), p. 139.

83. W.W. Sellers, *A History of Marion County, South Carolina, from its Earliest Times to the Present, 1901* (Columbia, S.C., 1902), pp. 19, 25; Boddie, *Williamsburg County,* pp. 41–42, 89–90; Gregg, *Old Cheraws,* pp. 109–112; Meriwether, *Expansion of SC,* p. 92; Rogers, *Georgetown County,* pp. 88, 91–92.

84. Schaper, "Sectionalism and Representation in South Carolina," p. 345; Sutherland, *Population Distribution,* p. 240; Brown, *Regulators,* pp. 40, 54–55.

85. Weir, "'Liberty and Property, and No Stamps,'" p. 95n; Greene, *Quest for Power,* Appendix, pp. 475–488; McCrady, *SC under Royal Government,* p. 797.

86. E. Rutledge to John Rutledge, Jr., 18 Feb. 1789, John Rutledge Papers, DU.

87. William Knox to Gov. William Henry Lyttelton, 5 March 1760, quoted in Sirmans, *Colonial South Carolina,* p. 320.

88. Hemphill and Wates, eds., *Extracts from Jours. of Prov. Cong.,* p. xxiii; Greene, *Quest for Power,* pp. 475–488.

89. Jensen, *Founding of a Nation,* p. 478; Walsh, *Charleston's Sons of Liberty,* p. 62; *SCG,* 11 July 1774, quoted in George Edward Frakes, *Laboratory for Liberty: The South Carolina Legislative Committee System, 1719–1776* (Lexington, Ky., 1970), p. 122.

90. McCrady, *SC under Royal Government,* p. 760; Walsh, *Charleston's Sons of Liberty,* p. 65.

91. Weir, "'Liberty and Property, and No Stamps,'" pp. 12–13; Arthur M. Schlesinger, *Prelude to Independence: The Newspaper War on Britain, 1764–1776* (New York, 1957), p. 127; Kinloch to John Laurens, 28 April 1776, quoted in Rogers, *Evolution of a Federalist,* p. 79; Henry Laurens to John Laurens, 4 Jan. 1775, "Letters from Henry Laurens to His Son," p. 271; same to same, 22 Jan. 1775, quoted in Hemphill and Wates, eds., *Extracts from Jours. of Prov. Cong.,* p. xxiii.

92. Johann David Schoepf, *Travels in the Confederation,* trans. and ed. Alfred J. Morrison (Philadelphia, 1911), pp. 198–199.

93. Laurens to Francis Kinloch, 10 March 1775, *Charleston Year Book,* 1882, 345–347; the Provincial Congress is quoted in Elisha P. Douglass, *Rebels and Democrats: The Struggle for Equal Political Rights and Majority Rule during the American Revolution* (Chapel Hill, 1955), pp. 37–38.

94. Francis Kinloch to Thomas Boone, 8 July 1786, Felix Gilbert, ed., ''Letters of Francis Kinloch to Thomas Boone, 1782–1788,'' *JSH* 8 (1942): 102.

NOTES
CHAPTER TWO

1. Jensen, *Founding of a Nation,* pp. 639–640.

2. For the quotations, see Gordon S. Wood, *The Creation of the American Republic, 1776–1787* (Chapel Hill, 1969), p. 129; for reference to the eight state constitutions, *ibid.*, p. 133.

3. "Journal of the South Carolina Provincial Congress," 11 Feb. 1776, in Force, ed., *American Archives,* Fourth Series, V, 570; Green, *Constitutional Development,* p. 61; for dates of entry into the Commons, see the Appendix in Greene, *Quest for Power,* pp. 475–488; for family relationships see the genealogical charts in Rogers, *Evolution of a Federalist,* pp. 401–406; for membership in the Provincial Congress, see Force, ed., *American Archives,* Fourth Series, IV, 27–28.

4. McCrady, *SC in the Revol., 1775–1780,* pp. 30–31, 88.

5. Drayton's remark is quoted in Clinton Lawrence Rossiter, *Seedtime of the Republic: The Origin of the American Tradition of Political Liberty* (New York, 1953), p. 384; and see Schlesinger, *Prelude to Independence,* p. 127.

6. Wallace, *Henry Laurens,* p. 105; Walsh, *Charleston's Sons of Liberty,* pp. 32–33; Rutledge and Lynch are quoted in Weir, " 'Liberty and Property, and No Stamps,' " p. 203.

7. "Journal of the Provincial Congress," in Force, ed., *American Archives,* Fourth Series, V, 565, 594, 597, 598; McCrady, *SC in the Revol., 1775–1780,* p. 112; Green, *Constitutional Development,* p. 61. The American Prohibitory Act is printed in Jensen, ed., *American Colonial Documents,* p. 853.

8. The constitution is printed in Thomas Cooper and David J. McCord, eds., *Statutes at Large of South Carolina* (10 vols., Columbia, S.C., 1836–1841), I; Force, ed., *American Archives,* Fourth Series, V.

9. Two errors account for most of the confusion regarding apportionment of representation. Edward McCrady, in his monumental work on *South Carolina in the Revolution, 1775–1780,* gave the backcountry 64 of the 202 representatives. But McCrady simply left out 12 representatives for St. Matthew and St. David, which he previously had treated as backcountry parishes. Several historians copied him. Others copied Schaper, who in "Sectionalism and Representation in South Carolina," pp. 359 and 367, gave the "up country" 58 representatives. But Schaper left out of his calculations the 18 representatives of Saxe-Gotha, St. Matthew, and St. David.

10. For colonial land policy see Sirmans, *Colonial South Carolina,* pp. 239–240.

11. The quotations, all from documents written in 1776, and the provisions of state constitutions can be found in Wood, *Creation of the American Republic,* pp. 132–143.

12. *Ibid.;* Green, *Constitutional Development,* p. 83; for the action of the Provincial Congress, see the "Journal," 18 March 1776, in Force, ed., *American Archives,* Fourth Series, V, 595.

13. The quotation is from a letter of William Hooper to the North Carolina Congress, 26 Oct. 1776, in Wood, *Creation of the American Republic,* p. 141.

14. On annual elections, see *ibid.*, p. 166.

15. The quotations are given in Wood, *Creation of the American Republic,* pp. 209, 215.

16. On the Powell affair see Smith, *South Carolina as a Royal Province,* pp. 388–390; McCrady, *SC under Royal Government,* pp. 715–721.

17. Because anyone who qualified for a seat in the lower house could sit in the upper or become governor, Francis Salvador, a Jew who had been elected to the First and Second Provincial Congresses, from where he moved into the first General Assembly, could have risen higher. Salvador was the first Jew to sit in a western Parliamentary body.

18. In 1775, the colonial council had suspended William Henry Drayton, chairman of the Provincial Congress writing the constitution. Smith, *South Carolina as a Royal Province,* pp. 400–401. Both Douglass, *Rebels and Democrats,* p. 42, and Green, *Constitutional Development,* p. 42, place all or most patronage powers in the General Assembly.

19. For the actions of other states and the quotation, from the New Jersey Constitution, see Wood, *Creation of the American Republic,* pp. 158, 158n, 160–161.

20. John Adams to James Warren, 22 April 1776, quoted in Dabney and Dargan, *William Henry Drayton,* p. 120; John Adams to Abigail Adams, 17 May 1776, L.H. Butterfield, ed., *The Adams Papers,* Series II, *Adams Family Correspondence* (2 vols., Cambridge, Mass., 1963), I, 411.

21. Hemphill *et al.,* eds., *Journals of the General Assembly,* 11 April 1776, pp. 52–55; Green, *Constitutional Development,* pp. 105–106.

22. Brown, *Strain of Violence,* p. 74.

23. Hemphill *et al.,* eds., *Journals of the General Assembly,* 12 Oct. 1776, p. 143; the quotations are from William Tennent, "Historic remarks on the session of Assembly began to be holden Tuesday, September 17th, 1776," in Newton B. Jones, ed., "Writings of the Reverend William Tennent, 1740–1777," *SCHM* 61 (1960): 189.

24. Hemphill *et al.,* eds., *Journals of the General Assembly,* Appendix II, p. 309, IV, p. 315; Tennent, "Historic Remarks," in Jones, ed., "Writings of Tennent," pp. 191–192.

25. Hemphill *et al.,* eds., *Journals of the General Assembly,* 12 Oct. 1776, p. 143, and Appendix I, pp. 302–303; Greene, *Quest for Power,* Appendix, pp. 475–488; Rogers, *Evolution of a Federalist,* pp. 113–114; Rogers, *Georgetown County,* pp. 48–52, 95.

26. Hemphill *et al.,* eds., *Journals of the General Assembly,* 14 Oct. 1776, pp. 148–149.

27. *Ibid.,* 17 Oct. 1776, p. 161; Tennent, "Historic Remarks," in Jones, ed., "Writings of Tennent," p. 18.

28. Tennent, "Historic Remarks," in Jones, ed., "Writings of Tennent," p. 107; Gervais to Henry Laurens, 16 March 1778, Raymond Starr, ed., "Letters from John Lewis Gervais to Henry Laurens, 1777–1778," *SCHM* 66 (1965): 29.

29. Tennent, "Historic Remarks," in Jones, ed., "Writings of Tennent," p. 192.

30. *Ibid.,* p. 193.

31. *Ibid.*

32. *Ibid.,* pp. 190, 192; McCrady, *SC in the Revol., 1775–1780,* pp. 206–207; David Ramsay, *The History of the Revolution of South-Carolina from a British Province to an Independent State* (2 vols., Trenton, N.J., 1785), I, 128.

33. McCrady, *SC in the Revol., 1775–1780,* pp. 206–207, 212–213; Tennent's speech is quoted in Green, *Constitutional Development,* p. 108.

34. For the attitudes of the Presbyterian and Baptist clergy see Durward Turrentine Stokes, "The Clergy of the Carolinas and the American Revolution" (Ph.D. dissertation, University of North Carolina, 1968), pp. 157–180, 213–228; for the fight over disestablishment see McCrady, *SC in The Revol., 1775–1780,* pp. 212–213; Green, *Constitutional Development,* p. 110.

35. *A Bill for Establishing the Constitution of the State of South-Carolina* (Charleston, 1777); the constitution is printed in Cooper and McCord, eds., *Statutes of South Carolina,* I.

36. For the Bullman quotation and the subsequent actions of the vestry, see Stokes, "The Clergy of the Carolinas," pp. 195–198.

37. The Reverend William Tennent had died of a fever in the fall of 1777, and Francis Salvador had been killed on an expedition against the Cherokees in July 1776. Jones, ed., "Writings of William Tennent," p. 133; Jacob R. Marcus. *The Colonial American Jew, 1492–1776* (3 vols., Detroit, 1970), III, 1308.

38. On the split between Gadsden and the Rutledges see Richard Walsh, ed., *Writings of Gadsden,* pp. 107n, 117.

39. Edward Rutledge was disgusted with the new Privy Council. See Rutledge to Thomas Pinckney, 17 Feb. 1779, Thomas Pinckney Letterbook, South Caroliniana Library, USC.

40. On impeachment in state constitutions, see Wood, *Creation of the American Republic,* pp. 141–143.

41. The lower house apparently forced the change by refusing to pass a tax bill until the Council agreed to the alteration. Green, *Constitutional Development,* p. 111.

42. The apportionment of representation among the sections was roughly the same in both houses: the backcountry elected 37.9 percent of the Senate and 37.6 percent of the lower house; Georgetown and Beaufort districts chose 17.2 percent of the Senate and 14.8 percent of the House; and Charleston District elected 44.8 percent of the Senate and 47.5 percent of the House.

43. On reapportionment in other states see Wood, *Creation of the American Republic,* p. 172.

44. Gervais to Henry Laurens, 16 March 1778, Starr, ed., "Letters of Gervais," p. 29; John Rutledge to Henry Laurens, 8 March 1778, Frank Moore, *Materials for History Printed from Original Manuscripts* (New York, 1861), pp. 103–105.

45. Rutledge is quoted in McCrady, *SC in the Revol., 1775–1780,* pp. 238–239, and Ramsay, *Revol. of SC,* I, 136; James Cannon to George Bryan, 14 March 1778, in Joseph Johnson, *Traditions & Reminiscences chiefly of the American Revolution in the South* (Charleston, 1851), pp. 156–157. Cannon's letter is a curious mixture of fact and misstatement. Cannon, for example, incorrectly identified Lowndes as the governor vetoing the constitution.

46. Rutledge to Henry Laurens, 8 March 1778, Moore, *Materials for History,* pp. 103–105. Green, citing the Cannon letter referred to above, states that it was only after Rutledge vetoed the constitution that the Assembly decided to strip the governor of the veto power. But that is clearly wrong. See Ramsay, *Revol. of SC,* I, 132; Rutledge to Laurens, 8 March 1778, Moore, *Materials for History,* p. 103; Gervais to Laurens, 16 March 1778, Starr, ed., "Letters of Gervais," p. 28.

47. In his letter to Laurens at the Continental Congress, Rutledge diplomatically withheld that argument. Ramsay, *Revol. of SC,* I, 136; Christopher Gadsden to William Henry Drayton, 7 March 1778, Walsh, ed., *Writings of Gadsden,* p. 122.

48. John Rutledge to Henry Laurens, 8 March 1778, Moore, *Materials for History,* p. 105; John Lewis Gervais to Henry Laurens, 16 March 1778, Starr, ed., "Letters of Gervais," p. 28; Christopher Gadsden to William Henry Drayton, 1 June 1778, Walsh, ed., *Writings of Gadsden,* p. 126; Gadsden to Peter Timothy, 8 June 1778, quoted in McCrady, *SC in the Revol., 1775–1780,* p. 272. Not too long before, Drayton had been elected president of the Provincial Congress and then chief justice by moderates attempting to silence him by removing him from the debating floor. Wallace, *Henry Laurens,* p. 219; Dabney and Dargan, *William Henry Drayton,* pp. 122–123.

49. John Lewis Gervais to Henry Laurens, 16 March 1778, Starr, ed., "Letters of Gervais," p. 28.

50. Laurens to John Laurens, 14 Aug. 1776, Moore, *Materials for History,* p. 31.

NOTES
CHAPTER THREE

1. Innes to Lord Dartmouth, 10 June 1775, Bargar, ed., "Charles Town Loyalism," pp. 133–134.

2. Christopher Gadsden to William Henry Drayton, 7 March 1778, Walsh, ed., *Writings of Gadsden,* p. 122.

3. Gadsden to William Henry Drayton, 14 Oct. 1778, *ibid.,* p. 159.

4. Lowndes to Henry Laurens, 17 June 1778 and 6 July 1778, Simms collection, roll 2, South Caroliniana Library, USC; McCrady, *SC in the Revol., 1775–1780,* pp. 266–267; Gadsden to Peter Timothy, 8 June 1778, Walsh, ed., *Writings of Gadsden,* p. 130. Lowndes's other son did soon die.

5. Gadsden to Peter Timothy, 8 June 1778, and Gadsden to Drayton, 15 June 1778, Walsh, ed., *Writings of Gadsden,* pp. 130, 133. According to printer John Wells, Jr., Edward Rutledge toned down objections to Lowndes, convincing people not to impeach the governor and Privy Council. Wells to Henry Laurens, 10 June 1778, Simms collection, roll 2, South Caroliniana Library, USC. But Gadsden himself had urged that the people try to have the officers impeached instead of continuing their mass protest. And Gadsden reported, in his letter to Drayton on 15 June, that he went out among the people, "found them chiefly a Mere Mob, with here and there some who ought not to have been [there], and," he added, "I was sorry to see there and had reason to suspect *that Day* much *Negative* Impulse." One can suspect that the "*Negative* Impulse" was provided by Edward Rutledge.

6. Gadsden to Thomas Bee, 5 Oct. 1778, and Gadsden to William Henry Drayton, 14 Oct. 1778, Walsh, ed., *Writings of Gadsden,* pp. 154–158, 159; John Wells, Jr. to Henry Laurens, 6 Sept. 1778, Simms collection, roll 2, South Caroliniana Library, USC. Bee was speaker of the House of Representatives.

7. Gadsden to Thomas Bee, 5 Oct. 1778, Walsh, ed., *Writings of Gadsden,* pp. 154–158; see also Gadsden to William Henry Drayton, 14 Oct. 1778, *ibid.,* p. 159.

8. Wells to Henry Laurens, 10 June 1778 and 6 Sept. 1778, Simms collection, roll 2, South Caroliniana Library, USC.

9. Gervais to Henry Laurens, 26 June 1778 and 21 Sept. 1778, Starr, ed., "Letters of Gervais," pp. 31–32, 36.

10. Gervais to Laurens, 21 Sept. 1778, *ibid.,* p. 36.

11. W. Robert Higgins, "A Financial History of the American Revolution in South Carolina" (Ph.D. dissertation, Duke University, 1970), pp. 41–42, 42n.

12. Lowndes to Henry Laurens, 7 Sept. 1778 and 22 Sept. 1778, Simms collection, roll 2, South Caroliniana Library, USC; Gadsden to William Henry Drayton, 9 Sept. 1778, Walsh, ed., *Writings of Gadsden,* p. 150; the French observer is cited in William C. Stinchcombe, *The American Revolution and the French Alliance* (Syracuse, N.Y., 1969), p. 60.

13. Hutson to Thomas Hutson, 30 June 1776, *Charleston Year Book,* 1895, pp. 323–325.

14. Clyde R. Ferguson, "Carolina and Georgia Patriot and Loyalist Militia in Action," in Crow and Tise, eds., *The Southern Experience in the American Revolution,* pp. 174–199; Brown to Governor Patrick Tonyn, [February] 1776, K.G. Davies, ed., *Documents of the American Revolution 1770–1783* (Colonial Office Series) (Irish University Press, 1972–), XII, 70; on the role of the American militia in general, see Don Higginbotham, "The American Militia: A Traditional Institution with Revolutionary Responsibilities," in Don Higginbotham, ed., *Reconsiderations on the Revolutionary War: Selected Essays* (Westport, Conn., 1978), pp. 83–103.

15. Zahniser, *Charles Cotesworth Pinckney*, pp. 19, 51.

16. Josiah Smith to James Poyas, 25 July 1777, and Smith to George Appleby, 23 March 1778, Josiah Smith Letterbook, UNC; Rogers, *Georgetown County*, pp. 118–119; Higgins, "Financial History of South Carolina," pp. 27–36; James Wright to Henry Clinton, 3 Feb. 1780, in Davies, ed., *Documents of the American Revolution*, XVIII, 46.

17. For the educational societies see the laws in Cooper and McCord, eds., *Statutes of South Carolina*, VIII, 114–119, 121; Gregg, *Old Cheraws*, pp. 280–284; for prewar educational opportunities see Bridenbaugh, *Myths and Realities*, pp. 100–101, 186; Sirmans, *Colonial South Carolina*, p. 232.

18. Higgins, "Financial History of South Carolina," pp. 34, 45; James Simpson to Lord George Germain, 30 Aug. 1780, Davies, ed., *Documents of the American Revolution*, XVIII, 156; see also Simpson to William Knox, 31 Dec. 1780, *ibid.*, 268.

19. Walsh, *Charleston's Sons of Liberty*, p. 78; Hart to Joseph Hart, 16 Feb. 1779, Oliver Hart Papers, South Caroliniana Library, USC.

20. Smith to George Appleby, 23 March 1778, Josiah Smith Letterbook, UNC; St. Philip's Church Vestry Journal, 3 Aug. 1779 and 8 Dec. 1779, WPA Transcripts, South Caroliniana Library, USC.

21. Walsh, *Charleston's Sons of Liberty*, pp. 77–79.

22. Hemphill *et al.*, eds., *Journals of the General Assembly*, 8 Sept. and 11 Sept. 1779, pp. 208–209, 226–227, 230; Cooper and McCord, eds., *Statutes of South Carolina*, IX, 679–680.

23. The pledges to resist were made by Henry Laurens and Josiah Smith. Laurens to James Laurens, 20 Oct. 1775, quoted in Wallace, *Henry Laurens*, pp. 217–218; Smith to James Poyas, 10 Jan. 1776, Josiah Smith Letterbook, UNC; Butler to [Rev. Weeden Butler], 15 March 1789, Pierce Butler Papers, British Museum, 16603.

24. John Richard Alden, *The South in the Revolution, 1763–1789* (Baton Rouge, La., 1957), pp. 235–236; Prevost to Lord George Germain, 10 June 1780, Davies, ed., *Documents of the American Revolution*, XVIII, 141.

25. Edward Rutledge to Thomas Pinckney, 17 Feb. 1779, Thomas Pinckney Letterbook, South Caroliniana Library, USC; Robert Woodward Barnwell, Jr., "Loyalism in South Carolina, 1765–1785" (Ph.D. dissertation, Duke University, 1941), p. 155; Ramsay, *Revol. of SC*, II, 31–33; James Simpson to Lord George Germain, 28 Aug. 1779, Alan S. Brown, ed., "James Simpson's Reports on the Carolina Loyalists, 1779–1780," *JSH* 21 (1955): 518.

26. Simpson to Lord Germain, 28 Aug. 1779, Brown, ed., "Simpson's Reports," p. 517. The Privy Council vote was five to three in favor of the proposal, with Gadsden in the minority. McCrady, *SC in the Revol., 1775–1780*, pp. 366–376.

27. For Campbell's call and the rebels' counterproclamation, see Ferguson, "Carolina and Georgia Patriot and Loyalist Militia in Action," p. 180; for the effect of rebel actions, see James Mark Prevost to Lord George Germain, 14 April 1779, Davies, ed., *Documents of the American Revolution*, XVII, 101.

28. Ferguson, "Carolina and Georgia Patriot and Loyalist Militia in Action," p. 182.

29. Augustine Prevost to Lord George Germain, 10 June 1779, Davies, ed., *Documents of the American Revolution*, XVII, 143.

30. Galloway to Dartmouth, 23 Jan. 1778, quoted in Quarles, *The Negro in the American Revolution*, p. 112; Richard W. Van Alstyne, *Empire and Independence: The International History of the American Revolution* (New York, 1965), pp. 191–198; Simpson to Lord Germain, 28 Aug. 1779, Brown, ed., "Simpson's Reports," p. 517.

31. Paul H. Smith, *Loyalists and Redcoats: A Study in British Revolutionary Policy*

(Chapel Hill, 1964), pp. 115–118; Germain to Clinton, 5 Aug. 1779, quoted in *ibid.*, p. 124. Germain had replaced Dartmouth as Secretary of State for the colonies.

32. Lee to Richard Henry Lee, 5 April 1776, *Lee Papers*, I, 379; Instructions to Brigadier General Armstrong, 10 April 1776, *ibid.*, p. 410.

33. Quarles, *The Negro in the American Revolution*, pp. 60, 90–91, 102–105.

34. Duncan, "Servitude and Slavery in Colonial South Carolina," pp. 472–476.

35. Gadsden to Sam Adams, 6 July 1779, Walsh, ed., *Writings of Gadsden*, p. 166; Hemphill *et al.*, eds., *Journals of the General Assembly*, 5 Feb. 1780, pp. 276–277.

36. Slaves were not alone in being 'volunteered.' In 1778 the state provided for the enlistment of "idle, lewd, disorderly men," beggars, and "straggling persons." Cooper and McCord, eds., *Statutes of South Carolina*, IV, 410–413, IX, 679–680.

37. Germain to Sir Henry Clinton, 27 Sept. 1779, quoted in Smith, *Loyalists and Redcoats*, p. 124; Clifford Shipton, "Benjamin Lincoln: Old Reliable," in George Athan Billias, ed., *George Washington's Generals* (New York, 1964), pp. 197–203; *New York Royal Gazette*, 21 June 1780, quoted in McCowen, *The British Occupation of Charleston*, p. 11.

38. The Charleston Address is printed in John Almon, *The Remembrancer, or Impartial Repository of Public Events* 10 (1780):83, and in Davies, ed., *Documents of the American Revolution*, XVIII, 102–104; the Georgetown Address is quoted in Rogers, *Georgetown County*, p. 123; Ramsay to Benjamin Lincoln, 29 Jan. 1788, *The Benjamin Lincoln Papers*, Massachusetts Historical Society, Microfilm Publication: Number 3, reel 9; Barnwell, "Loyalism in South Carolina," pp. 213–214.

39. Almon, *The Remembrancer* 10 (1780): 83; McCrady, *SC in the Revol., 1775–1780*, p. 537; Simpson to Sir Henry Clinton, 15 May 1780, Brown, ed., "Simpson's Reports," p. 517.

40. Almon, *The Remembrancer* 10 (1780): 83: Rogers, *Georgetown County*, p. 123.

41. Van Alstyne, *Empire and Independence*, p. 148; Eric Robson, *The American Revolution in its Political and Military Aspects, 1763–1783* (New York, 1955), pp. 183–197; Laurens to General Horatio Gates, 17 June 1778, in Edmund C. Burnett, ed., *Letters of Members of the Continental Congress* (8 vols., Washington, 1921–1936), III, 298–299.

42. *CEG*, 27 Oct. 1785 and 28 Oct. 1785.

43. The remarks of Elfe and others are quoted in Walsh, *Charleston's Sons of Liberty*, p. 94; McCrady, *SC in the Revol., 1775–1780*, p. 713.

44. Smith, *Loyalists and Redcoats*, p. 139. Ferguson was Inspector of the Militia.

45. The quotation is from Lord Rawdon to Lord Cornwallis, 7 July 1780, in *ibid.*, p. 133; on hopes for the restoration of civil government, see McCowen, *The British Occupation of Charleston*, pp. 16–19, 56.

46. Clinton to Cornwallis, 1 July 1780, quoted in Rogers, *Georgetown County*, p. 123; Instructions from Clinton to Major Ferguson, 22 May 1780, quoted in *ibid.*, p. 125; McCowen, *The British Occupation of Charleston*, p. 60.

47. Augustine Prevost to Lord George Germain, 10 June 1779, Davies, ed., *Documents of the American Revolution*, XVII, 143; Simpson to Henry Clinton, 15 May 1780, *ibid.*, XVIII, 95; James Mark Prevost to Lord George Germain, 14 April 1779, *ibid.*, XVII, 104.

48. Henry Clinton to Lord George Germain, 25 Aug. 1780, *ibid.*, XVIII, 153.

49. James Simpson to Lord George Germain, 13 Aug. 1780, *ibid.*, p. 138.

50. McCowen, *The British Occupation of Charleston*, pp. 131–132; McCrady, *SC in the Revol., 1775–1780*, pp. 618, 705–711.

51. General Clinton and Lord Rawdon are quoted in Smith, *Loyalists and Redcoats*, pp. 132–133.

52. McCrady, *SC in the Revol., 1775-1780,* p. 647; Cornwallis is quoted in Robert D. Bass, *The Green Dragoon: The Lives of Banastre Tarleton and Mary Robinson* (New York, 1957), p. 92. Bass's book, although containing no references to sources, is based on a great deal of research and contains several extremely valuable chapters on the war in South Carolina.

53. Exam[inatio]n [of] Deserters, 12 Jan. 1779, *Benjamin Lincoln Papers,* Microfilm, reel 3, part 1, MHS; on Sir James Beard, see [Louisa Susannah Wells], *The Journal of a Voyage from Charlestown, S.C., to London Undertaken . . . in the Year 1778* (New York, 1906), p. 53.

54. Henry Lee, *Memoirs of the War in the Southern Department of the United States* (New York, 1870 ed.), p. 165; McCrady, *SC in the Revol., 1775-1780,* pp. 522, 560; Bass, *Green Dragoon,* 81.

55. Tarleton is quoted in Bass, *Green Dragoon,* pp. 92, 110; Tarleton to "my dear sir," 5 Nov. 1780, and Tarleton to Cornwallis, 5 Aug. 1780, quoted in Rogers, *Georgetown County,* pp. 131, 129.

56. Rutledge is quoted in Bass, *Green Dragoon,* p. 111; McCrady, *SC in the Revol., 1775-1780,* pp. 816–817.

57. Wemyss's orders were from Lord Cornwallis and are quoted in Bass, *Green Dragoon,* p. 105; his reference to the "sedition shops" is quoted in Stokes, "The Clergy of the Carolinas," p. 180; McCrady, *SC in the Revol., 1775-1780,* p. 641.

58. McCrady, *SC in the Revol., 1775-1780,* pp. 710–711. Of Cornwallis and these hangings, Colonel Henry Lee wrote: "This sanguinary conduct, in the amiable, humane Cornwallis, evinces the proneness of military men, however virtuous, to abuse power." *Memoirs of the War,* p. 193.

59. Tarleton's justification is in a proclamation issued on 11 Nov. 1780, printed in Bass, *Green Dragoon,* pp. 111–112.

60. Rawdon to the earl of Hastings, 25 Sept. 1776, quoted in John Shy, "The Military Conflict Considered as a Revolutionary War," Stephen G. Kurtz and James H. Hutson, eds., *Essays on the American Revolution* (Chapel Hill, 1973), p. 135.

61. Stuart to his father, 16 Sept. 1778, quoted in *ibid.,* p. 146.

62. Burke to Arthur Middleton, 25 Jan. 1782, Barnwell, ed., "Correspondence of Arthur Middleton" (1925): 192; Kinloch to Thomas Boone, 1 Oct. 1782, Gilbert, ed., "Letters of Francis Kinloch," pp. 91–92; for Kinloch's thoughts in 1776, see his letter to John Laurens, 28 April 1776, quoted in Rogers, *Evolution of a Federalist,* p. 79.

63. Robert Scott Davis, Jr., "The Loyalist Trials at Ninety Six in 1779," *SCHM* 80 (1979): 172–181; *Royal Georgia Gazette,* 12 Aug. 1779, quoted in *ibid.,* 181.

64. Simpson to Henry Clinton, 15 May 1780, Davies, ed., *Documents of the American Revolution,* XVIII, 95.

65. *Ibid.;* Smith, *Loyalists and Redcoats,* pp. 129–130; Clinton's orders are quoted in Rogers, *Georgetown County,* p. 125.

66. James Simpson to Lord George Germain, 30 Aug. 1780, Davies, ed., *Documents of the American Revolution,* XVIII, 156.

67. For Tarleton and the "banditti," see Simpson to Germain, 13 Aug. 1780, *ibid.,* p. 138; for rebel cruelty, General Cornwallis to Lord George Germain, 19 Sept. 1780, *ibid.,* p. 169.

68. Cornwallis to Henry Clinton, 3 Dec. 1780, *ibid.,* p. 245.

69. John Shy, "American Society and its War for Independence," in Higginbotham, ed., *Reconsiderations on the Revolutionary War,* pp. 73–74.

70. Martin to Lord George Germain, 10 June 1780, Davies, ed., *Documents of the American Revolution,* XVIII, 107.

71. Rogers, *Georgetown County,* pp. 134–135; J.B.O. Landrum, *History of Spartanburg County* (Atlanta, Ga., 1900), pp. 184–189.

72. Edward McCrady, *The History of South Carolina in the Revolution, 1780-1783* (New York, 1902), pp. 467–474; Howe, *Presbyterian Church in SC,* I, 437; O'Neall and Chapman, *Annals of Newberry,* p. 200; Jack M. Sosin, *The Revolutionary Frontier, 1763-1783* (New York, 1967), pp. 128–129. On the partisan war in general, see the biographies by Robert D. Bass: *Gamecock: The Life and Campaigns of General Thomas Sumter* (New York, 1961); *Swamp Fox: The Life and Campaigns of General Francis Marion* (New York, 1959), and *Green Dragoon.* Alice Noble Waring, *The Fighting Elder, Andrew Pickens (1739-1817)* (Columbia, S.C., 1962), is also useful.

73. Brown, *Strain of Violence,* pp. 80–81; Greene to Andrew Pickens, 5 June 1781, Nathanael Greene Papers, Duke University; Greene to Gen. Robert Howe, 29 Dec. 1780, quoted in Ronald Hoffman, ''The 'Disaffected' in the Revolutionary South,'' in Alfred F. Young, ed., *The American Revolution: Explorations in the History of American Radicalism* (Dekalb, Ill., 1976), p. 294.

74. William Pierce to St. George Tucker, 20 July 1781, quoted in Charles Royster, *A Revolutionary People at War: The Continental Army and American Character, 1775-1783* (Chapel Hill, 1979), p. 278; Cornwallis to Major General Smallwood, 10 Nov. 1780, Charles Ross, ed., *Correspondence of Charles, First Marquis Cornwallis* (3 vols., London, 1859), I, 67.

75. Lord Balfour to Lord Cornwallis, 26 April 1781, quoted in Barnwell, ''Loyalism in South Carolina,'' p. 313; Watson is quoted in Russell P. Weigley, *The Partisan War: The South Carolina Campaign of 1780-1782* (Columbia, S.C., 1970), p. 48.

76. Compiled from figures in Howard H. Peckham, ed., *The Toll of Independence: Engagements & Battle Casualties of the Americana Revolution* (Chicago, 1974). A summary table is printed on page 130.

77. Gen. Nathanael Greene to Gov. William Greene, 22 April 1781, ''Revolutionary Correspondence from 1775 to 1782,'' Rhode Island Historical Society, *Collections* 6 (1867): 285–286.

78. McCrady, *SC in the Revol., 1780-1783,* p. 318; Schoepf, *Travels in the Confederation,* p. 163; Howe, *Presbyterian Church in SC,* I, 480–484; Gregg, *Old Cheraws,* pp. 302–306; Wemyss's remark is quoted in Bass, *Swamp Fox,* p. 58.

79. William Drayton, Remarks in a Tour through the Back Country of the State of South Carolina, 1784, William Drayton Journals, Charleston Museum. Drayton was a cousin of William Henry Drayton, the revolutionary leader who died in 1779. William Drayton had been chief justice of East Florida and had moved to England during the war. Rogers, *Evolution of a Federalist,* p. 113; Dabney and Dargan, *William Henry Drayton,* pp. 85–86.

80. Joseph Kershaw to Henry Laurens, 1 Feb. 1785, Emmett Collection, NYPL; Bass, *Gamecock,* p. 52; Howe, *Presbyterian Church in SC,* I, 496.

81. McCrady, *SC in the Revol., 1775-1780,* pp. 815–816; Ramsay, *Revol. of SC,* II, 159–160; Howe, *Presbyterian Church in SC,* I, 514, quoting a history of the church at Fishing Creek, which Howe believed to have been written by Simpson; Drayton, Remarks in a Tour, 1784, William Drayton Journals, Charleston Museum; William Moultrie, *Memoirs of the American Revolution, so far as it Related to the States of North and South Carolina, and Georgia* (2 vols., New York, 1802), II, 354.

82. John A. Chapman, *History of Edgefield County from the Earliest Settlements to 1897* (Newberry, S.C., 1897), p. 72; O'Neall and Chapman, *Annals of Newberry,* p. 163; McCrady, *SC in the Revol., 1775-1780,* p. 834; McCrady, *SC in the Revol., 1780-1783,*

pp. 18–20; Drayton, Remarks in a Tour, 1784, William Drayton Journals, Charleston Museum.

83. Rutledge to Thomas Pinckney, 17 Feb. 1779, Thomas Pinckney Letterbook, South Caroliniana Library, USC; Moultrie, *Memoirs of the American Revolution,* II, 355; Wallace, *Henry Laurens,* p. 423; Ralph Izard to Arthur Middleton, 30 May 1783, Barnwell, ed., "Correspondence of Arthur Middleton" (1926): 78; Pierce Butler to [James Iredell?], 15 May 1783, James Iredell Papers, DU; Rutledge to Arthur Middleton, 23 April 1782, Barnwell, ed., "Correspondence of Arthur Middleton" (1926): 14; Lee, *Memoirs of the War,* p. 351, for the description of the surrender of Fort Granby; for the removal of the church bells, see the copies of the correspondence which starts in the October 1782 meeting of the church vestry, Minute Book, St. Michael's Church, 1759–1824, WPA Transcripts, South Caroliniana Library, USC.

84. Hampton to Nathanael Greene, 27 July 1781, quoted in McCrady, *SC in the Revol., 1780–1783,* p. 425; Henderson to Governor Rutledge, 14 Aug. 1781, quoted in George Washington Greene, *The Life of Nathanael Greene, Major-General in the Army of the Revolution* (3 vols., New York, 1871), III, 377.

85. Izard to Mrs. Izard, 7 Oct. 1782, Burnett, ed., *Letters of Members of the Continental Congress,* VI, 497; Copy of General Leslie's instructions to Major Frasier, 27 March 1782, General Leslie Letterbook, Emmett Collection, NYPL.

86. McCowen, *The British Occupation of Charleston,* p. 109; Leslie to Sir Guy Carleton, 18 Oct. 1782, quoted in Quarles, *The Negro in the American Revolution,* p. 164; *ibid.,* p. 157.

87. Ramsay, *Revol. of SC,* II, 384; George Abbot Hall, collector of the port of Charleston, estimated the loss of slaves at 20,000. Enclosure in a letter of Ralph Izard to Thomas Jefferson, 10 June 1785, Julian P. Boyd, ed., *The Papers of Thomas Jefferson* (Princeton, 1950–), VIII, 199.

88. Joseph Clay to John Lewis Gervais, 28 Sept. 1779, *Letters of Joseph Clay, Merchant of Savannah, 1776–1793* (Georgia Historical Society, *Collections* 8 [1913]), p. 147; Sumter to Francis Marion, 28 March 1782, printed in Bass, *Gamecock,* pp. 142–144.

89. Madison is quoted in Quarles, *The Negro in the American Revolution,* p. 130.

90. Jeffrey J. Crow, "Slave Rebelliousness and Social Conflict in North Carolina, 1775 to 1802," *W&MQ,* 3rd Ser. 37 (1980): 86–87.

91. Quarles, *The Negro in the American Revolution,* pp. 119, 121; "Diary of Captain Hinrichs," in Bernard A. Uhlendorf, ed., *The Siege of Charleston* (Ann Arbor, Mich., 1938), p. 199; John Rutledge's comment about the blacks' prayers for British victory is quoted in George Bancroft, *History of the United States of America, from the Discovery of the Continent* (6 vols., New York, 1886 ed.), V, 413.

92. Ramsay, *Revol. of SC,* II, 32–33.

93. Quarles, *The Negro in the American Revolution,* p. 140; Ramsay, *Revol. of SC,* II, 67.

94. Sumter to Marion, 20 Feb. 1781, quoted in Quarles, *The Negro in the American Revolution,* p. 139; Pinckney to Arthur Middleton, 13 Aug. 1782, Barnwell, ed., "Correspondence of Arthur Middleton" (1926): 65.

95. Bull to Lord Hillsborough, 22 March 1781, quoted in McCowen, *The British Occupation of Charleston,* p. 103; Eliza Lucas Pinckney to Thomas Pinckney, 17 May 1779, quoted in Mary Beth Norton, " 'What an Alarming Crisis is This': Southern Women and the American Revolution," in Crow and Tise, eds., *The Southern Experience in the American Revolution,* p. 214.

96. Eliza Wilkinson, *Letters of Eliza Wilkinson, during the Invasion and Possession of Charleston, S.C. by the British in the Revolutionary War* (Arno Press Reprint, New York, 1969 [orig. publ. New York, 1839]), pp. 28–29.

97. Rev. Archibald Simpson's Journal, quoted in Howe, *Presbyterian Church in SC,* I, 465–466.

98. McCrady, *SC in the Revol., 1775–1780,* p. 232; Samuel Wise to Henry William Harrington, 22 Jan. 1778, in Gregg, *Old Cheraws,* p. 285. The fire destroyed almost all of the Charleston Library Society's remarkable collection of between 6,000 and 7,000 books.

99. Brown, *Strain of Violence,* pp. 76–77; Ramsay, *Revol. of SC,* II, 34.

100. Wilkinson, *Letters of Eliza Wilkinson,* p. 29; Mathews to Middleton, 25 Aug. 1782 and 1 Sept. 1782, Barnwell, ed., "Correspondence of Arthur Middleton" (1926): 70–72.

101. McCrady, *SC in the Revol., 1775–1780,* pp. 727, 729; McCrady, *SC in the Revol., 1780–1783,* p. 495.

102. Lee, *Memoirs of the War,* p. 525.

103. Ravenel, *Charleston,* pp. 294–295; McCowen, *British Occupation of Charleston,* pp. 71–72.

104. Zahniser, *Charles Cotesworth Pinckney,* pp. 64–66. The British and Americans in South Carolina had agreed to exchange some prisoners. Americans not exchanged were sent elsewhere to await future agreements.

105. McCrady, *SC in the Revol., 1775–1780,* pp. 716, 725–726; Ravenel, *Charleston,* p. 290. The worst time for these prisoners came when they were shipped to Philadelphia, where they met their families who had been hastily sent out of Charleston. The exiles were not allowed to lease their Charleston homes; they had little money to live on and were forced to borrow. The British had decided to punish unrepentant Carolinians. McCowen, *British Occupation of Charleston,* pp. 62–63; McCrady, *SC in the Revol., 1780–1783,* pp. 373–376.

106. Ravenel, *Charleston,* pp. 314–319; McCowen, *The British Occupation of Charleston,* pp. 66–68.

107. Gregg, *Old Cheraws,* pp. 357–361.

108. Wilkinson, *Letters of Eliza Wilkinson,* pp. 29–31.

109. Brown, *Strain of Violence,* p. 80; McCrady, *SC in the Revol., 1775–1780,* p. 641; Howe, *Presbyterian Church in SC,* I, 514; Kershaw to Henry Laurens, 1 Feb. 1785, Emmett Collection, NYPL; Marion, quoted in Bass, *Green Dragoon,* p. 112.

110. Rawdon to Francis, tenth Earl of Huntingdon, 5 Aug. 1776, in Henry Steele Commager and Richard B. Morris, *The Spirit of 'Seventy-Six: The Story of the American Revolution as Told by Participants* (2 vols., New York, 1958), I, 425. For a brief treatment of rape in the American Revolution, see Susan Brownmiller, *Against Our Will: Men, Women and Rape* (New York, 1975), pp. 115–121.

111. Ravenel, *Charleston,* p. 295, points out the often overlooked quality of the war in the lowcountry, where "there were few instances of the terrible *acharnement* between Whigs and Tories, which for three years made the upper districts — to speak mildly — a hell." Forrest McDonald, however, sets up his analysis of South Carolina's ratification of the federal constitution in 1788 by arguing that "the ravages of war were particularly great in the South Carolina low country. . . ." *We the People: The Economic Origins of the Constitution* (Chicago, 1958), p. 206.

112. Howard H. Peckham, *The War for Independence: A Military History* (Chicago, 1958), pp. 147–155, 160–163, 174–175.

NOTES

CHAPTER FOUR

1. Rutledge to Gen. Francis Marion, 2 Sept. 1781 and 15 Sept. 1781, Marion Papers, Bancroft Transcripts, NYPL; McCrady, *SC in the Revol., 1780–1783,* pp. 521–523. Rutledge's proclamation was dated 27 Sept. 1781.

2. Greene is quoted in Bass, *Gamecock,* p. 213, and in Greene, *Life of Nathanael Greene,* III, 344.

3. Bass, *Swamp Fox,* pp. 236–237; Bass, *Gamecock,* pp. 213–214; McCrady, *SC in the Revol., 1780–1783,* pp. 626–627, 638–639; Hoffman, "The 'Disaffected' in the Revolutionary South," in Young, ed., *The American Revolution,* p. 297.

4. Burke to Arthur Middleton, 14 May 1782, Barnwell, ed., "Correspondence of Arthur Middleton" (1925): 201.

5. Aedanus Burke to Arthur Middleton, 25 Jan. 1782, *ibid.,* 191; Sumter is quoted in Bass, *Gamecock,* p. 213, and Marion's men in Bass, *Swamp Fox,* p. 237, where mention is also made of Butler's previous actions; Gregg, *Old Cheraws,* pp. 375–376.

6. Benton to Gov. Mathews, 20 Aug. 1782, Marion Papers, Bancroft Transcripts, NYPL; McCrady, *SC in the Revol., 1780–1783,* pp. 638–639.

7. The quotation is from Nathanael Greene to Catherine Greene, 18 July 1781, in Greene, *Life of Nathanael Greene,* III, 351.

8. Rutledge to Gen. Francis Marion, 23 Nov. 1781, Marion Papers, Bancroft Transcripts, NYPL; Burke to Arthur Middleton, 25 Jan. 1782, Barnwell, ed., "Correspondence of Arthur Middleton" (1925): 193. But Burke wrote that Rutledge excluded "from voting all such persons as had not borne arms antecedent to the 27th September." William Moultrie, in his *Memoirs of the American Revolution,* also indicated that those who had taken protection could neither vote nor sit in the legislature. *Memoirs,* II, 304. Burke and Moultrie, however, are wrong. Rutledge's pardon granted those who rejoined the Americans within thirty days of his proclamation "a full and free pardon," and nothing was said about not including the right to vote. More conclusively, when Burke turned around in 1783 to denounce the way Rutledge had conducted this election, he attacked Rutledge's orders "not to admit any person to vote, but such as obeyed his extraordinary proclamation." Burke was now arguing that the elections should have been thrown open to all who could get to the polls, regardless of whether they had rejoined the Americans under Rutledge's proclamation of 27 September. He thought many Carolinians simply had not had the opportunity of taking advantage of the pardon because of the presence of the British. Aedanus Burke, *An Address to the Freemen of the State of South-Carolina* (Philadelphia, 1783), pp. 12–14. Some people who had at one time taken protection were elected to the legislature. Barnwell, "Loyalism in South Carolina," p. 232.

9. The quotation is in a letter from Edward Rutledge to Arthur Middleton, 14 April 1782, Barnwell, ed., "Correspondence of Arthur Middleton" (1926): 12. Francis Marion had been afraid that the election was "so soon entered on" that it could "not be full." To Gen. Greene, 1 Dec. 1781, quoted in Rogers, *Georgetown County,* p. 145. On political apathy in the colonial period see Sirmans, *Colonial South Carolina,* p. 246; McCrady, *SC under Royal Government,* p. 604.

10. Election Returns, 1781, Records of the General Assembly, SCA; Barnwell, "Loyalism in South Carolina," pp. 231–232. In the election for Charleston, Arthur Middleton, with thirteen votes, and Isaac Motte, with eight, were elected senators.

11. Rutledge to Arthur Middleton, 12 Dec. 1781 and 23 Jan. 1782, Barnwell, ed., "Correspondence of Arthur Middleton" (1925): 208, 210; Burke to Middleton, 25 Jan. 1782, *ibid.*, 193.

12. McCrady, *SC in the Revol., 1775–1780,* pp. 716, 723. The names of the members of the Jacksonborough Assembly may be found in the two Journals edited by A.S. Salley: *Journal of the House of Representatives of South Carolina, January 8, 1782–February 26, 1782* (Columbia, S.C., 1916), and *Journal of the Senate of South Carolina, January 8, 1782–February 26, 1782* (Columbia, S.C., 1941). The Senate Journal records the list of members who attend each day's meeting; the lower house's journal does not. Valuable lists of South Carolina officers, both of the Continental army and of the state forces, can be found in *Charleston Year Book,* 1893, 208–237. The military activities of the legislators are described in McCrady, *SC in the Revol., 1780–1783,* pp. 557–560. When McCrady wrote, however, the journals of the legislature for 1782 had not been found; he is, therefore, sometimes misleading.

13. Not all nineteen were present at the same time. Marion reported once having only thirteen senators, "the least number that can do business." Quoted in Bass, *Swamp Fox,* p. 227. A full senate consisted of twenty-nine members, but there was no election for British-held St. John.

14. Aedanus Burke to Arthur Middleton, 25 Jan. 1782, Barnwell, ed., "Correspondence of Arthur Middleton" (1925): 192.

15. McCrady, *SC in the Revol., 1780–1783,* p. 559; John B.O. Landrum, *Colonial and Revolutionary History of Upper South Carolina* (Greenville, S.C., 1897), pp. 76–78; Burke to Arthur Middleton, 25 Jan. 1782, Barnwell, ed., "Correspondence of Arthur Middleton" (1925): 192.

16. Apparently Laurens was supported by Thomas Ferguson and David Ramsay. Edward Rutledge to Arthur Middleton, 28 Jan. 1782 and 8 Feb. 1782, Barnwell, ed., "Correspondence of Arthur Middleton" (1926): 4; Aedanus Burke to Middleton, 25 Jan. 1782, *ibid.*, p. 194; Wallace, *Henry Laurens,* pp. 448–452. General Greene was a strong supporter of arming the slaves. Greene, *Life of Nathanael Greene,* III, 426–428.

17. The governor's address is printed in both legislative journals edited by Salley and in Almon, *The Remembrancer* 14 (1782): 137–140. A Charleston Tory criticized Rutledge's speech for being composed of "those Circumstances alone which contribute to the effect . . . regardless of whether these combinations ever really existed." *Royal Gazette,* 20–23 Feb. 1782, quoted in McCowen, *The British Occupation of Charleston,* p. 135n.

18. Burke to Arthur Middleton, 25 Jan. 1782, Barnwell, ed., "Correspondence of Arthur Middleton" (1925): 193; Edward Rutledge to Arthur Middleton, 12 Dec. 1781, and 28 Jan. 1782, *ibid.*, 209, 211–212. Gadsden's public reason for not accepting the post was that he had served the state for thirty years and that his age and infirmities were such that he could not serve the state properly. Walsh, ed., *Writings of Gadsden,* p. 193n. The letter Walsh quotes in this note is incorrectly attributed to Arthur Middleton. It was, however, sent to Middleton by Burke.

19. Almon, *The Remembrancer* 14 (1782): 140; Cooper and McCord, eds., *Statutes of South Carolina,* IV, 513. A creditor could sue, however, if he took an oath before a magistrate stating he had reason to believe his debtor intended to quit the state or send his property out of the state, or if the debtor refused to give bond with security.

20. Jackson Turner Main, *The Antifederalists: Critics of the Constitution, 1781–1788* (Chapel Hill, 1961), pp. 73–74.

21. Burke to Arthur Middleton, 14 May 1782, Barnwell, ed., "Correspondence of Arthur Middleton" (1925): 200–201; Grimké to [Gov. Benjamin Guerard], 12 Nov. 1783,

Governors Message, 2 Feb. 1785, enclosure, Records of the General Assembly, SCA; the act for opening the courts is not printed in the *Statutes of South Carolina.* It may be found in *Acts Passed . . . at Jacksonburg* (Philadelphia, 1782).

22. Burke to Arthur Middleton, 14 May and 6 July 1782, Barnwell, ed., "Correspondence of Arthur Middleton" (1925): 200–201, 204–205.

23. Burke to Arthur Middleton, 14 May 1782, *ibid.,* p. 202. For eighteenth-century opinion of England's Judge Jeffries, see H. Trevor Colbourn, *The Lamp of Experience: Whig History and the Intellectual Origins of the American Revolution* (Chapel Hill, 1965), p. 46. In 1784 the legislature passed acts confirming seizures of property that had been made by Generals Sumter and Pickens. That same year an American who had joined the British was sued in Camden for his wartime activities. He claimed to have been a subordinate (and apparently taking orders) while the plundering for which he was being sued was carried on and also that none of the property had been appropriated to his private emolument. Judge John Faucheraud Grimké, however, noted "that in treasons and trespasses, the highest and lowest offences, there are no accessaries or subordinate offenders. All are principals. . . ." The jury awarded the plaintiff £800. *Administrator of Whitaker against English,* in Elihu Hall Bay, *Reports of Cases Argued and Determined in the Superior Courts of Law in the State of South-Carolina, since the Revolution* (2 vols., New York, 1809, 1811), I, 15–16. See also *Porter against Dunn,* 1787, in which Judge Grimké, although indicating that neither the law of nations nor the rules of warfare justified taking property from the enemy, ruled that Porter was exonerated for his actions by the acts of 1784. *Ibid.,* 53–56.

24. Almon, *The Remembrancer* 14 (1782): 139; Cooper and McCord, eds., *Statutes of South Carolina,* IV, 516–525.

25. Barnwell, "Loyalism in South Carolina," pp. 361–362; Higgins, "Financial History of South Carolina," pp. 15–16; Hemphill *et al.,* eds., *Journals of the General Assembly,* 1 Sept. 1779, p. 186; Cooper and McCord, eds., *Statutes of South Carolina,* IV, 479–480.

26. Rutledge to Middleton, 8 Feb. 1782, Barnwell, ed., "Correspondence of Arthur Middleton" (1926): 3; Marion to Col. Peter Horry, 10 Feb. 1782, quoted in McCrady, *SC in the Revol., 1780–1783,* p. 583. McCrady did not believe that retaliation was a motive for the passage of the confiscation and amercement acts.

27. Burke to Arthur Middleton, 6 July 1782, Barnwell, ed., "Correspondence of Arthur Middleton" (1925): 203. In 1780 Burke introduced a petition into the lower house that asked for higher pay for the militia, better arrangements for their exchange when captured, a public store where they could purchase salt, and other reforms. Hemphill *et al.,* eds., *Journals of the General Assembly,* 4 Feb. 1780, p. 275.

28. Gadsden to Francis Marion, 17 Nov. 1782, Walsh, ed., *Writings of Gadsden,* pp. 195–196. Gadsden referred to the clause restricting the speculators as the 20th. It appears in the final act as section XIV. Cooper and McCord, eds., *Statutes of South Carolina,* IV, 521.

29. Account Book of the Commissioners of Forfeited Estates, 1782–1783, SCHS. Ferguson also joined with two others to purchase 6,640 acres formerly the property of Thomas Boone. And he bought another tract of 196 acres formerly belonging to David Yarborough.

30. Rogers, *Georgetown County,* pp. 158–159. By means of the confiscation law, one observer wrote, "the Wealthy are . . . invited to a dangerous Accumulation of Riches." George Turner to ____, 13 Oct. 1782, quoted in Jackson Turner Main, *Political Parties before the Constitution* (Chapel Hill, 1973), p. 274n.

31. Rutledge to Middleton, 28 Jan. 1782 and 8 Feb. 1782, Barnwell, ed., "Correspondence of Arthur Middleton" (1925): 212, (1926): 3.

32. Burke to Arthur Middleton, 14 May 1782, *ibid.* (1925): 199–200; for his comments

about Yorktown, see Burke to Middleton, 16 Oct. 1781, *ibid.*, 187. The letter must be misdated, since the British troops marched out of their garrison on 19 October.

33. Gadsden to Francis Marion, 17 Nov. 1782, Walsh, ed., *Writings of Gadsden*, pp. 194–195. Gadsden thought the attack on him "by a set of dirty tools, [was] set on by an artful cabal" of selfish men. In 1778 he had similarly identified an "artful and indefatigable cabal." See Gadsden to Thomas Bee, 14 Oct. 1778, and Gadsden to William Henry Drayton, 14 Oct. 1778, *ibid.*, pp. 154–158, 159.

34. Schoepf, *Travels in the Confederation*, p. 204.

35. Butler to James Iredell, 4 Feb. 1784, Griffith J. McRee, *Life and Correspondence of James Iredell, one of the Associate Justices of the Supreme Court of the United States* (2 vols., New York, 1857–1858), II, 88; Butler to [James Iredell?], 5 May 1783, James Iredell Papers, DU.

36. *Journal of the House of Representatives*, 21 Feb. 1787.

37. The quotation is from Edward Rutledge to Arthur Middleton, 8 Feb. 1782, Barnwell, ed., "Correspondence of Arthur Middleton" (1926): 3.

38. Journal of the House of Representatives, 4 Feb. and 7 Feb. 1783; *SCSGGA*, 13 Nov. 1784.

39. *SCSGGA*, 22 May 1784.

40. Alexander Garden, *Anecdotes of the Revolutionary War in America* (Charleston, 1822), p. 176; Francis Marion opposed the confiscation act. See Bass, *Swamp Fox*, p. 229.

41. Burke to Arthur Middleton, 25 Jan. 1782 and 14 May 1782, Barnwell, ed., "Correspondence of Arthur Middleton" (1925): 193, 200.

42. Gadsden to Francis Marion, 17 Nov. 1782, Walsh, ed., *Writings of Gadsden*, pp. 195, 197, 198. There were at least fourteen lawyers in the legislature at Jacksonborough: John, Edward, and Hugh Rutledge, John Faucheraud Grimké, John Laurens, Richard Beresford, Thomas Shubrick, James Smith, Aedanus Burke, Thomas Heyward, Jr., William Hasell Gibbes, Jacob Read, and John Ewing Colhoun, all in the lower house, and Benjamin Guerard, in the upper house. John Mathews, the governor, was also a lawyer. For lists of lawyers see McCrady, *SC under Royal Govt.*, pp. 475–476, 481n; Rogers, *Evolution of a Federalist*, pp. 112–116; John Belton O'Neall, *Biographical Sketches of the Bench and Bar of South Carolina* (2 vols., Charleston, 1859), II, 598–604.

43. Gadsden to Francis Marion, 17 Nov. 1782, Walsh, ed., *Writings of Gadsden*, p. 195.

44. Burke to Arthur Middleton, 25 Jan. 1782 and 14 May 1782, Barnwell, ed., "Correspondence of Arthur Middleton" (1925): 192–193, 197–199; Burke, *An Address to the Freemen of South Carolina*, p. 5.

45. The classes are neatly summarized in Barnwell, "Loyalism in South Carolina," p. 367.

46. *Ibid.*, pp. 367–368; Raymond G. Starr, "The Conservative Revolution: South Carolina Public Affairs, 1775–1790" (Ph.D. dissertation, University of Texas, 1964), p. 126.

47. Edward Rutledge to Arthur Middleton, 26 Feb. 1782, Barnwell, ed., "Correspondence of Arthur Middleton" (1926): 8.

48. *Ibid.*, 7–8. According to Edward Rutledge, Gadsden was most responsible for having Charles Pinckney's name placed on the amercement list. Charles Cotesworth Pinckney, who had not been at the legislature and who may have received his information from Edward Rutledge (both were married to sisters of Arthur Middleton), told his cousin, Charles Pinckney, that Gadsden "enumerated all your foibles and indiscretions." At the same time, Gadsden was defending his friend Rawlins Lowndes. In 1784 Gadsden justified his behavior by saying that he had put no man's name on the confiscation list but that he had succeeded

in having many transferred from the confiscated list to the amerced list. Charles Cotesworth Pinckney to [Charles Pinckney], 24 July 1782, Pinckney Family Papers, Box #1, LC; *SCSGGA,* 11 Sept. 1784.

49. Rutledge to Arthur Middleton, 26 Feb. 1782, Barnwell, ed., "Correspondence of Arthur Middleton" (1926): 6–7.

50. Burke to Arthur Middleton, 25 Jan. 1782, Barnwell, ed., "Correspondence of Arthur Middleton" (1925): 193; Burke, *An Address to the Freemen of South Carolina,* pp. 19, 24n.

51. Rutledge to Arthur Middleton, 26 Feb. 1782, Barnwell, ed., "Correspondence of Arthur Middleton" (1926): 8.

52. Mathews to Leslie, 12 April 1782, Emmett Collection, NYPL.

53. Laurens to [Thomas Bee], 14 April 1782, Henry and John Laurens Papers, LC. In Georgia, the legislature not only confiscated the estates of British sympathizers, but it seized also the debts due them as of April 1775. And debts owed to British merchants or citizens were to be paid to the state. Robert S. Lambert, "The Confiscation of Loyalist Property in Georgia, 1782–1786," *W&MQ,* 3rd Ser. 20 (1963): 82.

54. Ella Pettit Levett, "Loyalism in Charleston, 1761–1784," South Carolina Historical Association, *Proceedings,* 1936, 15–16; McCrady, *SC in the Revol., 1780–1783,* p. 584. McCrady thought that one might have expected more backcountry settlers to suffer confiscation of their property because the legislature was made up almost exclusively of lowcountry delegates. *Ibid.,* p. 587. But McCrady did not have access to the journals of the legislature; they indicate that the non-Charleston area dominated.

55. Garden, *Anecdotes of the Revolutionary War,* p. 179.

NOTES
CHAPTER FIVE

1. Gen. Leslie to Major Frasier, 27 March 1782, General Leslie Letterbook, Emmett Collection, NYPL.

2. *Ibid.;* Leslie to Gen. Nathanael Greene, 4 April 1782, Miscellaneous Letters, SCHS; Mathews to Gen. Leslie, 12 April 1782, Emmett Collection, NYPL.

3. John Laurens to Henry Laurens, 2 Feb. 1778, *The Army Correspondence of Colonel John Laurens in the Year 1777–8* (New York, 1867), pp. 115, 117.

4. Henry Laurens to John Laurens, 6 Feb. 1778, "Correspondence between Hon. Henry Laurens and his Son," p. 50; John Laurens to Henry Laurens, 2 Feb. 1778, *Army Correspondence of Col. John Laurens,* p. 115. Henry Laurens had made a large part of his fortune in the slave trade. In 1776, however, he wrote to John: "You know, my dear Son, I abhor Slavery," and he went on to write that he was devising means of manumitting his slaves. 14 Aug. 1776, Moore, *Materials for History,* p. 20; Sellers, *Charleston Business,* p. 146.

5. John Laurens to George Washington, 19 May 1782, Jared Sparks, ed., *Correspondence of the American Revolution; Being Letters of Eminent Men to George Washington* (4 vols., Boston, 1853), III, 506; the remark about a dead son was made originally, Adams said, by a Duke of Ormond. Adams to Henry Laurens, 6 Nov. 1782, Charles Francis Adams, ed., *The Works of John Adams* (10 vols., Boston, 1850–1856), VII, 658. For other reactions to John Laurens's death, see Wallace, *Henry Laurens,* p. 489. Even the Charleston *Royal Gazette,* on 17 Sept. 1782, praised Laurens's character.

6. The quotation is from the *SCGGA,* 9 Sept. 1784.

7. The quotation is from the *GSSC,* 6 Aug. 1783.

8. Articles of a Treaty, Respecting Slaves within British Lines, British Debts, Property Secured by Family Settlements, &c., American Papers Respecting the Evacuation of Charleston, 1782, LC. Some of the provisions of the treaty are printed in Ramsay, *Revol. of SC,* II, 376–378. The treaty of Paris is printed in Samuel Flagg Bemis, *The Diplomacy of the American Revolution* (New York, 1935), pp. 259–264. The problems caused by the prewar debt will be discussed in chapter eight.

9. Ramsay, *Revol. of SC,* II, 377; on the prewar debt see Baldwin, "The Debts Owed by Americans to British Creditors, 1763–1802," p. 96.

10. Gadsden to Francis Marion, 29 Oct. 1782, Walsh, ed., *Writings of Gadsden,* p. 186; Ramsay, *Revol. of SC,* II, 383–384.

11. Ramsay, *Revol. of SC,* II, 376–378.

12. Gadsden to Gov. Mathews, 16 Oct. 1782, Walsh, ed., *Writings of Gadsden,* p. 182.

13. Rutledge to Ralph Izard, 29 Oct. 1774, Deas, *Ralph Izard,* p. 24.

14. Gadsden to Gov. Mathews, 16 Oct. 1782, Walsh, ed., *Writings of Gadsden,* p. 182.

15. The Proclamation of 14 March 1782 is printed in Almon, *The Remembrancer* 14 (1782): 28–29; Mathews to Marion, 29 Aug. 1782 and Marion to Mathews, 24 Sept. 1782, Marion Papers, Bancroft Transcripts, NYPL. Marion thought that those trading with the British were people who the year before had taken advantage of Rutledge's pardon to join the rebel side.

16. Gadsden to Francis Marion, 29 Oct. 1782, Walsh, ed., *Writings of Gadsden,* p. 188; Gadsden to Marion, 17 Nov. 1782, Marion Papers, Bancroft Transcripts, NYPL.

17. The correspondence respecting the breaking of the treaty is printed in Ramsay, *Revol. of SC,* II, 379–384; McCowen, *The British Occupation of Charleston,* pp. 108–109; Leslie to Carleton, 18 Oct. 1782, quoted in Quarles, *The Negro in the American Revolution,*

p. 165; see also, Gadsden to Francis Marion, 21 Oct. 1782, Walsh, ed., *Writings of Gadsden*, p. 185.

18. The quotations are from Schoepf, *Travels in the Confederation*, p. 204, and Thomas Smith to Isaac Smith, 19 Aug. 1783, in Rogers, *Evolution of a Federalist*, p. 106.

19. Proclamation issued by Henry Barry, printed in the *Royal Gazette*, 7–11 April 1781.

20. The petition of the merchants is printed in Almon, *The Remembrancer* 15 (1783): 59–60.

21. Rutledge to Arthur Middleton, Aug. 1782, Barnwell, ed., "Correspondence of Arthur Middleton" (1926): 21–22. Rutledge expected the British to retaliate to a rejection of their proposals by burning Charleston. His answer would be to set fire to London. It was time, he felt, that the English experienced the horrors of war. *Ibid.*

22. Mathews's proposal-by-proposal answer to the petition is also printed in Almon, *The Remembrancer* 15 (1783): 59–60. Richard Walsh, in an explanatory footnote to one of Gadsden's letters, treats the "Treaty Respecting Slaves" and the agreement with the British merchants as one treaty. Walsh, ed., *Writings of Gadsden*, p. 179n.

23. Almon, *The Remembrancer* 15 (1783): 59–60, 62. The number fifty comes from a Senate committee report of 28 Feb. 1783. Both Ramsay, *Revol. of SC*, II, 372, and Moultrie, *Memoirs of the American Revolution*, II, 341–342, mistakenly report that Mathews allowed the merchants eighteen months. For the estimated value of the goods see Gervais & Owen to Leonard de Neufville, 13 April 1786, John de Neufville Papers, LC.

24. Charles Cotesworth Pinckney to Harriott [Pinckney], 23 Oct. 1782, Pinckney Family Papers, Undivided Box , LC; Gervais & Owen to Leonard de Neufville, 13 April 1786, John de Neufville Papers, LC.

25. Senate Journal, 30 Jan. 1783; see also *ibid.*, 24 Jan. and 17 Feb. 1783.

26. *Ibid.*, 19 Feb. 1783.

27. *Ibid.*, 19 Feb., 20 Feb., and 3 March 1783; House Journal, 22 Feb., 26 Feb., and 27 Feb. 1783.

28. Cooper and McCord, eds., *Statutes of South Carolina*, IV, 548–549; *PaPGA*, 16 Sept. 1783. In 1786 Edward Rutledge pointed out that special courts for aliens encouraged trade. *CEG*, 16 Feb. 1786.

29. Barnwell, "Loyalism in South Carolina," p. 343; House Journal, 17 March 1783; Privy Council Journal, 26 March, 9 April, 30 April, and 15 May 1783.

30. [Aedanus Burke], *A Few Salutary Hints, Pointing out the Policy and Consequences of Admitting British Subjects to Engross our Trade and Become our Citizens* (Charleston and New York, 1786). Burke is identified as the author of *A Few Salutary Hints* in George C. Rogers, Jr., "Aedanus Burke, Nathanael Greene, Anthony Wayne, and the British Merchants of Charleston," *SCHM* 67 (1966): 75–83.

31. Brailsford and Morris to Thomas Jefferson, 31 Oct. 1787, Richard Walsh, ed., "Letters of Morris & Brailsford to Thomas Jefferson," *SCHM* 58 (1957): 135–136.

32. Notes on the State Debt, Pierce Butler Papers, Box 6 (South Carolina Legislature), *HSP*. For more detailed information on the value of imports, see chapter seven. Forty percent is probably a low estimate for the share of the import trade handled by the postwar aliens. My method was as follows: The value of South Carolina's imports in 1784 was between £1,000,000 and £1,500,000. Beginning on 22 May 1784, the Book of Manifests and Entries in the South Carolina Archives lists all imports on which duties were paid. I added up entries of goods valued over £300. The total value of those goods imported after 22 May was £445,993. 11. 4½ sterling. The difference between that figure and the total value of goods imported would be made up of the value of goods imported before 22 May, imported in entries of under £300,

or imported in the coastal trade, since the products of other American states did not pay duties and were not entered in this book of entries. I attempted to isolate the value of the goods imported by those considered to be aliens for part of 1783 and 1784. (Some of the aliens of 1783 had become citizens by 1784.) To do this I added up the value of imports, still in amounts of over £300, entered under the names of merchants who petitioned the Senate in 1783, and those who were admitted as citizens by the Privy Council in 1783. And I included two merchants, Harry Grant and Samuel Midwood, mentioned by Rogers, *Evolution of a Federalist,* as being among those who came to the state in 1783. The imports of those merchants were valued at £184,178. 1. 10 sterling, roughly 41.3 percent of the total of £445,000. It may be, of course, that native merchants imported most of the coastal products and the goods entered under £300 in value. But I think it likely that the percentage of goods imported by "alien" merchants was in fact greater than 41 percent, for I have made no effort to discover the names of new merchants coming into Carolina in 1783 and 1784. In any event, small, native merchants had enough to complain about.

33. The quotation is from a letter of Gadsden to Francis Marion, 3 Nov. 1782, Walsh, ed., *Writings of Gadsden,* p. 189.

34. Joseph Clay to James Seagrove, 5 Feb. 1783, *Letters of Joseph Clay,* p. 173.

35. House Journal, 26 Feb., 27 Feb., and 3 March 1783.

36. *GSSC,* 6 May 1784.

37. Allan Westcott, "Alexander Gillon," in Allen Johnson and Dumas Malone, eds., *Dictionary of American Biography* (22 vols., New York, 1928–1958), VII, 296; Allan Nevins, *The American States during and after the Revolution, 1775–1789* (New York, 1924), p. 398.

38. House Journal, 4 Feb. and 7 Feb. 1783; James Lynah to Thomas Sumter, 14 Jan. 1783, Thomas Sumter Papers, Draper Manuscripts, Wisconsin Historical Society.

39. Cooper and McCord, eds., *Statutes of South Carolina,* IV, 553–554; Barnwell, "Loyalism in South Carolina," p. 373.

40. Kinloch to Thomas Boone, 1 Oct. 1782, Felix Gilbert, ed., "Letters of Francis Kinloch," pp. 91–92; Izard to Thomas Jefferson, 27 April 1784, Boyd, ed., *Jefferson Papers,* VII, 130. See also Pierce Butler to [James Iredell?], 5 May 1783, James Iredell Papers, DU.

41. Izard to Jefferson, 27 April 1784, Boyd, ed., *Jefferson Papers,* VII, 130; George C. Rogers, Jr., suggests that the desire to strengthen the conservative interest may have been a motive for allowing the banished to return. *Evolution of a Federalist,* p. 106.

42. Cooper and McCord, eds., *Statutes of South Carolina,* IV, 568–570.

43. Barnwell, "Loyalism in South Carolina," pp. 368–369. Barnwell points out that other historians have neglected the confiscation act of 1783. The names reported by the commanders are printed in Robert W. Barnwell, Jr., "Reports on Loyalist Exiles from South Carolina, 1783," South Carolina Historical Association, *Proceedings,* 1937, 43–46.

44. *SCWG,* 19 Dec. 1783. The move to establish a Chamber of Commerce was also connected with the British regulations respecting the West Indian trade. The regulations are discussed in chapter seven.

45. *Ibid.,* 19 July 1783.

46. *Ibid.,* 26 July 1783; Walsh, *Charleston's Sons of Liberty,* p. 29. The legislature indicated that ratification of the Preliminary Articles of Peace made further compacts with British merchants unnecessary. The merchants were free to remain forever if they chose. *SCGGA,* 12 Aug. 1783.

47. John Sandford Dart to Ralph Izard, 11 July 1783, quoted in Rogers, *Evolution of a Federalist,* pp. 104–105; Extract of a letter from Charleston, South Carolina, dated 11 July 1783, *PaPGA,* 24 July 1783.

48. Ramsay to Benjamin Rush, 11 July 1783, quoted in Rogers, *Evolution of a Federalist*, p. 105; Greene to Col. Pettit, 29 July 1783, Joseph Reed Papers, NYHS.

49. *SCGGA*, 27 Nov. 1784; see also the *GSSC*, 6 May 1784, and the *SCGGA*, 4 Sept. 1784.

50. Account Book of the Commissioners of Forfeited Estates, 1782–1783, SCHS.

51. Schoepf, *Travels in the Confederation*, p. 22; for the 1744 complaint, see Carl Bridenbaugh, *Cities in Revolt: Urban Life in America, 1743–1776* (New York, 1955), p. 88; the 1747 warning is quoted in Carl Bridenbaugh, *The Colonial Craftsman* (New York, 1950), p. 15; House Journal, 21 Feb. 1783; Senate Journal, 22 Feb. 1783.

52. House Journal, 8 March 1783; Walsh, *Charleston's Sons of Liberty*, pp. 124–126; *SCGGA*, 20 May 1783.

53. Bull to Lord Hillsborough, 22 March 1781, quoted in McCowen, *The British Occupation of Charleston*, p. 103; *Ordinances of the City Council of Charleston, South Carolina, Passed in the first Year of the Incorporation of the City* (Charleston, 1784), pp. 24–26.

54. Pierce Butler to [James Iredell?], 5 May 1783, James Iredell Papers, DU; see also Josiah Smith to Col. John Bayard, 16 May 1783, Josiah Smith Letterbook, UNC; on the price of flour see Pierce Butler to Thomas Fitzsimmons, 22 March 1783, Gratz Collection, Old Congress, HSP; on butter, *SCWG*, 1 March 1783; for high prices before the war, see Bridenbaugh, *Cities in Revolt*, p. 235. On 26 May 1783, the St. Philips Church Vestry granted relief to ninety-four people. St. Philips Church Vestry Journal, 1761–1795, WPA Transcripts, South Caroliniana Library, USC.

55. On the heat see William Pierce, Jr. to Dr. [Robert] Johnson, Aug. 1783, Emmett Collection, NYPL; on the four deaths, see Aedanus Burke's charge to the Grand Jury of Charleston, 9 June 1783, in Almon, *The Remembrancer* 15 (1783): 287.

56. The special session of the legislature, called for 7 July to consider continental affairs, finally got under way on 30 July, when the lower house mustered the necessary 69 members for a quorum. Not many more appeared before the end of the session. The legislature could not fill the lieutenant-governor's position, vacated by Richard Beresford who was sent to Congress, because the lower house was never able to find 102 members, a required majority, to attend an election. See the *CMP*, 12 Feb. 1787, for Gillon's complaint that only a few people had been present when Charleston was incorporated.

57. Cooper and McCord, eds., *Statutes of South Carolina*, VII, 97–101.

58. *GSSC*, 6 June 1785.

59. Cooper and McCord, eds., *Statutes of South Carolina*, VII, 97–101.

60. Bridenbaugh, *Cities in Revolt*, pp. 218–219; Walsh, *Charleston's Sons of Liberty*, p. 29.

61. Messages of Governor Guerard to the Senate and House of Representatives, 1 March and 9 March 1783 (nos. 210 and 227), Records of the General Assembly, SCA; Senate Report on the incorporation of Charleston, 16 March 1783, SCA.

62. *SCGGA*, 22 July 1783.

63. *SCGGA*, 19 July 1783.

64. *Ordinances of Charleston passed in the First Year of Incorporation of the City*, pp. 23–26.

65. *Ibid.*, pp. 6–9.

66. *Ibid.*, p. 2.

67. *Ibid.*, pp. 19–20.

68. The quotation is in a letter from Edward Rutledge to John Jay, 12 Nov. 1786. Henry P. Johnston, ed., *The Correspondence and Public Papers of John Jay* (New York, 1890–1893), III, 217.

NOTES
CHAPTER SIX

1. Main, "Government by the People," p. 396; *SCGGA,* 25 Sept. 1784.

2. For the representatives' wealth, see Main, "Government by the People," p. 404. The slight decline in the average wealth of the lowcountry members may have resulted from the increased representation for Charleston, Georgetown, and Beaufort districts and from the loss of property during the war. I have found only thirteen lowcountry election returns from the 1780s that include a tally of the votes along with the total number of voters and the names of those elected. These may be found in the Records of the General Assembly, SCA. For the 1790s there are more returns, with patterns similar to those cited in the text. Interesting lowcountry races occurred infrequently. When Thomas Tudor Tucker, a Virginia doctor who had moved to South Carolina, sought election to the lower house from St. George, Dorchester, in 1786, Ralph Izard campaigned against him and sent "one of his overseers to engage as many votes as he could for another party." Tucker lost, but shortly after he beat a cousin of Izard in a special election. Thomas Tudor Tucker to St. George Tucker, 8 April 1787, quoted in Rogers, *Evolution of a Federalist,* p. 128.

3. Main, "Government by the People," p. 403; on changes in the upper house see Jackson Turner Main, *The Upper House in Revolutionary America, 1763–1788* (Madison, Wis., 1967), pp. 114–117; on Cannon, see Walsh, *Charleston's Sons of Liberty,* p. 18.

4. Gadsden to Francis Marion, 29 Oct. 1782, Walsh, ed., *Writings of Gadsden,* p. 187; Henry Laurens to John Laurens, 22 Jan. 1775, quoted in Hemphill and Wates, eds., *Extracts of Jours. of Prov. Cong.,* p. xxiii.

5. Izard to Thomas Jefferson, 10 June 1785, "Letters of Ralph Izard," *SCHM* 2 (1901): 197; *GSSC,* 8 April 1784; Rutledge to John Jay, 21 May 1789, Johnston, ed., *Correspondence of Jay,* III, 368. Schoepf noticed a great many discontented army officers in South Carolina in 1784. He also noted, however, that military service had affected members of the upper class. "An esteemed lawyer," he wrote, "always appeared in public in black velvet, but with a white cockade to his hat, and a ribbon knot on his sword, for he had been a General, but was now again managing cases at law." Schoepf was surprised by the "liking for military show," since Americans "profess on all occasions a hatred for soldiers, or wish to appear as if they hated them." *Travels in the Confederation,* pp. 206–207.

6. Schoepf, *Travels in the Confederation,* p. 198; the reference to the "abilities" of ancient Romans was made in 1788 by James Lincoln, a backcountry representative. Jonathan Elliot, *The Debates in the Several State Conventions on the Adoption of the Federal Constitution* (2nd ed., 5 vols., Philadelphia, 1836), IV, 312.

7. Arthur Bryan to George Bryan, 9 April 1788, George Bryan Papers, HSP.

8. Lloyd to T.B. Smith, 7 Dec. 1784, John Lloyd Letters, Charleston Library Society; Rutledge to John Jay, 12 Nov. 1786, Johnston, ed., *Correspondence of Jay,* III, 217; *CMPDA,* 7 July 1786. The "clamour" was not completely unexpected.

9. Gillon to Nathanael Greene, 11 April 1783, Naval History Collection, NYHS.

10. *GSSC,* 15 Aug. 1785; *SCGPA,* 9 July and 3 Sept. 1785; the quotation is from *SCGPA,* 13 Aug. 1785.

11. *GSSC,* 2 June 1785; *SCGGA,* 16 Sept. 1784; *SCGPA,* 13 Aug. 1785; *GSSC,* 26 Sept. 1785.

12. *CnHd,* 2 May 1785.

13. *CEG,* 2 Sept. 1785. That limited, contemporary definition of freedom of the press corresponds to that set forth by William Blackstone. See Leonard W. Levy, *Freedom of Speech*

and Press in Early American History: Legacy of Suppression (New York, 1963 ed.), pp. 13–14.

14. *GSSC,* 3 Jan. 1785.

15. *GSSC,* 27 Aug. 1783; see also *SCGPA,* 1 Oct. 1785.

16. For a listing of South Carolina newspapers see Edwin Conner Lathem, comp., *Chronological Tables of American Newspapers, 1690–1820* (Barre, Mass., 1972), pp. 8, 9, 13, 21; Clarence Brigham, *History and Bibliography of American Newspapers, 1690–1820,* II, 1023–1053.

17. *GSSC,* 6 Aug. 1783. Ann Timothy served as state printer until her death in 1792. Peter Timothy's father, Louis, had published the *South Carolina Gazette* from 1732 to 1738. On his death, Peter's mother, Elizabeth, continued the newspaper's publication, becoming the "pioneer woman journalist in the colonies." Julia Cherry Spruill, *Women's Life and Work in the Southern Colonies* (Chapel Hill, 1938), pp. 263–264.

18. On high prices see W[illiam] Pollard to Thomas Day, 14 Feb. and 2 March 1784, Correspondence of William Pollard, Additional Mss. 35,655, Hardwicke Papers, CCCVII, BM; on banning exportation, *Glocester* [England] *Journal,* 16 Aug. 1784; Higgins, "Financial History of South Carolina," pp. 138–139.

19. John Lewis Gervais to Henry Laurens, 15 April 1784, Henry Laurens Papers, South Caroliniana Library, USC; Gervais to Laurens, 5 May 1784, Charles Francis Jenkins Collection, HSP; *SCGGA,* 1 July and 10 July 1784. The legislature had returned confiscated property to twelve of the thirteen.

20. *SCGGA,* 29 April 1784. Gillon was a member of the Privy Council and was present the day it gave its unanimous advice to the governor. Privy Council Journal, 28 April 1784, SCA.

21. Privy Council Journal, 12 July 1784, SCA; *SCGGA,* 10 July 1784. Wagner's estate had been taken off the confiscation list.

22. *CEG,* 1 Sept. and 3 Sept. 1785. At the same time, critics complained that the city government did nothing to quell the disturbances arising from the behavior of British sailors who defaced Dutch vessels and "rendezvous'd in the streets . . . contrary to law." *CEG,* 1 Sept. 1785.

23. Gervais to Laurens, 5 May 1784, Charles Francis Jenkins Collection, HSP; see also N. Pendleton to [Gen. Nathanael Greene], 18 April 1784, SCHS.

24. For the quotation from the petition and the treatment of Chambers and Cook, see Walsh, *Charleston's Sons of Liberty,* pp. 97, 118; for Rees's treatment, Gregorie, *Sumter County,* pp. 48–49; *GSSC,* 29 April 1784.

25. Ferguson to Lincoln, 25 July 1784, *Benjamin Lincoln Papers,* Microfilm reel 7, MHS; Thomas Waring, Sr., to Andrew Pickens, 22 July 1784, Waring & Hayne Accounts, SCHS; Read to [Benjamin Guerard], 4 Sept. 1784, Governors Message, 21 Jan. 1785, enclosure, item #37, Records of the General Assembly, SCA.

26. *SCGPA,* 3 Sept. 1785. Forrest McDonald writes that the merchants, who he thinks were the demonstrators, retaliated to the actions they disliked in 1784 with "a new wave of destruction. Violence reached a peak in July, when riots occurred almost nightly, but it continued sporadically until winter." *E. Pluribus Unum: The Formation of the American Republic, 1776–1790* (Boston, 1965), p. 103. As far as I know there is absolutely no evidence for such an extreme description.

27. *SCGGA,* 19 Oct. 1784; *CnHd,* 14 Feb. 1785. In January 1784 a special jury awarded £5 damages to a seaman who had been beaten by his captain with an iron poker. The captain's lawyer, an unidentified Pinckney, argued that "mariners were naturally a rough and turbulent set of man, and required curbing and restraint more than any other class in the community," but judges Pendleton and Burke ruled that masters were accountable when they used

dangerous weapons. *Flemming v. Ball,* 1784, in Bay, *Reports of Cases,* I, 3–6. Backcountry violence will be treated in chapter six.

28. *GSSC,* 6 Aug. 1783, 19 Aug. 1784, 27 Aug. 1783.

29. *SCGPA,* 9 July 1785; *GSSC,* 6 June 1785.

30. Lloyd to T.B. Smith, 7 Dec. 1784, John Lloyd Letters, Charleston Library Society; Rutledge to John Rutledge, Jr., 18 Feb. 1789, John Rutledge, Jr. Papers, DU.

31. *CEG,* 25 Aug. 1786; *CnHd,* 26 Nov. 1784.

32. *CnHd,* 26 Nov. 1784; *GSSC,* 27 Aug. 1783; *SCGGA,* 16 Sept. 1784.

33. *SCWG,* 19 July 1783; *SCGGA,* 13 May 1784.

34. The Regulators' "Remonstrance" is printed in full in Hooker, ed., *Carolina Backcountry,* pp. 213–233. On lawyers' fees, see also Henry Middleton to Arthur Middleton, 22 Sept. 1768, Barnwell, ed., "Correspondence of Arthur Middleton" (1926): 110. In 1767 eight of the forty-eight members of the lower house were lawyers.

35. Presentments of the Grand Jury of Ninety Six District, 26 Nov. 1783, and Clarendon County Petition, 1788, SCA. In 1784 the grand jury of Ninety Six complained that persons inimical to the United States were holding places of trust. *GSSC,* 20 Dec. 1784.

36. "Annotations on the Remonstrance," in Hooker, ed., *Carolina Backcountry,* pp. 237, 245; Weir, "'Liberty and Property, and No Stamps,'" pp. 406, 414; "Journal of Josiah Quincy," pp. 446–447. In 1772, the first time a session of the Circuit Court was held in Cheraw District, the grand jury complained of the lack of a collection of the laws of Great Britain and South Carolina. A Charleston grand jury made a similar complaint in 1774, as did another Cheraw grand jury in 1783. Gregg, *Old Cheraws,* pp. 197, 430; *SCG,* 3 Oct. 1774.

37. Gadsden to Francis Marion, 29 Oct. 1782, Walsh, ed., *Writings of Gadsden,* p. 187; Weir, "'Liberty and Property, and No Stamps,'" p. 415. In 1736 Louis Timothy had printed all the permanent laws passed in the colony through May 1734, and about a year later he brought out the temporary laws. David Duncan Wallace, *South Carolina: A Short History, 1520–1948* (Chapel Hill, 1951), p. 84.

38. Governors Message, 2 Feb. 1784, no. 276, Records of the General Assembly, SCA; Cooper and McCord, eds., *Statutes of South Carolina,* IV, 549; John Faucheraud Grimké, "Dedication," *The Public Laws of South-Carolina* (Philadelphia, 1790). The work of the legislature's commission was apparently not adopted, but Grimké, a member of the commission, published his compilation privately. Wallace, *South Carolina,* p. 416.

39. Weir, "'Liberty and Property, and No Stamps,'" p. 38; McCrady counted thirty-five members of the bar in South Carolina in 1775. *SC under Royal Govt.,* p. 480.

40. West to Reverend Samuel West, 23 July 1778, James S. Schoff, ed., *Life in the South, 1778–1779: the Letters of Benjamin West* (Ann Arbor, Mich., 1963), p. 32; Rogers *Evolution of a Federalist,* p. 119.

41. Rogers, *Evolution of a Federalist,* p. 119; Cooper and McCord, eds., *Statutes of South Carolina,* IV, 668–669.

42. Gadsden to Francis Marion, 3 Nov. 1782, Walsh, ed., *Writings of Gadsden,* p. 189; *SCSGDA,* 30 Nov. 1784. The lawyers who had served as governors were John Rutledge, John Mathews, and Benjamin Guerard. Rawlins Lowndes had been a judge.

43. Gadsden to Marion, 3 Nov. 1782, Walsh, ed., *Writings of Gadsden,* p. 189.

44. *GSSC,* 29 April 1784. Bee was closely connected with the Rutledge family. His wife, Sarah Smith, was the sister of Roger Smith, who had married Mary Rutledge, the sister of John, Hugh, and Edward. And Ann Smith, another sister of Sarah and Roger, had married Hugh Rutledge. Rogers. *Evolution of a Federalist,* Chart IV, p. 403.

45. *GSSC,* 8 April 1784.

46. *SCGPA,* 12 July 1785; *CnHd,* 26 Nov. 1784; Burke, *An Address to the Freemen of South Carolina,* pp. 14, 17.

47. *GSSC,* 6 June 1785; *SCGPA,* 21 May and 28 May 1785. Hutson is not mentioned by name in the articles. In 1794 Hutson resigned his position on the court of equity because he had "totally abandoned himself to the vice of habitual and excessive drinking." Committee Report on the conduct of Richard Hutson, Judge of the Court of Equity, 5 May 1794, General Assembly, Committee Report, 1794 #25, SCA.

48. *SCGGA,* 16 Sept. 1784; *CEG,* 25 Aug. 1786.

49. *GSSC,* 27 Aug. 1783, 19 Aug. 1784; *SCGGA,* 16 Sept. 1784.

50. *SCGGA,* 16 Sept. 1784; *SGSC,* 21 Aug. 1786; *GSSC,* 13 June 1785.

51. *SCGGA,* 4 Sept. 1784. "After regaining possession" of Charleston, one writer noted, "we were frequently, I had almost said every night, alarmed by fire, robberies, or riots: but since the Incorporation, by the establishment of a judicious, well-regulated Police, regularity, order, and good government, have been maintained. . . ." *SCGGA,* 27 Nov. 1784.

52. *SCGPA,* 11 Sept. 1784; *CnHd,* 30 May 1785. "BRUTUS" had earlier argued that "the dominion of justice" was more important than the "dominion of law." *GSSC,* 27 Aug. 1783.

53. *SCGGA,* 11 Sept. 1784; *GSSC,* 6 May 1784.

54. *SCGGA,* 10 July 1784; *GSSC,* 1 Sept. 1785; see also *SCGGA,* 27 Nov. 1784; *SCGPA,* 28 July 1784.

55. *SCGGA,* 25 Sept. 1784.

56. The quotation is in *SCGGA,* 20 Nov. 1784.

57. Greene to Col. Pettit, 29 July 1783, Joseph Reed Papers, NYHS; *SCGGA,* 27 Nov. 1784; see also *GSSC,* 6 May 1784; *SCGGA,* 4 Sept. 1784.

58. *CMPDA,* 11 April 1786.

59. *SCGPA,* 24 July 1784; see also *SCGGA,* 16 Sept. 1784.

60. Rutledge to John Jay, 12 Nov. 1786, Johnston, ed., *Correspondence of Jay,* III, 217.

61. *GSSC,* 29 April 1784; see also *GSSC,* 6 May 1784.

62. *GSSC,* 8 April 1784; McCrady, *SC in the Revol., 1775–1780,* pp. 238–239; Ramsay, *Revol. of SC,* I, 136; Izard to Thomas Jefferson, 10 June 1785, "Letters of Ralph Izard," p. 197. Izard's remark about the effect of moving the government inland was made in the House of Representatives on 1 March 1786 and printed in the *CEG,* 3 March 1786.

63. *GSSC,* 6 June 1785; House of Representatives, 9 Feb. 1787, in *CMP,* 12 Feb. 1787.

64. *SCGGA,* 4 Sept. 1784; *SCGPA,* 11 Sept. and 4 Sept. 1784.

65. *GSSC,* 17 Sept. 1783; *CMPDA,* 12 Sept. 1786; *CGDA,* 30 Sept. 1788; *SCGGA,* 14 Sept. 1784.

66. *SCGGA,* 9 Sept. 1784; *SCGPA,* 29 Sept. 1784. The estimate of Charleston's voting population is nothing more than a hopefully intelligent guess. In 1790, after six years of population growth, there were 2,810 free, white males over sixteen in the city. Many of them, British merchants and factors, merchants and factors of other countries, and males under twenty-one could not vote. In 1773, there had been approximately 11,000 inhabitants, including almost 6,000 Negro slaves. The males over sixteen probably numbered no more than 1,700. By 1784 there may have been fewer. The native population of the city had declined during the war, and the list of eligible voters had declined even more rapidly. Some Carolinians, remaining in the city while the British occupied it, had been disenfranchised by the Jacksonborough Assembly. For the population figures, see U.S. Bureau of the Census, *Heads of Families at the First Census of the United States taken in the Year 1790. South Carolina* (Washington, 1908) and E.B. Greene and Virginia D. Harrington, *American Population Before the Federal Census of 1790* (New York, 1932), p. 178n.

67. *SCGGA,* 16 Sept. 1784. Walsh, in *Charleston's Sons of Liberty,* p. 121, and *Writings of Gadsden,* pp. 224–225, note 6, incorrectly gives the results of the election as 387 votes for Hutson to 127 for Gillon. But Gillon got 260 votes, which was 127 less than Hutson. Walsh then goes on to state (in *Writings of Gadsden*) that the "defeat set back . . . [Gillon's] career politically. . . . Gillon retired to his plantation on the Congaree. In 1788, he entered the Congressional race but lost again. However, in 1793, he was elected to Congress." That description gives an entirely erroneous picture of Gillon's subsequent political career. His defeat not being so bad, he was not politically humiliated. In fact, in December 1784, less than three months after his loss to Hutson, Gillon was one of thirty representatives elected by Charleston to the state legislature. His vote total then placed him fourteenth on the list, behind such luminaries as Henry Laurens, Charles Cotesworth Pinckney, and Edward Rutledge, but ahead of Benjamin Guerard and John Mathews, the two previous governors. Furthermore, he was elected again from Charleston in 1786, although with fewer votes; that hardly mattered since he was chosen also by the district of Saxe-Gotha and chose to represent that area. Saxe-Gotha reelected him in 1788. And in 1789, he was elected lieutenant governor, but he declined the position, ostensibly because of ill health, but possibly because it was a position of little power.

68. *Ordinances Passed in the First Year of Incorporation of the City,* p. 34; Bridenbaugh, *Cities in Revolt,* p. 79; Cooper and McCord, eds., *Statutes of South Carolina,* IV, 562, 670–673; *GSSC,* 13 June 1785.

69. *SCGPA,* 2 April 1785; *GSSC,* 13 June and 2 June 1785.

70. Cooper and McCord, eds., *Statutes of South Carolina,* VII, 97–102. The Court of Wardens, however, did not have jurisdiction when a title of land was involved.

71. *GSSC,* 26 May and 2 June 1785.

72. *GSSC,* 2 June 1785; *SCGPA,* 1 Sept. 1785.

73. The City Council in 1786 prohibited any one from keeping more than two slaves for hiring out, "*except of any mechanic or handy-craft trade.*" Critics complained that it was impossible to tell whether the exception applied to masters who were mechanics or handicraftsmen or to slaves in those occupations. *SGSC,* 3 Aug. and 21 Aug. 1786; Sellers, *Charleston Business,* pp. 104–105. On the City Council's budget, see *GSSC,* 15 Aug. 1785; *CnHd,* 7 Sept. 1786; House of Representatives, 9 Feb. 1787, in *CMP,* 12 Feb. 1787.

74. On the incorporation of artisan societies, see Walsh, *Charleston's Sons of Liberty,* p. 123.

75. *SCGGA,* 19 Oct. 1784; *GSSC,* 15 Aug. 1785.

76. "Copy of a letter from a seafaring man, lately at Savannah, to his friend in this city [New York], dated May 6," *PaPDA,* 1 June 1790; House of Representatives, 9 Feb. 1787, in *CMP,* 12 Feb. 1787; *CnHd,* 26 July 1787.

77. On the problems of the poor, see *GSSC,* 4 July 1785.

78. Cooper and McCord, eds., *Statutes of South Carolina,* V, 38–39.

79. On escheators, *ibid.,* 49; on tax collectors, *ibid.,* 60; on denying state officials other positions, *ibid.,* 21.

80. *GSSC,* 14 July 1785; *Zylstra v. Corporation of Charleston,* 1794, in Bay, *Reports of Cases,* I, 389–391, 394.

81. Bay, *Reports of Cases,* I, 391–396. Waties was referring to the constitution adopted in 1790, but the same guarantee of a trial by jury was in the 1778 constitution.

82. *Ibid.,* 396–397.

83. *M'Mullen v. the City Council,* 1787, in Bay, *Reports of Cases,* I, 46–49.

84. *Zylstra v. Corporation of Charleston,* 1794, in Bay, *Reports of Cases,* I, 388.

NOTES
CHAPTER SEVEN

1. Grand Jury Presentments, Orangeburg District, 15 Nov. 1783, and Grand Jury Presentments, Ninety Six District, 26 Nov. 1783, SCA; *SCGGA,* 11 May and 13 Nov. 1784; *GSSC,* 20 Dec. 1784.

2. Quoted in Brown, *SC Regulators,* p. 139.

3. House Journal, 24 Feb. 1783; Senate Journal, 28 Feb. 1783.

4. Schoepf, *Travels in the Confederation,* pp. 198–200; *GSSC,* 29 July 1784, quoted in Main, *Political Parties before the Constitution,* p. 269n.

5. Tax returns, SCA; General William Henderson to Capt. John Henderson, 10 March 1784, Sumter Papers, Draper Manuscripts, Wisconsin Historical Society.

6. Calhoun to the Commissioners of the Public Treasury, 31 Jan. 1784, Commissioners of the Treasury, 1778–1791, Letters Received, SCA; Drayton, Remarks in a Tour, 1784, William Drayton Journals, Charleston Museum; Reverend Simpson's Journal, quoted in Howe, *Presbyterian Church in SC,* I, 466.

7. Simpson's Journal, quoted in Howe, *Presbyterian Church in SC,* I, 466.

8. Bratton to Guerard, 13 Feb. 1784, Governors Message, 26 Feb. 1784, enclosure, Records of the General Assembly, SCA; Drayton, Remarks in a Tour, 1784, William Drayton Journals, Charleston Museum; Burke to Guerard, 14 Dec. 1784, SCA.

9. Burke's remarks are from a charge to the Charleston Grand Jury, June 1783, in Almon, *American Remembrancer* 16 (1783): 286–287; Drayton, Remarks in a Tour, 1784, William Drayton Journals, Charleston Museum.

10. Grimké to [Gov. Guerard], 12 Nov. 1783, Governors Message, 2 Feb. 1785, enclosure, Records of the General Assembly, SCA.

11. Burke to Gov. Guerard, 11 Nov. 1784 and 17 Nov. 1784, *ibid.*

12. Grimké to [Gov. Guerard], 12 Nov. 1783, *ibid.*

13. Quarles, *The Negro in the American Revolution,* p. 174; Duncan, "Servitude and Slavery in Colonial South Carolina," p. 600; for Thomas Bee's letter to Governor John Mathews, 9 Dec. 1782, and the description of the maroon hideaway, see Michael Mullin "British Caribbean and North American Slaves in an Era of War and Revolution, 1775–1807," in Crow and Tise, eds. *The Southern Experience in the American Revolution,* pp. 240–241.

14. McCrady, *SC in the Revol., 1780–1783,* pp. 547–548; U.S. Bureau of the Census, *Heads of Families, 1790. South Carolina,* p. 9. In 1790 52.2 percent of the state's white population was under sixteen. The only state to have a higher proportion of young whites was Georgia, with 53.1 percent of its population under sixteen. Tennessee and Kentucky, not yet states, also had higher proportions of young. U.S. Bureau of the Census, *A Century of Population Growth From the First Census of the United States to the Twelfth, 1790–1900* (Washington, 1909), Table 34, p. 103. For a general picture of the numbers of children in the total population see Table 6-8, "Age Composition of the United States Population, By Regions, 1820–1950," in Donald J. Bogue, *The Population of the United States* (Glencoe, Ill., 1959), p. 113.

15. *SCGGA,* 11 May and 13 Nov. 1784.

16. Simpson's Journal, quoted in Howe, *Presbyterian Church in SC,* I, 466. The reference to the loss of inhabitants is in a message from Governor William Moultrie to the legislature, 16 Feb. 1785, Records of the General Assembly, SCA.

17. Cooper and McCord, eds., *Statutes of South Carolina,* V, 41–43; for acts of 1758 and 1778 which defined "vagrants" differently, see *ibid.,* IV, 51–52, 410–413.

18. Burke to Gov. Guerard, 14 Dec. 1784, SCA; entries under "Contingencies," Dec. 1783, in South Carolina Treasury, Ledgers and Journals, 1783–1791, reel 4, Colonial and State Records of South Carolina, Microcopy Number 5 [hereafter, Treasury Journals]; Lowndes to Henry Laurens, 22 Sept. 1778, South Carolina and Miscellaneous, Bancroft Transcripts, NYPL.

19. Cooper and McCord, eds. *Statutes of South Carolina,* IV, 284, 622; Presentments of the Grand Jury of Ninety Six District, in Hemphill *et al.*, eds., *Journals of the General Assembly,* 29 Jan. 1780, p. 256.

20. John Faucheraud Grimké to [Gov. Guerard], 12 Nov. 1783, Thomas Heyward, Jr. to Guerard, 11 Nov. 1784, Aedanus Burke to Guerard, 11 Nov. 1784 and 14 Dec. 1784, Governors Message, 2 Feb. 1785, enclosures, Records of the General Assembly, SCA; Docket for Georgetown and Ninety Six Districts, 1783–1784, SCA.

21. For payments to express riders carrying pardons and for McDonald's banishment, see "Contingencies," Nov. 1783, Nov. 1784, and Dec. 1784, Treasury Journals, reel 4.

22. Camden District, Journal of the Court of General Sessions, SCA.

23. Free inhabitants of Little River, petition . . . 17 March 1785, General Assembly, Petitions, 1785 #105, SCA.

24. Quarles, *The Negro in the American Revolution,* p. 174; message from Governor Thomas Pinckney, Senate Journal, 19 March 1787; for the use of Indians and the payment of rewards, see entries under "Expedition against Negroes," in the Treasury Journals, reel 4, between March 1787 and January 1788.

25. Lee to [James Madison], 20 Nov. 1784, James Curtis Ballagh, ed., *The Letters of Richard Henry Lee* (2 vols., New York, 1911, 1914), II, 300.

26. Cooper and McCord, eds., *Statutes of South Carolina,* IV, 590, 592, 706, 709; Account of Lands granted in the Secretary's Office from the 16th day of July 1784 . . . to the first day of January 1787, SCA; Higgins, "Financial History of South Carolina," pp. 221–224. The action favoring speculators is discussed in chapter eight below.

27. Pendleton's remarks were made in the lower house on 3 Feb. 1786 and printed in *CMPDA,* 4 Feb. 1786; *CGDA,* 4 March 1788; D. Huger Bacot, "The South Carolina Up Country at the End of the Eighteenth Century," *American Historical Review* 28 (1923): 690; U.S. Bureau of the Census, *Heads of Families, 1790. South Carolina,* p. 9. The settlement of South Carolina's backcountry in the immediate postwar years probably proceeded at the same pace, and for the same reasons, as the settlement of the Georgia backcountry. Georgia's growth was described by Savannah merchant Joseph Clay: "tis beyond conception the eagerness the people on this Continent discover to settle in Georgia," he wrote. Clay to Joachim Noel Famming, 23 April 1783, *Letters of Clay,* pp. 190–191.

28. McCrady, *SC in the Revol., 1775-1780,* p. 223; *SGSC,* 1 Oct. 1787; see also *SCGGA,* 24 July and 29 July 1784; *SCSGDA,* 4 Dec. 1784.

29. Petition of Chesterfield and Lancaster counties, 1787, SCA; Inhabitants of York County, Petition . . . 19 Oct. 1788, General Assembly, Petitions, 1788 #5, SCA.

30. Cooper and McCord, eds., *Statutes of South Carolina,* IV, 600–601, 746–747.

31. "Observations upon the Effects of Certain Late Political Suggestions," by the Delegates of Georgia, in Rev. George White, *Historical Collections of Georgia* (New York, 1855), p. 107; Lee to [James Madison], 26 Nov. 1784, Ballagh, ed., *Letters of Lee,* II, 300.

32. *GSSC,* 24 March 1785; Senate Journal, 17 Feb. 1785.

33. Gayle, "The Nature and Volume of Charleston Exports," SCHA, *Proc.,* 1937, p. 33; South Carolina's exports for the years 1783 to 1787 are listed conveniently in the Madison Papers, microfilm copy, LC, vol. 8, reel 4, following the letters of November 1787; the *PaPDA*

published the South Carolina exports for 1784, 1785, and 1786 on 18 May 1785, 20 March 1786, and 6 Jan. 1787; the exports of 1787 and 1788 are listed in an enclosure from George Miller to the Duke of Leeds, 28 Jan. 1790, BT 6/21, BPRO. Some of the tobacco exported by South Carolina was undoubtedly grown in North Carolina. George Abbott Hall noted that North Carolina paid for the goods it received through Charleston merchants with "Tobacco, Lumber and Naval Stores," and David Ramsay stated that South Carolina's specie enabled it to drain North Carolina of tobacco. George Abbott Hall, 31 Dec. 1784, Enclosure II, in letter from Ralph Izard to Thomas Jefferson, 10 June 1785, Boyd, ed., *Jefferson Papers,* VIII, 201; *CEG,* 29 Sept. 1785. According to Forrest McDonald's figures, the tobacco crop in 1769 was 0.5 percent as valuable as the rice crop. By 1783 it was 8 percent as valuable, 11 percent as valuable by 1785, and 28 percent as valuable by 1787. *We the People,* p. 209.

34. Cooper and McCord, eds., *Statutes of South Carolina,* IV, 327, 538, 604, 681, 749, VII, 532, 541–543, 545; Petition to the Senate from Ninety Six and Orangeburg, 16 Feb. 1786, SCA.

35. For the number of slave-holding families see the valuable Table 114, in *A Century of Population Growth,* pp. 290–291. Table 115, pp. 297–298, which classifies the families according to the numbers of slaves held, is also valuable, although I have not used it for my calculations. Some of the classes are too broad; for example, families owning ten to nineteen slaves, twenty to forty-nine, and so on are listed. My percentages are based on the figures in U.S. Bureau of the Census, *Heads of Families, 1790. South Carolina.*

36. Free inhabitants of Little River, petition . . . 17 March 1785, General Assembly, Petitions, 1785 #105, SCA. The back of the petition is dated 1783, but that is clearly a mistake, since item five of the petition states that the war had so "reduced the Inhabitants of this District . . . that the payment of a tax in money for the year 1785 . . . [would] be impossible. . . ." There is also, in the same legislative file, another copy of the petition, with corrected spelling, dated 1785.

37. Cooper and McCord, eds., *Statutes of South Carolina,* VII, 211–242. The county courts were abolished in 1799. Wallace, *South Carolina,* p. 337.

38. Almon, *The Remembrancer* 16 (1783): 33–34. James Mayson, a representative of Ninety Six District, had suggested moving the government inland in 1780. Hemphill *et al.,* eds., *Journals of the General Assembly,* 8 Feb. 1780, p. 287.

39. Senate, 9 March 1786, in *CMPDA,* 11 March 1786.

40. House of Representatives, 1 March 1786, in *CMPDA,* 3 March 1786.

41. On the Regulators' charge, see "Annotations on the Remonstrance," in Hooker, ed., *The Carolina Backcountry,* p. 237.

42. Burke to John Lamb, 21 June 1788, Lamb Papers, NYHS.

43. Rutledge's remarks are printed in *CnHd,* 28 March 1785; Izard's are in *CMPDA,* 3 March 1786.

44. *CnHd,* 28 March 1785; *CMPDA,* 3 March 1786.

45. Senate, 6 March and 9 March 1786, in *CMPDA,* 7 March and 11 March 1786.

46. House of Representatives, 14 March, 17 March, and 20 March 1786, in *CMPDA,* 15 March, 20 March, and 21 March 1786. According to one newspaper, the value of land around the new town rose 150 percent. *CMPDA,* 1 May 1786. On Sumter, see Gregorie, *Thomas Sumter,* pp. 203–205.

47. *SGSC,* 21 Aug. and 10 Aug. 1786.

48. *SGSC,* 10 Aug. 1786; *GSSC,* 24 Jan. 1785.

49. House of Representatives, 16 Feb. 1786, in *CEG,* 16 Feb. 1786.

50. *CMPDA,* 1 Nov. 1786; see also *SGSC,* 28 Sept. 1786. In a nineteenth-century court case, the judges ruled that the constitution of 1778 had been only an act of the legislature

and not binding on future legislatures. D.J. McCord, *Reports of Cases Determined in the Constitutional Court of South Carolina* (4 vols., Charleston, 1853), II, 354–360.

51. *SGSC,* 10 Aug. 1786; *CMPDA,* 1 Nov. 1786.

52. House Journal, 22 Jan. and 22 Feb. 1785; Senate Journal, 29 Sept. 1785; Free inhabitants of Little River, petition . . . 17 March 1785, General Assembly Petitions, 1785 #105, SCA. The report of the committee of the lower house is printed in *SCGPA,* 23 March 1785. In the opening paragraph, the word "property" is mistakenly used for "posterity." For the correct version, see *CnHd,* 28 March 1785. This report contains many of the ideas set forth by Thomas Tudor Tucker, writing as "PHILODEMUS," in his pamphlet *Conciliatory Hints, Attempting by a fair State of Matters, to remove Party-Prejudices. . . .* (Charleston, 1784). Tucker was a member of the lower house. Excerpts from the pamphlet are printed in *SGSC,* 7 Sept. 1786.

53. *SGSC,* 7 Sept. 1786; *SCGPA,* 23 March 1785.

54. Senate Journal, 21 March 1787. The House vote of 14 March 1787 was on a motion to postpone consideration of the committee report recommending the calling of a convention. While those who voted against postponing may not have been in favor of a convention, probably those voting in favor of postponing the report were against the idea of a convention.

55. House of Representatives, 3 Feb. 1786, in *CMPDA,* 4 Feb. 1786.

56. *Ibid.* Curiously, according to Judge Heyward one had to give ninety days notice of an intent to bring in a bill to alter the constitution at the next session of the legislature. In other words, the notice was given at one session, and the bill was introduced at the next session, at least ninety days after notice had been given. Pendleton accepted that requirement but said that the previous session had been a special one and so he could not have been expected to give notice then. Besides, he had given notice in the session preceding the special one. In 1783 Christopher Gadsden had said that in accordance with the 44th clause of the constitution he was giving notice that at the next sitting after ninety days he would bring in a bill to alter the constitution. What is curious about Gadsden's remark, Heyward's objection to Pendleton's proposal, and Pendleton's explanation of why he did not give notice according to the constitution, is that the constitution, as printed in 1778 and in subsequent years, does not mention the necessity of giving notice a session in advance. It simply says ninety days in advance. It was theoretically possible that one session could last longer than ninety days, although none did during the 1780s. And without that extra clause, it would have been possible for someone to give notice in the beginning of a session and introduce a bill ninety days later or to give notice in 1783 and not introduce a bill until 1785 or any other year. The copy of the 1778 constitution printed by the Historical Commission of South Carolina in 1953 was made from an engrossed original in the Commission's possession. That original apparently does not contain the phrase "next session." But contemporaries were certainly behaving and talking as though that phrase was in the constitution. For Pendleton's early notice see House Journal, 24 March 1785; for Gadsden's, House Journal, 30 Jan. 1783.

57. House of Representatives, Feb. 1786, in *CMPDA,* 4 Feb. 1786.

58. On the idea that superiority was unitary, see Bernard Bailyn, *The Ideological Origins of the American Revolution* (Cambridge, Mass., 1967), pp. 302–303; see also Timothy Ford's argument in 1794, summarized in John Harold Wolfe, *Jeffersonian Democracy in South Carolina* (Chapel Hill, 1940), p. 51.

59. House of Representatives, 3 Feb. 1786, in *CMPDA,* 4 Feb. 1786.

60. Tucker, *Conciliatory Hints,* p. 11; *SGSC,* 17 Aug. and 16 Nov. 1786.

61. Gadsden to John Adams, 24 July 1787, Walsh, ed., *Writings of Gadsden,* p. 244.

62. House of Representatives, 3 Feb. 1786, in *CMPDA,* 4 Feb. 1786.

63. House of Representatives, 21 Feb. 1786, in *CEG,* 21 Feb. 1786.

64. Senate Journal, 21 March 1787.

NOTES

CHAPTER EIGHT

1. Izard to Arthur Middleton, 30 May 1783, Barnwell, ed., "Correspondence of Arthur Middleton" (1926): 78; Butler to [Thomas Fitzsimons], 18 May 1783, Gratz Collection, Old Congress, HSP; David Ramsay to Benjamin Rush, 9 Sept. 1783, quoted in Rogers, *Evolution of a Federalist,* p. 101. Butler, a planter, was himself constantly alert for opportunities in trade, relaying commercial information to a friend, the Philadelphia merchant Thomas Fitzsimons. See his letters to Fitzsimons, 18 May, 24 May, and 29 Oct. 1783, Gratz Collection, Old Congress, HSP.

2. General Greene complained that people were "so attentive to private pursuits" that they forgot the enemy might return. To Charles Pettit, 3 April 1783, Joseph Reed Papers, NYHS.

3. Bridenbaugh, *Myths and Realities,* pp. 79, 81, 88–92.

4. *SCGGA,* 20 May 1783; Bridenbaugh, *Myths and Realities,* p. 92.

5. "The St. George's Club," *SCHM* 7 (1906): 93.

6. *Ibid.,* 88–91; *SCGDA,* 30 Dec. 1784; *SCGGA,* 24 April 1784.

7. Joseph W. Barnwell, ed., "Diary of Timothy Ford, 1785–1786," *SCHM* 13 (1912): 191; Schoepf, *Travels in the Confederation,* p. 218. Ford noted that men as young as twenty-two had "wracked" their bodies.

8. *SCGGA,* 7 Feb. 1784; *GSSC,* 22 April 1784; the imports are from Notes on the state debt, Pierce Butler Papers, Box 6 (South Carolina Legislature), HSP.

9. Schoepf, *Travels in the Confederation,* p. 168; Thomas Reese, *An Essay on the Influence of Religion in Civil Society* (Charleston, 1788), p. 69; Barnwell, ed., "Diary of Timothy Ford," pp. 189–190. A decade later La Rochefoucauld Liancourt made similar remarks. A Carolinian "rarely has fewer than twenty [slaves] . . . in his stable, in his kitchen, and attendant upon his table. A child has a number of negro children to attend him, and comply with all his humours. . . ." *Travels Through the United States of North America . . . in the Years 1795, 1796, and 1797* (2nd ed., 4 vols., London, 1800), II, 378–379.

10. Gervais and Owen to Leonard De Neufville, 13 April 1786, John De Neufville Papers, LC; Notes on the state debt, Pierce Butler Papers, Box 6 (South Carolina Legislature), HSP.

11. Notes on the state debt, Pierce Butler Papers, Box 6 (South Carolina Legislature), HSP.

12. Burke, *A Few Salutary Hints, Pointing out the Policy and Consequences of Admitting British Subjects to Engross our Trade and Become our Citizens* (Charleston and New York, 1786), p. 4. Burke wrote this pamphlet anonymously. Rogers, "Aedanus Burke, Nathanael Green, Anthony Wayne, and the British Merchants of Charleston," pp. 75–83.

13. *CEG,* 1 Sept. 1785; Brailsford and Morris to Thomas Jefferson, 31 Oct. 1787, Richard Walsh, ed., "Letters of Morris & Brailsford," *SCHM* 58 (1957): 135–136.

14. Baldwin, "The Debts Owed by Americans to British Creditors, 1763–1802," p. 96.

15. Ramsay, *History of SC,* II, 428; Lord Sheffield, *Observations on the Commerce of the American States* (6th ed., London, 1784), pp. 248–249.

16. George Abbott Hall, 31 Dec. 1784, enclosure II in letter from Ralph Izard to Thomas Jefferson, 10 June 1785, Boyd, ed., *Jefferson Papers,* VIII, 201.

17. For Butler's loan see McDonald, *We the People,* p. 82, and Gervais and Owen to Leonard De Neufville, 13 April 1786, John De Neufville Papers, LC; on Gadsden and Gillon, see *SCGGA,* 11 Sept. 1784; on the Dutch in general, Lord Sheffield, *Observations,*

pp. 248–249. Dutch trade and credit are treated in Albert Ludwig Kohlmeier, "The Commerce Between the United States and the Netherlands, 1783–1789," *Studies in American History* 12 (1925): 1–47.

18. Brailsford and Morris to J.J. Berards & Co., Oct., 1787, Walsh, ed., "Letters of Morris & Brailsford," p. 141.

19. *GSSC,* 8 April 1784.

20. Hall, 31 Dec. 1784, enclosure II in letter from Ralph Izard to Thomas Jefferson, 10 June 1785, Boyd, ed., *Jefferson Papers,* VIII, 201.

21. Brailsford and Morris to Thomas Jefferson, 31 Oct. 1787, Walsh, ed., "Letters of Morris & Brailsford," pp. 135–136. In 1779 Chevalier de la Luzerne described the French merchants who were trading to America as "a Parcell of little Rascals, *petits Coquins,* and Adventurers who have sold the worst Merchandises, for great Prices." Quoted in Stinchcombe, *The American Revolution and the French Alliance,* p. 201.

22. Ramsay to Benjamin Rush, 9 Sept. 1783, quoted in Rogers, *Evolution of a Federalist,* p. 101. Timothy Ford commented on the slaves around the table. Barnwell, ed., "Diary of Timothy Ford," pp. 142–143.

23. Hall, 31 Dec. 1784, enclosure II in letter from Ralph Izard to Thomas Jefferson, 10 June 1785, Boyd, ed., *Jefferson Papers,* VIII, 199.

24. George Abbott Hall, 13 Jan. 1785, in John Drayton, *A View of South-Carolina, as Respects Her Natural and Civil Liberties* (Charleston, 1802), pp. 166–167. Hall's figures indicate that in 1783 1,003 Negroes were imported from Africa and the West Indies and 167 from St. Augustine. For 1784 he listed 4,020 slaves from Africa and the West Indies and 1,372 from St. Augustine, a total for the two years of 6,562. Pierce Butler's notes on the state debt list the number of Negroes imported in 1784 as 4,922 and estimates their sale at £50 each. Pierce Butler Papers, Box 6 (South Carolina Legislature), HSP.

25. Lord Sheffield, *Observations,* pp. 154–155, 195.

26. Hall, 31 Dec. 1784, enclosure II in letter from Ralph Izard to Thomas Jefferson, 10 June 1785, Boyd, ed., *Jefferson Papers,* VIII, 200. One vessel carrying 293 slaves entered Charleston from the French possession of Cape Francois, was captained by Louis Castandet, and was named *Le Leger. SCGGA,* 20 May 1784. In July 1785 two ships of the Royal Company of Denmark were in Charleston with slaves. *PaPDA,* 30 July 1785. On the Rhode Island slave trader see Elizabeth Donnan, "The New England Slave Trade after the Revolution," *New England Quarterly* 3 (1930): 256.

27. Gervais and Owen to Leonard De Neufville, 13 April 1786, John De Neufville Papers, LC; Barnwell, ed., "Diary of Timothy Ford," p. 193.

28. Butler to [James Iredell?], 5 May 1783, James Iredell Papers, DU; Smith to Col. John Bayard, 16 May 1783, and Smith to Bayard, 12 July 1783, Josiah Smith Letterbook, UNC; see also Butler to [Thomas Fitzsimons], 18 May 1783, Gratz Collection, Old Congress, HSP.

29. Isaac Teasdale to Andrew Clow, 13 May 1785, Andrew Clow Letters, DU. The wholesale prices of imported items worked out by George Rogers Taylor in his "Wholesale Commodity Prices at Charleston, South Carolina, 1732–1791, 1796–1861," indicate a general rise in prices in 1785, but these figures are of little value since they are tabulations of prices of rum, sugar, molasses and other relatively unimportant South Carolina imports. He has no figures for the prices of dry goods.

30. *PaPDA,* 5 Oct. and 16 Nov. 1785. For 133 slaves sold in the summer of 1785 a Rhode Island trader received an average of £53 sterling each, but he had to extend credit until 1787. Jacob Rodriguez Rivera to Capt. Nathaniel Briggs, 13 Sept. 1785, Jacob Rader Marcus, ed., *American Jewry: Documents: Eighteenth Century, Primarily Hitherto Unpublished Manuscripts* (Cincinnati, Ohio, 1959), pp. 446–447.

31. *SCGGA,* 19 July 1783; *GSSC,* 17 July 1784. Aedanus Burke voiced the objections of the native merchants again when he wrote: "as well might a pigmy be compared to a giant, as the impoverished miserable funds of an American merchant, who lost his fortune in the war, to the immense capitals of British traders." *A Few Salutary Hints,* p. 9.

32. Wells to ______, 13 Aug. 1765, South Carolina Box, Charleston Folder, NYPL; Josiah Smith to George Austin, 8 June 1773, and Smith to John Ray, Jr., 10 June 1773, Josiah Smith Letterbook, UNC.

33. *GSSC,* 17 July 1784; Butler to [Thomas Fitzsimons], 18 May 1783, Gratz Collection, Old Congress, HSP; Smith to Col. John Bayard, 12 July 1783, Josiah Smith Letterbook, UNC; House of Representatives, 8 Feb. 1786, in *CMPDA,* 9 Feb. 1786.

34. Taylor, "Wholesale Commodity Prices," Table I, p. 372; Butler to [Thomas Fitzsimons], 18 May 1783, Gratz Collection, Old Congress, HSP.

35. Laurens to ____ Fisher, 27 Feb. 1766, quoted in Wallace, *Henry Laurens,* p. 121; Smith to George Austin, 11 April 1774, Josiah Smith Letterbook, UNC; on fear of Congress's power over trade see, for example, the comments of legislators printed in *CMPDA,* 9 Feb. 1786, and the remarks of Charles Pinckney at the Constitutional Convention in 1787. Max Farrand, ed., *The Records of the Federal Convention of 1787* (rev. ed., 4 vols., New Haven, 1937), II, 420, 449.

36. Sellers, *Charleston Business,* p. 157.

37. Smith to Joseph Clay, 11 Nov. 1772, and Smith to Clay, 29 June 1773, Josiah Smith Letterbook, UNC.

38. The merchant's remark is in Richard Pares, *Yankees and Creoles: The Trade between North America and the West Indies before the American Revolution* (London, 1956), p. 8. On England's postwar mercantile policy, see Herbert C. Bell, "British Commercial Policy in the West Indies, 1783–1793," *English Historical Review* 31 (1916): 429–441.

39. The figures are from tables included by George Abbott Hall in his account of South Carolina's trade, which was sent by Ralph Izard to Thomas Jefferson in his letter of 10 June 1785, Boyd, ed., *Jefferson Papers,* VIII, 202–203.

40. Butler to [Thomas Fitzsimons], 18 May 1783, Gratz Collection, Old Congress, HSP; Izard to Jefferson, 4 April 1787, "Letters of Ralph Izard," p. 202. From 31 October 1767 to 6 June 1768, 14,745 barrels of rice were shipped to Lisbon. Gayle, "The Nature and Volume of Exports from Charleston, 1724–1774," p. 26.

41. George Abbott Hall's tables in Izard to Jefferson, 10 June 1785, Boyd, ed., *Jefferson Papers,* VIII, 202–203.

42. *Ibid.,* p. 200; Ralph Izard to Thomas Jefferson, 1 July 1786, "Letters of Ralph Izard," p. 198.

43. Hall, 31 Dec. 1784, in Izard to Jefferson, 10 June 1785, Boyd, ed., *Jefferson Papers,* VIII, 200; Brailsford and Morris to Thomas Jefferson, 31 Oct. 1787, enclosure I, Walsh, ed., "Letters of Morris and Brailsford," p. 139.

44. Brailsford and Morris to Thomas Jefferson, 10 March 1789, Walsh, ed., "Letters of Morris and Brailsford," pp. 143–144.

45. Gervais and Owen to Leonard De Neufville, 13 April 1786, John De Neufville Papers, LC.

46. Lloyd to Francis Simmons, 30 Jan. 1785, John Lloyd Letters, Charleston Library Society.

47. Merrill Jensen, *The New Nation: A History of the United States during the Confederation, 1781–1789* (New York, 1950), p. 216.

48. House Journal, 26 Sept. 1785.

49. Extract of a letter from London, 15 Aug. 1784, *SCSGGA,* 9 Nov. 1784; Elias Ball to Elias Ball, Jr., 9 July 1785, Ball Family Papers, South Caroliniana Library, USC.

50. Laurens to James Bourdieu, 9 June 1785, South Carolina and Miscellaneous, Bancroft Transcripts, NYPL.

51. *SCGPA,* 21 May 1785.

NOTES
CHAPTER NINE

1. *CnHd,* 30 Sept. 1785; *Glocester Journal,* 15 Aug. 1785; Barnwell, ed., "Diary of Timothy Ford," p. 193. The description of Maham's actions is from a "Memorial of Aedanus Burke to the Senate," 1 March 1786, Records of the General Assembly, Petitions, 1786, #71, SCA. Maham was sentenced by a court, on which Burke sat, to three months' imprisonment, to pay a fine of £100, and to give bonds for his good behavior for seven years, he for £2,000 and each of two securities for £1,000. He accused his judges of "injustice and oppression." The legislature noted that Maham's action was "very reprehensible" and testified its "approbation of the . . . judges," but nevertheless refunded the fine and discharged his recognizance. Maham, it said, had been "carried away by a sudden gust of passion, and not actuated by any motives of contempt to the judicial power. . . ." Senate Report, 6 March 1786, *ibid.* During the war Maham had the idea of building a tower of logs to enable Marion's men to fire down into Fort Watson, which the British subsequently surrendered. Shortly afterwards Light Horse Harry Lee used the same tactic against another British fort which also surrendered. Bass, *Gamecock,* pp. 155–156, 182.

2. *CnHd,* 22 Aug. 1785; *CEG,* 1 Oct. 1785; see also Gov. Moultrie's message to the legislature, House Journal, 26 Sept. 1785. One newspaper mentioned that there had been "several instances lately of the Sheriff's deputies being compelled to eat the writs of a whole district." *CnHd,* 30 Sept. 1785. Only the Maham incident, however, was described by several sources.

3. Joshua Ward to Isaac King, 14 May 1785, Joshua Ward Letters, South Caroliniana Library, USC. Ward referred to Mr. Duboise. He probably meant Isaac Dubose who represented St. James Santee. According to Ward, Dubose was arrested when the Assembly adjourned.

4. Ramsay, *History of SC,* II, 428; Inhabitants of Saint Johns Parish, Petition . . . 15 Feb. 1787, General Assembly, Petitions, 1787 #32, SCA; Hall, 31 Dec. 1784, enclosure II in Ralph Izard to Thomas Jefferson, 10 June 1785, Boyd, ed., *Jefferson Papers,* VIII, 199; the number of imported slaves is from a debate in the House of Representatives, 5 Oct. 1785, in *CEG,* 18 Oct. 1785.

5. Ramsay, *History of SC,* II, 428; *PaPDA,* 27 June 1785; Thomas Ferguson to Benjamin Lincoln, 2 Feb. 1786, *Benjamin Lincoln Papers,* Microfilm, reel 7, MHS; *PaPDA,* 1 July and 2 Sept. 1786.

6. *PaPDA,* 18 May 1785, 20 March 1786, 6 Jan. 1787; Gayle, "The Nature and Volume of Charleston Exports," p. 30; Gervais and Owen to Leonard De Neufville, 13 April 1786, John De Neufville Papers, LC.

7. Smith to James Poyas, 7 Dec. 1772 and 25 Jan. 1774, Josiah Smith Letterbook, UNC; see also David Ramsay to Henry Laurens, 3 Dec. 1787, Society Collections, HSP; *CnHd,* 16 Nov. 1786. A similar situation existed in prewar Virginia also; debtors had considerable power over merchants. "If one Merchant will not comply with their Desires, they fly to another," wrote Robert Carter Nicholas in 1773. Quoted in Evans, "Planter Indebtedness and the Coming of the Revolution in Virginia," p. 523.

8. *Boston Gazette & the Country Journal,* 25 Oct. 1784; *PaPDA,* 4 April 1786.

9. "Message to the Legislature," House Journal, 26 Sept. 1785; for Pringle's remarks see House of Representatives, 16 Feb. 1787, in *Mass. Gaz.,* 27 March 1787; for Burke's comments see House of Representatives, 21 Feb. 1786, in *CMPDA,* 22 Feb. 1786; Laurens to James Bourdieu, 9 June 1785, South Carolina and Miscellaneous, Bancroft Transcripts, NYPL.

10. House of Representatives, 27 Sept. 1785, in *CEG,* 28 Sept. 1785.

11. William Bratton to Mr. Bleak [Blake], 9 June 1785, Patrick Calhoun to the Commissioners of the Public Treasury, 31 Jan. 1784, and William Murrell to Messrs. Blake and Bocquet, treasurers, 2 May 1785, Commissioners of the Treasury, 1778–1791, Letters Received, SCA.

12. "Statement of Taxes Received by District, 1783–1785," Governors Message, 1787, SCA. The "Statement" is dated 19 Feb. 1787.

13. *Ibid.*, for the sums planters paid; the amounts they should have paid are taken from another statement, "Amount of Taxes paid into the Treasury for the year 1785," SCA. Apparently this statement represents the taxes paid for 1785 as of 1790, for the total corresponds with the total listed on a separate "Aggregate Amount of the Taxes paid into the Treasury from anno 1783 to 1789, both years inclusive," in the same file. Most of 1785's taxes were paid between February 1787 and sometime in 1790. It is possible that the planters and others continued to make payments after this return was made out, and therefore the amounts they should have paid may have been even larger.

14. *CnHd,* 30 May 1785.

15. *GSSC,* 1 Sept. 1785; *SCGGA,* 25 Sept., 10 July, and 27 Nov. 1784; see also *SCGPA,* 28 July 1784.

16. "Message to the Legislature," House Journal, 26 Sept. 1785; House of Representatives, 16 Feb. 1787, in *Mass. Gaz.,* 27 March 1787.

17. Burke's remarks in the lower house, 21 Feb. 1786, are in *CMPDA,* 22 Feb. 1786; *SGSC,* 22 Feb. 1787. In 1789 Edward Rutledge wrote: "if in Republics the general sense of the community, I mean the sense of feeling, is against the operation of laws, it is almost impossible to coerce obedience. . . ." Rutledge to John Jay, 21 May 1789, Johnston, ed., *Correspondence of Jay,* III, 368.

18. Kinloch to Thomas Boone, 14 March 1786, Gilbert, ed., "Letters of Francis Kinloch," p. 99; Lloyd to T.B. Smith, 15 April 1786, John Lloyd Letters, Charleston Library Society. "The rich man's refuge" is a phrase of David Ramsay. *CGDA,* 2 Nov. 1788.

19. Cooper and McCord, eds., *Statutes of South Carolina,* IV, 513, for the act of 1782; *ibid.,* VI, Appendix, 627–628, for the act of 1783.

20. Gervais to Henry Laurens, 16 Dec. 1783, Gervais Mss., NYHS; Izard to Jefferson, 1 July 1786, "Letters of Ralph Izard," p. 199; for the relevant parts of the 1782 treaty see Ramsay, *Revol. of SC,* II, 377.

21. Moultrie to John Jay, 21 June 1786, *The Diplomatic Correspondence of the United States of America from . . . 1783 to . . . 1789* (3 vols., Washington, 1837), II, 786–787.

22. Burke, *A Few Salutary Hints,* pp. 4–5; Barnwell, ed., "Diary of Timothy Ford," p. 195. One of the most extreme statements was made by Patrick Calhoun in 1786. He said then: "pray, whose voice was it that called for the negro merchants or importers of dry goods? Who sent for them to come among us? Nobody." House of Representatives, 15 March 1786, in *CMPDA,* 16 March 1786.

23. Barnwell, ed., "Diary of Timothy Ford," p. 195; see also *CnHd,* 16 Nov. 1786.

24. *GSSC,* 29 Sept. 1785; Farr to ____, 27 Aug. 1785, R.W. Gibbes Autograph Book, South Caroliniana Library, USC; House of Representatives, 30 Sept. and 10 Oct. 1785, in *CEG,* 30 Sept. and 10 Oct. 1785. Thomas Farr was a member of the legislature but not present at the special session.

25. House of Representatives, 5 Oct. 1785, in *CEG,* 18 Oct. 1785. The colonial measure to prohibit the slave trade took the form of high duties on imported slaves. Ramsay had supported John Laurens's attempt to raise Negro troops.

26. House of Representatives, 1 Oct. and 5 Oct. 1785, in *CEG,* 1 Oct. and 18 Oct. 1785.

27. The votes were forty-seven to fifty-one and forty-eight to sixty-three. *Ibid.*

28. House Journal, 7 Oct. 1785; Senate Journal, 8 Oct. 1785. Slaves were still being sold so quickly in the summer of 1785 that by 13 Sept. news had already arrived in Newport of the sale of 133 slaves who had entered Charleston in mid-August. Only 7, "ruffage," were unsold. Jacob Rodriguez Rivera to Capt. Nathaniel Briggs, 13 Sept. 1785, Marcus, ed., *American Jewry: Documents: Eighteenth Century,* pp. 446–447.

29. House of Representatives, 29 Sept. 1785, in *CEG,* 29 Sept. 1785.

30. *GSSC,* 19 Sept. 1785.

31. House of Representatives, 21 Feb. 1786, in *CMPDA,* 22 Feb. 1786.

32. Guerard's plan is printed in *CEG,* 4 Oct. 1785; for the debate on it see *CEG,* 29 Sept. 1785. Other states had already considered fighting the depression with paper money acts. Pennsylvania passed such a bill in the spring of 1785. Jensen, *The New Nation,* pp. 314–323.

33. *CEG,* 1 Oct. 1785.

34. *CEG,* 3 Oct. 1785.

35. Cooper and McCord, eds. *Statutes of South Carolina,* IV, 714.

36. *Ibid.,* pp. 710–712; the bill was introduced by Thomas Pinckney; it was essentially the same as Pendleton's earlier version, except that Pendleton had called for transferring property at two-thirds its value. *CEG,* 29 Sept. and 6 Oct. 1785.

37. Sirmans, *Colonial South Carolina,* pp. 142, 154, 166.

38. *GSSC,* 10 Nov. 1785; "Extract of a letter from a merchant in Charleston, . . . 16th of July, 1786," *Mass. Gaz.,* 12 Jan. 1787.

39. "Occurrences from 5 January to 2 February 1787," Endorsed Intelligence from New York, 12 March 1787, from Sir George Youngs, FO 4/5, BPRO, LC transcripts; *PaPDA,* 16 June 1787; *Mass. Gaz.,* 12 Jan. 1787. Thomas Bee mentioned in the lower house that people were buying pine barren to offer to their creditors. *CMPDA,* 22 Feb. 1786. There was precedent for the "infamous" law. Richard Pares described similar legislation in England's West Indian colonies. *Merchants and Planters* (Cambridge, 1960), p. 46. Massachusetts passed a valuation act in 1640. Property seized for debt was to be valued by three "understanding and indifferent men." But that law allowed the creditor to choose the property. Bernard Bailyn, *The New England Merchants in the Seventeenth Century* (Cambridge, Mass., 1955), p. 48.

40. Russell to Christopher Champlin, 6 March 1786, *Commerce of Rhode Island, 1726–1800* (Massachusetts Historical Society, *Collections* 69–70 [1914–1915]), II, 274; Russell to Stephen Deblois, 8 March 1786 and 7 April 1786, Slavery Mss., Box II, NYHS; Kinloch to Thomas Boone, 14 March 1786, Gilbert, ed., "Letters of Francis Kinloch," p. 99; Lloyd to T.B. Smith, 15 April 1786, John Lloyd Letters, Charleston Library Society.

41. House of Representatives, 21 Feb. 1786, in *CMPDA,* 22 Feb. 1786.

42. *CnHd,* 16 Nov. 1786.

43. Cooper and McCord, eds., *Statutes of South Carolina,* IV, 725–726; Russell to Stephen Deblois, 7 April 1786, Slavery Mss., Box II, NYHS.

44. "Message to the Legislature," House Journal, 26 Sept. 1785.

45. The individual tax returns for Lexington County and the people between the Broad and Catawba are in Tax Returns, 1788, SCA. The Clarendon County tax list is in the South Caroliniana Library, USC; it is undated but the total corresponds with what is listed for Clarendon on the "Amount of Taxes paid into the Treasury for the year 1788," in the SCA file. For the land sales see the "Account of lands granted in the Secretary's Office from the 16th day of July 1784 . . . to the first day of January 1787," SCA. The individual land sales,

listed alphabetically and then by date, are in the Treasury Book of Land Office Accounts and General Taxes Received, SCA.

46. Christ Church return, 1788, Tax Returns, SCA.

47. The loans are listed in the Mortgage Books and Loan Office Books, SCA. Some people borrowed more than the maximum £250 allowed by the law. Frequently a few people joined together in one transaction and borrowed more than £250. For example, on 17 May 1786, Richard and Wade Hampton and James Webber borrowed £750. That same day Wade Hampton joined with four others to borrow £1,000. Four days before, he and Thomas Taylor borrowed £250, while on 19 May he joined with John Lawson to borrow £125 and with two other people to borrow £500. Each such multiple transaction listed the names and residences of the borrowers. I simply divided the sum borrowed by the number of people involved, and credited each district with its share. That may not be accurate since the people may not have been borrowing equal amounts, but there was no other way of handling the multiple entries. The loan office books have 381 entries for the period between 21 March and 1 Aug. 1786, but about 450 people were involved.

48. On the district auditors see Higgins. "Financial History of South Carolina," p. 176.

49. House of Representatives, 16 Feb. 1787, in *Mass. Gaz.*, 20 March 1787.

50. Cooper and McCord, eds., *Statutes of South Carolina,* IV, 590, 592, 706, 709.

51. In addition to the petitions from Orangeburg, and Lancaster and Chesterfield, see the petition from the Inhabitants of the Great and Little Lynches Creeks, 17 Jan. 1789, General Assembly, Petitions, 1789 #105, SCA.

52. House of Representatives, 22 Oct. 1788, in *CGDA,* 3 Nov. 1788.

53. Senate, 17 Feb. 1786, in *CMPDA,* 18 Feb. 1786; *CMPDA,* 24 March 1786, and 30 Jan. 1787. A bill to prohibit the slave trade which had been defeated during the spring meeting of the legislature in 1785 was brought up again at the fall meeting.

54. Senate, 17 Feb. 1786, in *CMPDA,* 18 Feb. 1786; Senate Journal, 22 Feb. 1786; House of Representatives, 21 Feb. 1786, in *CEG,* 21 Feb. 1786; on Rutledge's debts, see Ward to Isaac King, 14 May 1785, Joshua Ward Letters, South Caroliniana Library, USC.

55. House of Representatives, 21 Feb. and 28 Feb. 1786; in *CMPDA,* 22 Feb. 1786, and *CnHd,* 2 March 1786.

56. *CMPDA,* 30 Jan. 1787.

57. Senate, 12 Feb. 1787, in *CMPDA,* 13 Feb. 1787. Perhaps while ruling on the act in 1787, Burke recalled a remark he had made in 1786; not even "5000 troops," he then said, "could enforce obedience to the Common Pleas." House of Representatives, 21 Feb. 1786, in *CMPDA,* 22 Feb. 1786.

58. Gervais and Owen to John De Neufville, 16 Aug. 1786, in John De Neufville Papers, LC.

59. House of Representatives, 15 March 1786, in *CMPDA,* 16 March 1786; Senate Journal, 21 March and 22 March 1786; *CMPDA,* 23 March 1786; Rogers, *Evolution of a Federalist,* pp. 139–140.

60. *CEG,* 30 March 1786; *CMPDA,* 1 April 1786.

61. *PaPDA,* 16 June and 22 June 1786; Notes on the state debt, Pierce Butler Papers, Box 6 (South Carolina Legislature), HSP. The estimate of imports in these notes corresponds quite closely with that given by "Appius" in *SGSC,* 5 March 1787, if one adds to the newspaper's figures the value of imported slaves.

62. *PaPDA,* 22 May, 29 June, and 19 Aug. 1786. In September 1786 the depreciation was 30 percent. According to Gervais and Owen, the decline was caused by traders from Philadelphia and New York who arrived in Charleston with much-needed corn and, finding no produce to carry back, understandably demanded specie rather than the Carolina medium.

By November, however, when the new crop of rice began appearing on the market, resulting in a greater demand for the paper, part of the value was recovered. The depreciation then was 20 percent. Gervais and Owen to John De Neufville, 15 Sept. 1786, and Gervais and Owen to Leonard De Neufville, 2 Nov. 1786, John De Neufville Papers, LC; *PaPDA,* 15 Nov. 1786.

63. *CEG,* 3 Oct. 1785; Senate Journal, 22 March 1787; *Mass. Gaz.,* 16 Feb. 1787. In 1788 Pierce Butler objected to Ramsay's "extraordinary ideas on the magic power of brisk circulation." *CGDA,* 13 Feb. 1788.

64. Senate Journal, 19 Feb. 1787; House Journal, 19 Feb. and 12 March 1787; Ramsay to Henry Laurens, 26 July 1787, Society Collections, HSP.

65. For the debates, see *Mass. Gaz.,* 23 March and 27 March 1787.

66. *Mass. Gaz.,* 27 March 1787.

67. The quotation is from Ward to Isaac King, 28 March 1787, Joshua Ward Letters, South Caroliniana Library, USC.

68. Cooper and McCord, eds., *Statutes of South Carolina,* V, 36–38; Miller to Lord Carmarthen, 10 July 1787, FO 4/5, BPRO, LC transcripts; Gadsden to George Washington, 13 May 1787, Walsh, ed., *Writings of Gadsden,* p. 242.

69. House Journal, 17 March 1787.

70. Miller to Lord Carmarthen, 10 July 1787, FO 4/5, BPRO, LC transcripts.

71. Forrest McDonald described the special session and its work in the following way: "About a hundred legislators, almost all from the lowcountry (the backcountry did not even bother to send representatives), gathered in Charleston on September 27, 1785. Under the leadership of the Rutledges, the Pinckneys, Ralph Izard, Pierce Butler, and others high in the aristocracy, the legislature enacted a radical debtor-relief program over the feeble protests or resignation of the merchants and backcountry planters." *E Pluribus Unum,* p. 104. His account in *We the People,* p. 210, is the same. He is right in emphasizing the lowcountry's role in the passage of debtor legislation, but wrong in singling out individuals. Pierce Butler did not attend the session, Ralph Izard and Edward Rutledge worked hard only for a prohibition of the slave trade, John Rutledge and Charles Cotesworth Pinckney fought against paper money, and both denounced the "pine barren" act in 1786.

72. Cooper and McCord, eds., *Statutes of South Carolina,* V, 37.

73. Ramsay to Jefferson, 7 April 1787, Boyd, ed., *Jefferson Papers,* XI, 279.

NOTES
CHAPTER TEN

1. David Ramsay to Thomas Jefferson, 7 April 1787, Boyd, ed., *Jefferson Papers,* XI, 279; Christopher Gadsden to George Washington, 13 May 1787, Walsh, ed., *Writings of Gadsden,* p. 242; see also Henry William Desaussure to Reverend Jedidiah Morse, 12 Sept. 1787, Gratz Collection, HSP; Thomas Pinckney to John Adams, 10 July 1787, Adams, ed., *Works of John Adams,* VIII, 443.

2. Laurens to John Lewis Gervais, 4 March 1784, South Carolina and Miscellaneous, Bound Volume, Bancroft Transcripts, NYPL; see also Laurens to John Mathews, 9 March 1784, *ibid.;* Ralph Izard to Thomas Jefferson, 1 July 1786, "Letters of Ralph Izard," p. 198; *GSSC,* 4 March 1784; Jensen, *The New Nation,* p. 402. In 1782 the Jacksonborough legislature, which was not controlled by the lowcountry, granted Congress the right to levy a 5 percent impost. Two years later, by an overwhelming vote of eighty-seven to twenty-eight, legislators passed again a similar bill. The act was not to go into effect until the other states passed the same kind of legislation. *GSSC,* 18 March 1784; *Providence Gazette & Country Journal,* 17 April 1784; David Ramsay to Reverend Dr. Gordon, 23 June 1784, Ramsay folder, NYPL. The legislature had repealed the grant of 1782 in 1783, but that action came after Virginia repealed its law and after General Greene had provoked Carolinians with some outspoken critcisms. The repeal did not represent permanent anti-Congress feeling. *PaPGA,* 26 April 1783; Greene to Charles Pettit, 3 April 1783, Joseph Reed Papers, NYHS.

3. *CEG,* 20 Sept. 1786; Minutes, Charleston Chamber of Commerce, 19 May 1784, 13 July and 1 Aug. 1785, SCHS. For an account of a general meeting of citizens called by the Chamber of Commerce, see *SCGPA,* 13 Aug. 1785. See also *GSSC,* 1 Sept. 1785; *CEG,* 11 Oct. 1785; House Journal, 26 Sept. 1785; Senate Journal, 29 Sept. 1785.

4. House Journal, 11 Oct. 1785; *CEG,* 11 Oct. 1785; House of Representatives, 3 Feb. and 8 Feb. 1786, in *CMPDA,* 4 Feb. and 9 Feb. 1786. Some accounts of the debates in the lower house also appeared in the *PaPDA,* 10 March 1786. For Camden's petition, see General Assembly, Petitions, 1786 #57, SCA; *CEG,* 4 Feb. 1786.

5. *SCGPA,* 13 Aug. 1785; Brailsford and Morris to Thomas Jefferson, 31 Oct. 1787, Walsh, ed., "Letters of Morris & Brailsford," pp. 134–138; Senate Journal, 25 Feb. 1788; Walsh, *Charleston's Sons of Liberty,* p. 127.

6. *GSSC,* 12 Aug. 1784.

7. Senate Journal, 6 Feb. 1786; *CMPDA,* 9 Feb. 1786.

8. Farrand, ed., *Records of the Federal Convention,* II, 452, I, 30–31.

9. Robert L. Meriwether, "John Rutledge," *DAB,* XVI, 258–260; J.G. DeR Hamilton, "Charles Cotesworth Pinckney," *DAB,* XIV, 614–616; see also Zahniser, *Charles Cotesworth Pinckney.* Thomas Pinckney, Charles Cotesworth's brother, was governor of South Carolina when the convention met. Louis Otto, the French chargé d'affaires, described Rutledge as "the proudest and most imperious man in the United States." Quoted in Clinton Rossiter, *1787: The Grand Convention* (New York, 1966), p. 130. Henry Laurens was also elected to the Convention, but he decided not to attend. He was sixty-three, his health poor, and he had undoubtedly had enough of politics and travel.

10. J. Harold Easterby, "Charles Pinckney," *DAB,* XIV, 611–614.

11. Robert L. Meriwether, "Pierce Butler," *DAB,* III, 364–365. On the education of Butler's son in England, see the correspondence from Butler to Rev. Weeden Butler, Add. Mss., 16,603, BM. By 1789 Butler was apparently opposed politically to the Rutledges and Pinckneys. J.B. Cutting to [John Rutledge, Jr.,], 21 Feb. 1789, John Rutledge, Jr., Papers, UNC.

12. Kinloch to Thomas Boone, 8 July 1786, Felix Gilbert, ed., "Letters of Kinloch," p. 102; Thomas Pinckney to Harriott Pinckney Horry, 16 Sept. 1786, quoted in Rogers, *Evolution of a Federalist,* p. 143; Edward Rutledge to John Jay, 12 Nov. 1786, Johnston, ed., *Correspondence of Jay,* III, 217. For the travelers see Rogers, *Evolution of a Federalist,* pp. 141–142.

13. Gorham is quoted in Edmund Cody Burnett, *The Continental Congress* (New York, 1941), p. 644; see also Jensen, *The New Nation,* pp. 415, 418. For New Jersey's actions, including its refusal to meet the requisition even after rescinding the February resolution, see Richard P. McCormick, *Experiment in Independence: New Jersey in the Critical Period, 1781–1789* (New Brunswick, 1950), pp. 218–251.

14. Pinckney's ideas are from a pamphlet he wrote apparently from a speech prepared for the Constitutional Convention. The "Observations on the Plan of Government Submitted to the Federal Convention in Philadelphia, on the 28th of May, 1787," was reprinted in the *SGSC* in October and November 1787. It is also printed in Farrand, ed., *Records of the Federal Convention,* III, 106–123. The quotation is on page 106.

15. Elliot, *Debates,* IV, 255–274, 281; Butler to Elbridge Gerry, 3 March 1788, Elbridge Gerry Personal Miscellaneous Papers, LC.

16. Charles Pinckney, "Observations," in Farrand, ed., *Records of the Federal Convention,* III, 115; Elliot, *Debates,* IV, 282, 327.

17. *CMPDA,* 4 Feb. 1786.

18. *SCGGA,* 16 Sept. 1784; Alexander Gillon to Nathanael Greene, 11 April 1783, Naval History Collection, NYHS; *GSSC,* 8 April and 29 April 1784.

19. For the views of Rutledge, C.C. Pinckney, and Butler on debtor legislation see chapter eight; for Charles Pinckney, see Elliot, *Debates,* IV, 336. According to Forrest McDonald, "all four delegates who attended the Convention had supported paper money and debtor-relief laws." *We the People,* p. 35. He is obviously wrong.

20. Farrand, ed., *Records of the Federal Convention,* I, 48, 50, 58, 132, 137, 142–143, 155, 359–360. On fifteen of sixteen important votes, the South Carolina delegates voted together. McDonald, *We the People,* Table, pp. 102–103.

21. Farrand, ed., *Records of the Federal Convention,* I, 358–360. After South Carolina voters chose two opponents of the Constitution to represent them in 1789, Charles Pinckney called election by the people "the greatest blot in the constitution." Pinckney to Rufus King, 26 Jan. 1789, C.R. King, *Life and Correspondence of Rufus King* (6 vols., New York, 1894–1900), I, 359.

22. Farrand, ed., *Records of the Federal Convention,* I, 215–216, II, 290, 293.

23. *Ibid.,* I, 386, 391, 428, 429, 434. Rutledge's opinion is not recorded.

24. Elliot, *Debates,* IV, 302; Wood, *Creation of the American Republic,* pp. 504–505, 510–511.

25. On Tucker's duel and election, see Rogers, *Evolution of a Federalist,* p. 28; for his support of a state convention, see his pamphlet, *Conciliatory Hints, Attempting by a Fair State of Matters, to Remove Party Prejudice* (Charleston, 1784); Grimké to General Harrington, 16 Jan. 1789, Harrington Collection, UNC ; Pinckney to Rufus King, 26 Jan. 1789, King. *Life of King,* I, 359.

26. Ramsay to Benjamin Lincoln, 29 Jan. 1788, in Francis Bowen, *Life of Benjamin Lincoln* (Boston, 1855), p. 411; Desaussure to Reverend Jedidiah Morse, 11 Feb. 1788, Desaussure Mss., NYHS; Butler to Elbridge Gerry, 3 March 1788, Elbridge Gerry Papers, LC. Apparently Reverend Morse thought enough of Desaussure's letter to send copies to newspapers. Extracts appeared in at least two papers: *The New-Haven Gazette, and the Connecticut Magazine,* 6 March 1788, and the *PaPDA,* 14 March 1788.

27. David Ramsay to Benjamin Lincoln, 29 Jan. 1788, in Bowen, *Lincoln*, p. 410; Ramsay to Benjamin Rush, 17 Feb. 1788, Robert L. Brunhouse, ed., "David Ramsay on the Ratification of the Constitution in South Carolina, 1787–1788," *JSH* 9 (1934): 553; Henry William Desaussure to Reverend Jedidiah Morse, 11 Feb. 1788, Desaussure Mss., NYHS. While the legislature unanimously agreed to call a convention, it decided to hold it in Charleston by only a one vote margin, with Lowndes voting in the majority.

28. Rutledge to Jay, 20 June 1788, Johnston, ed., *Correspondence of Jay*, III, 339.

29. Burke to John Lamb, 23 June 1788, Lamb Papers, NYHS; Jno. Wilson to Samuel Wilson, 10 July 1788, Glenn Collection, UNC. This is a typed copy of a letter still in a private collection.

30. Rogers, *Evolution of a Federalist*, p. 154.

31. Elliot, *Debates*, IV, 340; Charles W. Roll, Jr., "We, Some of the People: Apportionment in the Thirteen State Conventions Ratifying the Constitution," *JAH* 56 (1969): Table IV, 26.

32. Main, *The Antifederalists*, pp. 218–219; *SGSC*, 29 May 1788.

33. Jno. Wilson to Samuel Wilson, 10 July 1788, Glenn Collection, UNC.

34. Burke to John Lamb, 23 June 1788, Lamb Papers, NYHS.

35. Elliot, *Debates*, IV, 316–317; *PaPDA*, 5 March 1788.

36. McDonald, *We the People*, pp. 217–220, 228–229. For dates of admission, see O'Neall, *Bench and Bar*, II, 601–602; for Burke, *DAB*, III, 280. McDonald lists John Bowman as a merchant, indicating that he was a slave trader. I have found only one record in the customs books indicating that Bowman imported slaves. They might well have been for his own large plantations. McDonald also attempts to increase the importance of Antifederalist merchants by writing that they "were the principal leaders of the opposition in the ratifying convention." *We the People*, p. 215. If so, it was completely silent leadership. I have found no record that any one of the four Antifederalist merchants he names, including Bowman, ever spoke at the ratifying convention.

37. The property holdings are based on McDonald's information. My interpretation of the data, however, is different from McDonald's. It hardly seems accurate to say that "the Federalists and the anti-Federalists were both largely men of wealth and [that] they had, proportionately, about the same amounts of the same kinds of property, the most important of which were land and slaves." Not when such a greater percentage of Antifederalists than Federalists were small farmers and not when there was such a great difference in slaveholding, even between large Federalist and large Antifederalist planters. Nor does it seem accurate to say that "only a handful of delegates held more than $5,000 in securities. . . ." Twenty-two (eighteen Federalists and four Antifederalists) is more than a handful. The quotations are from *We the People* pp. 234–235. The public securities held by Carolinians may have played a role in diminishing opposition to, or creating support, for, the Constitution. At Philadelphia John Rutledge had argued that assumption of state debts was necessary since the states had given up the impost, an argument later repeated before the new Congress by Aedanus Burke, an Antifederalist and a Rutledge opponent. Farrand, ed., *Records of the Federal Convention*, II, 327; Wolfe, *Jeffersonian Democracy in South Carolina*, p.56n.

38. To the best of my knowledge, no one, in trying to analyze South Carolina's opposing sides in economic terms, has pointed out the obvious: that the economic division between Federalists and Antifederalists outside the ratifying convention was even greater than the marked division within it.

39. Boddie, *Williamsburg*, pp. 136, 173–175.

40. Elliot, *Debates*, IV, 273–274; Ramsay to Benjamin Lincoln, 29 Jan. 1788, in Bowen, *Lincoln*, pp. 410–412.

41. Farrand, ed., *Records of the Federal Convention,* II, 420, 449.

42. *Ibid.,* 451. The quotation is Butler's. For the compromise, see Merrill Jensen, *The Making of the American Constitution* (Princeton, 1964), pp. 91–94.

43. Elliot, *Debates,* IV, 286. Carolinians had not complained about the loss of fugitive slaves, but some people might have remembered that a Massachusetts court had freed slaves stolen by the British in 1779 and recaptured by a Massachusetts vessel. The slaves' owners complained that it was "a measure mischievous & ruinous to these southern States." Governor Benjamin Guerard told the Carolina legislature in 1785 that Massachusetts's action "may materially injure individuals of our country & the country herself eventually," adding, too, the revealing comment that the South Carolina legislature would have quickly returned the blacks and not have worried about "any refined judicial & religiously scrupulous opinion." Guerard to [the Senate], 23 Feb. 1784, and Guerard to Mr. Speaker, 24 Jan. 1785, Governors Messages, SCA.

44. Elliot, *Debates,* IV, 265. Charles Pinckney led the fight in the Confederation Congress, united Southern representatives, and defeated Jay's scheme. Nevertheless, Pinckney was content with the two-thirds requirement in the Constitution. Jensen, *The New Nation,* pp. 171–173; Burnett, *The Continental Congress,* p. 658.

45. Elliot, *Debates,* IV, 319, 326; Ramsay to Benjamin Rush, 10 Nov. 1787, Brunhouse, ed., "Ramsay on the Constitution," p. 552.

46. Elliot, *Debates,* IV, 338.

47. *Ibid.,* 313; *SGSC,* 28 Jan. 1788.

48. Burke to John Lamb, 23 June 1788, Lamb Papers, NYHS.

49. Kinloch to Thomas Boone, 26 May 1788, Gilbert, ed., "Letters of Kinloch," pp. 104–105; David Ramsay to Benjamin Rush, 17 Feb. 1788, Brunhouse, ed., "Ramsay on the Constitution," p. 557; *CGDA,* 10 March 1788.

50. Elliot, *Debates,* IV, 313, 332–333, 337.

51. *Ibid.,* 274.

52. Butler was then talking about a valuation law. House of Representatives, 16 Oct. 1788, in *CGDA,* 17 Oct. 1788.

53. It was James Lincoln who, lamenting "the want of [his] abilities" to oppose the Constitution and "such men," praised their "eloquence and learning." Elliot, *Debates,* IV, 312.

54. Charles Pinckney, "Observations," Farrand, ed., *Records of the Federal Convention,* III, 115.

55. Elliot, *Debates,* IV, 337; *CGDA,* 20 May 1788; Burke, *An Address to the Freemen of South Carolina,* p. 15; Elliot, *Debates,* IV, 271.

56. *CGDA,* 19 May and 20 May 1788. Many of these Antifederalist objections are not reported in Elliot's *Debates,* which historians have generally relied on. They are, however, reported in the daily accounts of the ratifying convention given in the *City Gazette.*

57. Elliot, *Debates,* IV, 314.

58. *Ibid.,* IV, 313; *CGDA,* 20 May 1788; *CMPDA,* 9 Feb. 1786; Farrand, ed., *Records of the Federal Convention,* I, 409.

59. *CGDA,* 20 May 1788.

60. Elliot, *Debates,* IV, 288.

61. Rutledge's remark on the constitution of 1778 is quoted in Ramsay, *Revol. of SC,* I, 136; for his remark in the convention see Farrand, ed., *Records of the Federal Convention,* I, 359.

62. Elliot, *Debates,* IV, 304.

63. *Ibid.,* IV, 319, 327, 329.

64. *Ibid.*, 327, 302.

65. *CGDA,* 19 May and 20 May 1788; Butler to Rev. [Weeden] Butler, 5 May 1788, Butler Papers, Add. Mss., 16,603, BM.

66. *SCGPA,* 13 Aug. 1785; *CnHd,* 26 Nov. 1784.

67. Brailsford and Morris to Thomas Jefferson, 31 Oct. 1787, Walsh, ed., "Letters of Morris and Brailsford," pp. 134–138.

68. Elliot, *Debates,* IV, 157, 169.

69. Pinckney to Rufus King, 21 June 1788, King Mss., NYHS.

NOTES

CHAPTER ELEVEN

1. Elliot, *Debates,* IV, 338; Burke to John Lamb, 23 June 1788, Lamb Papers, NYHS; *CGDA,* 24 May 1788; see also Charles Cotesworth Pinckney to Rufus King, 21 June 1788, Rufus King Mss., NYHS. According to Alexander Garden, Aedanus Burke, traveling in the backcountry after the Constitution was ratified, asked some wagon drivers their opinion of the new government. Their reply was unanimous: "We abominate it, and to such a degree, that should the President . . . on any emergency . . . call us into the field, we would refuse obedience to a man." Burke lectured them on their civil responsibilities, while admiring their independence. *Anecdotes of the Revolutionary War,* pp. 178–179.

2. *SGSC,* 2 June 1788; *CGDA,* 11 June and 19 June 1788.

3. Izard to Thomas Jefferson, 3 April 1789, "Letters of Ralph Izard," pp. 203–204; Rutledge to John Jay, 20 June 1788, Johnston, ed., *Correspondence of Jay,* III, 339; Kinloch to Thomas Boone, 26 May 1788, Gilbert, ed., "Letters of Kinloch," p. 105.

4. Grimké to General Harrington, 16 Jan. 1789, Harrington Collection, UNC.

5. "Civis" [David Ramsay], "An Address to the Freemen of South Carolina on the subject of the Federal Constitution, Proposed by the Convention which met in Philadelphia, May, 1787," reprinted in Paul L. Ford, *Pamphlets on the Constitution of the United States* (Brooklyn, N.Y., 1888), pp. 373–380; Ramsay to Lincoln, 29 Jan. 1788, in Bowen, *Lincoln,* p. 411; Ramsay to Benjamin Rush, 21 April 1788, Brunhouse, ed., "Ramsay on the Constitution," p. 554.

6. Charles Cotesworth Pinckney to Rufus King, 21 June 1788, Rufus King Mss., NYHS.

7. House of Representatives, 23 Oct. 1788, in *CGDA,* 8 Nov. 1788.

8. House Journal, 21 Feb. 1788; on the legislation of 1785 see chapter eight above.

9. Arthur Bryan to George Bryan, 9 April 1788, George Bryan Papers, HSP.

10. House of Representatives, 16 Feb. 1787, in *Mass. Gaz.,* 27 March 1787.

11. See, for example, *CGDA,* 11 Feb., 13 Feb., and 20 Feb. 1788.

12. Elliot, *Debates,* IV, 266, 290; House of Representatives, 20 Feb. 1788, in *CGDA,* 23 Feb. 1788.

13. Elliot, *Debates,* IV, 266, 270.

14. For both petitions, see General Assembly, Petitions, 1787, 1788, SCA.

15. *CGDA,* 20 Feb. and 23 Feb. 1788.

16. House of Representatives, 18 Feb. 1788, in *PaPDA,* 20 March 1788; House of Representatives, 20 Feb. 1788, in *CGDA,* 23 Feb. 1788.

17. Butler to Elbridge Gerry, 3 March 1788, Elbridge Gerry Papers, LC; *CGDA,* 13 Feb. 1788; Butler to Thomas Fitzsimons, 15 Feb. 1788, Gratz Collection, Old Congress, HSP. H.W. Desaussure wrote that some people who thought the debt enormous and others who simply wanted not to pay their debts "have called out ruin — destruction, opposition, civil war & every other evil." To Jedidiah Morse, 11 Feb. 1788, Desaussure Mss., NYHS. New Jersey's valuation law was repealed eight months after it was enacted. McCormick, *Experiment in Independence,* p. 205. In a series of articles in February 1788, "A PILGRIM" found historical justification for legislative action in the fact that the Romans had interfered between creditors and debtors. *CGDA,* 4 Feb., 5 Feb., 11 Feb., and 12 Feb. 1788.

18. *CGDA,* 21 Feb. and 23 Feb. 1788.

19. Senate Journal, 18 Feb. 1788; House Journal, 21 Feb. 1788.

20. Senate Journal, 12 Feb. and 18 Feb. 1788.

21. Rutledge to ______, 4 March 1788, Edward Rutledge Personal Papers Misc., LC.

22. Ramsay to Benjamin Lincoln, 31 March 1788, *Benjamin Lincoln Papers,* Microfilm, reel 9, MHS; House Journal, 21 Oct. 1788; Senate Journal, 17 Oct. 1788.

23. Memorial of Aedanus Burke to the Senate, 1 March 1786, General Assembly, Petitions, 1786 #71, SCA; *CnHd,* 30 Sept. 1785; *CGDA,* 16 Oct. 1788.

24. See General Assembly, Petitions, 1788, #24, #83, SCA.

25. House of Representatives, 21 Oct. 1788, in *CGDA,* 24 Oct. 1788; David Ramsay to Benjamin Lincoln, 20 June 1788, *Benjamin Lincoln Papers,* Microfilm, reel 9, MHS; House of Representatives, 21 Oct. 1788, in *CGDA,* 28 Oct. 1788; Arthur Bryan to George Bryan, 9 April 1788, George Bryan Papers, HSP.

26. *Boston Gazette & the Country Journal,* 25 Oct. 1784; PaPDA, 4 April 1786; *Gentleman's Magazine* 58 (1788): 460, quoted in Thomas S. Ashton, *Economic Fluctuations in England, 1700–1800* (Oxford, 1959), p. 166n; *CGDA,* 12 July 1788; see also *CGDA,* 14 July 1788.

27. David Ramsay to Benjamin Lincoln, 20 June 1788, *Benjamin Lincoln Papers,* Microfilm, reel 9, MHS; House of Representatives, 21 Oct. 1788, in *CGDA,* 28 Oct. and 29 Oct. 1788.

28. Ramsay had noted in March that creditors had "generally foreborn to bring suits" in order to prevent new debtor legislation. To Benjamin Lincoln, 31 March 1788, *Benjamin Lincoln Papers,* Microfilm, reel 9, MHS.

29. House of Representatives, 22 Oct. 1788, in *CGDA,* 3 Nov. 1788; for the sentiments of the backcountry, see General Assembly, Petitions, 1788, SCA.

30. Inhabitants of St. Bartholomews Parish, Petition . . . 7 Oct. 1788, General Assembly, Petitions, 1788 #3, SCA.

31. House Journal, 21 Oct. 1788.

32. House of Representatives, 21 Oct. 1788, in *CGDA,* 27 Oct. 1788.

33. House of Representatives, 21 Oct. 1788, in *CGDA,* 29 Oct. 1788; *CGDA,* 8 Nov. 1788. David Ramsay wrote Henry Laurens that "indigo will not sell at all only in small quantities to northern traders." 7 Dec. 1787, Society Collections, HSP.

34. In 1787 Carolina exported 65,195 barrels of rice and 974,050 pounds of indigo, in 1788, 82,400 barrels of rice and 833,550 pounds of indigo. Enclosure in George Miller to the Duke of Leeds, 28 Jan. 1790, BT 6/21, BPRO.

35. Tobacco exports from South Carolina were: 2,305 hogsheads in 1785, 3,929 hogsheads in 1786, 5,493 hogsheads in 1787, and 5,993 hogsheads in 1788. *Ibid.* For the vote on the slave trade, see House Journal, 17 March 1787.

36. Rutledge to ______, 4 March 1788, Edward Rutledge Personal Papers Misc., LC; House of Representatives, 20 Feb. and 22 Oct. 1788, in *CGDA,* 23 Feb. and 4 Nov. 1788.

37. House of Representatives, 20 Feb. 1788, in *CGDA,* 23 Feb. 1788; *PaPDA,* 16 June and 22 June 1786; *SGSC,* 5 March 1787; for Pinckney's remarks made in the House of Representatives, 21 Oct. 1788, see *CGDA,* 31 Oct. 1788.

38. House of Representatives, 21 Oct. 1788, in *CGDA,* 28 Oct. 1788.

39. House of Representatives, 21 Oct. and 23 Oct. 1788, in *CGDA,* 24 Oct. and 10 Nov. 1788.

40. *CGDA,* 24 Oct., 27 Oct., 8 Nov., and 13 Nov. 1788. Strangely, Charles Pinckney thought the Constitution binding but argued that intervention was necessary; he said also, however, that the other delegates to Philadelphia did not think that the constitution was already partly operative. *CGDA,* 15 Nov. 1788.

41. House of Representatives, 21 Oct. 1788, in *CGDA,* 24 Oct. 1788; Senate Journal, 20 Oct. 1788.

42. House of Representatives, 21 Oct. 1788, in *CGDA,* 28 Oct. 1788.

43. House of Representatives, 21 Oct. 1788, in *CGDA,* 27 Oct. 1788.

44. *CGDA,* 13 Feb. and 21 Feb. 1789. Lincoln also tried to make the money more available to backcountry settlers by suggesting that "for the greater ease of the citizens, . . . commissioners be appointed and the money loaned out in each district. . . ."

45. General Assembly, Petitions, 1788, SCA; House of Representatives, 16 Oct. and 22 Oct. 1788, in *CGDA,* 17 Oct. and 4 Nov. 1788; House Journal, 23 Oct. 1788.

46. Cooper and McCord, eds., *Statutes of South Carolina,* V, 88–92; *CGDA,* 11 Nov. and 20 Nov. 1788. In Congress, Smith worked to convince people that the bill was "absolutely necessary for the salvation of the country." Smith to Edward Rutledge, 21 June 1789, William Loughton Smith Papers, SCHS. For a protest from British merchants, see their Memorial to the Marquis of Carmarthen, 24 Feb. 1789, FO 4/7, BPRO, LC transcripts.

47. House Journal, 2 Nov. 1788.

48. House of Representatives, 22 Oct. 1788, in *CGDA,* 4 Nov. 1788.

49. *CGDA,* 20 Nov. 1788.

50. Ward to Isaac King, 2 Jan. 1789, Joshua Ward Letters, South Caroliniana Library, USC; *CGDA,* 13 Nov. 1788. In 1789 some people in Edgefield County, Ninety Six District, complained that property was still selling at one-fifth or one-sixth its value and that they needed a circulating medium. Inhabitants of Edgefield County, Petition . . . 17 Oct. 1788, General Assembly, Petitions, 1788 #3, SCA.

51. Schoepf, *Travels in the Confederation,* p. 198.

52. House of Representatives, 12 Feb. 1789, in *SGSC,* 16 Feb. 1789.

53. *SGSC,* 7 Feb. 1788; Burke to John Lamb, 23 June 1788, Lamb Papers, NYHS; Elliot, *Debates,* IV, 317; House of Representatives, 22 Jan. 1789, in *CGDA,* 26 Jan. 1789.

54. House of Representatives, 22 Jan. 1789, in *CGDA,* 24 Jan. and 26 Jan. 1789; for Butler's appreciation of the backcountry see his letters to Rev. Weeden Butler, 18 July and 16 Nov. 1788, Butler Papers, Add. Mss., 16,603, BM.

55. House of Representatives, 22 Jan. 1789, in *CGDA,* 24 Jan. and 26 Jan. 1789; *Acts, Ordinances, and Resolves of the General Assembly of the State of South-Carolina, passed in March, 1789* (Charleston, 1789), p. 16.

56. Schaper, "Sectionalism and Representation in South Carolina," p. 380

57. Zahniser, *Charles Cotesworth Pinckney,* p. 109; see also the treatment in Starr, "The Conservative Revolution," pp. 280–282.

58. See chapter one above.

59. The quotations are from Tennent, "Historic Remarks," in Jones, "Writings of Tennent," pp. 107, 192. Fletcher Green thought that the constitution of 1778 gave the backcountry so little power that it considered remedying the situation through a foreceful revolution. *Constitutional Development,* p. 119. I have seen no contemporary evidence that justifies such a belief.

60. Green, *Constitutional Development,* pp. 119–120; *SGSC,* 7 Sept. 1786.

61. While historians have not generally seen the constitution of 1790 as a democratic advance, they have confusingly thought that the property requirements for officeholding were reduced by the new constitution. Green, *Constitutional Development,* p. 122; D. Huger Bacot, "Constitutional Progress and the Struggle for Democracy in South Carolina following the Revolution," *South Atlantic Quarterly* 24 (1925): 64; Wolfe, *Jeffersonian Democracy in South Carolina,* p. 46; Starr, "The Conservative Revolution," p. 280. Chilton Williamson, however, wrote that the property tests for officeholders "were revised drastically upward." *American Suffrage: From Property to Democracy, 1760–1860* (Princeton, 1960),

p. 132. It is easy to see why most people reached the conclusion that the requirements were reduced: the 1778 constitution expressed the property requirements in currency, the 1790 constitution in sterling. Green and Wolfe, for example, note the reduction in property requirements for governor from £10,000 to £1,500, for senator from £2,000 to £300. Neither mentions the change from currency to sterling. The convention simply rewrote the requirements in sterling. The requirement for representatives in 1778 was "the same as mentioned in the Election Act," and that meant 500 acres and ten slaves, which was the same as the requirement in 1790.

62. Again historians have incorrectly seen a change in this provision, thinking that the constitution of 1790 first allowed citizens to substitute payment of a tax as an alternative to owning land. But the constitution of 1778 granted the suffrage to people who owned fifty acres of land or a town lot, or people who paid a tax equal to the amount paid on fifty acres of land. Actually, this provision in 1790 seems to have raised the requirement although no one realized it. The tax on fifty acres in 1783 was 2s. 4p. But in 1784 the tax was changed to an advalorem rate, and the lowest tax on fifty acres was 6p. Apparently that act's potential effect on suffrage was not widely known. Perhaps the property requirement was never enforced anyway.

63. For the alien acts see Cooper and McCord, eds., *Statutes of South Carolina,* IV, 600–601, 746–747.

64. Father Carroll to Don Jose Ignacio Viar, 20 April 1790, in Thomas F. Hopkins, "St. Mary's Church, Charleston, South Carolina: The First Catholic Church in the Original Diocese of Charleston," *Charleston Year Book,* 1897, p. 438; *CGDA,* 10 July 1788.

65. For the oath requiring clergymen and teachers to deny allegiance to foreign powers, see Senate Journal, 11 Feb. 1786; for Pinckney's opposition, and the opposition of Thomas Bee, who argued that under their constitution South Carolina "was held out as an asylum for all the sons of freedom from all parts of the world," see House of Representatives, 16 Feb. 1786, in *CEG,* 16 Feb. 1786; Reese's remarks are in his *Essay on the Influence of Religion,* p. 33.

66. Smith to Rutledge, 28 June 1790, 4 July 1790, and 8 Aug. 1790, quoted in Starr, "The Conservative Revolution," pp. 281–282.

67. Edward Rutledge to Arthur Middleton, 28 Jan. 1782, Barnwell, ed., "Correspondence of Arthur Middleton" (1925): 212; *CGDA,* 20 May 1788.

68. Zahniser, *Charles Cotesworth Pinckney,* pp. 107–108; House of Representatives, 13 Feb. 1787, in *CMPDA,* 14 Feb. 1787.

69. Gadsden to Adams, 24 July 1787, Walsh, ed., *Writings of Gadsden,* p. 244; *SGSC,* 3 June 1790.

70. *SCGPA,* 29 Sept. 1784; Free inhabitants of Little River, Petition . . . 17 March 1785, General Assembly, Petitions, 1785 #105, SCA.

71. Green, *Constitutional Development,* p. 121.

72. Green wrote that "the low country stood firm to the last and prevented any reapportionment." *Constitutional Development,* p. 121. Schaper and Wolfe made similar comments. Schaper, "Sectionalism and Representation in South Carolina," p. 380; Wolfe, *Jeffersonian Democracy,* p.47.

73. House Journal, 21 Feb. 1787; House of Representatives, 12 Feb. 1789, in *SGSC,* 16 Feb. 1789.

74. Gadsden to Thomas Morris, 30 May 1790, Walsh, ed., *Writings of Gadsden,* p. 251; *City Gazette,* quoted in Starr, "The Conservative Revolution," p. 277.

75. See Letters of Acceptance and Declinature of those elected delegates to the 1790

Constitutional Convention, Governor: Correspondence Received, 1789, SCA. Only two backcountry delegates sent letters saying they would not serve. In February the governor requested that he be notified as soon as possible by people who were not going to fill their seats, but some of the letters were not sent until late March. *SGSC,* 15 Feb. 1790.

76. Schaper, "Sectionalism and Representation in South Carolina," p. 377.

77. Christopher Gadsden to Thomas Morris, 30 May 1790, Walsh, ed., *Writings of Gadsden,* pp. 251–252; Smith is quoted in Starr, "The Conservative Revolution," p. 277.

78. The quotation is from Edward Rutledge to John Jay, 21 May 1789, Johnston, ed., *Correspondence of Jay,* III, 368.

79. Richard H. Kohn, *Eagle and Sword: The Federalists and the Creation of the Military Establishment in America, 1783–1802* (New York, 1975), pp. 128–138; *Acts and Resolutions of the General Assembly of the State of South-Carolina Passed in April, 1794* (Charleston, 1794), pp. 1–7; House Journal, 18 Dec. 1793, 3 May 1794. While I have combined the votes of the distant lowcountry parishes, on both these militia votes Georgetown supported the backcountry and Beaufort the Charleston area.

80. Schaper, "Sectionalism and Representation in South Carolina," p. 426. The 1777 draft of the constitution of 1778 had provided for the popular election of sheriffs. *A Bill for Establishing the Constitution of the State of South-Carolina* (Charleston, 1777).

81. Jefferson to Thomas Mann Randolph, 5 Dec. 1800, quoted in Noble E. Cunningham, *The Jeffersonian Republicans: The Formation of Party Organization, 1789–1801* (Chapel Hill, 1957), p. 231.

82. Wolfe, *Jeffersonian Democracy,* pp. 54–155.

83. Cunningham, *The Jeffersonian Republicans,* pp. 231–234; Wolfe, *Jeffersonian Democracy,* p. 153.

84. Pinckney to Thomas Jefferson, 12 Oct. 1800 and 16 Oct. 1800, J. Franklin Jameson, ed., "South Carolina in the Presidential Election of 1800," *AHR* 4 (1898–1899): 114–115.

85. Pinckney to Jefferson, 22 Dec. 1800, *ibid.,* p. 126.

86. Zahniser, *Charles Cotesworth Pinckney,* pp. 228–229.

87. Peleg Wadsworth to Jacob Burnett, 10 Dec. 1800, quoted in Cunningham, *The Jeffersonian Republicans,* p. 239.

88. *SGSC,* 7 Feb. 1788.

89. House Journal, 23 Jan. 1787.

90. *SGSC,* 7 Feb. 1788; Burke to Governor Guerard, 14 Dec. 1784, SCA.

91. *SGSC,* 7 Feb. 1788; the reference to the "devastations" of the war is from a Winton County petition of 1788. General Assembly, Petitions, 1788 #2, SCA.

92. *SGSC,* 7 Feb. 1788.

93. Charge to the Grand Jury of Camden District, Dec. 1790, SCA.

94. *Ibid.; SCGGA,* 10 July and 27 Nov. 1784.

95. Charge to the Grand Jury of Camden District, Dec. 1790, General Assembly, Presentments, 1790, #3, SCA.

96. Alexander Gillon to Nathanael Greene, 11 April 1783, Naval History Collection, NYHS; *SCGGA,* 16 Sept. 1784.

97. Reese, *Essay on the Influence of Religion,* p. 77.

98. Representation of the People of Pendleton County, 10 July 1794, SCA.

Bibliography

PRIMARY SOURCES

Manuscripts

South Carolina Department of Archives and History, Columbia*
Book of Manifests and Entries, 1784–1787
Books of Manifests and Entries, 1787–1789:
Coasting Trade of the United States
France and Dominions
Great Britain and Dominions
Holland, Denmark, Sweden, Prussia and Dominions
Spain, Portugal and Dominions
Commissioners of the Treasury, 1778–1791, Letters Received
Confiscated Estates, Public Sales, 1782–1795 [1788]
Governor: Corresponsence Received
Journal of Treasury Department, January 1783–May 1790
Loan Office Mortgage and Bond Books
Privy Council Journals, 1783–1786
Privy Council Journal, rough copy, 1783–1789

Records of the General Assembly
Committee Reports
Election Returns
Governors Messages [and Enclosures]
Petitions
Presentments
Sainsbury Transcripts of Records in the British Public Record Office Relating to South Carolina, 1663–1782, 36 volumes
Tax Returns
Treasury Book of Land Office Accounts and General Taxes Received

South Caroliniana Library, University of South Carolina, Columbia
Ball Family Papers
Patrick Calhoun Manuscript
Clarendon County Tax List [1788]
John Lewis Gervais Papers
Robert Wilson Gibbes Autograph Book
Oliver Hart Papers
Henry Laurens Papers
Manigault Family Papers
Minute Book, St. Michael's Church, 1759–1824, WPA Transcripts
Charles Cotesworth Pinckney Papers
Thomas Pinckney Letterbook, 1779–1798
David Ramsay Manuscripts
Read Family Papers
John Rutledge Papers

*The South Carolina Department of Archives and History is currently reorganizing many of the manuscript collections listed above.

St. Paul's Parish, Board of Commissioners of Roads, Minutes, 1783–1839
St. Philip's Church Vestry Journal, 1761–1795, WPA Transcripts
Simms Collection
Vestry Book, St. John's Parish, Colleton, 1738–1817, WPA Transcripts
Joshua Ward Letters
New-York Historical Society
H. W. Desaussure Manuscripts
James Duane Papers
John Lewis Gervais Manuscripts
Rufus King Manuscripts
John Lamb Papers
Miscellaneous Manuscripts:
John Julius Pringle
Naval History Collection
Nathaniel Pendleton Papers
Joseph Reed Papers
Slavery Manuscripts, Box II
New York Public Library
Emmett Collection:
General Alexander Leslie Letterbook
Miscellaneous Letters:
Richard Beresford; William Hasell Gibbes; Richard Hutson; Ralph Izard; Joseph Kershaw; John De Neufville; William Pierce, Jr.; Charles Cotesworth Pinckney; John Mathews; John Rutledge; William Smith
Francis Marion Papers, Bancroft Transcripts
David Ramsay Folder
South Carolina and Miscellaneous, Bound Volume, Bancroft Transcripts
South Carolina Box
Historical Society of Pennsylvania, Philadelphia
George Bryan Papers
Pierce Butler Papers
Dreer Collection
Gratz Collection
Charles Francis Jenkins Collection
Henry Laurens Letterbook and Papers
Society Collections
Library of Congress
American Papers Respecting the Evacuation of Charleston, 1782
Thomas Bee Letters
British Public Record Office Transcripts, Foreign Office: FO 4/5, 6, 7
Levinius Clarkson, William Neate: Letters to Each Other and to David Van Horne
Journals of the South Carolina House of Representatives and Senate, 1783–1790 (Microfilm Collection of Early State Records)
Henry Laurens Papers
Henry and John Laurens Papers
James Madison Papers (Microfilm)
John De Neufville Papers

Personal Papers, Miscellaneous:
Elbridge Gerry; James Grant; Ralph Izard; Gouverneur Morris; Edward Rutledge; John Rutledge; William Loughton Smith
Pinckney Family Papers
William Loughton Smith Papers

Duke University
John Banks Papers
Calhoun Family Papers
James Chestnut Letters and Papers
Andrew Clow Letters
Nathanael Greene Papers
Hogg & Clayton Letterbook and Accounts, 1762–1771
James Iredell Papers
William Murrell Letterbook
John Rutledge, Jr. Papers
Josiah Edward Smith Papers
Edward Telfair Papers

University of North Carolina
Preston Davie Collection
Leonidas Chalmers Glenn Collection
Henry William Harrington Collection
George Hooper Papers
John Rutledge, Jr. Papers
Josiah Smith Letterbook

South Carolina Historical Society, Charleston
Account Book of the Commissioners of Forfeited Estates, 1782–1783
Chestnut-Miller-Manning Papers
Manigault Papers
Minutes, Charleston Chamber of Commerce
Miscellaneous Letters:
Pierce Butler; Gervais & Owen; Gen. Alexander Leslie; Nathaniel Pendleton; William Loughton Smith Papers; Waring & Hayne Accounts, 1778–1821

Charleston Library Society
Thomas Farr Letter
John Lloyd Letters
John Rutledge Papers

Charleston Museum
William Drayton Journals

Wisconsin Historical Society
Thomas Sumter Papers, Draper Manuscripts

British Museum, London
Correspondence from Pierce Butler to Rev. Weeden Butler, Additional Manuscripts, 16,603
Correspondence of William Pollard, Additional Manuscripts, 35,655, Hardwicke Papers, CCCVII

British Public Record Office, London
Board of Trade Papers:
BT 6/21
BT 6/85 American Intercourse with Great Britain, 1784–1786
BT 6/86 American Intercourse: Customs House Accounts, 1783–1784
Customs 17/8

Printed Government Records

Acts Passed at a General Assembly begun and holden at Jacksonburg, in the State of South Carolina, on the 8th of January, 1782, continued to the 26th day of February of the Same Year (Philadelphia, 1782).

Acts and Ordinances of the General Assembly of the State of South Carolina, passed in the Year 1783 [Jan. 6–Nov. 17, 1783], [Charleston, 1783].

Acts, Ordinances, and Resolves of the General Assembly of the State of South Carolina, passed in the year 1784 (Charleston, 1784).

Acts, Ordinances, and Resolves, of the General Assembly of the State of South-Carolina; passed in March, 1785 (Charleston, 1785).

[Acts and Ordinances of the General Assembly of the State of South Carolina, Sept. 20–Oct. 12, 1785], (Charleston, 1785).

Acts, Ordinances, and Resolves of the General Assembly of the State of South-Carolina, passed in March, 1786 (Charleston, 1786).

Acts, Ordinances, and Resolves, of the General Assembly of the State of South-Carolina; passed in March, 1787 (Charleston, 1787).

Acts and Ordinances of the General Assembly of the State of South-Carolina, passed in February, 1788 (Charleston, 1788).

Acts and Ordinances of the General Assembly of the State of South-Carolina, passed in October and November 1788 (Charleston, 1789).

Acts, Ordinances, and Resolves, of the General Assembly of the State of South-Carolina passed in March, 1789 (Charleston, [1789]).

Bay, Elihu Hall, *Reports of Cases Argued and Determined in the Superior Courts of Law in the State of South-Carolina, since the Revolution,* 2 vols. (New York, 1809, 1811).

A Bill for Establishing the Constitution of the State of South-Carolina (Charleston, 1777).

Cooper, Thomas and David J. McCord, eds., *Statutes at Large of South Carolina,* 10 vols. (Columbia, S.C., 1836–1841).

DeSaussure, Henry William, *Reports of Cases Argued and Determined in the Court of Chancery of the State of South Carolina, from the Revolution, to December, 1813, Inclusive,* 4 vols. (Philadelphia, 1854).

The Diplomatic Correspondence of the United States of America, from the Signing of the Definitive Treaty of Peace, 10th September, 1783, to the Adoption of the Constitution, March 4, 1789. 3 vols. (Washington, 1837).

Elliot, Jonathan, *The Debates in the Several State Conventions on the Adoption of the Federal Constitution, as recommended by the General Convention at Philadelphia, in 1787, together with the Journal of the Federal Convention, Luther Martin's Letter, Yates's Minutes, Congressional Opinions, Virginia and Kentucky Resolutions of 98–99, and other Illustrations of the Constitutiuon,* 2nd ed., 5 vols. (Philadelphia, 1836).

Farrand, Max, ed., *The Records of the Federal Convention of 1787,* rev. ed., 4 vols. (New Haven: Yale University Press, 1937).

Gregorie, Anne King, ed., *Records of the Court of Chancery of South-Carolina, 1671-1779,* with an introduction by J. Nelson Frierson, American Legal Records, vol. 6)(Washington: American Historical Association, 1950).

Grimké, John Faucheraud, *The Public Laws of South-Carolina* (Philadelphia, 1790).

Hemphill, William Edwin and Wylma Anne Wates, eds., *Extracts from the Journals of the Provincial Congresses of South Carolina, 1775-1776* (Columbia, S.C.: South Carolina Archives Department, 1960).

Hemphill, William Edwin *et al.*, eds., *Journals of the General Assembly and House of Representatives, 1776-1780* (Columbia, S.C.: Published for the South Carolina Department of Archives and History by the University of South Carolina Press, 1970).

McCord, D.J., *Reports of Cases Determined in the Constitutional Court of South Carolina,* 4 vols. (Charleston, 1853).

Ordinances of the City Council of Charleston, South Carolina, Passed in the First Year of the Incorporation of the City (Charleston, 1784).

Salley, A. S., ed., *Journal of the House of Representatives of South Carolina, January 8, 1782-February 26, 1782* (Columbia, S.C.: Printed for the Historical Commission of South Carolina by the State Company, 1916).

———, ed., *Journal of the Senate of South Carolina, January 8, 1782-February 26, 1782* (Columbia, S.C.: Printed for the Historical Commission of South Carolina by the State Company, 1941).

South Carolina General Assembly, *Second Report of* [the Committee of] *Ways and Means* (Charleston, 1785).

U. S. Bureau of the Census, *A Century of Population Growth from the First Census of the United States to the Twelfth, 1790-1900* (Washington: Government Printing Office, 1909).

U. S. Bureau of the Census, *Heads of Families at the First Census of the United States taken in the Year 1790. South Carolina* (Washington: Government Printing Office, 1908).

Letters, Memoirs, Pamphlets, Travel Accounts, Collections, etc.

Adams, Charles Francis, ed., *The Works of John Adams, Second President of the United States: With a Life of the Author, Notes and Illustrations,* 10 vols. (Boston, 1850-1856).

Address and Rules of the South-Carolina Society for Promoting and Improving Agriculture and other Rural Concerns (Charleston, 1785).

Almon, John, *The Remembrancer, or Impartial Repository of Public Events, 1775-1784,* 17 vols. (London, 1775-1784).

The Army Correspondence of Colonel John Laurens in the Year 1777-8, Now First Printed from Original Letters Addressed to his Father, Henry Laurens, President of Congress, with a Memoir by William Gilmore Simms (New York, 1867).

Ballagh, James Curtis, ed., *The Letters of Richard Henry Lee,* 2 vols. (New York: Macmillan, 1911, 1914).

Bargar, B.D., ed., "Charles Town Loyalism in 1775: The Secret Reports of Alexander Innes," *SCHM* 63 (1962): 125-136.

Barnwell, Joseph, ed., "Correspondence of Hon. Arthur Middleton, Signer of the Declaration of Independence," *SCHM* 26 (1925): 183-213; 27 (1926): 1-29, 51-80, 107-155.

______, ed., "Diary of Timothy Ford, 1785–1786," *SCHM* 13 (1912): 132–147, 181–204.

Boyd, Julian P., ed., *The Papers of Thomas Jefferson* (Princeton: Princeton University Press, 1950—).

Brissot De Warville, J. P., *New Travels in the United States of America, 1788,* trans. Mara Soceanu Vamos and Durand Echeverria, ed. Durand Echeverria (Cambridge, Mass.: Belknap Press of Harvard University Press, 1964).

Brown, Alan S., ed., "James Simpson's Reports on the Carolina Loyalists, 1779–1780," *JSH* 21 (1955): 513–519.

Bruchey, Stuart, ed., *The Colonial Merchant: Sources and Readings* (New York: Harcourt, Brace & World, 1966).

Brunhouse, Robert L., ed., "David Ramsay on the Ratification of the Constitution in South Carolina, 1787–1788," *JSH* 9 (1943): 549–555.

Burke, Aedanus, *An Address to the Freemen of South-Carolina* (Philadelphia, 1783).

[Burke, Aedanus], *A Few Salutary Hints, Pointing out the Policy and Consequences of Admitting British Subjects to Engross our Trade and Become our Citizens. Addressed to Those who either risqued or lost their all in bringing about the Revolution* (Charleston, 1786).

Burnett, Edmund C., ed., *Letters of Members of the Continental Congress,* 8 vols. (Washington: The Carnegie Institution of Washington, 1921–1936).

Butterfield, L. H., ed., *The Adams Papers,* Series II, *Adams Family Correspondence,* 2 vols. (Cambridge, Mass.: Belknap Press of Harvard University Press, 1963).

Carroll, Bartholomew Rivers, ed., *Historical Collections of South Carolina; embracing many rare and valuable pamphlets, and other documents, relating to the history of that state from its first discovery to its independence, in the year 1776,* 2 vols. (New York, 1836).

"Charleston in 1774," *SCHM* 47 (1946): 179–180.

Charleston Yearbooks, 1883–1948 (Charleston, 1884-1951).

Clark, Elmer T., ed., *The Journal and Letters of Francis Asbury,* 3 vols. (Nashville, Tenn.: Abingdon Press, 1958).

Cohen, Hennig, "Four Letters from Peter Timothy, 1755, 1768, 1771," *SCHM* 55 (1954): 160–165.

"Colonel Robert Gray's Observations on the War in Carolina," *SCHM* 11 (1910): 139–159.

Commager, Henry Steele and Richard B. Morris, eds., *The Spirit of 'Seventy-Six: The Story of the American Revolution as told by Participants,* 2 vols. (Indianapolis: Bobbs-Merrill, 1958).

Commerce of Rhode Island, 1726–1800 (Massachusetts Historical Society, *Collections* 69–70 [1914–1915]).

"Correspondence between Hon. Henry Laurens and his Son, John, 1777–1780," *SCHM* 6 (1905): 3–12, 47–52, 103–110, 137–160.

Cross, Jack L., ed., "Letters of Thomas Pinckney, 1775–1780," *SCHM* 58 (1957): 19–33, 67–83, 145–162, 224–242.

Curwen, Samuel, *The Journal and Letters of Samuel Curwen, an American in England, from 1775–1783,* 4th ed. (Boston, 1864).

Davies, K. G., ed., *Documents of the American Revolution 1770–1783* (Colonial Office Series) 21 vols. (Irish University Press, 1972—).

Deas, Anne Izard, *Correspondence of Mr. Ralph Izard, of South Carolina, from the year 1774 to 1804; with a short memoir* (New York, 1844).
"Diary of Captain Hinrichs," in Bernhard A. Uhlendorf, trans. and ed., *The Siege of Charleston with an Account of the Province of South Carolina: Diaries and Letters of Hessian Officers from the von Jungkenn Papers in the William L. Clements Library* (Ann Arbor: University of Michigan Press, 1938).
Dubose, Samuel, "Reminiscences of St. Stephen's Parish, Craven County, and Notices of her old Homesteads," in Theodore Gaillard Thomas, ed., *A Contribution to the History of the Huguenots of South Carolina* (New York, 1887).
Drayton, John, *A View of South-Carolina, As Respects her Natural and Civil Liberties* (Charleston, 1802).
Force, Peter, ed., *American Archives,* Fourth Series, 6 vols. (Washington, 1837–1846).
Ford, Paul L., ed., *Pamphlets on the Constitution of the United States* (Brooklyn, N.Y., 1888).
Garden, Alexander, *Anecdotes of the Revolutionary War in America, with Sketches of Character of Persons the Most Distinguished, in the Southern States, for Civil and Military Services* (Charleston, 1822).
______, *Anecdotes of the American Revolution, Illustrative of the Talents and Virtues of the Heroes and Patriots who acted the most Conspicuous Parts Therein.* Second Series (Charleston, 1828).
Gentleman's Magazine, 1783–1788.
Gibbes, R. W., ed., *Documentary History of the American Revolution: Consisting of Letters and Papers relating to the Contest for Liberty, Chiefly in South Carolina, from Originals in the Possession of the Editor, and other Sources,* 3 vols. (New York, 1853–1857).
Gilbert, Felix, ed., "Letters of Francis Kinloch to Thomas Boone, 1782–1788," *JSH* 8 (1942): 87–105.
[Glen, James], "A Descriptive Account of South Carolina" (1761), in B.R. Carroll, ed., *Historical Collections of South Carolina. . . ,* 2 vols. (New York, 1836).
Hooker, Richard J., ed., *The Carolina Backcountry on the Eve of the Revolution: The Journal and Other Writings of Charles Woodmason, Anglican Itinerant* (Chapel Hill: Published for the Institute of Early American History and Culture at Williamsburg, Virginia, by the University of North Carolina Press, 1953).
"Izard-Laurens Correspondence," *SCHM* 22 (1921): 1–11, 39–52, 73–88.
Jameson, J. Franklin, ed., "South Carolina in the Presidential Election of 1800," *American Historical Review* 4 (1898–1899): 111–129.
Jensen, Merrill, ed., *American Colonial Documents to 1776* (*English Historical Documents,* ed. David C. Douglas, IX [London: Oxford University Press, 1955]).
Johnson, Elmer Douglas, trans., "A Frenchman Visits Charleston in 1777," *SCHM* 52 (1951): 88–92.
Johnston, Henry P., ed., *The Correspondence and Public Papers of John Jay,* 4 vols. (New York: G.P. Putnam's Sons, 1890–1893).

Jones, Newton B., ed., "Writings of the Reverend William Tennent, 1740–1777," *SCHM* 61 (1960): 129–145, 189–209.

"Journal of Josiah Quincy, Junior, 1773," Massachusetts Historical Society, *Proceedings* 49 (1915–1916): 424–481.

La Rochefoucauld Liancourt, *Travels through the United States of North America . . . in the Years 1795, 1796, and 1797,* 2nd ed., 4 vols. (London, 1800).

Lee, Henry, *Memoirs of the War in the Southern Department of the United States,* 1870 ed. (New York).

The Lee Papers (New-York Historical Society, *Collections* 5–6 [1872–1873]).

"Letters from Governor Sir James Wright to the Earl of Dartmouth and Lord George Germain, Secretaries of State for America, from August 24, 1774, to February 16, 1782," Georgia Historical Society, *Collections* 3 (1873): 180–378.

"Letters from Henry Laurens to William Bull of Philadelphia," *SCHM* 24 (1923): 53–68; 25 (1924): 23–35, 77–87.

"Letters from Hon. Henry Laurens to his Son John, 1773–1776," *SCHM* 3 (1902): 86–96, 134–149, 207–215; 4 (1903): 26–35, 99–107, 215–220, 263–277.

"Letters of General Francis Marion," *Charleston Yearbook,* 1895, 326–332.

Letters of Joseph Clay, Merchant of Savannah, 1776–1793 (Georgia Historical Society, *Collections* 8 [1913]).

"Letters of Ralph Izard," *SCHM* 2 (1901): 194–204.

Benjamin Lincoln Papers (Massachusetts Historical Society, Microfilm Publication: Number 3, Boston, 1967).

McMurtie, Douglas, ed., "The Correspondence of Peter Timothy, Printer of Charlestown, with Benjamin Franklin," *SCHM* 35 (1934): 123–129.

MacPherson, David, *Annals of Commerce, Manufactures, Fisheries, and Navigation. . . ,* 4 vols. (London, 1805).

Marcus, Jacob Rader, ed., *American Jewry: Documents: Eighteenth Century, Primarily Hitherto Unpublished Manuscripts,* American Jewish Archives Publications, no. 9 (Cincinnati, Ohio: Hebrew Union College Press, 1959).

Mitchell, John Hinckley, *Mitchell-Boulton Correspondence, 1787–1792, relative to coinages for South Carolina & the United States* (Princeton: Princeton University Press, 1931).

Moody, Robert Earle and Charles Christopher Crittenden, "The Letter-Book of Mills & Hicks (Nathaniel Mills and John Hicks), August 13th, 1781, to August 22nd, 1784, at Charles Town (South Carolina), St. Augustine (East Florida), New York (New York), and Granville (Nova Scotia)," *North Carolina Historical Review* 14 (1937): 39–83.

Moore, Frank, *Materials for History Printed from Original Manuscripts* (New York, 1861).

Moultrie, William, *Memoirs of the American Revolution, so far as it Related to the States of North and South-Carolina, and Georgia,* 2 vols. (New York, 1802).

"Narrative of John Cruden His Majesty's Commissioner of Sequestered Estates in South Carolina," in Paul Leicester Ford, ed., *Winnowings in American History* (New York, 1890).

"Original Letters from General Francis Marion and General William Moultrie, 1781–1788," *Charleston Yearbook,* 1898, 380–385.

[Ramsay, David], "Civis," "An Address to the Freemen of South Carolina on the subject of the Federal Constitution, Proposed by the Convention which met in Philadelphia, May, 1787," in Paul L. Ford, ed., *Pamphlets on the Constitution of the United States* (Brooklyn, N.Y., 1888), 373–380.

______, *The History of the Revolution of South-Carolina from a British Province to an Independent State,* 2 vols. (Trenton, N.J., 1785).

______, *The History of South Carolina, from Its First Settlement in 1670, to the Year 1808,* 2 vols. (Charleston, 1809).

Reese, Thomas, *An Essay on the Influence of Religion in Civil Society* (Charleston, 1788).

"Revolutionary Correspondence from 1775 to 1782," Rhode Island Historical Society, *Collections* 6 (1867), 105–300.

Salley, A. S., ed., "Diary of William Dillwyn during a Visit to Charleston in 1772," *SCHM* 36 (1935): 1–6, 29–35, 73–79, 107–110.

______, ed., *Colonel William Hill's Memoirs of the Revolution* (Columbia, S.C.: Printed for the Historical Commission of South Carolina by the State Company, 1921.

Schoepf, Johann David, *Travels in the Confederation,* trans. and ed. Alfred J. Morrison (Philadelphia: W.J. Campbell, 1911).

Schoff, James S., ed., *Life in the South, 1778-1779: the Letters of Benjamin West* (Ann Arbor: University of Michigan Press, 1963).

John, Lord Sheffield. *Observations on the Commerce of the American States,* 6th ed. (London, 1784).

Sparks, Jared, ed., *Correspondence of the American Revolution; Being Letters of Eminent Men to George Washington, From the time of his Taking Command of the Army to the End of his Presidency,* 4 vols. (Boston, 1853).

Starr, Raymond, ed., "Letters from John Lewis Gervais to Henry Laurens, 1777–1778," *SCHM* 66 (1965): 15–37.

"Stephen Mazyck to Philip Porcher, June 14, 1783," *SCHM* 38 (1937): 11–14.

Thomas, Theodore Gaillard, ed., *A Contribution to the History of the Huguenots of South Carolina: Consisting of Pamphlets by Samuel Dubose . . . and Prof. Frederick A. Porcher* (New York, 1887).

Tobler, John, *The South Carolina and Georgia Almanack, for the Year of our Lord 1786 . . .* (Charleston, 1786).

[Tucker, Thomas Tuder], "PHILODEMUS," *Conciliatory Hints, Attempting, by a Fair State of Matters, to Remove Party Prejudices; — offering a Few Reflections on the Various Forms of Government; — Pointing out the Preference to be given to the Republican or Democratic System; — And Proposing a Convention by Delegates for the Purpose of Accomodating our Constitution more Perfectly to the Principles of Equal and Permanent Freedom: submitted to the Consideration of the Citizens of the Commonwealth of South-Carolina. By Philodemus. Foe to All Party but the Public Weal* (Charleston, 1784).

Uhlendorf, Bernhard A., trans. and ed., *The Siege of Charleston with an Account of the Province of South Carolina: Diaries and Letters of Hessian Officers from the von Jungkenn Papers in the William L. Clements Library* (Ann Arbor: University of Michigan Press, 1938).

Walsh, Richard, ed., "Letters of Morris & Brailsford to Thomas Jefferson," *SCHM* 58 (1957): 129–144.

______, ed., *The Writings of Christopher Gadsden, 1746–1805* (Columbia, S.C.: University of South Carolina Press, 1966).

Webber, Mabel L., ed., "Josiah Smith's Diary, 1780–1781," *SCHM* 34 (1933): 31–39, 67–84, 138–148, 194–210.

[Wells, Louisa Susannah], *The Journal of a Voyage from Charlestown, S. C., to London Undertaken during the American Revolution by a Daughter of an Eminent American Loyalist in the Year 1778 and Written from Memory only in 1779* (New York: Printed for the New-York Historical Society, 1906).

Wilkinson, Eliza, *Letters of Eliza Wilkinson, during the Invasion and Possession of Charlestown, S. C. by the British in the Revolutionary War* (Arno Press Reprint, New York, 1969 [orig. publ. New York, 1839]).

Wright, Louis B. and Marion Tinling, eds., *Quebec to Carolina in 1785–1786, Being the Travel Diary and Observation of Robert Hunter, Jr., a Young Merchant of London* (San Marino, California: The Huntington Library, 1943).

Newspapers

Boston Gazette & the Country Journal, 1783–1786
Charleston Evening Gazette, 1785–1786
Charleston Morning Post and Daily Advertiser, 1786–1787
City Gazette, or the Daily Advertiser, 1788–1789
Columbian Herald, 1784–1787
Gazette of the State of Georgia, 1784, 1786–1787
Gazette of the State of South-Carolina, 1783–1785
Glocester [Gloucester, England] *Journal,* 1783–1785
Massachusetts Gazette, 1786–1787
New-Haven Gazette, and the Connecticut Magazine, 1788
Pennsylvania Packet & Daily Advertiser, 1785–1789
Pennsylvania Packet, or the General Advertiser, 1783–1784
Providence Gazette & Country Journal, 1784
[Charleston] *Royal Gazette,* 1781–1782
Royal South Carolina Gazette, 1780–1782
Salem [Massachusetts] *Gazette,* 1785
South Carolina Gazette, 1775
South Carolina Gazette, and General Advertiser, 1783–1784
South Carolina State Gazette and Daily Advertiser, 1784
South Carolina Gazette & Public Advertiser, 1784–1785
South Carolina State Gazette and General Advertiser, 1784
South-Carolina Weekly Gazette, 1783–1784
State Gazette of South-Carolina, 1785–1788

SECONDARY SOURCES

Books and Articles

Alden, John Richard, *The South in the Revolution, 1763–1789* (Baton Rouge: Louisiana State University Press, 1957).

Andreano, Ralph Louis and Herbert D. Werner, "Charleston Loyalists: A Statistical Note," *SCHM* 60 (1959): 164–168.

Ashton, Thomas S., *Economic Fluctuations in England, 1700–1800* (Oxford: Clarendon Press, 1959).

Bacot, D. Huger, "Constitutional Progress and the Struggle for Democracy in South Carolina following the Revolution," *South Atlantic Quarterly* 24 (1925): 61–72.

______, "The South Carolina Middle Country at the End of the Eighteenth Century," *South Atlantic Quarterly* 23 (1924): 50–60.

______, "The South Carolina Up Country at the End of the Eighteenth Century," *American Historical Review* 28 (1923): 682–698.

Bailyn, Bernard, *The Ideological Origins of the American Revolution* (Cambridge, Mass.: Belknap Press of Harvard University Press, 1967).

______, *The New England Merchants in the Seventeenth Century* (Cambridge, Mass.: Harvard University Press, 1955).

Bancroft, George, *History of the United States of America, from the Discovery of the Continent,* 1886 ed., 6 vols. (New York).

Barnwell, Robert Woodward, Jr., "Reports on Loyalist Exiles from South Carolina, 1783," South Carolina Historical Association, *Proceedings,* 1937, 43–46.

Bass, Robert D., *Gamecock: The Life and Campaigns of General Thomas Sumter* (New York: Holt, Rinehart and Winston, 1961).

______, *The Green Dragoon: The Lives of Banastre Tarleton and Mary Robinson* (New York: Holt, 1957).

______, *Swamp Fox: The Life and Campaigns of General Francis Marion* (New York: Holt, 1959).

Bell, Herbert C., "British Commercial Policy in the West Indies, 1783–1793," *English Historical Review* 31 (1916): 429–441.

Bemis, Samuel Flagg, *The Diplomacy of the American Revolution* (New York: D. Appleton-Century Co., 1935).

Betts, Albert Deems, *History of South Carolina Methodism* (Columbia, S. C.: Advocate Press, 1952).

Billias, George Athan, ed., *George Washington's Generals* (New York: W. Morrow, 1964).

Boddie, William Willis, *History of Williamsburg: Something about the People of Williamsburg County, South Carolina, from the First Settlement by Europeans about 1705 until 1923* (Columbia, S. C.: The State Co., 1923).

Bogue, Donald J., *The Population of the United States* (Glencoe, Illinois: Free Press, 1959).

Bowen, Francis, *Life of Benjamin Lincoln* (Boston, 1855).

Bowes, Frederick, *The Culture of Early Charleston* (Chapel Hill: University of North Carolina Press, 1942).

Bridenbaugh, Carl, *Cities in Revolt: Urban Life in America, 1743–1776* (New York: Knopf, 1955).

______, *The Colonial Craftsman* (New York: New York University Press, 1950).

______, *Myths and Realities, Societies of the Colonial South* (Baton Rouge: Louisiana State University Press, 1952).

Brown, Douglas Summers, *A City Without Cobwebs: A History of Rock Hill, South Carolina* (Columbia, S.C.: University of South Carolina Press, 1953).

Brown, Richard Maxwell, *The South Carolina Regulators* (Cambridge, Mass.: Belknap Press of Harvard University Press, 1963).

Burnett, Edmund Cody, *The Continental Congress* (New York: The Macmillan Company, 1941).

Buron, Edmund, "Notes and Documents: Statistics on Franco-American Trade, 1778–1806," *Journal of Economic and Business History* 4 (1932): 571–580.

Chapman, John A., *A History of Edgefield County from the Earliest Settlements to 1897* (Newberry, S.C.: E.H. Aull, 1897).

Colbourn, H. Trevor, *The Lamp of Experience: Whig History and the Intellectual Origins of the American Revolution* (Chapel Hill: Published for the Institute of Early American History and Culture at Williamsburg, Virginia, by the University of North Carolina Press, 1965).

Crow, Jeffrey J., "Slave Rebelliousness and Social Conflict in North Carolina, 1775 to 1802," *W&MQ*, 3rd Ser. 37 (1980): 79–102.

______, and Larry E. Tise, eds., *The Southern Experience in the American Revolution* (Chapel Hill: University of North Carolina Press, 1978).

Cunninghamm, Noble E., *The Jeffersonian Republicans: The Formation of Party Organization, 1789–1801* (Chapel Hill: Published for the Institute of Early American History and Culture at Williamsburg, Virginia, by the University of North Carolina Press, 1957).

Dabney, William M., "Drayton and Laurens in the Continental Congress," *SCHM* 60 (1959): 74–82.

______, and Marion Dargan, *William Henry Drayton & the American Revolution* (Albuquerque, N.M.: University of New Mexico Press, 1962).

Davidson, Chalmers G., *Friend of the People: The Life of Dr. Peter Fayssoux of Charleston, South Carolina* (Columbia, S.C.: Medical Association of South Carolina, 1950).

Davis, Robert Scott Jr., "The Loyalist Trials at Ninety Six in 1779," *SCHM* 80 (1979): 172–181.

Dickerson, Oliver M., *The Navigation Acts and the American Revolution* (Philadelphia: University of Pennsylvania Press, 1951).

Donnan, Elizabeth, "The New England Slave Trade after the Revolution," *New England Quarterly* 3 (1930): 251–278.

______, "The Slave Trade into South Carolina before the Revolution," *American Historical Review* 33 (1928): 804–829.

Douglass, Elisha P., *Rebels and Democrats: The Struggle for Equal Political Rights and Majority Rule during the American Revolution* (Chapel Hill: University of North Carolina Press, 1955).

Drayton, John, *Memoirs of the American Revolution, from its commencement to the year 1776, inclusive; as relating to the state of South-Carolina: and occasionally refer[ring] to the states of North-Carolina and Georgia* (Charleston, 1821).

Evans, Emory G., "Planter Indebtedness and the Coming of the Revolution in Virginia," *W&MQ*, 3rd Ser. 19 (1962): 511–533.

Ferguson, Clyde R., "Carolina and Georgia Patriot and Loyalist Militia in Action," in Jeffrey J. Crow and Larry E. Tise, eds., *The Southern Experience in the American Revolution* (Chapel Hill: University of North Carolina Press, 1978), 174–199.

Frakes, George Edward, *Laboratory for Liberty: The South Carolina Legislative Committee System, 1719–1776* (Lexington, Ky.: University Press of Kentucky, 1970).

Gayle, Charles Joseph, "The Nature and Volume of Exports from Charleston, 1724–1774," South Carolina Historical Association, *Proceedings,* 1935, 25–33.

Gray, Lewis Cecil, *History of Agriculture in the Southern United States to 1860,* 2 vols. (Washington: The Carnegie Institution of Washington, 1933).

Green, Edwin L., *A History of Richland County* (Columbia, S.C.: The R.L. Bryan Company, 1932).

Green, Fletcher M., *Constitutional Development in the South Atlantic States, 1776–1860: A Study in the Evolution of Democracy* (Chapel Hill: University of North Carolina Press, 1930).

Greene, Evarts B. and Virginia D. Harrington, *American Population before the Federal Census of 1790* (New York: Columbia University Press, 1932).

Greene, George Washington, *The Life of Nathanael Greene, Major General in the Army of the Revolution,* 3 vols. (New York, 1871).

Greene, Jack P., "Bridge to Revolution: the Wilkes Fund Controversy in South Carolina, 1769–1775," *JSH* 29 (1963): 19–52.

______, "The Gadsden Election Controversy and the Revolutionary Movement in South Carolina," *Mississippi Valley Historical Review* 46 (1959): 469–492.

______, *The Quest for Power: The Lower Houses of Assembly in the Southern Royal Colonies, 1689–1776* (Chapel Hill: Published for the Institute of Early American History and Culture at Williamsburg, Virginia, by the University of North Carolina Press, 1963).

______, "'Slavery or Independence': Some Reflections on the Relationship Among Liberty, Black Bondage, and Equality in Revolutionary South Carolina," *SCHM* 80 (1979): 193–214.

______ and Richard M. Jellison, "The Currency Act of 1764 in Imperial-Colonial Relations, 1764–1776," *W&MQ, 3rd Ser. 18 (1961): 485–518.*

Gregg, Alexander, *History of the Old Cheraws: containing an account of the Aborigines of the Pedee, the First White Settlements, their Subsequent Progress, Civil Changes, the Struggle of the Revolution, and Growth of the Country Afterward; Extending from about A. D. 1730 to 1810, with Notices of Families and Sketches of Individuals* (New York, 1867).

Gregorie, Anne King, *History of Sumter County, South Carolina* (Sumter, S.C.: Library Board of Sumter County, 1954).

______, *Thomas Sumter* (Columbia, S.C.: R.L. Bryan Company, 1931).

Harrington, Virginia D., *The New York Merchant on the Eve of the Revolution* (New York: Columbia University Press, 1935).

Haywood, C. Robert, "Mercantilism and South Carolina Agriculture, 1700–1763," *SCHM* 60 (1959): 15–27.

Higginbotham, Don, "The American Militia: A Traditional Institution with Revolutionary Responsibilities," in Don Higginbotham, ed., *Reconsider-*

ations on the Revolutionary War: Selected Essays (Westport, Conn., 1978), 83–103.

______, ed., *Reconsiderations on the Revolutionary War: Selected Essays* (Westport, Conn.: Greenwood Press, 1978).

Hopkins, Thomas F., "St. Mary's Church, Charleston, S.C.: The First Catholic Church in the Original Diocese of Charleston," *Charleston Yearbook*, 1897, 427–502.

Horry, Peter and M.L. Weems, *The Life of Gen. Francis Marion*, 1854 ed. (Philadelphia).

Howe, George, *History of the Presbyterian Church in South Carolina*, 2 vols. (Columbia, S.C., 1870, 1873).

Jensen, Merrill, *The Founding of a Nation: A History of the American Revolution, 1763–1776* (New York: Oxford University Press, 1968).

______, *The Making of the American Constitution* (Princeton, N.J.: Van Nostrand, 1964).

______, *The New Nation: A History of the United States during the Confederation, 1781–1789* (New York: Knopf, 1950).

Johnson, Allen and Dumas Malone, eds., *Dictionary of American Biography*, 22 vols. (New York: C. Scribner's Sons, 1928–1958).

Johnson, Guion Griffis, *A Social History of the Sea Islands with Special Reference to St. Helena Island, South Carolina* (Chapel Hill: University of North Carolina Press, 1930).

Johnson, Joseph, *Traditions & Reminiscences chiefly of the American Revolution in the South* (Charleston, 1851).

Johnson, William, *Sketches of the Life and Correspondence of Nathanael Greene, Major General of the Armies of the United States, in the War of the Revolution*, 2 vols. (Charleston, 1822).

Jordan, Winthrop D., *White Over Black: American Attitudes toward the Negro, 1550–1812* (Chapel Hill: Published for the Institute of Early American History and Culture at Williamsburg, Virginia, by the University of North Carolina Press, 1968).

King, C.R., *Life and Correspondence of Rufus King, Comprising his Letters, Private and Official, his Public Documents and his Speeches*, 6 vols. (New York: G.P. Putnam's Sons, 1894–1900.

Kirkland, Thomas and Robert M. Kennedy, *Historic Camden*, Part I: *Colonial and Revolutionary* (Columbia, S.C.: The State Company, 1905).

Kohlmeier, Albert Ludwig, "The Commerce between the United States and the Netherlands, 1783–1789," *Studies in American History Inscribed to James Albert Woodburn, Ph. D., LL. D., professor emeritus of American History in Indiana University*, by his former students, Indiana University Studies, 12 (Bloomington, 1925), 1–47.

Kurtz, Stephen G. and James H. Hutson, eds., *Essays on the American Revolution* (Chapel Hill: Published for the Institute of Early American History and Culture at Williamsburg, Virginia, by the University of North Carolina Press, 1973).

Labaree, Benjamin Woods, *The Boston Tea Party* (New York: Oxford University Press, 1964).

Labaree, Leonard Woods, *Royal Government in America: A Study of the British Colonial System before 1783* (New Haven: Yale University Press, 1930).

Lambert, Robert S., "The Confiscation of Loyalist Property in Georgia, 1782–1786," *W&MQ,* 3rd Ser. 20 (1963): 80–94.

Landrum, John B.O., *Colonial and Revolutionary History of Upper South Carolina, Embracing for the most part the Primitive and Colonial History of the Territory Comprising the Original County of Spartanburg with a General Review of the Entire Military Operations in the Upper Portion of South Carolina and Portions of North Carolina* (Greenville, S.C., 1897).

______, *History of Spartanburg County* (Atlanta, Ga.: Franklin Printing and Publishing Company, 1900).

Lathem, Edwin Conner, comp., *Chronological Tables of American Newspapers, 1690–1820: Being a tabular guide to holdings of newspapers published in America through the year 1820* (Barre, Mass.: American Antiquarian Society, 1972).

Levett, Ella Pettit, "Loyalism in Charleston, 1761–1784," South Carolina Historical Association, *Proceedings,* 1936, 3–17.

Levy, Leonard W., *Freedom of Speech and Press in Early American History: Legacy of Suppression* (New York: Harper & Row, 1963 ed.).

Logan, John H., *A History of the Upper Country of South Carolina* (Charleston, 1859).

McCormick, Richard P., *Experiment in Independence: New Jersey in the Critical Period, 1781–1789* (New Brunswick, N.J.: Rutgers University Press, 1950).

McCowen, George Smith, Jr., *The British Occupation of Charleston, 1780–1782* (Columbia, S.C.: Published for the South Carolina Tricentennial Commission by the University of South Carolina Press, 1972).

McCrady, Edward, *The History of South Carolina in the Revolution, 1775–1780* (New York: The Macmillan Company, 1901).

______, *The History of South Carolina in the Revolution, 1780–1783* (New York: The Macmillan Company, 1902).

______, *The History of South Carolina under the Royal Government, 1719–1776* (New York: The Macmillan Company, 1899).

McDonald, Forrest, *E Pluribus Unum: The Formation of the American Republic, 1776–1790* (Boston: Houghton Mifflin, 1965).

______, *We the People: The Economic Origins of the Constitution* (Chicago: University of Chicago Press, 1958).

McRee, Griffith J., *Life and Correspondence of James Iredell, one of the Associate Justices of the Supreme Court of the United States,* 2 vols. (New York, 1857–1858).

Main, Jackson Turner, *The Antifederalists: Critics of the Constitution, 1781–1788* (Chapel Hill: Published for the Institute of Early American History and Culture at Williamsburg, Virginia, by the University of North Carolina Press, 1961).

______, "Government by the People: The American Revolution and the Democratization of the Legislatures," *W&MQ,* 3rd Ser. 23 (1966): 391–407.

______, *Political Parties before the Constitution* (Chapel Hill: Published for the Institute of Early American History and Culture at Williamsburg, Virginia, by the University of North Carolina Press, 1973).

______, "Social Origins of a Political Elite: The Upper House in the Revolutionary Era," *The Huntington Library Quarterly* 27 (1964): 147–158.

______, *The Social Structure of Revolutionary America* (Princeton: Princeton University Press, 1965).

______, *The Upper House in Revolutionary America, 1763–1788* (Madison, Wis.: University of Wisconsin Press, 1967).

Marcus, Jacob R., *The Colonial American Jew, 1492–1776,* 3 vols. (Detroit: Wayne State University Press, 1970).

Meade, Robert Douthat, *Patrick Henry: Patriot in the Making* (Philadelphia: Lippincott, 1957).

Meriwether, Robert L., *The Expansion of South Carolina, 1729–1765* (Kingsport, Tenn.: Southern Publishers, Inc., 1940).

Minchinton, Walter E., "Richard Champion, Nicholas Pocock, and the Carolina Trade," *SCHM* 65 (1964): 87–97.

Morris, Richard B., *The Peacemakers: The Great Powers and American Independence* (New York: Harper & Row, 1965).

Mullin, Michael, "British Caribbean and North American Slaves in an Era of War and Revolution, 1775–1807," in Jeffrey J. Crow and Larry E. Tise, eds., *The Southern Experience in the American Revolution* (Chapel Hill: University of North Carolina Press, 1978), 235–267.

Nadelhaft, Jerome, "Ending South Carolina's War: Two 1782 Agreements Favoring the Planters," *SCHM* 80 (1979): 50–64.

______, "The 'Havoc of War' and its Aftermath in Revolutionary South Carolina," *Histoire Sociale* 12 (1979): 97–121.

______, "The Somersett Case and Slavery: Myth, Reality, and Repercussions," *Journal of Negro Hisotry* 51 (1966): 193–208.

Nevins, Allan, *The American States during and after the Revolution, 1775–1789* (New York: The Macmillan Company, 1924).

Norton, Mary Beth, "'What an Alarming Crisis is This': Southern Women and the American Revolution," in Jeffrey J. Crow and Larry E. Tise, eds., *The Southern Experience in the American Revolution* (Chapel Hill: University of North Carolina Press, 1978), 203–234.

Okoye, F. Nwabueze, "Chattel Slavery as the Nightmare of the American Revolutionaries," *W&MQ,* 3rd Ser. 37 (1980): 3–28.

O'Neall, John Belton, *Biographical Sketches of the Bench and Bar of South Carolina,* 2 vols. (Charleston, 1859).

______ and John A. Chapman, *The Annals of Newberry in Two Parts* (Newberry, S.C., 1892).

Pares, Richard, *Merchants and Planters* (Cambridge: Published for the Economic History Review at the University Press, 1960).

______, *Yankees and Creoles: The Trade between North America and the West Indies before the American Revolution* (London: Longmans, Green, 1956).

Peckham, Howard H., ed., *The Toll of Independence: Engagements & Battle Casualties of the American Revolution* (Chicago: University of Chicago Press, 1974).

______, *The War for Independence: A Military History* (Chicago: University of Chicago Press, 1958).

Pinckney, Charles Cotesworth, *The Life of General Thomas Pinckney* (Boston, 1895).

Quarles, Benjamin, *The Negro in the American Revolution* (Chapel Hill: Published for the Institute of Early American History and Culture, Williamsburg, Virginia, by the University of North Carolina Press, 1961).
Ravenel, Harriet Horry, *Eliza Pinckney* (New York: C. Scribner's Sons, 1902).
______, *Charleston: The Place and the People* (New York: The Macmillan Company, 1906).
______, *Life and Times of William Lowndes of South Carolina, 1782-1822* (Boston: Houghton, Mifflin & Company, 1901).
Reynolds, Emily Bellinger and Joan Reynolds Faunt, compilers, *Biographical Directory of the Senate of the State of South Carolina, 1776-1964* (Columbia, S.C.: South Carolina Archives Department, 1964).
______, compilers, *The Senate of the State of South Carolina, 1776-1962* (Columbia, S.C.: Senate of the General Assembly of the State of South Carolina, 1962).
Robson, Eric, *The American Revolution in its Political and Military Aspects, 1763-1783* (New York: Oxford University Press, 1955).
Rogers, George C., Jr., "Aedanus Burke, Nathanael Greene, Anthony Wayne, and the British Merchants of Charleston," *SCHM* 67 (1966): 75–83.
______, *Charleston in the Age of the Pinckneys* (Norman, Okla.: University of Oklahoma Press, 1969).
______, *Evolution of a Federalist: William Loughton Smith of Charleston (1758-1812)* (Columbia, S.C.: University of South Carolina Press, 1962).
______, *The History of Georgetown County, South Carolina* (Columbia, S.C.: University of South Carolina Press, 1970).
Roll, Charles W., Jr., "We, Some of the People: Apportionment in the Thirteen State Conventions Ratifying the Constitution," *Journal of American History* 56 (1969): 21–40.
Rossiter, Clinton, *1787: The Grand Convention* (New York: Macmillan, 1966).
______, *Seedtime of the Republic: The Origin of the American Tradition of Political Liberty* (New York: Harcourt, Brace, 1953).
Royster, Charles, *A Revolutionary People at War: The Continental Army and American Character, 1775-1783* (Chapel Hill: Published for the Institute of Early American History and Culture at Williamsburg, Virginia, by the University of North Carolina Press, 1979).
Rutland, Robert Allen, *The Ordeal of the Constitution: The Antifederalists and the Ratification Struggle of 1787-1788* (Norman, Okla.: University of Oklahoma Press, 1965).
Ryan, Frank W., Jr., "The Role of South Carolina in the First Continental Congress," *SCHM* 60 (1959): 147–153.
"The St. George's Club," *SCHM* 7 (1906): 88–91.
Salley, A.S., Jr., *The History of Orangeburg County, South Carolina from its first Settlement to the Close of the Revolutionary War* (Orangeburg, S.C.: R.L. Berry, 1898).
Schaper, William A., "Sectionalism and Representation in South Carolina," American Historical Association, *Annual Report,* 1900, I, 243–463.
Schlesinger, Arthur Meier, *The Colonial Merchants and the American Revolution, 1763-1776,* Studies in History, Economics and Public Law, ed. by

the Faculty of Political Science of Columbia University, v. 182 (New York, 1918).

______, *Prelude to Independence: The Newspaper War on Britain, 1764-1776* (New York: Knopf, 1957).

Sellers, Leila, *Charleston Business on the Eve of the American Revolution* (Chapel Hill: University of North Carolina Press, 1934).

Sellers, W. W., *A History of Marion County, South Carolina, from its Earliest Times to the Present, 1901* (Columbia, S. C.: R. L. Bryan Company, 1902).

Sheridan, Richard B., "The British Credit Crisis of 1772 and the American Colonies," *Journal of Economic History* 20 (1960): 161–186.

Shipton, Clifford, "Benjamin Lincoln," in George Athan Billias, ed., *George Washington's Generals* (New York: W. Morrow, 1964), 193–211.

Shy, John, "The American Revolution: The Military Conflict Considered as a Revolutionary War," in Stephen G. Kurtz and James H. Hutson, eds., *Essays on the American Revolution* (Chapel Hill: Published for the Institute of Early American History and Culture, Williamsburg, Virginia, by the University of North Carolina Press, 1973), 121–156.

______, "American Society and its War for Independence," in Don Higginbotham, ed., *Reconsiderations on the Revolutionary War: Selected Essays* (Westport, Conn.: Greenwood Press), 72–82.

Singer, Charles Gregg, *South Carolina in the Confederation* (Philadelphia: Privately Printed, 1941).

Sirmans, M. Eugene, *Colonial South Carolina: A Political History, 1663-1763* (Chapel Hill: Published for the Institute of Early American History and Culture at Williamsburg, Virginia, by the University of North Carolina Press, 1966).

______, "The South Carolina Royal Council, 1720–1763," *W&MQ*, 3rd Ser. 18 (1961): 373–392.

Smith, D. E. Huger, "Commodore Alexander Gillon and the Frigate South Carolina," *SCHM* 9 (1908): 189–219.

Smith, Paul H., *Loyalists and Redcoats: A Study in British Revolutionary Policy* (Chapel Hill: Published for the Institute of Early American History and Culture at Williamsburg, Virginia, by the University of North Carolina Press, 1964).

Smith, W. Roy, *South Carolina as a Royal Province, 1719-1776* (New York: The Macmillan Company, 1903).

Sosin, Jack M., *The Revolutionary Frontier, 1763-1783* (New York: Holt, Rinehart and Winston, 1967).

Spruill, Julia Cherry, *Women's Life and Work in the Southern Colonies* (Chapel Hill: University of North Carolina Press, 1938).

Stinchcombe, William C., *The American Revolution and the French Alliance* (Syracuse: Syracuse University Press, 1969).

Stoessen, Alexander R., "The British Occupation of Charleston, 1780–1782," *SCHM* 63 (1962): 71–82.

Sutherland, Stella H., *Population Distribution in Colonial America* (New York: Columbia University Press, 1936).

Taylor, George Rogers, "Wholesale Commodity Prices at Charleston, South Carolina, 1732–1791, 1796–1861," *Journal of Economic and Business History* 4 (1932): 357–377, 848–876.

Townsend, Leah, *South Carolina Baptists, 1670-1805* (Florence, S.C.: The Florence Printing Company, 1935).
Van Alstyne, Richard W., *Empire and Independence: The International History of the American Revolution* (New York: Wiley, 1965).
Wallace, David Duncan, *The Life of Henry Laurens, with a sketch of the life of Lieutenant-Colonel John Laurens* (New York: G.P. Putnam's Sons, 1915).
———, *South Carolina: A Short History, 1520-1948* (Chapel Hill: University of North Carolina Press, 1951).
Walsh, Richard, *Charleston's Sons of Liberty: A Study of the Artisans, 1763-1789* (Columbia, S.C.: University of South Carolina Press, 1959).
———, "Christopher Gadsden: Radical or Conservative Revolutionary?" *SCHM* 63 (1962): 195-203.
Ward, Christopher, *The War of the Revolution,* ed. by John Richard Alden, 2 vols. (New York: Macmillan Company, 1952).
Waring, Alice Noble, *The Fighting Elder: Andrew Pickens (1739-1817)* (Columbia, S.C.: University of South Carolina Press, 1962).
Weigley, Russell F., *The Partisan War: The South Carolina Campaign of 1780-1782* (Columbia, S.C.: Published for the South Carolina Tricentennial Commission, by the University of South Carolina Press, 1970).
Weir, Robert M., "'The Harmony We Were Famous For'; An Interpretation of Pre-Revolutionary South Carolina Politics," *W&MQ,* 3rd Ser. 26 (1969): 473-501.
White, George, *Historical Collections of Georgia* (New York, 1855).
Williamson, Chilton, *American Suffrage: From Property to Democracy, 1760-1860* (Princeton: Princeton University Press, 1960).
Wolfe, John Harold, *Jeffersonian Democracy in South Carolina* (Chapel Hill: University of North Carolina Press, 1940).
Wood, Peter H., "'Taking Care of Business' in Revolutionary South Carolina: Republicanism and the Slave Society," in Jeffrey J. Crow and Larry E. Tise, eds., *The Southern Experience in the American Revolution* (Chapel Hill: University of North Carolina Press, 1978), 268-293.
Woody, Robert H., "Christopher Gadsden and the Stamp Act," South Carolina Historical Association, *Proceedings,* 1939, 3-12.
Zahniser, Marvin R., *Charles Cotesworth Pinckney: Founding Father* (Chapel Hill: Published for the Institute of Early American History and Culture at Williamsburg, Virginia, by the University of North Carolina Press, 1967).

Dissertations

Baldwin, Benjamin R., "The Debts Owed by Americans to British Creditors, 1763-1802" (Ph. D. dissertation, University of Indiana, 1932).
Barnwell, Robert Woodward, Jr., "Loyalism in South Carolina, 1765-1785" (Ph. D. dissertation, Duke University, 1941).
Duncan, John Donald, "Servitude and Slavery in Colonial South Carolina, 1670-1776" (Ph. D. dissertation, Emory University, 1971).
Higgins, W. Robert, "A Financial History of the American Revolution in South Carolina" (Ph. D. dissertation, Duke University, 1970).
Knepper, David Morton, "The Political Structure of Colonial South Carolina, 1743-1776" (Ph. D. dissertation, University of Virginia, 1971).

Nadelhaft, Jerome J., "The Revolutionary Era in South Carolina, 1775–1788" (Ph. D. dissertation, University of Wisconsin, 1965).

Starr, Raymond G., "The Conservative Revolution: South Carolina Public Affairs, 1775–1790" (Ph. D. dissertation, University of Texas, 1964).

Stokes, Durward Turrentine, "The Clergy of the Carolinas and the American Revolution" (Ph. D. dissertation, University of North Carolina, 1968).

Weir, Robert McCulloch, "'Liberty and Property, and No Stamps'; South Carolina and the Stamp Act Crisis" (Ph. D. dissertation, Western Reserve University, 1966).

Index

E
263
S7
N32

Nadelhaft, Jerome Joshua,
1937-
The disorders of war:

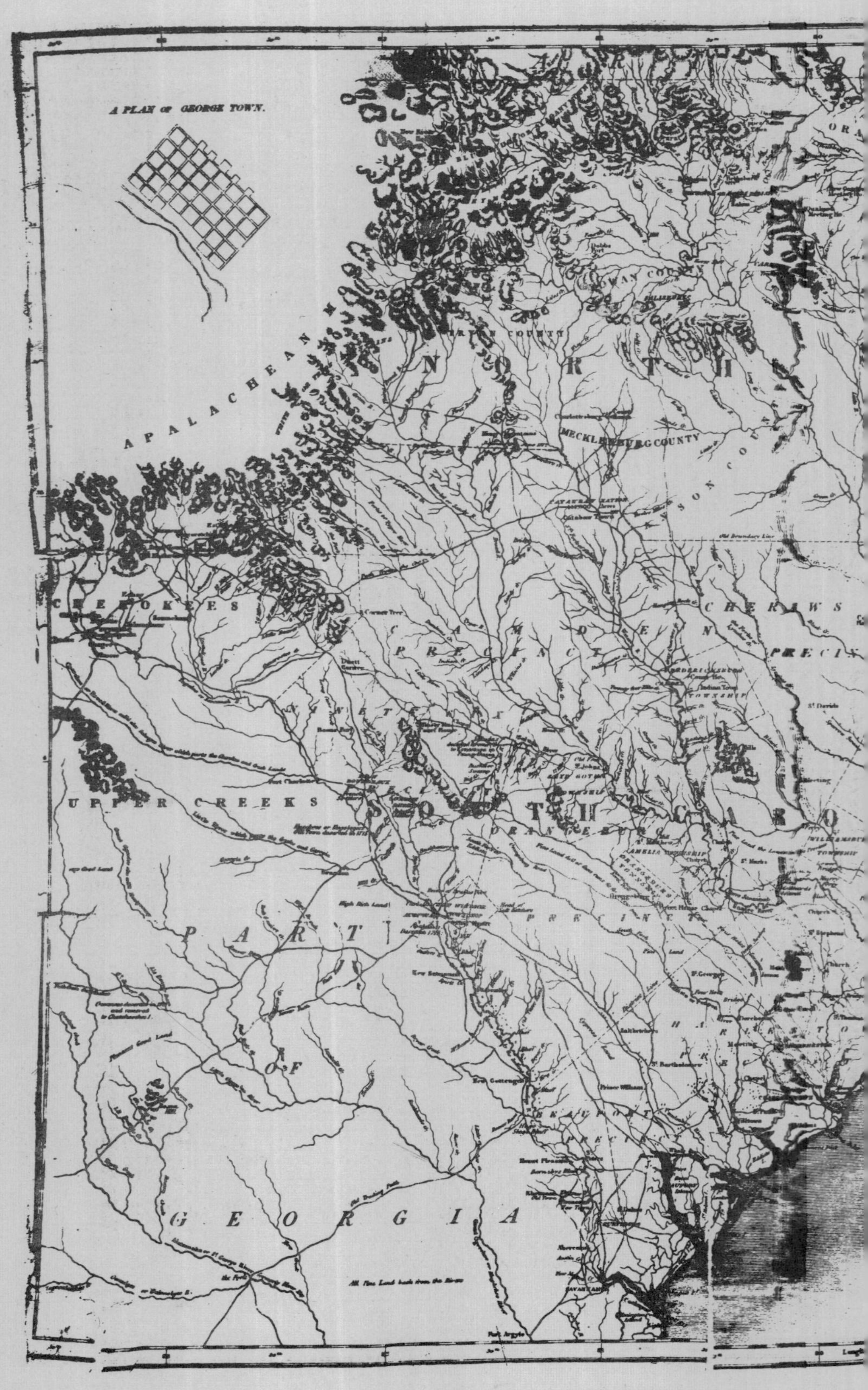

A PLAN OF GEORGE TOWN.
APALACHEAN
N O R T H
TRYON COUNTY
MECKLENBURG COUNTY
CHEROKEES
UPPER CREEKS
C A M D E N
P R E C I N C T
CHERAWS
Old Boundary Line
S O U T H
O R A N G E B U R G
P R E C I N C T
AMELIA TOWNSHIP
ORANGEBURG TOWNSHIP
P A R T
O F
G E O R G I A
Fort Charlotte
High Rich Land
New Gottengen
Prince William
St. Bartholomew
All Pine Land back from the Rivers
Fort Argyle
SAVANNAH